WHITE MEN AREN'T

WHITE MEN AREN'T

Thomas DiPiero

DUKE UNIVERSITY PRESS

Durham & London 2002

An earlier version of chapter 2

appeared as "Missing Links: White-

ness and the Color of Reason in the

Eighteenth Century," *The Eighteenth

Century: Theory and Interpretation* 40,

no. 2 (summer 1999). Part of chapter 5

appeared as "White Men Aren't,"

Camera Obscura 30 (1994).

CONTENTS

ACKNOWLEDGMENTS

This book originated out of a curiosity to determine whether the observations I had read in a great deal of feminist scholarship concerning men and their desires—observations made largely, although in no way exclusively, by women—were true. My curiosity turned to frustration when I realized that if I couldn't determine whether the observations were true about me, then there wasn't any hope for determining their veracity for men in general. I nevertheless continued interrogating situations in which I or others I knew (not all of whom, by the way, were men) did or did not evince the particular features deemed characteristic of masculinity. Thus was born a hypothesis of masculine hysteria, which, if it didn't yet have the clinical or theoretical backing, nevertheless had the particular advantage that it just felt right.

Fortunately for me, a great number of people were willing to put up with the hysteria. It is often the case that one's closest friends are not one's best readers. Emotional or affective proximity sometimes seems to oppose critical distance. My friends, however, have been only too happy to tell me when I don't make any sense; my students seemed to consider it their duty, and those in "Contemporary French Thought," "Constructions of Masculinity," and "Freud and Lacan" helped shape significant portions of this book.

Friends and colleagues at the University of Rochester in the Department of Modern Languages and Cultures and the Department of English, as well as in the interdepartmental programs in Visual and Cultural Studies and the Susan B. Anthony Institute collaborate in producing a lively intellectual climate, and a great deal of this book grew out of our discussions and debates. I am also indebted to specific people for their special help. In particular I thank Sue Gustafson, Cilas Kemedjio, Trevor Hope, Joel Morales, Noreen Javornik, Tim Walters, Kien Ket Lim, Michael Holly, Douglas Crimp, Claudia Schaefer, Darby English, Eva Geulen, Babacar Camara, Beth Newman, Kathleen Parthé, and Mohammed Bamyeh (who did me the added favor of making me realize I needed a much bigger house). To Pat Gill, who is sometimes me, there is no need to express thanks, because she'll finish this sentence for me anyway. Randall Halle valiantly defended my defense of the phallus, and John Michael let me get away with nothing, which requires more energy than anyone should have to expend. Thanks also to Richard Estell, who showed me that you actually can learn how to see, and to Sharon Willis, who over the years has done me the tremendous favor of reading me especially well. I thank Rajani Sudan for her theoretical insights, and also and especially for asking difficult questions totally in the dark. I thank Jeff Hilyard for still hearing the saxophone music after so many years.

INTRODUCTION: BELIEVING IS SEEING

I object to a strategy which situates men in such a
way that the only speaking positions available to
them are those of tame feminist or wild antifemi-
nist. —K. K. Ruthven, *Feminist Literary Studies*

Sometime during the early 1990s, the dead white male, that extraordinarily prolific author who wrote most of the books featured in
high-school and college curricula across the United States, died. Another white male took his place, but this one wasn't dead—he was angry.
Suddenly angry white men were popping up everywhere, and what they
were mad at, at least according to the dozens of newspaper and magazine articles reporting the phenomenon, was the decline in their value,
both cultural and economic, to the general population. From the front
pages of the *New York Times* and the *Wall Street Journal*, feature stories
in *Time* and *Newsweek*, and from discussion groups on the Internet, we
have learned that angry white men resent the imposition of affirmative
action and the so-called reverse discrimination it produces. They de-
plore the competing definitions of family, history, and politics that arise
along with increasingly diverse—and increasingly vocal—minority populations. Perhaps most of all, however, they rage against the mutating
definition of white masculinity itself as it responds to shifting social,
political, and economic tides.

There is really nothing new about white men being angry, however.
In fact, anger seems to be constitutive of the identity. Even if we go as
far back in time as Homer's *Iliad*, what we see is that white men—or at
least men belonging to those cultures that would later be identified as
white—are not only angry, but confused about who they are supposed to
be as well. "Sing, goddess, the anger of Peleus' son Achilleus," the *Iliad*
opens, and that perhaps first of angry white men must later decide
whether revenge or a burgeoning form of compassion should be what

characterizes his culture's heroic male. But Achilleus is hardly an isolated example: Ariosto's sixteenth-century *Orlando Furioso* was pretty mad, and we cannot forget Peter Finch's character Howard Beale (he was "mad as hell," we recall) in Sidney Lumet's *Network,* or Sylvester Stallone's Rambo.[1] Moving to real life, the wrath of individuals such as terrorists Timothy McVeigh and Unabomber Ted Kazinski correlates the fury of the KKK, the more recent rural militiamen, and the angry young high school boys who began shooting their classmates and their parents in the 1990s, with perhaps the most spectacular and gruesome scene occurring at Columbine High School in Colorado during the spring of 1999.

By all accounts, at least according to the popular press, angry white males are fuming over the cultural changes that conspire to eject them from the social order's defining center. The features that have traditionally not only characterized but distinguished the white male seem no longer important. Possessing physical strength, heading a household, working outside the home, and having sole access to the most respected and profitable arenas of culture are all features that either no longer pertain exclusively to white males or that are no longer particularly valued. Consequently, the white male appears no longer to be the focus of identification, and it seems increasingly true that such a focus no longer exists. But if the center can no longer hold, it's not necessarily the case that things fall apart: the same categories that maintained the white male in the culture's identificatory focus certainly continue both to endow and constrain people with identities today, but as we have seen most notably in the realm of virtual reality, people seem to be developing the ability to assume different and even multiple or conflicting identities. What we are currently experiencing in the anger of the white male, then, might be the contradiction caused by the enduring historical weight of an identity no longer invested with the preeminence it once enjoyed, and the contemporary push toward opening up new raced, gendered, and sexual identities that do not take the white male as their normative ground. If that isn't enough to anger those who feel cheated out of occupying a center stage, it just might be enough to make them hysterical: as I will show, in fact, the identity "white male" is about nothing if not a form of hysteria.[2]

In this book, I take a close look at the complex nature of the white male identity, with particular emphasis on white masculinity as a response to specific cultural phenomena.[3] While white masculinity constitutes a hegemonic force in contemporary social, political, and economic domains, we need to analyze it as a symptomatic reply to cultural demands, not as a self-generating ahistorical entity somehow able endlessly to reproduce itself.[4] We need to be careful, in other words, not to construct white masculinity as an apodictic force with no exterior. We must take care not to conflate a hegemonic force in culture with the source or prime motivator in that culture—simply put, the identity in question cannot perform the taxonomically impossible task of defining itself. Finally, we need to take care, at the most fundamental level, not to equate an identity, which is the product of cultural activity, with that activity itself. In contradistinction to a great many studies of masculinity, then, I insist not only on the cultural conditions inhering in the production of specific strains of masculinity—in this case, white masculinity—but also on the cultural work that white masculinity continually performs in order to retain its hegemony. There are, consequently, two extremes of white masculinity, neither of which is for any practical purposes readily available to us: on the one hand is the figure of hegemonic stability to which all other forms of identity are explicitly or implicitly compared; and on the other hand there is the identity as it is lived by real human beings. It is precisely because these two so rarely match up that white males are so often angry: sustaining the contradiction between how the culture defines them and how they experience their lives, white males are often frustrated by their inability to live up to cultural ideals. Indeed, studies in the 1940s and 1950s indicated that over-identification with cultural ideals of masculinity produced antisocial, even criminal behavior.[5]

It seems likely, in fact, that no one is really supposed to live up to the ideals our culture constructs for white men. If we take a look at models of masculinity suggested in psychoanalysis or popular culture, for example, it seems fairly obvious that the figures that men are enjoined to emulate are models of impossible identification. Throughout the psychoanalytic writings of Sigmund Freud, for example, the male child is continually frustrated by his inability to possess what his father has. The principal conflict that psychoanalysis describes—the Oedipus complex, which will come under close scrutiny in chapter 1—produces a situation in which the young male child is required to be simultaneously like and unlike the father: Freud maintains that the superego tells the young male, " 'You *ought to be* like this (like your father).' It also comprises the prohibition: 'You *may not be* like this (like your father)—that is, you may not do all that he does; some things are his prerogative.' "[6] If inhabiting masculinity involves disentangling the threads of conflicting cultural values, it also involves recognizing how those values are incarnated in the male body.[7] Little Hans, Freud's famous five-year-old analysand with a morbid fear of horses, feared that his own penis would never measure up to his father's.[8] But conflicting cultural signals concerning what a man is supposed to be are not limited in psychoanalysis to the young male child. Freud tells us that the little girl passing through her society's civilizing processes learns that "a husband is . . . never anything but a proxy, never the right man; the first claim upon the feeling of love in a woman belongs to someone else, in typical cases to her father; the husband is at best a second".[9] For both the little boy and the little girl, it seems, the father is an unattainable ideal, a too-perfect model that sets them up for failure.

The basic premise informing my excavation of the white male identity is that the principal poles of identification—whiteness, maleness— are impossible ones, since according to the cultural logic that has defined them, no one could ever be completely white and/or completely male.[10] The ideal white male figure, in other words, is not simply a fiction, like the father in psychoanalysis's heuristic tales, but a fiction constructed to prohibit comprehensive identification. Throughout the course of this book I will examine the manner in which ideal white and male figures are constructed, with an eye toward understanding precisely how and why they are impossible ones. To analyze the social construction of the white male I will often be using models drawn from psychoanalysis, principally because I believe that the processes through which we adopt or reject the models of identity our cultures put forth operate on a largely unconscious level, but a level that nevertheless informs our most fundamental ways of signifying and knowing, and hence the ways we live our social, economic, and political lives. But placing stock in the operations of unconscious thought processes need not imply a wholesale acceptance of specific models of psychoanalysis: one of the aims of this book is to understand the cultural prejudices inhering in both Freudian and Lacanian psychoanalysis and the blind spots those prejudices produce. As I interrogate the construction of the white male identity, beginning roughly at the end of the seventeenth century, I will be simultaneously investigating some of the consequences that ensue from the presuppositions informing psychoanalysis and its theories of gender.

It may be interesting to note that many of the earliest studies of masculinity came not from the perspective of psychoanalysis, but from that of sociology. The work of Victor Seidler, David Morgan, Andy Metcalf, Martin Humphries, R. W. Connell, and Harry Brod come to mind immediately as part of a new generation of scholars working in the field of gender studies and directing their attentions nearly exclusively to masculinity.[11] Rather than present a list of what I consider to be the most notable studies on masculinity from the past twenty or so years, I will cite what I consider to be the most influential works in the field at moments in my argument more appropriate to the subject matters at hand. Likewise, the scholarship on race, and what is especially germane here, whiteness studies, has increased dramatically just in the past few years, and in order to avoid an overwhelming list of titles at this juncture, I will include discussion of many of the signal works at relevant moments. As I hope will become clear, however, this book is not simply the conjunction or intersection of "race" and "gender," as if the two were simply ingredients one could unproblematically add in a recipe of human identity. The whiteness and masculinity I will be looking at here are not only mutually dependent; they are overdetermined and articulated in such a way that each becomes more complex by association with the other.

White Men Aren't looks at the white male identity in several different moments of history. It is not intended to present a seamless narrative of the origins of that identity and its subsequent development throughout history, primarily because such a history would leave out or conflate as much as it included. Instead, I have chosen times and places that seem significant for the development of white masculine hegemony, fully recognizing, of course, that explanatory narratives often produce exactly what they're trying to describe. Indeed, I will argue in chapter 1 that such a phenomenon is precisely what lies behind Freud's production of the Oedipus complex, particularly as that complex involves the active obfuscation of forms of identity that do not pertain to gender.[12] Psychoanalysis has traditionally taken gender to be the fundamental difference informing the production of subjectivity. Indeed, the Freudian reading of Oedipus typifies most other interpretations of the classic tragedy—including the more traditional literary ones—in its active obfuscation of forms of difference the work quite explicitly underscores. Form mirrors function in such readings of *Oedipus* in that the work that goes into not seeing ethnic, civic, and other kinds of difference operating in Sophocles' tragedy correlates modern productions of whiteness as an invisible or empty marker of identity.

In chapters 2 and 3 I look at the uneasy relationship western European travelers, anthropologists, and naturalists maintained with people they considered to be radically unlike themselves—for the most part Africans and, to a lesser extent, Asians and Americans—and ask how and why they identified specific morphological features as enough unlike their own to consider these people fundamentally different. In other words, how do we recognize similarity and how do we identify difference, particularly when the terrain on which we are operating is by and large new? What caused Europeans to focus on skin color, particular facial features, or hair when trying to determine whether a specific cultural group was principally like or unlike them? Why did they see difference, and not sameness? What metaphors, necessarily grounded in their own cultural systems of meaning, informed the manner in which they saw and understood other peoples?[13] How do we locate difference, and what does it mean when we (think we) find it?[14] Finally, how and why do we marshal specific features based on the contingencies of our own cultural classificatory systems into the engulfing and presumably trans-human taxonomic systems we call "race" and "gender"?

Chapter 4 is devoted to the Lacanian phallus, that organ that seems to bear an uneasy and ambivalent relationship to an anatomical marker of difference—in fact, to what is normally taken to be *the* anatomical marker of difference: the penis. Extrapolating from my reading of *Oedipus the King*, I will argue that to conflate phallus and penis is to perform two simultaneous and related operations: on the one hand such a conflation casts all forms of difference in terms of sexual difference, and in the process masks a host of different social identifiers; and on the other hand the conflation of signifier of difference with male anatomy reproduces a form of masculine hegemony that figures masculinity either as seamless and integral, or as something that needs to be exposed or dismantled. I will show that to fail to consider the phallus as a signifier operating in any (and potentially every) domain of difference is to obfuscate the crucial operations that invest bodies with signification, and hence to naturalize the very forms of domination that critiques aimed at aligning the phallus with the penis have sought to expose. Such critiques ironically end up defending the very form of phallic power they generally seek to repudiate. Finally, in chapter 5 I will more fully address what I call the hysteria of white masculinity. Beginning with nineteenth-century fears and anxieties over what constitutes whiteness and whether the "white race" might be contaminated by nonwhite blood, I will address the more sophisticated manifestations of those concerns prevalent in contemporary culture: the African American or Latino conscripted to tell the white man who or what the latter is, and to know more about his identity than he himself apparently does.

White Men Aren't begins with the simple premise that the systems of classification that we take to be fundamental—the mantra of gender, race, and class that we have heard so much about of late—not only mean something different in different historical and cultural contexts, but that they might have no meaning at all for the specific social groups they are meant to characterize. Whether by casting all difference as representable through a specific set of cultural metaphors—indeed, by casting difference as representable at all—or by imposing labels through brute force, white masculinity ascends to a position of power and cultural predominance. The power that this identity assumes—and it is important to remember that like all identities white masculinity is not so much a thing as it is a complex encoded response to cultural phenomena—derives in large part from the fact that in most areas of Western culture a single unit or measure of value gives expression to many others. White masculinity's hegemony arises because it causes different kinds of subjectivity to become expressions of the central position that it represents; manifestations of difference get subsumed into terms not only designed to represent the central position, but restricted to such use, in much the same way, for example, that a film can be expressed in terms of its narrative but at the cost of its filmic specificity. In other words, white masculinity assumes what we might call the least common denominator of subjective identity, since part of its mythology has long been that it is an identity in which expressions of other identities are crystallized.

It seems crucial, if not by now almost gratuitous, to stress that the issue here is not biological, even if for several hundred years naturalists, anthropologists, philosophers, and jurists tried to demonstrate that it is, as I will discuss in chapters 2 and 3. Rather, the issue is a cultural one and it is a subjective one, by which I mean it pertains to how people think themselves and their relationships to their communities and to the world. But scientific explanations quite often lend legitimacy to the most outrageous ideological propaganda, since the things that appear to be natural or empirically observable generally also seem to be without political content. For example, the nineteenth-century anthropologist Arthur de Gobineau deployed the discourses of science and equality predominant in his time to "prove" that white people were the most beautiful. "Taking the white race as the standard of beauty," he writes, "we perceive all others more or less receding from that model. There is, then, an inequality in point of beauty among the various races of men, and that inequality is permanent and indelible."[15] One of the questions we need to formulate, then, concerns the extent to which empirical observations are themselves already steeped in the politics of what their ostensible objectivity is called on to prove. Simon LeVay, a neurobiologist investigating the "cause" of homosexuality, perhaps unwittingly demonstrates the manner in which scientific discourse blinds itself to its own workings when he writes that "it is not unrealistic to expect a gene or genes influencing sexual orientation to be identified within the next few years, since there are at least three laboratories in the United States alone that are working on the topic."[16] What this kind of science thinks it will find is determined in advance by the epistemological frameworks that themselves give rise to investigation in the first place.[17]

But scientific investigation into the nature of human identity, be it race, gender, or sexuality, is only a symptom, and not a cause, of the phenomenon I am investigating. We need to determine the manner in which the abstractions we produce to describe the material world around us are necessarily already inflected by that world. Furthermore, we must understand how the world is affected by our abstractions. As Margaret Homans puts it, "The discourses of race and of gender in this country have historically been characterized by debates about the body: about the ontological status as well as the interpretability of biological difference."[18] As the above citations from Gobineau and LeVay indicate, the material and the ideal—which also turn out to be the two fundamental and completely imbricated components of signification in the forms best known as signifier and signified, a point to which I will return in chapter 4—inflect one another in unexpected and sometimes far-reaching ways when it comes to human identities and their bodily markers. If nobody has ever really been fully white or completely male, then what we have is a gap separating our signifying and our socio-political practices. This means that we have a designation of human identity—white male—that apparently has no real referent in the world in which we live. On the one hand it seems hardly surprising that such might be the case, since it is probably no more likely that any other identity for which we have a name perfectly corresponds to real individuals, but on the other hand it seems particularly ironic that the standard by which all others have traditionally been measured and through which all are made into fictionalized others is itself an impossible and nonexistent model.

As I have postulated, both whiteness and masculinity are built around an anxiety of insufficiency.[19] Whether we approach that issue from the psychoanalytic perspective I mentioned above, which holds that males are continually enjoined both to emulate their fathers and to fear their punishing power, or from the numerous examples we can observe in everyday life in which males are called on to "Be a man!" it seems clear that for most men there is always at least the hint of an anxiety that we could be just a little more masculine, whether in the disposition of our bodies or our behavior, with examples ranging from the leanly muscled SoloFlex boy to the archly self-reliant Marlboro Man. In fact, the 1980s gave rise to a new form of exaggerated, heavily muscled warrior hero in popular culture, first with Sylvester Stallone's Rambo and Rocky, and then continuing on with Arnold Schwarzenegger's many incarnations, at least one of which—the Terminator—honed masculinity to an inhuman perfection. In similar fashion, whiteness has assumed a position of impossible emulation, but the significance of that fact seems not generally recognized. I will discuss that issue in greater detail in chapter 3, but for now I might simply point out the famous "one drop of blood" rule, which developed in the eighteenth century in the American south and has yet to disappear completely. This rule specifies that no person with any identifiable nonwhite heritage whatsoever—however distant in the past and however culturally similar to European, especially Anglo-Saxon traditions—can be identified as properly white. Since no one can ever be absolutely sure of his or her ancestry (who could ever account for the sexual dalliances of ancestors long dead?), a great deal of racial consternation and hysteria arises in the people for whom such pedigree matters. Whiteness and masculinity thus pose all sorts of possibilities of not measuring up or of coming up short. With regard to masculinity, Anne Fausto-Sterling argues that this phenomenon begins with a boy's first day on earth: "At birth, then, masculinity becomes a social phenomenon. For proper masculine socialization to occur, the little boy must have a sufficiently large penis. There must be no doubt in the boy's mind, in the minds of his parents and other adult relatives, or in the minds of his male peers about the legitimacy of his male identification."[20] Thus, I might argue that if one can never be too thin or too rich, as the advertising industry continually likes to remind us, neither can one be too white or too male.

In this study, then, I look at the conjunction of whiteness and masculinity for two principal, mutually informing purposes. First, I want to attempt an articulation of to whom or what the particular descriptor "white male" actually refers. It is devastatingly simple merely to point to someone who appears to be both white and male and say, "There he is." But the apparent simplicity of that operation is part of the problem. Like LeVay's confidence that he will find what he's looking for because he knows in advance what the answer will be, it turns out that we need to know what a white guy is before we can see him. The proof behind that assertion lies in the fact that the person to whom we might unproblematically point as the incarnation of white masculinity has been historically variable—in some cases quite radically. In the early years of this century, for example, Irish and Italian immigrants were not generally considered white, even though both groups today would most likely be considered white by nearly everyone for whom such a designation has meaning.[21] Perhaps more startlingly, it took a Supreme Court decision to determine whether Bhagat Singh Thind, a native of India who was applying for American citizenship, was white. He wasn't. The Supreme Court held that "the words 'free white persons' are words of common speech, to be interpreted in accordance with the understanding of the common man."[22] Thus it is not simply the case that we can unproblematically—or even reliably—identify who white males are. In fact, white masculinity seems to be determined at least as much by what people believe or know as it is by the physical characteristics that would appear to define it.[23] In other words, if it were simply the case that any person who appeared to be a white male simply *was* a white male, the identity would have no problematic political or ideological dimension since there would be no question of a legitimacy to which some people were not entitled.[24] That is why we cannot simply and unproblematically point to the person who seems both white and male: you have to know what he looks like before you can actually see him.[25]

One goal of this study is thus to determine what a white male is, and to do that I will invoke a number of biological, anthropological, and legal sources, all of which attempt in one way or another to describe whiteness, masculinity, or both. I will be looking at different historical moments, not in order somehow to produce a linear history of the white male, but to show that the identity position is dynamically produced, and that who and what a white male has been has changed dramatically over the years and for a variety of reasons. With that in mind, a second goal of this study is to analyze the complex relationship between signification and human identity. If it is the case that the identities we ascribe to particular features of the body overflow the parts or traits that supposedly give them meaning, then it is also the case that those identities are products of human knowledge, which is in turn governed by relationships of power.[26] In what might at first appear to be a dizzying *mise en abîme* of mutually informing and inflecting components, in which corporeal features give rise to identities, which in turn articulate parts of the body deemed to be significant, we can identify a process whereby a dominant discourse—one that is able to regulate to a very large but by no means absolute extent the production and exchange of meaning—covers the tracks of its own production. That is, what I am pursuing is the manner in which a specific discursive practice emerges and sustains itself as an ostensibly transparent medium for indexing the world, in the process obfuscating the specific symbolic dimensions it is unable to accommodate. In chapter 2, for example, I will show that one of the West's most enduring "transparent" media, the discourse of reason, correlates particular morphological features prized in Enlightenment Europe, among which we find white skin.

I will argue that the symbolic dimensions that fall outside of the dominant discourse's purview, or of what it is able to represent, form a sort of perimeter or constitutive outside that in turn defines its interior. In the case of white masculinity as a dominant discourse, what falls under the category of the unrepresentable from within that discourse is precisely any positive—positive, in the sense of formally laid down or prescribed—definition or description of what it is. White masculinity seems to abject from itself everything that differs from it, forcing the responsibility of differential definition on whatever seems to be its "other," a phenomenon we will see in its most extreme forms in chapter 5. Thus, in a formulation that has become almost axiomatic, Luce Irigaray observed back in 1974 that "We can assume that any theory of the subject has always been appropriated by the 'masculine,'" arguing that the default subject is male, and that the female becomes the marked or differentiated variety.[27] Similarly, Toni Morrison writes of the default variety of racial identity, specifying that "American means white, and Africanist people struggle to make the term applicable to themselves with ethnicity and hyphen after hyphen after hyphen."[28] In short, as the ostensibly unmarked gendered and racial identity, white masculinity causes those identities that it excludes from itself to define it.[29]

White masculinity occupies a hegemonic position in contemporary American culture, and it will be the burden of this study to investigate precisely what this hegemony is and how it operates. Hegemony, of course, refers to a preponderant influence or power over others. But it is important to distinguish hegemony from brute force. Hegemony differs from coercion in that it involves the production of meaning as a way of unifying and ordering people (the word "hegemony" itself derives from a Greek word meaning "leader"). A hegemonic position as I will be using the term quilts together portions or fragments of meaning from different realms, in the process forming a way of knowing that becomes a world view for a given community. One example of this phenomenon can be found in Benedict Anderson's account of how the coalition between Protestantism and print-capitalism created new reading publics in Europe in the sixteenth century. Those reading publics mobilized the people composing them for politico-religious purposes, Anderson argues, and capitalism and print combined to form what he calls "monoglot mass reading publics"; from those publics specific languages of power arose.[30] For the time being I will leave aside the various means that allow a group to achieve hegemony because what I want to stress is the fact that the very act of interweaving together various domains of signification transcends those domains themselves; not only does hegemony produce new meaning in the links that it forges, but it causes the linked elements to accrue new meaning by virtue of the associative paths uniting them.

Hegemony is consequently a process of articulation in both senses of that word. That is, hegemony not only joins together different discursive strands or pockets of social meaning; it also expresses, through that very act of joining together, new possibilities and new ways of thinking.[31] As a hegemonic identity that casts other identities as inadequate substitutes or failed approximations of itself, white masculinity has for the past three hundred years—since, that is, roughly the time that the identity "white" has come into the picture[32]—governed not only questions of racial and gender identity, but also broader issues of signification in domains not generally associated with the color of one's skin, or the arrangement of one's genitalia or, indeed, the manner in which one presents oneself to the world as a member of a particular sexed or raced group.[33] What I will attempt to show, in other words, is the manner in which white masculinity, as a hegemonic identity, has anchored tremendous numbers of elements of a shared symbolic order, such that white masculinity becomes what psychoanalysis calls a nodal point, an anchor in the constant slippage of meaning. As such, by partially fixing the continued differential interplay of signifiers, it infiltrates those signifiers and informs their meaning. When this happens, certain signifiers function as master signifiers. Like a dollar bill, which expresses very little if anything at all about itself but can nevertheless express the exchange value of everything else, these signifiers have little if any meaning of their own, but reflect instead the signification of a host of other cultural artifacts.

The question we need to consider concerns how some signifiers get elevated to this function. We need to find a way to understand not only how we can speak of white masculinity as anything other than what Marjorie Garber has called a "phallic redundancy," but how specific political and ideological processes contribute to causing white masculinity to appear as a seamless, monolithic entity.[34] Kaja Silverman has proposed the concept of the "dominant fiction" as a means of understanding how an ideologically invested subject position covers over the disjunctions in its own composition. In her *Male Subjectivity at the Margins* she demonstrates that male subjectivity, like the version of female subjectivity that some strains of psychoanalysis have posited, is founded on a lack; it is only the deployment of particular ideological "fictions," she argues, that covers that lack. "The normative male ego," she writes "is necessarily fortified against any knowledge of the void upon which it rests."[35] That fortification in turn relies on a "dominant fiction," a phenomenon that she defines, in part, as "above all else the representational system through which the subject is accommodated to the Name-of-the-Father. Its most central signifier of unity is the (paternal) family, and its primary signifier of privilege the phallus."[36] Silverman's dominant fiction derives from ideological critique, especially of the Althusserian variety, in which a subject is hailed by particular social and political structures. Recognizing itself in those structures, the subject reproduces them in its daily life. In Silverman's dominant fiction, fiction with all its narrative implications takes the forefront: dependent on such narrative devices as *vraisemblance* and realism, the dominant fiction "consists of the images and stories through which a society figures consensus; images and stories which cinema, fiction, popular culture, and other forms of mass representation presumably both draw upon and help to shape."[37]

In a similar vein, Ernesto Laclau and Chantal Mouffe use "hegemony" to "allude to an absent totality, and to the diverse attempts at recomposition and rearticulation which, in overcoming . . . original absence, made it possible for struggles to be given a meaning."[38] Laclau and Mouffe call for a renunciation of the concept of society, if by "society" we mean the concept of a unified, organic, and integral civic or cultural body. Like an overarching narrative that provides meaning by finding points of intersection among specific elements and abjecting whatever does not mesh, the "absent totality" they refer to is a fiction whose ideological mission is to mask its very fictitiousness. That is, the social absent totality works by obfuscating the considerable work that goes into making it appear seamlessly natural and self-evident. Thus, Laclau and Mouffe ask us to "consider the openness of the social as the constitutive ground or 'negative essence' of the existing, and the diverse 'social orders' as precarious and ultimately failed attempts to domesticate the field of differences."[39] In other words, they propose that we understand "society" not as a closed or completed system, but as an ever-evolving testimony to the very impossibility of such a thing, since every perceived group that composes "society" is itself a frustrated attempt to constitute such a system. There are always, in other words, components or meanings of a group identity that either disrupt that identity or fail to be incorporated into it. Hegemony works by fixing identity and meaning as much as possible, even though a complete fixity is impossible. They write:

> The impossibility of an ultimate fixity of meaning implies that there have to be partial fixations—otherwise, the very flow of differences would be impossible. Even in order to differ, to subvert meaning, there has to be *a* meaning. If the social does not manage to fix itself in the intelligible and instituted forms of a *society*, the social only exists, however, as an effort to construct that impossible object.[40]

I will be considering hegemony in a manner designed to amalgamate the two positions I have just elaborated: the narrative construction of a unified meaning that incorporates disparate elements under a single rubric, jettisoning meanings or components that do not apply; and the social and political act of constructing the illusion of a unified social group by propounding a system of cultural, political, ideological, and personal belief systems that can be accepted as nearly universally valid or "realistic" for a given group of people.[41] Benedetto Fontana makes an explicit connection between these mental and political components when he writes, "Hegemony establishes a direct and intimate connection between knowledge and the subject to which it is addressed. The nature of the knowledge is determined by both the act of addressing and the subject that is addressed."[42]

Throughout *White Men Aren't* I will be considering the manner in which white masculinity arose and is sustained as a form of knowledge despite its presentation as a corporeal reality. Furthermore, in spite of my interest here in psychoanalysis—or, rather, as I hope to show, because of it—I will be working against the orthodox premise that sexual difference is the founding or fundamental difference in human subjectivity.[43] I would argue instead that difference is a social and signifying product of human interaction, and that as such no significant real, a priori characteristics precede our apprehension of them. What we will find throughout *White Men Aren't* is that the very recognition of difference implies a ground on which that difference matters, and that what we see as empirically and verifiably different in the real is already structured by the parameters governing our signifying systems. What I think we need to avoid, and what I fear the insinuation that sexual difference is the most fundamental human difference can lead to, is the assumption that sexual difference *is* anything at all prior to our representation of it. We have come to be comfortable with separating "sex" from "gender," in which the former term relates more or less to one's biological category and the latter to one's lived expression of it. More radical than that dialectical opposition, sexual difference as a primary and non- or pre-symbolic reality would be an uncontested and invariable fact of life.

Are there facts or entities that escape or precede our representation of them, facts that inhere absolutely in the realm of the real? Here I am taking the real to be that which resists the symbolic absolutely, that which lies completely outside of language, and that which is knowable only through the agency of the symbolic and on terms established in the symbolic.[44] Thus, whatever may be out there — be it the *X-Files'* truth, sexual difference, or black holes—we can only understand it through the mediation of concepts that our languages allow us to deploy. We will never know the thing in itself, and that is why, I would argue, to take sexual difference as somehow most fundamental misses the crucial fact that this is a difference that we have installed in and through language as well as in and on bodies. To construe sexual difference as primary or fundamental is to assume that we can somehow draw a line separating precisely that social area where sex differentiates itself from, say, power or, what will be principally under consideration here, race. It is also to obfuscate the fact that difference is constructed in the first place.[45] As Judith Butler writes, "The 'sex' which is referred to as prior to gender will itself be a postulation, a construction, offered within language, as that which is prior to language, prior to construction. But this sex posited as prior to construction will, by virtue of being posited, become the effect of that very positing, the construction of construction."[46] Consequently, even if it were the case that sexual difference belongs to the real, our understanding of it can only ever be, as Silverman in fact notes, ideological.

As I have indicated, much of what I am arguing about white masculinity derives from psychoanalysis, but I should make clear from the outset that I will be using some of the tools psychoanalysis provides without necessarily subscribing to all of its tenets. Furthermore, I will be using some of those tools in areas they were not necessarily designed to probe, in particular within the domain traditionally referred to as "race."⁴⁷ One of my goals will be to determine the extent to which psychoanalysis can be used as a philosophy and theory of representation extending well beyond—or, I suppose, depending on one's perspective, well short of—the purely personal and subjective, generally gendered research it was designed to facilitate. Furthermore, I will investigate some of psychoanalysis's blind spots, those areas that it takes for granted as uncontested, natural points of departure. Finally, I want to investigate the discourse of difference normally taken to be fundamental, both in psychoanalysis and in, I would venture, the culture at large: sexual difference. By looking at some of the fundamental texts of psychoanalysis, and also by looking at the manner in which other forms of difference have been articulated, I hope to show that not only do we strive to impose on whiteness and on masculinity a single and linear narrative and a unified meaning, but that in so doing we inadvertently participate in the production of white masculinity as a hegemonic discursive identity.

I alluded above to a correlation between white masculinity and hysteria, and throughout *White Men Aren't* I will defend and elaborate that claim. Some aspects of my argument will no doubt strike some readers as an unorthodox application of psychoanalytic theory to inappropriate domains of subjective identity. However, I will show not only how hysteria fittingly characterizes many of the fundamental components of white masculinity, but also why it might be politically and ethically efficacious to expand the term's specificity beyond femininity (with which it has often been primarily associated) to a domain completely outside that of sexual difference. On the one hand I believe that hysteria as both Freud and Lacan defined it can teach us much about ambiguous and ambivalent identities, and on the other hand even within the realm of sexual difference it seems clear that hysteria can reveal a great deal about masculinity. Many of the earliest debates surrounding hysteria focused on women, even though as many as 25 percent of nineteenth- and early twentieth-century case studies on hysteria concerned men. In some of their earliest remarks concerning hysteria, Breuer and Freud maintained that "hysterics suffer mainly from reminiscences," and they concluded that hysteria represented a failure or breach of spoken language; when the subject was unable to give utterance to some troubling event, the event retained its affect and manifested itself in bodily symptoms.⁴⁸

Throughout the lengthy debates concerning hysteria—beginning, perhaps, with two of psychoanalysis's most famous cases, Anna O. and Dora—one of the political issues never adequately resolved has been the extent to which hysteria as a form of bodily signification that disrupts traditional, male-dominated discourse represents a feminist challenge to that discourse. In the mid-1970s, Hélène Cixous and Catherine Clément explicitly formulated the debate: Cixous called Dora "the name of a certain troubling force,"[49] and argued that the hysteric, "with her manner of interrogating others . . . manages to bring down the men who surround her . . . by interrogating them, by ceaselessly returning to them the image that truly castrates them. . . . The hysteric, in my eyes, is the ideal woman (la femme-type) in all of her strength."[50] Clément, however, does not share Cixous's enthusiastic optimism, arguing that if one considers hysterics in the context of all social deviants it is clear that such deviance does not disrupt social structure, but only serves to reinforce it. Why, she asks, should one limit the "troubling force" to which Cixous refers only to hysterics and more specifically to femininity? The obsessional—typically male—accomplishes a certain destructive work, she points out. The hysteric, she concludes, cannot be revolutionary.[51]

Many scholars have linked a burgeoning feminist movement in the nineteenth century with the first appearances of female hysteria. Charles Bernheimer, for example, notes that Victorian women experienced anger and frustration toward a culture that gave them few outlets for expression. He argues that "women transformed their repressed hostility and desire into physical symptoms that simultaneously acknowledged and disowned those feelings."[52] Claire Kahane ties hysteria to early feminism's disturbance of gender categories and to the changes in forms of representation that those disturbances occasioned. Although Freud believed that hysterical symptoms would disappear when patients undergoing psychoanalysis could tell their own stories, Kahane points out that Freud never specified how women could possess their own stories when virtually all discursive outlets available to them made women the objects, rather than the subjects of narration.[53] Dianne Sadoff finds that psychoanalytic practice dominated by men produces the female hysteric for the male analyst's visual and erotic pleasure. She writes that "Lacan and his followers 'praised' the disease, reducing its symptomatology to an always already available female sexuality and the hysterical transference to a demand for love, as distinct from need or desire."[54] In her study of hysteria, Dianne Hunter has argued that in the early part of the twentieth century the surrealists recognized hysteria's disruptive force and that hysteria was "a discourse of femininity addressed to patriarchal thought."[55] In fact, Hunter goes so far as to call Bertha Pappenheim (Anna O.'s real name) "a forebear of psychoanalytic feminism."[56] Joel Kovel maintains that given the structure of psychoanalysis's attention to patients' speech, hysteria was bound to stake a place for a resistant feminist discursive practice: "Once the opening had been made to the 'talking cure,' it was only a matter of time before women would claim the power of speech and use it to define their own reality against that established by the prevailing order of things."[57]

Yet, some others do not find in hysteria the liberating potentials elaborated above. If Clément worried about the specifically feminine dimension of the cultural disruption that Cixous lauded, Jane Gallop reads Clément and Cixous's *La jeune née* as posing an open question on the subject of hysteria: "Throughout *La jeune née* the hysteric, particularly Dora, functions as an insistent question the two women writers are asking: Is she a heroine or a victim?"[58] Similarly, Jacqueline Rose asks whether the questions that arise from the study of hysteria can ever be answered, and she goes so far as to suggest that what hysteria teaches us is that desire itself is, in fact, a question. Rose stipulates that the study of hysteria will reveal less about the potential for a specifically feminine discourse or *écriture feminine* than it might about the impossibility of locating woman in a discourse that continually strives to foreclose the question of desire.[59] Concerned with what she argues is the impossibility of women's occupying the position of either subject or object of desire, Rose warns that we must nevertheless always bear in mind "the persistence of the question of desire *as* a question."[60] Toril Moi is among the most emphatically skeptical over claims that hysteria offers the possibility for feminine resistance when she writes that "Hysteria is not, *pace* Hélène Cixous, the incarnation of the revolt of woman forced to silence but rather a declaration of defeat, the realization that there is no other way out."[61]

I intend to show how the political and ethical debates surrounding the question of hysteria briefly outlined above apply as well to white masculinity.[62] While I will not strive to insert that identity directly into today's specifically feminist discussions about hysteria, I do want to underscore at this juncture not only the theoretical justifications for my claim that white masculinity operates through a form of hysteria, but the ethical ones as well. Certain very obvious dissimilarities separate white masculine hysteria from the variety delineated above; the most obvious lies no doubt in etiology. While the female hysteria arising largely in nineteenth-century Europe is generally attributed to women's inability to give vent to desire and their concomitant frustration with the cultural avenues for expression made available to them, there seems to be scant evidence that mainstream masculinity has faced similar frustrations.[63] Furthermore, if primarily female hysteria as analyzed by Freud and his followers focused on a breakdown of discursive language and the predominance of a somatic signifying system governed by symptoms and repressed memories, the aspects of hysteria I will center on with respect to white masculinity emphasize the identity's interrogation of its presumed others. That is, just as Rose emphasizes "the question of desire *as* a question," I will pinpoint the implicit and explicit manners in which white masculinity has asked those unlike itself to return to it an image of its identity. Following a Lacanian understanding of hysteria as one of four principal discourses, I will emphasize the manner in which that discourse focuses on the lack in the Other. Lacanian psychoanalytic theory teaches that the hysteric subject attempts to keep the Other's desire unsatisfied in order to be the desired object; I will show how since at least as far back as the seventeenth century (when the identity "white male" first began to exist qua identity), and continuing on today, white masculinity projected onto its presumed others a morphological and subjective lack that it then proceeded to fill. I will argue throughout *White Men Aren't* that the maneuver of externalizing fragmentation or division onto an other while simultaneously demanding of that other knowledge of white masculinity causes hysteria to join mastery. That, I will emphasize, is what lies behind the identity's enduring ideological strength.

It is surely obvious that I am not adhering to an orthodox Freudian or Lacanian perspective on hysteria. While retaining the Freudian observation that hysteria expresses through morphological symptoms a subject's conflicts concerning sexual difference, I am also dependent on the Lacanian discourse of hysteria, a discourse often structured in the form of a question, and one that interrogates its other about its own nature and constitution.[64] But if psychoanalysis has a lot to teach us about how unconscious forces operating largely if not exclusively through the domain of sexual difference can inform human subjectivity, it also has something to learn about other forms of difference that, I will be arguing throughout this book, seem equally able to inflect the unconscious in far-reaching ways. Thus, if I eschew an orthodox psychoanalytic line, it is in order to understand better the forces at work influencing human subjectivity, as well as the theories that we use to describe it. The tools psychoanalysis has provided give us tremendous power to understand how systems of representation, human subjectivity, and unconscious or otherwise obfuscated forces mutually affect one another, and as Ernesto Laclau has argued, psychoanalysis shares many of its strategies and basic assumptions with historical materialism, including an emphasis on struggle and antagonism and the affirmation that certain aspects of the social are implicitly opaque.[65] Throughout *White Men Aren't* I will look at some of the ways in which historical and psychoanalytic approaches can complement one another and, mindful of the disclaimer that those are generally incompatible analytical tools, I will nevertheless allow them to illuminate not only the cultural artifacts on which I bring them to bear, but the suppositions and limitations that they make about and on one another.

Psychoanalysis has fixed on the Oedipus complex as one of the fundamental components of masculinity, and so that is the first place I will turn to investigate not only how race and masculinity might inform one another in this time-honored formula for the production of sexual difference, but also how psychoanalysis might enrich its understanding of fundamental difference by looking beyond the sexual. In the following chapter, I will show that Freud was not only predisposed to view the world in a particular way—in a way that would cause him to assign an unequivocal meaning to a text that I will demonstrate is far more ambivalent than Freud allows—but that the psychoanalysis evolving from Freud's reading participates in a form of hermeneutical hegemony. That is, the standard Freudian reading of the Oedipus myth produces a unified narrative of what masculinity is supposed to be, but as I will show, Sophocles' *Oedipus Rex* is a very particular rendition of what was at the time a well-known story, one that complicates to a very great extent the way fifth-century Athenians understood their culture and their heritage. Sophocles' version of the story is perhaps less a version of the myth than it is a perversion: Sophocles adds a striking element to the story that seems not to have been found in its other, earlier tellings, and that element—which amounts to a possible acquittal for Oedipus of the guilt of killing his father—has much more to do with an evolving notion of what it meant to be a citizen of Athens than it does with what it means to be male. Thus, I will argue, traditional discourses of sexual difference have been put into play in order to account for political and civic difference. What gets lost in the process is much of Sophocles' striking ambiguity and ambivalence concerning what it meant to be a fifth-century Athenian man. What is gained is perhaps a whole set of assumptions about masculinity that psychoanalysis does not discover, as Freud assumed, but actually produces in the process.

Clearly, our ideological investments are in the way the hegemonic narratives we take to be realistic structure the world instead of simply reflecting what we want or need to believe. In other words, when we produce systems of meaning such as the hegemonic narratives I have been describing, we always and as a necessary result exclude other, competing meanings. Surely the scientist who confidently asserts that the answer to a prickly ideological question will be decided in the laboratory *because several laboratories are investigating the issue* is no different from the rest of us: we are all predisposed to see in specific, culturally determined ways, even when those ways seem so fundamental as to appear absolutely natural and given. By looking at the blind spots in cultural theory, we can learn a great deal about the sorts of leaps in sense that hegemonic narratives cause us to make in order to make their own positions seem natural and legitimate. I now want to turn to one of Western culture's most famous, self-blinded men—Oedipus, the king—in order to determine what sorts of hegemonic leaps of logic Oedipus makes to sustain sense and order in his world, and how we as Sophocles' readers have been induced to make those same leaps in order to maintain the meaning of identities in our lives.

1. COMPLEX OEDIPUS:

READING SOPHOCLES, TESTING FREUD

Oedipus might have already had a complex, but
certainly not the one to which he was to give his
name.—Jacques Lacan, *L'envers de la psychanalyse*

Although he is no doubt best known in the popular imagination for
his work on the Oedipus complex, Sigmund Freud had surprisingly little to say about the Greek tragedy from which the psychological
phenomenon draws its name. Freud was a psychoanalyst, not a classi-
cist; he directed the bulk of his interpretive efforts not to the written
word, but to his analysands' dreams and slips of the tongue. He does
pepper his writings with references to ancient and modern works of
literature, however, frequently displaying his traditional liberal education.[1] Regarding Sophocles' tragedy, from which he borrowed the name
of his most popularly recognized psychological discovery, he writes:
"*Oedipus Rex* is what is known as a tragedy of destiny. Its tragic effect is
said to lie in the contrast between the supreme will of the gods and the
vain attempts of mankind to escape the evil that threatens them. The
lesson which, it is said, the deeply moved spectator should learn from
the tragedy is submission to the divine will and realization of his own
impotence."[2] Freud's characterization of *Oedipus Rex* as a "tragedy of
destiny" follows traditional readings of the ancient tragedy. Generations of high school and college students have dutifully penned those
words in blue books, reproducing an interpretation that, however useful and to some extent reassuring, misses something of the curious
ambiguity regarding fate and its power in Sophocles' work. For although at face value the play is about Oedipus's discovery that he killed
his father and slept with his mother, the work closes without ever definitively proving the guilt of its hapless hero.

That challenges traditional interpretations of *Oedipus Rex,* of course, and according to the myth on which Sophocles based his tragedy there is no doubt at all about what Oedipus did. In fact, myriad readers havefound Sophocles' originality to consist not in modification of the mythic material, but in the specific peripeteia he brings to it to prolong suspense. Walker Burkert points out, for example, that the tradition behind the Oedipus story emphasizes the entire family and the curse brought down on it. He writes that "the singularity—indeed the audacity—of Sophocles' play is that this whole family context has nearly become invisible."[3] Overlooking Sophocles' originality, Freud himself described the work's action as "nothing other than the process of revealing, with cunning delays and ever-mounting excitement—a process that can be likened to the work of psycho-analysis—that Oedipus himself is the murderer of Laius, but further that he is the son of the murdered man and of Jocasta."[4] Yet, most readers, including Freud, pay little heed to one small detail in Sophocles' treatment of the material: although Oedipus was alone when he slew a man "at a place where three roads meet,"[5] the only living witness to Laius's murder testified that "the robbers they encountered were many and the hands that did the murder were many; it was no man's single power" (ll. 121–24). That detail obsesses Oedipus throughout the tragedy—even when he begins to suspect his own involvement in the murder, he tells Jocasta, "You said that [the witness] spoke of highway *robbers* who killed Laius. Now if he uses the same number, it was not I who killed him. One man cannot be the same as many" (ll. 844–45). However, when Oedipus sends for the herdsman who witnessed the crime, his interrogation centers exclusively on the identity of the infant that the herdsman received from Laius, the infant whom he had sent away to be raised by another man. The question of whether one man or many killed the king never arises, and consequently in Sophocles' treatment of the material it becomes impossible to determine whether Oedipus did, in fact, murder his father.[6]

Determining whether one man or many killed the king is not simply a matter of splitting hairs, because although the herdsman's testimony establishes Oedipus as the son of Laius, it does nothing to incriminate him in the murder.[7] The question, then, is why in Sophocles' version of the story does Oedipus jump to the conclusion that he is his father's murderer? In addition, why have readers, Freud included, jumped to that same conclusion for over two thousand years? Answering these questions will help us understand how Freud's description of the Oedipus complex actually *performs* the very phenomenon that it purports to elucidate. Indeed, the phenomenon Freud describes in the Oedipus complex—that young males long to do away with their fathers in order to enjoy exclusive possession of their mothers—is a symptom, and not a fundamental deep structure, of modern masculinity, particularly as it is represented in literature and culture.[8] Instead, Freud's Oedipus complex and the various discursive structures it implicates buffer the masculinity they describe from the emptiness, antagonism, and hysteria on which they are actually based. Despite the fact that it hinges on castration, the Oedipus complex actually produces a unified narrative of male wholeness that, as we will see, masks a more fundamental set of cultural conflicts, conflicts involving sexuality as well as other forms of social and political identity, including national and ethnic identity.

Even though Sophocles' tragedy does not necessarily represent what Freud believed it did—that Oedipus killed his father and slept with his mother—conventional (mis)interpretations of that tragedy can help us understand the production of a single and unified narrative of masculine gender identity, particularly as that identity has been staged in Western culture. To identify as a male in Western culture is to be held in the thrall of diametrically competing forces. To be masculine is to attempt identification with a figure that is itself designed to be inimitable. That figure, commonly referred to as the father, incarnates an image of stability, mastery, power, and knowledge.[9] The reading of *Oedipus the King* to follow demonstrates that in its attempt to provide a taxonomy of gender identification through the use of the Oedipus complex, Freudian psychoanalysis not only reproduces the very forms of acculturated gender identification it claims to be cataloging, in the process inadvertently naturalizing a highly fragmented, multiply articulated identity, but it also defends against fundamental personal antagonisms at the heart of nearly all complex human identities. Put quite simply, one man *can* be the same as many, in marked contradistinction to Oedipus's claim; in fact, that multiplicity is virtually impossible to avoid. Contemporary psychoanalysis, however, works to produce a more or less single narrative of a unified masculine identity.

Furthermore, in this reading of Oedipus—a reading I fully acknowledge goes against the grain of most treatments of the tale—not only did

Freud privilege a sexual economy in his reading of the story, but he did so at the expense of other forms of political and social difference we can see operating. While it is undeniably true that Oedipus identifies as the man who killed his father and had sex with his mother, the play also carefully highlights the changing role of the patriarch in fifth-century Athens, and it interrogates as well differences attributable to the status of "foreigner."[10] Hortense J. Spillers has recently called for a psychoanalytic theory empowered to account for subjects' unequal access to language, discourse, and culture, observing that "such an understanding would conduce toward a systematic materialist reading, which would establish 'race,' in turn, in perspective with other strategies of marking and stigmata."[11] This chapter proposes the groundwork for just such an enterprise, and by way of beginning, it looks at the sorts of difference that most contemporary psychoanalytic theory subsumes under sexual difference. In addition, it investigates the hegemonic process whereby the discourse of sexual difference obscures the operations of difference no less crucial, and no less fundamental.

As I have already mentioned, conventional readings of Greek tragedy emphasize an abstract antagonism between human will and divine fate. Peter D. Arnott sums up the traditional view of that conflict in concise fashion: "The protagonist struggles against fate and usually loses."[12] One has to wonder, however, what the point would be of a dramatic representation simply showing human beings repeatedly struggling against omnipotent gods and then losing. Indeed, Joel D. Schwartz asks, "Were the Greeks simply sloppy thinkers when they maintained . . . that freedom of the will is compatible with a belief that the gods routinely intervene in human affairs?"[13] The answer, of course, is no. Schwartz argues, as do many others, that Greek tragedy expresses otherwise inarticulable contradictions; it is a vehicle through which problems facing Athens and its citizens could be expressed, particularly when the concepts tragedy addressed may not have been available in discursive speech.

In addition to its artistic role, Greek tragedy fulfilled the political function of engaging citizens and others in the process of interrogating values and beliefs. The antagonisms depicted on stage encoded seemingly irresolvable tensions traversing Athenian democracy, tensions such as those arising when traditional institutions such as religion and family conflicted with civic developments such as justice and written law, and when the reorganization of customary tribal units into democratic, more or less centralized forms of government replaced older, aristocratic ones. The Athenian audience for whom Sophocles wrote would have experienced all of these tensions; they would have felt the tug of contradiction in these private and public aspects of their lives. Charles Segal writes that "tragedy, while affirming the interrelatedness of all parts of the human and divine order, also has the peculiarity of calling into question the normative codes themselves."[14] Tragic representation, in other words, is a public ritual that helps coalesce a complex of values, attitudes, and beliefs. At the same time, however, because tragedy is itself a determinate cultural practice, the illusion that it organizes other such practices in organic fashion is laid bare. One of tragedy's characteristic functions is thus to expose the complex discursive networks responsible for many cultural institutions in order to better foster debate about the nature of those institutions.

One might argue, of course, that nearly any complex work of representation produced and consumed in even a moderately multifarious society accomplishes the sort of "calling into question" of cultural codes that Segal describes. But the cultural and political situation in fifth-century Athens presents a very specific case: tragedies formed part of a public ceremony of religious worship, and they took place within the context of ritual displays of civic strength. Tragedy was, therefore, a highly political event, charged with unifying the Athenian population. Furthermore, radical political changes in the early part of the fifth century B.C.E. dramatically altered daily life. Cleisthenes of Athens overthrew the oligarchic government in power and reorganized the state, both in the number and distribution of its smaller administrative units. He divided Attica into parishes based not on traditional hereditary lines, but on geography, thus diminishing the influence of family power and local interest.[15] The radical reforms that moved Athens from aristocratic to democratic rule also included an overhaul of the judicial system and the institution of the *Ecclesia,* an assembly of citizens charged with deciding issues of civic justice and other political concerns.[16] Greek tragedy—*Oedipus the King* perhaps foremost among them—constituted a formal and ritualistic public examination of the changes punctuating the culture, especially as those changes involved how Athenians saw themselves as belonging to a specific political group.

The changes sweeping through Athens during the fifth century—

during the same period, that is, in which *Oedipus Rex* was staged for the first time—heralded the development of what we generally think of as relational politics. Affiliations and allegiances gradually shifted away from family and blood ties, away that is, from an aristocratic form of government, and toward political representation based more on geography and civic delegation than on kin. Whereas previously aristocratic domination had sustained itself through religious and cultural tradition backed up by military and economic power, in the democratically evolving Athens of the fifth century, constitutionally based laws promoted public discussion and debate. Greek cities had become too large and too diverse to continue to be governed simply by tradition, heads of household, or religious figures.[17] As Pierre Vidal-Naquet has argued, however, the political developments characterizing fifth-century Athens did not in themselves constitute the originality of the Greek city-state. In addition to the elements listed above, what distinguished the Athenian experiment was the fact that these phenomena "rose to the level of consciousness; the Greeks were aware of the 'crisis of sovereignty' even if only in comparing themselves to the empires nearby."[18] It was philosophic rationality, the rejection of the stultifying aspects of blind adherence to tradition, and perhaps most important, the tremendous value placed on logic, order, and reason, that characterized the Greeks of Sophocles' time.

It is clearly well beyond the scope of this study to do a history of Greece and its theater. What I want to emphasize, however, is the dramatic shift in cultural identity underway when Sophocles staged his *Oedipus the King* in 427 B.C.E. Athenians had only recently begun to conceive of their position in society—indeed, their very identities—as negotiable instruments, as entities that evolved and transmuted in response to public and private circumstances and to the discourses that supported them.[19] As Jean-Pierre Vernant argues, tragedy articulated the cultural anxiety attending the emerging democracy's confrontation with tradition: "The tragic sense of responsibility emerges when human action has already become an object of reflection, of internal debate, but has not yet acquired sufficient autonomy to be fully self-sufficient."[20] Consequently, contra Freud, we need to keep the political situation of fifth-century Athens in mind when we read *Oedipus the King*, because the tension between traditional social organization and the newly emerging one marks the tragedy explicitly. Oedipus himself represents the tension between two competing social systems, since, as we will see, he rejects traditional forms of knowledge in favor of newly legitimized forms of reason, yet at the same time the rulership to which he aspires is only available in traditional aristocratic forms.

We note the tension between the traditional and the innovative midway through the play when Jocasta observes that Oedipus does not think the way the rest of the citizens of Thebes do. She despairs, in fact, that "Oedipus excites himself too much at every sort of trouble, not conjecturing, like a man of sense, what will be from what was" (ll. 914–16). Here Jocasta explicitly laments the fact that Oedipus does not seem bound, the way the rest of the Thebans do, to a model of thinking rigidly tethered to the past. Unaware of or unimpeded by tradition, Oedipus the outsider can fathom possibilities unavailable to those restricted by traditional paradigms of thought; at the same time, however, and by that very token, he has little access to his city's cultural history. Culturally determined narrative models decree, of course, not only how specific events are to be interpreted—indeed, they decree what constitutes an event in the first place—but also how causal linear episodes provide individuals and communities with a sense of who they are and what their roles in the world are. Oedipus is both foreigner and citizen in Thebes. As a newcomer who rules the city, he personifies conflicting epistemological domains, since he has effectively brought to the city a new way of thinking, and he has done so in the guise of both a victor and a ruler. But as we see, his cultural difference makes him an imposing, even alarming figure: "Now when we look to him we are all afraid," Jocasta wails; "he's pilot of our ship and he is frightened" (ll. 922–23).

Oedipus's fear might be discomforting, but his ability to think in a manner unfamiliar to the citizens of Thebes is precisely what made him most welcome there in the first place. Only Oedipus was able to solve the Sphinx's riddle, a feat that on the surface involved little more than basic metaphoric thinking. Specifically, solving the riddle entailed substituting a dynamic view of humanity for a static one; it involved understanding that human identity is fundamentally multifarious and evolving ("What walks on four legs in the morning, two legs at noon, and three legs in the evening?"). As the axial figure linking two cultures, both geographically and historically, Oedipus embodies complex subjectivity while at the same time appearing to be the only person able to recognize its representation.

Yet, for as much as Oedipus may have understood the diversity of identity when it was posed as a riddle, he seems woefully unable—or unwilling, one might claim—to fathom complex subjectivity when confronted with it directly. When a messenger arrives to relate the news of the death of Polybus, Oedipus's presumed father, Oedipus tells him of the prophecy that he would kill his father and lie with his mother. The messenger answers that "Polybus was no kin to you in blood" (l. 1016), which provokes for Oedipus another frustrating enigma, one akin to his assertion that "one man cannot be the same as many": "How can my father be my father as much as one that's nothing to me?" (ll. 1017–18). Oedipus's question rivals the Sphinx's in logical complexity, and like the Sphinx's riddle, his conundrum, like that of Athens itself, once again involves competing or conflicting identities inhering in a single individual. How does one reconcile contradictory social and familial functions? It seems important to stress that Oedipus's question is not rhetorical, and that it does not simply mark his frustration when assailed with the overwhelming predicament toward which all the facts seem to be pointing. Rather, Oedipus struggles to find a way to negotiate an identity for himself when none is appropriate or ready-made.

As Sophocles nuances the traditional myth, jumping to the conclusion that he killed his father and slept with his mother is the ideal way for Oedipus to negotiate such an identity. Put quite bluntly, Oedipus would rather assume a criminal identity than risk having none at all.[21] He prefers to think of himself as a committer of regicide and incest rather than as a bastard or as a man with no organic or cultural tie to the city he lives in and rules. In fact, the blind prophet Teiresias taunts Oedipus with his lack of organic or historical tie to Thebes when he asks, "Do you know who your parents are? Unknowing you are an enemy to kith and kin" (ll. 415–16). Correlatively, as Oedipus recounts the events leading up to his murder of the old man, everything begins when "there was a dinner and at it a man, a drunken man, [who] accused me in his drink of being a bastard" (ll. 777–80).[22] As we have seen, Oedipus's interrogation of the herdsman establishes his identity as the son of Laius; it fails, however, to implicate him as his father's murderer. Consequently, when Oedipus fails to ask the herdsman the crucial question—was it one man or was it many who killed Laius?—we might speculate that, with his biological heritage positively confirmed, Oedipus now needs to establish for himself a cultural identity, one that specifies his relationship both to his father and to his city. That is, by not asking the decisive question of whether one man or many killed King Laius, Oedipus can insert himself into the history and culture of a group—the city of Thebes—by legitimizing its narratives and assuming them to be unironically true. He gets to occupy the position of cultural innovator simultaneously part of and distinct from the city that he rules. Thus, by refraining from asking the determining question Oedipus remains captivated in a concurrent acceptance and rejection of the patrimony, desiring to rule as king but doing so in a decidedly nontraditional manner. And, because his relationship to tradition is so remarkably ambivalent, Sophocles' Oedipus, the character that embodies competing cultural and historical traditions, is quite unusual: unlike the typical male whom Freud describes who wants to do away with his father, Sophocles' Oedipus desires *to have already killed his father*.[23]

There are two related conclusions we can draw from Sophocles' manipulation of the Oedipus myth, but before considering them I want to address the potential objections that I am "reading too much into" Sophocles' work or failing to respect the tradition in which he wrote. Both objections would imply that I am overemphasizing a particular textual detail to the point of distorting the work completely; they would suggest, I think, that we all know what the Oedipus story is "really about," and that any attempt to refocus emphasis simply perverts the work's meaning. Sandor Goodhart maintains that "to suggest that Oedipus may not have killed Laius is to play havoc with a legend that for twenty-eight hundred years has remained curiously intact."[24] But I want to be clear about what I am suggesting here. I am not suggesting that Oedipus did not kill Laius, only that as Sophocles presents the myth he has left room for equivocation and interpretation, a fact that should not surprise, given the social and political complexities prevalent when the work was produced. I want to remain faithful to one of the most basic tenets of literary analysis, the one that says, as E. R. Dodds reminds us about *Oedipus the King*, or any other literary work for that matter, that "what is not mentioned in the play does not exist."[25] Thus, since Sophocles leaves open to question the issue of Oedipus's guilt, we need not only to respect the work's ambiguity, but to reflect on what it means. What I am arguing is simply that *Oedipus the King* modifies the material on which it is based, much in the same way, for example, that *West Side Story* modifies *Romeo and Juliet*, which in turn modifies the story of Pyramus and Thisbe. It seems clear that the stories we repeat about ourselves and our past evolve over time to account for cultural change; in the Athens for which Sophocles wrote his version of *Oedipus the King*, new models of government and comportment based on internal argument and debate superceded revealed beliefs and received modes of regulation and conduct.

Thus, the first conclusion we can draw from Sophocles' execution of the Oedipus drama concerns its interaction with the culture in which it was produced. The character of Oedipus in many ways stands in for the evolving Athenian culture in which *Oedipus the King* was created, most notably in that both the character and the city value and profit from reasoned debate and logical deduction over traditional received knowledge.[26] Clearly, the conflict between a self-reliant, philosophical approach to resolving problems and the traditional method of relying on received wisdom comes to the fore immediately: In the play's opening speech Oedipus refers to himself as "Oedipus, whom all men call the Great" (l. 8), but the priest to whom he is speaking reminds him that "it was God that aided you, men say, and you are held with God's assistance to have saved our lives" (ll. 38–39). Demonstrating his hubris—or perhaps more in line with the argument I am trying to make, his originality and his independence—Oedipus boasts that "the riddle's answer was not the province of a chance comer. It was a prophet's task. . . . But I came, Oedipus, who knew nothing, and I stopped her. I solved the riddle by my wit alone" (ll. 394–98). Oedipus emphasizes that he had no access to tradition and that he solved the riddle exclusively through his own resourcefulness, consequently epitomizing the burgeoning Athenian values of reasoned dialog and self-determination, removed from the constricting influence of revealed truths or patrimonial wisdom.[27] In fact, as *tyrannos* of Thebes, Oedipus has seized power by force of his own intellect; he has not inherited it. What is particularly striking, however, is a further paradoxical feature of Oedipus's complex and contradictory set of identities: he is simultaneously self-made *tyrannos* and hereditary king, since he is also, and unbeknownst to him, Thebes's legitimate aristocratic ruler.

If Sophocles' Oedipus displays the contradictory values of an evolving democratic city and reflects the tension accompanying the demise of traditional knowledge, the second conclusion we can draw from this version of the tale involves Oedipus the individual. Jean-Joseph Goux has shown that the Oedipus myth in general illustrates the breakdown of other forms of tradition, particularly those involving initiation and ritual. He argues that typical mythic initiation scenarios depict neophytes learning from a wise initiator suitable responses to the trials they will undergo.[28] Initiates must remember their lessons until the ordeal comes, and then act appropriately. Standard initiation rituals generally involve a king who fears replacement by a younger man, whom he consequently banishes; the youth escapes, but eventually finds himself in a similar situation with a different king who, instead of imposing death, prescribes instead perilous tasks. When the hero accomplishes his tasks, he is rewarded with the king's daughter.[29] In the Oedipus myth, however, the initiation ritual is perverted, and the scandal of the Oedipus drama lies precisely in the near total distortion of the conventions of initiation. First, there is a complete absence of any king or authority figure who gives the young initiate a reason to act heroically.[30] Then, when the time to act comes, Oedipus invents the correct response himself, bypassing or completely disregarding the inheritance of knowledge that traditionally constitutes the transmission of culture. Furthermore, Goux maintains, initiates generally perform a heroic deed involving a victory over a threatening enemy. In the Oedipus myth, however, the hero triumphs not only without the help of traditional knowledge, but also without any remarkable feats of physical prowess: Oedipus prevails with only a word—the answer to the riddle. Finally, Oedipus does not even get to slay his enemy the Sphinx: instead, she commits suicide.[31]

In Goux's reading of traditional initiation rituals the young male undergoes a trial that distances him from the world of women and inducts him into the domain of men. The youth enters the founding male line of his society and takes part in the culture established by his dead male ancestors.[32] Consequently, in standard initiation tales "authority of the paternal type (the royal mandate) is . . . not opposed to the masculine subject's radical desire, but instead allows its realization."[33] That view directly opposes Freud's picture of an antagonistic intergenerational relationship, of course, and Goux maintains that as a perversion of ritual the Oedipus drama invalidates or in any case refuses to recognize the patrimonial culture normally sustained through the transmission of specific forms of desire. When Oedipus triumphs over the Sphinx he not only displays his superior intellect and capacity for new and creative ways of thinking; he also negates traditional forms of knowledge and short-circuits normal initiation rituals in what constitutes scandal and blasphemy to the initiated. Oedipus gets high marks for creativity and original thinking from those who value reason and cognition, but he fails miserably in the domain of cultural history and received paradigms of knowledge.

Sophocles' *Oedipus the King* consequently constitutes a complex reexamination of both public and private modes of thought. It concatenates the civic issues of reasoned public debate with the domestic matter of how young males accede to culturally appropriate masculinity. What makes this conflict laden with significance is the fact that the tension between traditional social organization and the newly emerging one is generally encoded as a drama about the production of gender. Specifically, that tension gets cast in terms of a father-son relationship, or perhaps more specifically still, in terms of a son's emergence into the status of adult male. While the traditional initiation ritual that Goux describes involves the boy's distancing from his mother and the world of women, it also involves the young man's simultaneous convergence with and distancing from the father. The engendering of a young male as culturally masculine, in other words, holds him in the thrall of a father figure. He is enjoined to identify with that figure while at the same time forbidden to emulate him absolutely.

I will return in a moment to discuss the significance of casting civic and national identity in strictly gendered terms, as most psychoanalytic readings of Sophocles have done. I want to emphasize, however, that as Sophocles tells the traditional Oedipus myth, the conflict between traditional forms of knowledge and ways of knowing that derive from logic and reason comes to figure generational masculine conflict. What characterizes this conflict is Oedipus's strong desire to identify as Laius's murderer while simultaneously insisting on his own unassisted resolution of the Sphinx's riddle. On the one hand, his refusal to pose the potentially exculpating question of how many robbers descended on Laius shows the extent to which Oedipus wants to believe the prophecy that predicted he would kill his father. The coming to pass of that prophecy would place Oedipus in a specific cultural order by inserting him into history and tradition. On the other hand, Oedipus wants to be the man who, without any help from older, more experienced cultural initiates, succeeds in a ritualistic trial designed to test his mettle. Oedi-

pus is caught, in other words, between tradition and innovation, between identifying with the father and rejecting or invalidating him.
Furthermore, when Oedipus jumps to the conclusion that he has already killed his father, he establishes a specific relationship to him that
works quite differently from the model that Freud proposed: in Freud's
scenario the youth is engaged in a continuing impulse to murder the
father until he reconciles himself to accepting a metaphoric substitution of the father's prized possession. Sophocles' Oedipus breaks free
from the drama of sexual jealousy and control characterizing the father-
son relationship because he has the rare opportunity to compete with
the father on equal footing and, rarer still, he wins. Finally, in whichever
version of the tale we subscribe to, Sophocles' or the traditional one,
Oedipus never really gets to participate in the event itself, either because he was unaware of whom he was killing, or because he never
really did it in the first place.

What this suggests is that the event itself matters far less than the
significance attached to it, or, perhaps more pointedly, that the event
only becomes an event after a synthesis of apparently related "effects"
is recognized and negotiated. Freud himself observed this same phenomenon in his famous case history of the Wolf Man. The Wolf Man
dreamed of six or seven white wolves perched in a walnut tree in front of
his bedroom window; the wolves had their ears pricked at attention, and
the dreamer feared being eaten up by the wolves.[34] Freud's renowned
analysis of this dream and its dreamer postulates that the four-year-
old boy must at some early point have witnessed his parents having
intercourse—a "primal scene"—and that the child's misunderstanding
of the biomechanics involved led to a series of neuroses involving anal
eroticism and fear of castration. But the Wolf Man's analysis is interesting less for what it reveals about how early memories influence later life,
and more for the manner in which recollections are produced like
stories from an ensemble of psychically collectable narrative material.
Freud states the case quite boldly: "So far as my experience hitherto
goes, these scenes from infancy are not reproduced during the treatment as recollections, they are the products of construction."[35]

We therefore need to understand both the manner in which the
aboriginal event is inferred from states of affairs deemed to be effects of
that event and the reasons for which that event seems necessary in the
first place. In his own analysis of primal events constructed in analysis,

Freud considers them to be "products of the imagination, which find their instigation in mature life, which are intended to serve as some kind of symbolic representation of real wishes and interests, and which owe their origin to a regressive tendency, to an aversion from the problems of the present."[36] The event presumed to be both at the origins and at the heart of a current state of affairs, in other words, is really itself little other than a representation, a backward formation of what, given how things are, must have been. And while this would seem to be a perfectly natural way of conceptualizing cause and effect relationships, it is crucial to point out that the constructions produced in these sorts of narrative analysis restrict any speculation about the past to some image of the present. As Freud himself remarks in the *Interpretation of Dreams*, "To explain a thing means to trace it back to something already known."[37]

By way of a brief example of this phenomenon, we might look at another Freudian text, one to which I will return in greater detail later. In *Totem and Taboo*, Freud relies on another myth, this time that of the primal horde. Freud's point in this essay is to explain the origins of the incest taboo, and to do so he fabricates, along with Charles Darwin and J. J. Atkinson, a story of what conditions must have been like for the young males who, subject to the power of the oldest and strongest male, were prevented from mating. In this essay Freud is attempting to understand the series of events that lead up to the incest taboo, that psychic and social principle that ostensibly informs all of Western culture. The problem, however, is that he describes the events leading up to the establishment of the incest taboo in terms of conditions resulting from that taboo:

> Atkinson (1903) seems to have been the first to realize that the practical consequence of the conditions obtaining in Darwin's primal horde must be exogamy for the young males. Each of them might, after being driven out, establish a similar horde, in which the same prohibition upon sexual intercourse would rule owing to its leader's jealousy. In course of time this would produce what grew into a conscious law: "No sexual relations between those who share a common home."[38]

The simple point I want to make here, and on which I will elaborate later, is the following: The incest taboo is arguably the fundamental organizing principle of Western culture (for psychoanalysis, at least). Psychic events and predilections are organized according to principles relative to the incest taboo, and specific features such as gender characteristics or family structure find their motivation and their roots there. Since the incest taboo coordinates the sexual dynamics obtaining as the result of a specific traumatic event—the brothers' joining together to kill the father—it makes little sense to describe pre-totemic group males in terms of cultural stereotypes characterizing the aggressive and sexually jealous males that the primal myth is meant to have produced. In other words, although the myth purports to describe how the incest taboo originates, it relies on contemporary conceptions about gender and sexuality to formulate its own prehistory. It pinpoints a moment that heralded in a radically new gender dynamic—the moment at which young males banded together and killed the primal father—and yet it describes the strain of masculinity that preceded that event in terms of the modern stereotypes of masculinity that the event itself ostensibly produced.[39]

In a similar manner the traditional reading of *Oedipus the King* rehearses the project of casting an explanatory narrative in terms of the thing being explained, such that the very event deemed responsible for a given state of affairs seems always already determined by that state. What we fail to see in a culturally determined reading such as this is the simple fact that our perceptions of the way things are—and this comprises phenomena as complex as causal sequences of events or gender characteristics—are motivated by culturally and politically determined notions of what should or could happen in a given situation. We believe that Sophocles' Oedipus killed his father because tradition and the apparent logic of the plot tell us that; the point here, however, is that the logic of the plot is itself already cast in an Oedipal tone. We tend not to consider that a nuanced version of the myth might reveal not only something about the culture in which it was produced, but facts about our own assumptions in the process of reading, and about the narrative structures that order the way we perceive the world.[40]

I would thus argue that our jumping to the conclusion that Oedipus killed his father—the same conclusion to which the principal character jumps, it must be noted—glosses over a significant subtlety that Sophocles places before us. That subtlety concerns the possibility for multiple identities, as well as Oedipus's peculiarly conflicted and contradictory

position with respect to cultural transmission and to the socially legitimized version of masculinity implicated therein. Oedipus is caught in a
double bind, an impasse that places him squarely in the middle of two
competing forms of cultural identity. On the one hand there is the
traditional paternalistic variety, in which older members of the society
govern through strength and received knowledge; and on the other
hand there is the sort that functions through reasoned debate and that
values innovative intellectual responses unfettered by established paradigms. Sophocles' Oedipus wants the power and privilege of the one
without the ritualistic ordeal of the other. He wants the rights and
prerogatives of an initiate, but spurns initiation. In short, Oedipus is
a cultural hysteric, unwilling and unable to situate himself squarely into
a single identity, even though that is precisely what he thinks he is
doing.[41]

By casting himself as the principal character in the story the proph-
ets told, Oedipus legitimizes that story as the single and unique truth
about himself and about his culture. Paradoxically, however, by validat-
ing the prophecy and presuming that he killed his father, Oedipus
simultaneously abrogates the very process of initiation that would allow
him to occupy the position of king and husband he holds. That is, only
through the traditional initiation ritual can a man become king and
marry the prized female, and there are numerous examples from classical mythology onward to back this up: Perseus, Jason, most of the
bildungsroman tradition, and even contemporary adventure films such
as *Speed, Chain Reaction,* or even *Ocean's Eleven.* By placing himself in
presumed equality with the father and then defeating him Oedipus
gains the coveted position of king, but only by perverting the ritualistic
process through which a youth accedes to culturally sanctioned masculinity. Ironically, then, when you win, you lose: if you actually manage
to defeat the father, you cannot remain in the position he occupied
because you gained that position through illegitimate means. In the
new cultural order that Oedipus inaugurates, initiation, it seems, is
always failed initiation.

Finally, Oedipus's desire to have killed the father goes beyond instituting a new order based not on tradition, but on the son's unique
authority. It introduces the element of filial competition with the father,
and the desire to have defeated him establishes the son's relationship to
the father as one of equality. In other words, the desire to have killed the

father represents an attempt to transcend an interdiction, to neutralize whatever power or authority the father may have possessed. When Oedipus jumps to the conclusion that he has killed his father, he is erecting a culturally significant story in the place of an absence—the absence of his own identity within the social and historical order of the city he has come to rule, and the absence of a single, coherent narrative to account for his presence within that city. Oedipus has come to fill the paternal function through illegitimate means, and the only way for him to justify his position is to invent a plausible fiction simultaneously to mask his lack of cultural antecedent and to account for how he got into his current position.

I argued earlier that Oedipus's story is symptomatic of hegemonic masculine identity, particularly as psychoanalysis has theorized it. To the extent that a symptom articulates by simultaneously joining and expressing strands of signification, Oedipus's story is significant in its production of a tale designed specifically to cover over an original absence—in this case, Oedipus's lack of identity within a particular history and culture. His construction of an originary conflict, even—or perhaps especially—one about which he has no certain memory, casts the event itself as subsequent to its interpretation. That is, because Oedipus's story needs to have a point, and because the tragedy about him has to be tragic, he must have killed his father, or else there is no reason to tell the tale.[42] Cynthia Chase goes so far as to suggest that Oedipus is not only "the one person in history *without* an Oedipus complex" but also that he is "the one person who actually enacts patricide and incest [and who] completely misses the experience—until after the fact, when the parrincest is inscribed as a palimpsest and becomes readable for the first time."[43] For Chase, Oedipus's murder of Laius is a sort of primal scene, one that makes sense only after other significant events enter into the story to configure the meaning of what later comes to be the founding moment of the tale. In any event, what is emphasized in these readings is the introduction of a narrative structure to Oedipus's life, a structure that, it cannot be overemphasized, casts the putative narrative causes of the story in terms of the effects they are supposed to have produced.

Sophocles' *Oedipus the King* reveals the truth about desire, then, but it is not the sexually aggressive masculine desire that Freud believed he found. The desire operating in this work is the desire for coherence; it is the desire to fill the yawning void we call the real with the articulated meanings that hegemonic narratives produce. Thus, *Oedipus the King* is about a character who strives to insert himself into a cultural tradition by allowing the force of narrative structure to impose identity on him. Furthermore, as leader of his people, that character provides a political dimension to the imposition of narrative meaning. Finally, and perhaps most crucial for the point I am making concerning the necessary imbrication of other forms of identity with what we take to be gender identity, as readers of the tragedy we perform the same narrative and ideological work when we identify Oedipus as the guilty party and as the emblem of masculine desire and subjectivity that Freud found him to be. In other words, it is simply not the case that Freud's interpretation of Sophocles relates some fundamental truth about masculine desire, as though there existed some sort of masculinity prior to its historical and cultural expression. Freud's interpretation first covers up the truth of that desire by causing a reassuring narrative logic to supplant the fundamental anxiety actually at the heart of the tale, an anxiety about the underlying lack constitutive of any subjectivity whatsoever. Then Freud's interpretation of *Oedipus the King* installs in that lack a story deemed universal in which males want to compete with their fathers for mating privileges.

What makes this a story about *masculinity*, and not just subjectivity in general, is precisely the fact that in a heteronormative economy the only thing that males could compete for qua males would be mating privileges, that is, something related strictly to the particular arrangement of the male body. Consequently, when Freud reads *Oedipus the King*, he is able to collapse onto the apparent naturalness of the body a host of other sorts of multiple differences, in the process applying to those differences a gendered nuance. The telling of the story, the assumption that Oedipus must have killed his father, effects hegemonic masculinity because it casts the son as the father's equal, and at the same time it depicts the initiation ritual as fundamentally flawed and perverted. Furthermore, the telling of the story brings together in a single epistemological framework a host of disparate elements and causes them to relate to one another by imposing a common set of signifiers.

Bernard Knox maintains that the oracle predicting that Oedipus would one day kill his father and sleep with his mother must be true, since "if the oracles and the truth are not equated the performance of the play has no meaning."[44] However, I have been contending that the play derives its meaning not from the continuation of traditional knowledge, but from the application of different narrative meanings to situations in which they may not apply. *Oedipus the King*, like its eponymous hero, installs meaning where meaning is lacking, and that is precisely the play's significance; it is also what the Oedipus complex does. In other words, it is the attempt to provide a comprehensive narrative account for the fragmented individual and social contradictions obtaining in Oedipus, in his family and associates, and in his culture that renders the play meaningful. This is the play's fundamental gesture: it interrogates the stability of meaning by depicting a hero who opts for a particular interpretation—and a nasty one, at that—rather than face the potential incoherence of his own existence within the culture he inhabits.

As Goux shows, that is also how the standard Freudian interpretation of *Oedipus the King* proceeds. Goux maintains that one latches onto castration and the paternal threat rather than face the horrifying reality of absolute absence, an absence whose lack of qualities or connections would nullify the subject associated with it. Arguing that "the most decisive form of castration [is] . . . a confrontation with the lack of the Thing,"[45] he writes:

> The Oedipus complex constitutes a veil that dissimulates the overwhelming radicality of that desire and that castration. The Oedipus complex has the function of repressing castration. Faced with the absence of the Thing (the primordial object of desire that the mother situates but with which she cannot be identified), the Oedipus complex positions paternal conflict as a veil. The Oedipal subject is protected by the paternal threat (which makes him believe that the object of his desire for absolute jouissance is simply forbidden) from the radical confrontation with castration and death.[46]

To confront the lack of the thing is to risk subjective annihilation, since it is precisely one's relationship to the thing as object of desire that grants one subjective consistency and substance in the first place.[47] The subject is defined, in other words, by what it desires, and what it lacks is thus constitutive. In a formulation similar to Goux's, Slavoj Žižek argues that "what we call 'subjectivization' (recognizing oneself in inter-pellation, assuming an imposed symbolic mandate) is a kind of defense mechanism against an abyss, a gap, which 'is' the subject."[48] Oedipus and his heir, the typical male subject, prefer prohibition and coercion to absence and emptiness, but it is important not to underestimate the radical nature of the emptiness they fear, since this is an empti-ness that goes well beyond the monotony of ennui and reaches into the depths of existential nothingness. To confront the absence of the thing is to dissociate as a subject. Oedipus and the typical—principally psychoanalytic—male subject construe in place of that yawning absence a structured narrative designed to conceal fundamental emptiness. That hegemonic narrative operates by erecting a plausible fiction de-signed to unify the diverse members of a group under a single, nor-malizing cultural apparatus. Hegemonic narratives become true, or more properly speaking "realistic," not because they more adequately describe the world, but because for a variety of historical and political reasons they are better able to insert themselves between subjects and the world in which they live.

So what does the apparent discrepancy between Freud's reading of *Oedipus the King* and the one that I have been proposing reveal? How do hegemonic narratives come into play to influence how we think our-selves and our relationships to features such as gender and race that we have come to consider fundamental to our identity? And how, precisely, does white masculinity embody a specific form of hegemonic narrative, subsuming into itself features not normally associated with gender or race as they are narrowly defined? As we will now see, these questions converge precisely on the issue of how the individual possessing or performing the identity in question deals with antagonism—conflicting or contradictory vectors of social meaning—and where that antagonism comes from.[49]

Antagonism, as I will be using the term, refers to a disruption or a blockage in one's sense of identity. It can be purposeful or incidental, but in general it offers a competing interpretation or perspective on the things we take to be fundamentally defining of ourselves. Antagonism arises on individual or group levels when incompatible meanings or demands for response attempt to inhabit the same psychic, social, or economic space.[50] There need be nothing logical or particularly pene-trating about this incompatibility or competing interpretation—as Žižek has shown, it is most often self-contradictory: "To the racist, the 'other' is either a workaholic stealing our jobs or an idler living on our labor, and it is quite amusing to notice the haste with which one passes from reproaching the other with a refusal to work to reproaching him for the theft of work."[51] The crucial thing about antagonism is that it must disrupt the flow of meaning or signification that gives one a sense of identity. What is antagonistic must therefore appear to come from without; it must pose a threat to any synthesis of meaning that would allow it to coexist with that which it appears to threaten.[52] As Ernesto Laclau and Chantal Mouffe put it, antagonism "situates itself within the limits of language and can only exist as the disruption of it—that is, as metaphor" (125).[53] Or, to paraphrase Žižek again, the paradox behind what I am referring to as antagonism is that the very thing that I take to be fundamental to my sense of identity, and hence unavailable to the other, is precisely that thing that the other seems to threaten in me.

In Freud's reading of *Oedipus the King,* and, it must be stated, in most psychoanalytic accounts of gendered subjectivity, the male subject faces an antagonism in the guise of the father who represents all of the things he would like to be, but who simultaneously prohibits him from achieving full satisfaction.[54] As the male subject introjects the father's authority and prohibitions in the form of the superego, the fundamental masculine antagonism inheres within the subject himself. As Freud expresses this dilemma, the male subject receives two competing injunctions: "You *ought to be* like this (like your father)"; and "you *may not be* like this (like your father) . . . you may not do all that he does; some things are his prerogative."[55]

Masculine gender identity for Freud is consequently inherently and internally antagonistic, and even if Freud had no recourse to the definition of antagonism that I am developing here, his description of male subjectivity, particularly as it germinates in the Oedipus complex, emphasizes internal contradiction. In *The Ego and the Id* he stresses that "an ambivalent attitude to his father and an object relation of a solely affectionate kind to his mother make up the content of the simple positive Oedipus complex in a boy,"[56] and later, in the "Dissolution of the Oedipus Complex," he argues that the ambivalence to competing external forces takes up residence in the subject himself: "If the satisfaction of love in the field of the Oedipus complex is to cost the child his penis, a conflict is bound to arise between his narcissistic interest in that part of his body and the libidinal cathexis of his parental objects."[57] The point here is that what Freud describes happening in the little boy— the introjection of conflicting events nevertheless clustered around his gendered identity—is the same phenomenon I am claiming we see happening in Sophocles' Oedipus, with the notable difference that the latter is required to synthesize details extending well beyond gender and into a far broader spectrum of social and political concepts.

Freud felt from his very first writings about the Oedipus complex that the phenomenon was universal. Attempting to explain the "riveting power of *Oedipus Rex*" and why this particular tragedy of destiny is so much more compelling than any of the others, Freud writes in a letter to Fliess: "But the Greek legend seizes on a compulsion which everyone recognizes because he feels its existence within himself. Each member of the audience was once, in germ and in fantasy, just such an Oedipus, and each one recoils in horror from the dream-fulfillment here transplanted into reality, with the whole quota of repression which separates his infantile state from his present one."[58] Later, he would remark that the Oedipus complex "is determined and laid down by heredity," and that the phenomenon "is bound to pass away according to programme when the next pre-ordained phase of development sets in."[59] Freud went even further in underscoring the unidirectional, unwavering line of human psychic development: on two separate occasions he pronounced his often-quoted "anatomy is destiny" admonition, and we might take all of this as indication that for Freud, not only is the Oedipus complex universal and unavoidable, but it inheres in the masculine subject as a fraught and never-ending inner antagonism separating his erotic longings from his cultural aspirations.[60] Freud privileges the irreducibly material aspects of the human psyche in his theories of erotic development and attachment; the features that characterize the unconscious life of the mind derive nearly exclusively in the last instance from the specific physical arrangement of our bodies and from the manner in which cultural practices dictate our uses of them.

While it would be difficult to disagree with the claim that our psychic dispositions have a material foundation and that the body and the mind influence one another in complex, generally unconscious ways, what I now want to investigate are other avenues for conceptualizing the manner in which the Oedipus complex is installed in the human psyche, and what sorts of discourses such a complex might articulate. Whether

Freud is right to claim that the Oedipus complex is nearly universal, and/or that it is hereditarily determined is of less interest here than the desire for a unified narrative of cultural identity that the theory itself expresses, and the figure of the father incarnating complex contradictory social identities. And, even though the figure of the father provides the masculine subject with an antagonistic set of demands to internalize, that figure nevertheless remains emblematic of the desire for a master narrative, since all components, however contradictory, remain distinctly attached to the father himself. The father, in Freud's schema, becomes, like the dollar bill I have alluded to, the currency of meaning, the thing that allows unlike elements to compare themselves by converting their meaning into signifiers he makes available. What remains, however, is the question of what gets lost in the conversion, and what gets added.

As I have shown, Sophocles' Oedipus tries to articulate a set of differing discourses in order to provide himself a narrative able to account for his cultural and historical determinations, but the crucial difference between Sophocles' Oedipus and the one that Freud relates lies precisely in the absence of the figure of a master. Because the title character in *Oedipus the King* desires to have already killed his father, despite the existence of evidence to the contrary, he differs radically from the masculine subject in Freud's Oedipus complex, who remains defined in large part by the desire to kill the father. Thus, what we see in Sophocles' work is the repudiation of a master figure and the annihilation of tradition, whereas in Freud the masculine subject installs tradition and the master within himself. The difference is subtle, yet crucial: what is perhaps most significant for the point I am trying to elaborate here is that while Freud's Oedipus internalizes an antagonism that comes to him from the same source—the father—Sophocles' Oedipus must compose a tale of his own identity by bringing together discursive strands from a wide variety of sources. In *Oedipus the King* the title character agonizes over the question of how one man can be the same as many, emphasizing the act of articulation, in which the telling of the tale expresses individual identity by bringing together strands from various sources. In addition, he strives to assert his independence and the value of his own critical thinking over traditional modes of knowledge while simultaneously attempting to be a hereditary ruler. Entering the city as an outsider—and both Teiresias and Oedipus himself explicitly emphasize his foreignness[61]—Oedipus constructs a hegemonic narrative that weaves together strands of meaning extending well beyond the purview of gender and into the discourses of national or ethnic identity, history, and cultural unity.

The point we need to draw from all of this is that it certainly seems true, as Freud claimed, that fundamental antagonisms pertaining to the way we live our bodies inform the organization of our psyches at the most basic level. But what I am contesting is the contention that such a psychic organization needs to take place strictly or even largely along gender lines. I have been arguing that difference of whatever variety is a product not of the interplay of elements pre-existing our apprehension of them somewhere in the real, but of significant cultural choices, themselves the product of history, that are then mapped onto the human body as representative of the real, as a means, that is, of naturalizing or legitimizing those choices. Indeed, we can find ample evidence of this in the work of Freud himself, and a few comparatively simple examples might help clarify this complexity. In "Some Psychological Consequences of the Anatomical Distinction Between the Sexes" (1925), Freud implicitly underscores the remark he had made a year earlier that "anatomy is destiny" when he writes that little girls "notice the penis of a brother or playmate, strikingly visible and of large proportions, at once recognize it as the superior counterpart of their own small and inconspicuous organ, and from that time forward fall victim to the envy for the penis."[62] This is the sort of remark that has made Freud an easy mark for psychoanalysis's detractors. If the girl "at once recognizes" the penis as "superior," it seems that Freud believes not that the penis is culturally invested with the sorts of meaning he describes, but that it somehow is naturally endowed with such a superiority. The voluminous criticism stemming from Freud's anatomical assumptions interrogate not only the implicit sexism in psychoanalytic investigation, but topics as diverse as the nature of signification, the heterosexist imperative at work in Freud's writing, and the status of psychoanalysis as political and/or philosophical critique.[63]

Another example can help us understand not only the complexity of this phenomenon, but some of the other social registers at play in the production of difference and the manner in which that difference appears to reside in the body. In the "History of an Infantile Neurosis" (the Wolf Man) to which I referred briefly above, Freud elaborates a stunningly complex psychic operation in which a very young child witnesses his parents engaged in *coitus a tergo*. As a result of this observation, the child develops, among other things, a castration anxiety, an erotics centered largely if not exclusively on the anus, a fear of wolves, a love of maids (especially when they are on all fours), and a religious obsession that causes him to pronounce the words "God" and "shit" together. Yet, in spite of the almost mind-numbing array of distinctions that this extremely young child is supposed to be able to make, Freud dismisses the idea that the images of the family's mute water-carrier and maid, who were for the Wolf Man surrogate parents, represented for the boy any sort of intention to debase his mother and father, "even though it is true that both parents have come to be represented [by the Wolf Man] as servants." Freud continues: "A child pays no regard to social distinctions, which have little meaning for it as yet; and it classes people of inferior rank with its parents if they love it as its parents do."[64] While I find Freud's analysis of the Wolf Man to be compelling and persuasive, I must admit that it strikes me as hard to believe that any child capable of making the sorts of remarkably subtle and complex sexual distinctions Freud describes could not also recognize the far less subtle differences obtaining in social class.[65]

A final example can show how culturally produced meaning appears to inhere in the bodies that reflect them. In a passage related to the one I cited above that deals with children's perceptions of the anatomical distinction between the sexes, Freud writes of the little boy and his concerns. Discovering that not all creatures possess a penis, and hence that he is implicitly in danger of losing his own, the boy falls victim to castration anxiety. "The little boy undoubtedly perceives the distinction between men and women," Freud writes, "but to begin with he has no occasion to connect it with any difference in the genitals."[66] What we have here is Freud's startlingly explicit admission that the child's recognition of cultural difference—what I might broadly call "gender" here—necessarily precedes his recognition of anatomical difference. That is, the child has already formed the categories "men" and "women," but he has not assigned any anatomical feature as the marker of distinction governing those categories. Consequently, what this means is that the child must understand gender difference before he can map it onto anatomy. Genital difference thus comes to confirm the sorts of social distinctions that the child has already been able to make between men and women.

At issue here is the reason why Freud can state categorically and out of hand that a child pays no regard to differences attributable to things such as social class, but yet seems able—indeed driven—to differentiate fine shades of meaning in sexual matters, meanings that a good many adults would have trouble negotiating. The standard psychoanalytic response to this question would be to demonstrate that since the unconscious is structured according to sexual fantasies involving distinctions just such as these, not only is it not surprising that a child could produce metaphoric substitutions of the sort Freud describes, it is well nigh expected. But as we have observed, "believing is seeing." That is, as I argued above and in the introduction, the cultural and epistemological preconditions for observing specific phenomena need to be met before we can "see" the phenomenon in question. That is how we can explain, for example, the fact that systems of gender or racial oppression could exist for centuries before a population even begins to recognize the phenomenon. Since we never confront an object of observation directly, but must always pass through the lens of representation, any observation is necessarily culturally skewed. In the case of the little boy whom Freud describes, it is the cultural difference distinguishing the manner in which men and women live their lives that leads the boy to search for an anatomical foundation, which is then presumed to be anterior or causal. Thus, the anatomical foundation of difference—broadly speaking, the premise that sexual difference is the fundamental or primary difference—turns out to be a cultural phenomenon, one that maintains its own coherence and consistency by obfuscating the other operations that support it.

The point I think we now need to consider is whether—given the cultural production of gender we have just observed—it is possible to disarticulate gender from the various other social, historical, and cultural institutions with which it is necessarily not only associated, but, indeed, produced. What could make us so confident that when we speak of gender we have been able to isolate it from other, equally constitutive and fundamental categories? I would argue, in fact, that when we call in our theoretical enterprises for examinations of the intersections of such entities as gender and race, we should first understand that they were never really separate in the first place.[67] That is, social and cultural categories such as race and gender, like all categories or divisions of knowledge, are all part of the vast archeology of knowledge that cultures erect. Since neither gender nor race pre-exists the categories that name them—since, that is, they are not part of the real— it is we who have artificially disarticulated them by causing them to appear to have crystallized out of the nearly infinite permutation of human identity features we have been able to construct.

Any strategies for reading texts or events necessarily emphasize particular components and downplay or disregard others, of course. I have tried to show, taking the particular example of psychoanalysis as my model, how explanatory or elucidative systems can often participate in the hegemonic narratives they would purport merely to describe.[68] In the particular case at hand, I have looked at the manner in which psychoanalysis causes differences not principally or even generally associated with gender to express themselves according to contemporary logics of sexual difference. Not only does such a strategy de-emphasize other dynamics and conflicts obtaining in the text or even in question; by casting such dynamics as readable only through the template of sexual difference, it also accomplishes the hegemonic maneuver of filtering out specific layers of information and promoting or otherwise emphasizing material or relationships relevant to a particular ideological agenda. Freudian psychoanalysis helps sustain the hegemony of the masculine subject by subsuming under the rubric of gender political conflicts that extend well into the domain of nation, of class, of epistemological traditions, and of specific rituals encoded far more for a civic identity than a sexual one. Freudian psychoanalysis installs in the place of a dread centering on the lack of proper social identity a nexus of anxieties focusing almost exclusively on bodily integrity and the predominance accompanying the constructed yet socially valued wholeness of the ideal male body.

Two significant consequences derive from the imposition of sexual difference as the principal articulation of all difference onto a host of other significant social identifiers. On the one hand, the restrictive focus on gender to the near exclusion of other identity features produces a belabored stress on the binary opposition between male and female. This belabored stress causes nearly all social tension to conform to this opposition, and at the same time provides an unnecessary and unwarranted valuation on males as the dominant side of a binary that artificially excludes more subtle social distinctions to which men, by virtue of their gender alone, have no legitimate claim. In other words, the overvaluation of gender works in favor of men because it excludes competing, perhaps more subtle social markers with which men qua men have no particular relationship. On the other hand, because of the manner in which contemporary, mainly Freudian psychoanalysis has leveraged the other social markers I elaborated above into the category of sexual difference, and because it has done so over a vast historical span, it has created a palimpsest of gender. Layers of social dynamics involving issues of identity unrelated to sexual difference not only find expression solely through the lens of gender in the hegemonic move I just described; it is also the case that our current ways of thinking about gender have wrapped up in them, and in ways not always easy to disarticulate, the other identity issues such as nation, class, and epistemological heritage discussed above. That means not only that gender is inflected *by* these things, but also and more significant for my project here, that it is largely comprised *of* these things, even if through time the various discrete components have effaced their particular specificity in behalf of the larger phenomenon.[69] In short, not only is gender historically (and culturally) produced; it also has a genealogy, one built on interacting social components responding to one another and articulating one another as more features add themselves to the mix and obfuscate the individual identities of those elements that preceded them in the mix historically. What remains is a vast amalgamation of social features, greater, no doubt, than the sum of its parts, that together present as sexual difference in a process that, because it reduces a large array of characteristics to the binary opposition male/female, promotes the predominance of men as a group because it minimizes the number of potential competing positions.

When I argued at the beginning of this chapter that Freud's description of the Oedipus complex actually performs the very phenomenon that it purports to elucidate, I was referring to this very process. That is, I am referring to the production of a hegemonic narrative, one that, as I argued in the introduction, establishes its own primacy, its own legitimate claim to provide an adequate account in symbolic form for the order and structure of the world, and does so by organizing at a very basic level the manner in which signifiers interact with one another to produce meaning. In fact, Jacques Lacan's definition of Greek tragedy, using the specialized terminology and interests for which he has become famous, emphasizes the difference between individual and community readings of an event: "Tragedy represents the relationship of man to speech, in so far as that relationship seizes him in his fate—a conflictual fate inasmuch as the chain that ties man to the signifying law is not the same at the level of the family and at the level of the community."[70] In the following chapter I will investigate early forays into personal and community identity by examining the early modern articulation of the category of race. By looking at various travel narratives and anthropological investigations into the nature of humanity and the possibility of classifying it, I will show how the production of hegemonic narratives worked to overcome specific strands of antagonisms. Furthermore, I will show that, much as we saw here, a phenomenon that presents as "race" actually contains a host of other social indicators, wrapped up together in a historically produced series that deletes the specificity of each constituent part. As we will see, that is precisely where the category of "race" achieves so much of its social power.

2. MISSING LINKS

Men mistook the order of their ideas for the order
of nature, and hence imagined that the control which
they have, or seem to have, over their thoughts, permitted them to exercise a corresponding control over
things.—J. G. Frazer, *The Golden Bough*

M odern readers of Sophocles' *Oedipus the King* adopt the title character's interpretive strategies and produce a hegemonic narrative
that installs meaning in the place of absence. That narrative simultaneously naturalizes a specific identity and masks the work required to
sustain it. A similar process occurred in early modern Europe when
people confronted the emptiness of identity and forged a hegemonic
narrative to prevent what amounts to psychic collapse. Empirical and
scientific discussions of human difference that began in the seventeenth century and remain with us today perform the labor not only of
naturalizing oppressive political agendas, but of articulating an identity
in the gap opened by the defamiliarizing encounter of different groups
of people.

In fact, that is what is at the heart of white racial thinking. Having
passed variously as logic and reason, it is at bottom an organized form
of thought that functions to create an identity consisting of defensively
defining itself almost exclusively as absence. That is, whiteness is not
only the ostensible absence of color, it has also traditionally been viewed
as the absence of any positive defining characteristics.[1] Whiteness, according to this line of thinking, is what nonwhiteness is not. However,
this chapter will show that whiteness is neither the empty category
it has for so many centuries purported to be, nor an identity tied exclusively to the body. Whiteness is above all a mode of knowing and a
mode of thinking, and it operates in the amorphous social space located
somewhere between the material and abstract world constituted by the

interaction of body and signifier. An overdetermined phenomenon, white racial thinking functions much like the thinking I identified as Oedipal in chapter 1. That is, just as psychoanalysis has subsumed other forms of identity into the category of gender, white racial thinking causes differences and capacities not traditionally associated with race to be subsumed into that category. Furthermore, it owes its very existence to an attempt at dealing with an original or fundamental absence, a move we saw to be constitutive of Oedipal thinking. It may come as somewhat of a surprise, however, to learn that white racial thinking's confrontation with an original absence works in a manner diametrically opposed to Oedipus's similar run-in, as we will see. And, as I will show, we are dealing with a kind of encounter with the real, a phenomenon in which markedly ideological entities are ejected out of the symbolic and projected onto the real, particularly as this process concerns the body and our signification on and about it.

I am borrowing the term "encounter with the real" from Jacques Lacan, who in turn borrows the concept from Aristotle.[2] In *The Four Fundamental Concepts of Psychoanalysis,* Lacan reminds us that Aristotle uses the *tuché* in his search for cause, and he speaks of the concept variously. The first point to keep in mind, he argues, is that Freud's fascination with the function of fantasy led to a search for the real event provoking the repetition of signifiers constituting the fantasy. Thus, Lacan writes, "The real is beyond the *automaton,* the return, the coming-back, the insistence of the signs, by which we see ourselves governed by the pleasure principle. The real is that which always lies behind the automaton."[3] If the real in itself is not to be encountered, however, the *tuché* gives us that point at which the fantasy's signifying chain confronts the real: "The function of the *tuché,* of the real as encounter—the encounter in so far as it may be missed, in so far as it is essentially the missed encounter—first presented itself in the history of psychoanalysis in a form that was in itself already enough to arouse our attention, that of trauma."[4] From the domain of trauma Lacan derives the fundamentally unassimilable nature of the tuché, as well as the fact that the real always makes itself known to us through repetition of symptomatic signs.[5] For Lacan, the tuché as encounter with the real is unassimilable because it occupies the nebulous zone where the symbolic and the real meet for the human subject, that point of indeterminacy where language's naming and creating capacities intersect and blur. The traumatic real as that which motivates the repetition of certain symbolic encapsulations of an originary moment is recognizable precisely in that repetition, even if it can never be apprehended in the brute form of its own existence. The real as trauma presents itself as "determining all that follows," Lacan maintains, but in spite of its determining capacity, the encounter itself is always missed.

To show why the encounter with the real is always missed, Lacan points to Freud's analysis of the Wolf Man. Here we see Freud's frustrated attempt to find the real encounter at the heart of a complex symbolic nexus of symptoms. "What is the first encounter, the real, that lies behind the phantasy?" Lacan asks in legion with Freud. By way of an answer, he offers the almost stunningly counterintuitive postulate that "throughout this analysis, this real brings with it the subject, almost by force, so directing the research that, after all, we can today ask ourselves whether this fever [to know the real behind the fantasy], this presence, this desire of Freud is not that which, in his patient, might have conditioned the belated accident of his psychosis."[6] Once we get through the almost traumatic turns of Lacan's prose, we can ask: How could the subject have desired to know what lies behind the fantasy without suspecting that the fantasy masked something more fundamental in the first place? In other words, to desire to know the truth behind the symptom, the reality behind the appearances, is already to have sought a cause, a link uniting symbolic and real events. Something, in short, has to bind the way we represent the world to the world itself, even if that bond remains largely symbolic. In the absence of any such bond, the world and our representations of it would have no connection whatsoever, and, like psychotics, we would face a terrifying and hostile sea of unrelated signifiers whose relationship to one another would be utterly random. In an epistemological structure similar to the "believing is seeing" model I evoked in the introduction, the subject possessed by trauma inscribes itself on that trauma; the brute reality of the trauma is thus forever lost to us because it is inaugurated in a field of meaning that prevents us from ever seeing it in its own reality. To put this in the simplest possible terms, to look for the traumatic origin of a particular symptom is to be already caught up in the symbolic structure that such a trauma would have produced. From this, two basic possibilities arise: either I find what I'm looking for, much like the laboratory scientists we noted earlier; or I fail in my search, doomed from the outset because the trauma I seek is part of the real, not the symbolic, and hence not completely assimilable or available to any signifying system.

I have evoked the issue of trauma here not because I think that Europeans who traveled to other locales were somehow traumatized by the people they saw there, but because I believe that to search for the *cause* of racial thinking is to be caught in the same sort of epistemological trap. One creates the differences one sees, but the creation of those differences—that is, their *cause*—is lost in a signifying network that may, in fact, condition its own existence. Furthermore, trauma, like certain forms of law that I will address shortly, is concerned with how signifying systems play out across bodies, a phenomenon directly implicated in the question of race, particularly in seventeenth- and eighteenth-century treatments of it. In any event, I am not interested in justifying Europeans' reactions to the people they saw, but in investigating some of the empirical characteristics inhering in the ostensibly empty category "white." If my reading of Sophocles dramatizes the production of a hegemonic narrative that not only covers the tracks of its own production, but also fills in the nothingness at its core, my analysis of the production of white racial thinking will emphasize similar narratives at work in seventeenth- and eighteenth-century accounts of intracultural encounters. Although Oedipus was unable to sustain his self-blindness to the means by which he acceded to power, this has not posed a problem for white consciousness. European encounters with others often contributed to constituting in white consciousness those others as "raced," and indeed, Europeans as "white" in the first place. Two discourses allowed the production of white racial thinking through a fantasy network that provided the illusion of access to the real: on the one hand is the discourse of science, in which what comes to the fore are reasons and causes for the way the material world functions, particularly as that concerns human variation; and on the other hand is the discourse of law that strives to legitimize ideological positions in part by appearing merely to describe the social phenomena that it in fact orders. These two forms of discourse became racialized when they moved to confound symbolic interpretations of the real with the real itself. At bottom, however, we encounter one inevitable conclusion: whiteness is not a mode of being, but one of knowing; it is intimately bound up not only with the discourses of law I have already invoked, but those of logic and reason as well.

I want to preface my discussion of seventeenth- and eighteenth-century encounters between cultures, however, with a brief look at the sorts of thinking I take to be typical of white racial consciousness, something that I believe will help show the extent to which whiteness is a matter of knowing. Significant portions of the law are devoted to racial classification, and it is worth underscoring the resemblance between the encounter with the real and the law's attempt to cause the body and the various ideologically laden discourses about it to coincide. I mentioned in the introduction the case before the Supreme Court in 1922 in which Bhagat Singh Thind applied for American citizenship as a "white person."[7] A native of India, Thind had argued that he was a Caucasian in the anthropological understanding of the term, and consequently "white"; the Court maintained, however, that "it may be true that the blond Scandinavian and the brown Hindu have a common ancestor in the dim reaches of antiquity, but the average man knows perfectly well that there are unmistakable and profound differences between them today."[8] (The Court never specified what those differences are.) It would be difficult to find a more explicit contradiction in the legal and commonsensical definitions of race: on the one hand laws had been proposed precisely to establish positive criteria for racial determination, and on the other hand those criteria were simply abandoned when they conflicted with everyday perceptions.[9]

Contradictions between formal and customary ways of classifying human groups lead to "believing is seeing." That is, when shifting dynamics in human interaction cause new categories to emerge or when they alter the position or meaning of existing categories, beliefs vanquish logic and reason, a phenomenon recognized as far back as the fifth century B.C.E., when Thucydides remarked that because of civil war in Corcyra, "Words, too, had to change their usual meanings."[10] Thus, even though laws were proposed to outline racial identity, they often had unexpected results. Of all the laws composed to regulate and define racial makeup, the first and perhaps most bizarre dates back to 1785, when the Commonwealth of Virginia legally defined the Negro as a person with one black parent or black grandparent. Legislators apparently missed the fact that the definition was ironically recursive, unable to account for the race of the very people used to determine the race of the petitioner. That is, how do you know if the parents or grandparents were black, unless, according to this definition, you can show that *their* parents or grandparents were black? The issue reaches back into the generations indefinitely.[11] At some point, observation based on common sense, or on what a given individual's racial identity "obviously" was, had to hold sway, and common sense, or what everyone "knew" about race supplanted official legislation ostensibly based on scientific fact. Thus, tacit assumptions concerning what constituted whiteness diverged from its legal definitions, particularly since those latter definitions admitted as white any people who were as much as one-fourth black. White common sense, in other words, began to distinguish those who were *legally* white from those who were "really" white. What resulted was the famous "one-drop of blood" rule, which stipulated that no person with *any* African heritage whatsoever could be white.[12] Virginia's evolving definition of the Negro thus demonstrated the extent to which racial identity emerges not from the people classified, but from the classifiers, since they are free to change the terms and conditions of classification at any moment.[13]

The ironic fact that emerges from court involvement in deciding identity is that neither people who "look" white nor those who fit the "definition" of white are necessarily "really" white. Yet, if neither appearance nor anthropological classification could serve as reliable indicators of whiteness, the conclusiveness of both the "one drop" rule and the Thind decision demonstrates that, even if no one could define it, it seemed that everyone knew what whiteness was. Whiteness is a matter of common knowledge, subject to change but nevertheless always binding in situations ranging from public restrooms to Supreme Court decisions. Indeed, the Supreme Court made this point in no uncertain terms when it held in the same year as the Thind decision that "the average man, without being able to define a white person, understands distinctly what the term means."[14] Astonishingly fluid, then, yet perplexingly rigid, whiteness is a protean legal and scientific concept whose early stages and mutations will serve as the material of this chapter. At once a measure of morphological variety and an arbitrary indicator of social origin and privilege, whiteness nevertheless encodes a great deal more than the color of one's skin, and it is precisely because it does that it has such a tenacious hold on identity. Far from being an empty category, and however "normative" whiteness may be perceived to be, as a historically produced denomination it obfuscates its own construction and constitution—much in the way, for example, that narrative realism does—in order to appear simply natural and self-evident, a comparison that I will bring to the fore in this chapter.[15]

The task at hand now is to look at the manner in which European culture of the seventeenth and eighteenth centuries produced a hegemonic narrative concerning racial and gender identity, and at how they naturalized the narratives they produced in their own bodies and in those of the various peoples they studied. I have been arguing that hegemonic narratives produce, generally in overdetermined fashion, the links missing among collections of disparate elements in order to produce meaning. Here we will look at what European and American travelers and anthropologists found to be, for want of a better word, the missing links between themselves and what they took to be higher and lower forms of life.[16] It will become clear that the missing links these observers believed they found supply the links missing in their stories and theories necessary to make culturally different groups of people meaningful to the way they understood themselves.[17]

I recognize that the analysis to follow issues from a decidedly European, even "white" perspective; consequently, some discussion of that perspective is in order. To illuminate some part of the genealogy of "whiteness," I will be looking principally at what are—for want of better terminology—Europeans' or westerners' perceptions of themselves and of others. But even to say that reproduces many of the problems inherent in attempting a genealogy of whiteness, since to correlate whiteness with Europeans begs the question of what whiteness is: if we investigate it through the lens of the very group responsible for the category and its effects, we recognize whiteness as natural, synonymous with a particular geographic territory, and, thus, not ideologically disputable. We end up relying on nothing but an unspoken notion of what whiteness is, and we consequently participate in reproducing whiteness as exclusion, since we rely on intuition, rather than evidence. As we will see, whiteness and a specific cultural, class, and sexed identity have come to define one another in a dizzying recursiveness that makes whiteness appear to be simply a matter of common sense. But it is precisely the recourse to common sense that demonstrates the degree to which the category "whiteness" is much more properly social than biological—if it exists primarily as a form of knowledge, and not as an empirically measured phenomenon, then it becomes an ideological instrument to be manipulated by the group of people who created it and who profit from it.[18]

I should also point out at this juncture that I will not be relying on any of the economic arguments that many scholars have used to try to understand the roots of racism in Western thinking. Many historians have looked at racism, especially in the U.S., as an expression of economic conflict. While it was true that Africans in the New World shared the burden of forced labor with indentured servants, they were removed both culturally and historically from the conflicts that English servants had faced. The cost of keeping an African slave alive for life, versus what it cost to maintain an English servant for five years, played a role, as did the political fact that ever-growing numbers of white, free, economically disadvantaged, and armed former indentured servants were gathering in the south. Many economic historians have pointed out that the kind of labor required in the north was not conducive to slavery. Since no one seems to feel particularly comfortable asserting whether racism caused slavery or slavery begat racism, we generally find speculations such as Winthrop Jordan's that "they seem rather to have generated each other."[19] While these arguments are persuasive and, of course, significant ways of understanding the tremendous complexities involved in the question of "race," this chapter addresses modes of thinking and methods of representing. Although I realize, of course, that I am to some extent creating a false division in separating the economic from the symbolic, it is in order to investigate a dimension of white racial thinking that has heretofore been largely ignored.[20]

As we just saw from the brief examples of the law and what everyone is supposed to accept as unquestionably true, it is often difficult to gauge the extent to which something as apparently self-evident as common sense is steeped in cultural values and prejudices. Likewise, the sorts of categories we use to define what a person can be are culturally and historically informed. Most of the scientific and juridical categories we use to define identity, for example, whether racial, civic, or philosophic, date to the eighteenth century. Similarly, most Western notions of equality derive to a very great extent from principles of natural justice and human law from that same period, in such documents as the American Bill of Rights, or the French *Déclaration des droits de l'homme et du citoyen,* as well as from the political writings of Montesquieu,

Rousseau, Hume, and Locke, to name just the most obvious. Furthermore, most modern notions of the individual as a political and psychological entity emerged at that same time. The human subject, no longer utterly subjected to absolutist authority or blind tradition, nevertheless remains, for all of the equality and reason associated with it in Enlightenment discourse, a culturally and historically specific entity. Thus, despite the fact that many of our modern notions of equality and rationality date back to the eighteenth century, we should avoid the temptation of regarding those concepts as the teleological expression of social practices reaching their organic culmination, and consider instead how they formed in tandem with other eighteenth-century discourses.

One of the clearest ways of demonstrating the intimate connection among what appear today to be separate discourses is, as we have already briefly seen, the law. But one of the things we need to keep in mind about the form and function of the law is that they evolved rather dramatically as concepts during the seventeenth and eighteenth centuries. Louis Althusser explains this evolution as follows:

> Its modern meaning (the sense of *scientific law*) only emerged in the works of the physicists and philosophers of the sixteenth and seventeenth centuries. And even then it still carried with it the traits of its past. Before taking the new sense of a constant relation between phenomenal variables, i.e. before relating to the practice of the modern experimental sciences, law belonged to the world of religion, morality and politics. It was, in its meaning, steeped in exigencies arising from human relations. Law thus presupposed human beings, or beings in the image of man, even if they surpassed it. The law as a *commandment*.[21]

What we note in particular about the law in the eighteenth century is that it denoted for people the way things *must* be on both an empirical and a political level.[22] Like literary verisimilitude during the same period, which expressed not necessarily what readers considered plausible in a given situation, but instead what they considered ideologically appropriate, law bore an ambiguous relationship to reality because it marked the line between the way things were and the way they ought to be.[23] As Peter Gay puts it, the imperfections of positive laws "proved the assertions of natural law to be organized wishes rather than current realities, moral imperatives rather than generalizations from experience."[24] The evolving definition of the law in the seventeenth and eighteenth centuries, in other words, correlates the encounter with the real—in both cases ideologically invested signifying systems come into contact with a bodily materiality.

The law consequently provided a convenient intersection of human knowledge and the natural world, such that each seemed somehow to inform the other, if only in ambiguous or unstated fashion. In many respects the law functioned as the tuché or encounter with the real, since it operated precisely to quilt the imperatives of a moral or cultural agenda to the apparently incontrovertible aspects of the real. We can see a clear example of how the law ambiguously and sometimes ironically united the social and natural worlds in Montesquieu's *Spirit of Laws*. For Montesquieu, law cemented social relations, even when those relations were equivocal or internally contradictory.[25] There would seem to be no better illustration of such a scenario than the paternal function in a heavily controlled culture: "In well-policed societies, the father is he whom laws, through the ceremony of marriage, have declared must be such *(devoir être tel)*, because they find in him the person whom they seek."[26] Strikingly, this definition of the father omits any reference to procreation, focusing instead solely on statutory relationships. Montesquieu's use of the ambiguous modal verb "must" *(devoir)* underscores the extent to which biological paternity has little at all to do with one's status as father. "Must" here neatly divides the father's identity somewhere between a probability and a command. In other words, in the societies that Montesquieu describes, the laws declare that a woman's husband *probably is* the father of her child, but more important, they indicate that this man *has to be* the father; otherwise, we presume, the social structures that depend on the legitimacy of offspring could threaten to collapse. Furthermore, well regulated societies give the law absolute autonomy to dictate social relationships, regardless of the biological facts that might contradict them. That autonomy joins with the certainty that the law will find whatever it is looking for—and in this instance, the man who fits the law's *definition* of paternity is the father precisely because he is the man whom the law seeks. The law, in this case, always gets its man.

In a somewhat more pointed formulation, this time from Montesquieu's earlier *Persian Letters,* the Persian sultan Rica writes home from Paris, explaining that the authority granted to Western law to specify familial affiliations not only structures social relations, but lies at the heart of the way people think and understand: "According to the law observed here, every child born in marriage is considered to belong to the husband. He might well have good reasons for not believing it, but the law believes for him, and it relieves him from examination and from doubt."[27] What seems particularly significant here is the law's capacity not simply to regulate behavior through force or coercion, but to alter the way in which people perceive the real world around them and their place in it. That is, the law can resolve contradictions in the social world and install a buffer between people and the world, a buffer that patches social discrepancies with the apparently seamless interface I have been calling a hegemonic narrative. The law does not simply prescribe relationships, in other words; it determines and produces them.[28]

The practice of allowing the law to determine social or familial relationships is ancient, of course. In the *Republic*, for example, Plato suggests that "all the children who are born in the tenth and seventh month after a man became a bridegroom he will call sons if they are male, daughters if they are female, and they will call him father. . . . Those born during the time when their fathers and mothers are having children they will call their brothers and sisters."[29] Plato designed his laws for the formation of kinship structures to make it easy for the wives of his ideal city's guardians to have children, but what we see here is the elaboration of a hegemonic narrative designed to preserve what have come to be called family values. That is, what is most important in Plato's legal formulation is the familial and communal unity the law establishes, regardless of the biological realities that might otherwise threaten those things. During the Renaissance, François Rabelais toyed with a similar idea by causing the mother of his famous Gargantua to be pregnant with the child for eleven months: "For that long, indeed for longer, can women carry children, especially when it's a masterpiece, someone who in his time is destined for great deeds."[30] Rabelais goes on to list a dozen or so famous long-term pregnancies, and he adds that "the ancient Pantagruelists have confirmed what I say and have declared not only possible, but also legitimate, the child born of a woman in the eleventh month after the death of her husband."[31] The point here is that the law legitimates specific forms of behavior as well as the conditions that result from that behavior and it does so in the construction of a hegemonic narrative in which plausibility follows a political, and not necessarily empirically based, agenda. Individual identity and group unity derive from what people accept as likely, normal, or valid.

If Montesquieu offers us an explicit case in point of the phenomenon in which human law seemed written to naturalize or legitimize certain ideological modes of behavior, however, there are numerous examples of similar, albeit less manifest situations in which seventeenth- and eighteenth-century thinkers attempted to align what they saw with what they believed.[32] Since so much of scientific and commonsensical "believing is seeing" centers on human variation and its significance, we need to understand how and why observers classified people the way they did, and how the assumptions underwriting the classification, perhaps even more than the resulting classifications themselves, are part of a racialized discourse giving substance to the identity "white." The first thing we need to keep in mind is that the equation of human difference and hierarchy is a comparatively recent phenomenon. A brief look at earlier cross-cultural encounters might help illustrate this.

People began to notice and to catalog differences among themselves and others long before the early modern period, of course, and their reactions to the differences they noted varied widely. Despite the many sorts of differences people might have encountered, it was complexion, in particular that of the dark-skinned inhabitants of sub-Saharan Africa, that seems most often to have attracted the attention of ancient Europeans and North Africans.[33] Egyptian, Old Testament, and Greek and Roman sources refer to those inhabiting the upper Nile Valley as "black," "burnt-faced," or "colored" as early as the third millenium B.C.E.[34] Although the dark skin typical of this region was proverbial at least as far back as the sixth century B.C.E. (as demonstrated in the often-cited passage from Jeremiah 13:23: "Can the Ethiopian change his skin or the leopard his spots?"), there is generally no evidence to suggest that the ancients used morphological difference to encode moral or intellectual ascendancy. However, it is true that Ethiopians and other dark-skinned peoples were singled out as both physically and culturally unusual in Greek poetic literature as early as Homer and Hesiod,[35] and they are no less remarkable in historical documents. In his *Histories,* Herodotus describes the Ethiopians variously as "the tallest and best-looking people in the world" and the longest-lived, often attaining the age of one hundred and twenty.[36] Herodotus also notes distinct varieties among the Ethiopians, observing that the eastern Ethiopians "were just like the southern Ethiopians, except for their language and their hair: their hair is straight, while that of the Ethiopians in Libya is the crispest and the curliest in the world."[37] Whatever their moral or physical distinction, the Ethiopians were also according to Herodotus among the most culturally idiosyncratic people on earth. The "Ethiopian holemen, or troglodytes," he reports, hunt "in four-horse chariots, for these troglodytes are exceedingly swift of foot—more so than any people of whom we have any information. They eat snakes and lizards and other reptiles and speak a language like no other, but squeak like bats."[38]

Although the Ethiopians' physical appearance seemed to outsiders to correlate their unusual cultural activities, it is important to underscore the lack of a perceived causal connection between the two domains as well as the absence of any inferred cultural superiority.[39] Yet, if morphology did not dictate moral, cultural, or intellectual worth, the Greeks did nevertheless recognize hierarchical differences among human beings—it was simply not the case that those differences bore the same essential weight that early modern and later classifiers attributed to them, nor was it the case that appearance had much to do with hierarchy.[40] Herodotus's countryman Aristotle, for example, although far less likely to report on unusual physical variations, did recognize human variation and theorize about it, and one of the principal variations obvious to a Greek was condition of servitude. About the slave Aristotle wrote: "Those whose condition is such that their function is the use of their bodies and nothing better can be expected of them . . . are slaves by nature. . . . For the 'slave by nature' is he that can and therefore does belong to another."[41] He went on to state that "there are some who are slaves everywhere, others who are slaves nowhere. And the same is true of noble birth."[42]

But to be a "slave by nature" did not imply to Aristotle what a similar formulation would mean to American slaveholders over two thousand years later, for the simple and obvious reason that Greek slavery had a history all its own. Like their predecessors the Mycenaeans, the Greeks kept slaves, but unlike perhaps most of the other Greek city-states, Athens had developed a complex economy utterly dependent on slave labor. In fact, it seems likely that nearly half the population of Athens were slaves.[43] We need to remember, however, that slaves in Athens not only engaged in all activities available to free persons—except, of course, holding public office—but also that they were permitted to retain a portion of their earnings gained through the exercise of their specific talents and crafts. Thus, it was not unusual to find a slave better off materially than a free citizen.[44] In fact, in the *Republic* Plato poses a rhetorical question concerning slavery that indicates that the Greeks did not view slavery as an innate condition, but rather as a function of civic identity: "Is it right for Greeks to enslave Greek cities, or should they, as far as they can, not even allow any other city to do so, and make a habit of sparing the Greek race as a precaution against being enslaved by the barbarians?"[45] Enslavement of a fellow Greek seems to constitute a sort of narcissistic wound to Plato's municipal pride. But his fear that Greek cities might be reduced to slavery emphasizes that such a condition is political, and not natural or innate.

Similarly, the writer known as Old Oligarch underscores the political nature of slavery when he writes: "If it were legal for a free man to strike a slave, a metic, or a freedman, an Athenian would often have been struck under the mistaken impression that he was a slave, for the clothing of the common people there is in no way superior to that of the slaves and metics, nor is their appearance."[46] Slaves differed from citizens in no essential way, in other words. Furthermore, not only did outward appearance provide no clue concerning what amounts to a purely civic status, but the law prohibited citizens from mistreating slaves. Finally, despite Aristotle's implication that the slave differs in some fundamental way from the free citizen, it is important to understand that he considered slavery a condition, and not an identity, as it was later understood, especially in North America. In the *Nichomachean Ethics* he makes the distinction clear:

> For where there is nothing common to ruler and ruled, there is not friendship either, since there is not justice; e.g. between craftsman and tool, soul and body, master and slave; the latter in each case is benefited by that which uses it, but there is no friendship or justice towards lifeless things. But neither is there friendship towards a horse or an ox, nor to a slave *qua* slave. . . . *Qua* slave . . . one cannot be friends with him. But *qua* man one can.[47]

Aristotle's distinction between the condition of slavery, which reduces to a civic or national identity, and essential humanity, which is unchangeable, demonstrates the complete disjunction Greeks established between morphology and human worth. As David Brion Davis describes the problem of slavery in ancient Greece, "Externally, the servant might be the instrument of his master's will, but internally, in his own self-consciousness, he remained a free soul."[48]

Reports by astonished observers of Africans' dark complexions and the possible significance continued well beyond the classical period. In the second-century *Tetrabiblos*, Ptolemy characterized the inhabitants of the various climes, noting that those who lived "from the equator to the summer tropic, since they have the sun over their heads and are burned by it, have black skins and thick, wooly hair, are contracted in form and shrunken in stature, are sanguine of nature, and in habits are for the most part savage because their homes are continually oppressed by heat; we call them by the general name Ethiopians."[49] While a detailed history of westerners' encounters with dark-skinned people lies well beyond the scope of this study, I want to emphasize that although for Greeks and Romans the color black *may* have evoked negative characteristics—and as far back as the first century the devil is referred to as the Black One, for example—response to black-skinned people was far from unequivocal.[50] As Frank M. Snowden Jr. points out, Ethiopians in fact became a symbol for the inclusiveness of Christianity at least as early as Origen (died 254? c.e.), who preached that whom God created he created equal. Snowden writes: "Ethiopians in fact became an important symbol of Christianity's ecumenical mission. Building on classical color usages, the Christian writers developed an exegesis and a black-white imagery in which Ethiopians illustrated the meaning of the Scriptures for *all* men."[51] Furthermore, Nancy Stepan has shown that in the ancient world blackness was often associated with physical or moral beauty.[52]

Europeans' association of moral and intellectual wretchedness with dark complexion seems to have become fixed in the popular imagination during the Middle Ages. Ironic portraits of ideal ugliness dot medieval epics,[53] and in the twelfth-century *Chronicle of the Ducs of Normandie*, by Benoît de Sainte-More, the author describes the inhabitants of the tropical zones as follows:

> It happens that in regions
> In which all day it is hot and burning
> Are the venimous vermine,
> Dreaded, cruel and heinous,

And the beasts deadly and fierce
And the people of all sorts
Who have no law, nor any reason,
Righteousness or discretion,
Who only know evil, not good
And who are more criminal than dogs,
Black, without chins, large and horned
And hairy down to the ground,
With hanging ears. . . .[54]

These literary examples can help gauge predominant attitudes, since like the celebrated Homeric similes they provide familiar points of reference to establish cultural norms, even if those norms relate principally to the home culture. John Block Friedman has argued that Africans—whether Amazons, Saracens, or Ethiopians—served as a sort of ethical pivot, sometimes teaching valuable lessons and sometimes serving as bad moral examples. He identifies talmudic traditions in which Amazons teach ironic lessons on vanity, as well as Christian conversion tales. He writes: "A 'good' Saracen was less the product of an exotic civilization than a pair of alien eyes in which Europeans could see their own values mirrored. Yet to see these men freshly, in literary or artistic context, allowed the Westerner to call his own values into question and so . . . to redefine his traditional conception of humanity."[55]

From this extremely abbreviated account of encounters among different human populations in the distant past I want to emphasize two crucial points. The first is that the association of moral and intellectual qualities with physiognomic characteristics is a comparatively recent phenomenon. As we have seen, although the ancients noticed and remarked on what appeared to them bizarre physical differences, they did not uncompromisingly bind morphology to character. The second point is that when corporeal features began to correlate for observers the more intangible and abstract features associated with personality, intellect, and comportment—roughly in the middle years of the seventeenth century—it became possible to trace, as Snowden and Friedman have shown, the anxieties and displacements operating in observers' characterizations of unfamiliar peoples.

Even the very earliest reports of European contact with Turks, Arabs, or Africans infuse notions of social or ideological identity with conceptions of bodily integrity or difference. How they understand the correlation of culture and morphology, of knowledge and nature, however, is a complex matter. Of note are two particular, somewhat competing discursive strategies of understanding difference that we can see in the seventeenth and eighteenth centuries. On the one hand, and generally earlier on in this historical period, we find Europeans' attempts to explain or rationalize the differences they noted in the people whom they visited, a gesture that implicitly (and sometimes explicitly) recognizes a standard from which the people identified as significantly different have departed; and, on the other hand, and generally later on in this period, perhaps becoming more frequent beginning about the first quarter of the eighteenth century, we note the assumption that difference has no cause, and indicates not a departure from a norm, but a taxonomic reality, the way things simply are. These two ways of reporting and understanding difference complement the encounter with the real and the evolving interpretation of law in the eighteenth century that we noted above, since in both cases ways of knowing directly impinge on ways of being and ways of seeing. Just as the law marked an uneasy tension between ought and is, signaling the intervention of a signifying system into the way people understood reality, causality (or lack thereof) of difference introduced the domain of discursive interpretation into what had been considered a strictly empirical system of observing nature and its people. Consequently, Western observers began to see what they believed. White racial thinking in its early forms thus consisted in constructing morphological difference, aligning it with a determinate cultural practice, and then, in its next stage, effacing the social dimension such that the body seemed to chart human moral, intellectual, aesthetic, and ethical difference.

The earliest reports of European travel to faraway lands include descriptions of the people encountered, of course, and we find two basic formulas: these people looked different, and their difference could be explained; or, some prodigious accident of nature produced the difference, and that's just how they looked. But, in both cases, observers began to theorize a cause for the human variation they noted. More often than not in accounts that antedate roughly the middle years of the seventeenth century, when Europeans noted physical differences between themselves and those of other cultures or geographic locales, they considered the variation to be deliberately produced by members of the culture in a considered attempt to distinguish themselves.[56] Cultural modification of the body seems to have indicated to early modern Europeans that social and political institutions invaded and corrupted the ostensibly "natural" domain of the biological, a domain in which all people were originally equal and the same, and one that interested a great many European and American thinkers, particularly as they attempted to develop theories concerning the question of human equality.[57] And while predominant attitudes and beliefs about the superiority of western European culture may have caused them to scorn other cultures, Europeans nevertheless maintained a fundamental respect for others' power and presence in the world.[58]

One concrete example of the manner in which Europeans mapped culture onto the body before the eighteenth century can be found in Christian attitudes toward Islam and the practice of circumcision. In 1621, John Rawlins reported the facts surrounding the Turkish capture of an English ship:

> For there had beene five hundred [English] brought into the market for the same purpose [to be sold as slaves] and above a hundred hansome youths compelled to turne Turkes, or made subject to more viler prostitution. . . . And so many even for feare of torment and death, make their tongues betray their hearts to a most fearful wickednesse, and so are circumcised with new names, and brought to confesse a new Religion.[59]

Although the Muslim practice of circumcising Christians was by no means unheard of, it is not entirely clear from Rawlins's unusual language ("circumcised with new names") whether the Muslim names that the English are forced to adopt serve as the agent of circumcision, which would render it a metaphorical one; or whether a knife or other such instrument is the agent of their marking, such that a real, physical circumcision accompanies the adoption of a Muslim name. It is more than likely, however, given prevailing attitudes about Muslim barbarism, that Rawlins viewed the mutilation of the men's Christian names as an affront equally as serious as the mutilation of their bodies.[60] What is particularly significant in this report is the manner in which a modification of the body appears to correlate a crucial change in what that body houses: Rawlins seems to believe that forced circumcision and con-version to Islam necessarily produce a concurrent internal alteration.

Examples abound in which European travelers not only reported difference, but tried to account for it as well, and if circumcision was one way to modify a part of the human body, other, more generalized practices were also theorized. The sixteenth-century traveler John Leo, for example, noticed that Africans' complexions were not uniformly the same color; along with many other observers, he used this fact to sug-gest that people were all originally born with the same or similar com-plexion, but that cultural practice changed their skin pigmentation.[61] In his *Observations of Africa* Leo explained differing skin tones by noting that "the Inhabitants of Necaus are very rich, liberall, and curious in their apparell. . . . Their women are white, having black haires and a most delicate skinne, because they frequent the Bath-stoves so often."[62] In similar fashion, Jean Barbot opens his two-volume study on Guinea [1688] by attempting proleptically to answer the reader's questions con-cerning the morphological differences between Europeans and the peo-ple he observed:

> Why are the peoples of Nigritie and Guinea black, as are many other nations of southern Africa? Further, you wish me to inform you about which Europeans gained the honour of discovering these burning climates, and when they did so. . . . It is necessary to revert to the issue of defining Africa in general, and why it is so called. This will serve as an introduction to what I will tell you about the blackness of those peoples whose lands and customs I will be describing to you.[63]

By way of an answer to the first and most immediate question, Barbot finds, as did Leo, that ablutions and other ritualistic hygienic behavior cause dark skin color. The natives of Senegal, he remarks, "have an at-tractive, shiny black skin, which comes from their washing and anoint-ing it."[64]

These sorts of tales of human variation resulting from culturally determined and deliberate modification of the body are far from un-common in the seventeenth and eighteenth centuries, and they are also geographically widespread. In the opening years of the seventeenth century, an unnamed traveler to Jamestown had the following to say about the natives of the region:

They goe all naked save their privityes, yet in coole weather they weare deare skinns . . . : some have leather stockinges up to their twysters, & sandalls on their feet, their hayre is black generally. . . . Their skynn is tawny not so borne, but with dying and paynting them selves, in which they delight greatly. The women are like the men, onely this difference; their hayre groweth long all over their heades save clipt somewhat short afore, these do all the labour and the men hunt and goe at their pleasure.[65]

These observers appear to have believed not only that the human body is easily modified, but that the changes wrought could be passed on to offspring. Although by no means all early European observers attributed the morphological differences they noted to cultural practices, the belief was firmly enough established that even at the end of the eighteenth century well-respected men of science still occasionally held to this theory.[66]

What these observations show us is that some of the earliest forays into what we might call racialized discourse correlate culture with the body. Furthermore, we see a collateral attempt to explain morphological and cultural variation as expressions of one another.[67] It is important to underscore, however, that while racial thinking took on many different forms, it was generally aligned with an attempt to locate the cause for difference even when causality was not explicitly evoked. Sometimes deviation, or departure from some tacitly recognized norm, takes the place of causality, especially in eighteenth-century observations. In his *History of British West Indies* (1794), for example, Bryan Edwards compares Africans to baboons, but claims the comparison implies no belief in these people's inferiority. Furthermore, if he believes that Africans' difference has no apparent cause—if by cause we understand a determined and reasoned course directing a specific outcome of events—he does nevertheless seem to believe that something happened, perhaps providentially, to have made them different from him.

I cannot help observing too, that the conformation of the face, in a great majority of them, very much resembles that of the baboon. I believe indeed there is, in most of the nations of Africa, a greater elongation of the lower jaw, than among the people of Europe; but this distinction I think is more visible among the Eboes, than in any other Africans. I mean not however to draw any conclusion of natural inferiority in these people to the rest of the human race, from a circumstance which perhaps is purely accidental, and no more to be considered as a proof of degradation than the red hair and high cheek bones of the Natives of the North of Europe.[68]

Comparisons of different human groups to animals become more frequent the later we proceed in the eighteenth century and into the nineteenth century, as we will see in chapter 3. What interests me here, however, is Edwards' almost off-hand remark concerning the source of difference ("a circumstance which perhaps is purely accidental"). Rather than appearing to be the determined work of human endeavor, difference here is a chance occurrence, and as is typical in eighteenth-century theories (and we will see more of this in a moment) the differing body becomes part of the real, or of natural necessity. A component of the natural world, difference that results independent of human thought and activity can reveal something of the natural order; the only problem was that there was considerable disagreement about precisely what was revealed. In sum, what we see in these first kinds of observations I have described is the belief, generally expressed through recourse to known or unknown causality, that an identifiable human divergence has occurred, and that without external intervention, generally in the form of some culturally specific activity, people would be more or less the same.

The issue of causality might become clearer if we look at the sorts of human variation Europeans noted that seemed to have no apparent cause. If early modern beliefs about human variation were based largely (but not exclusively, as we will see) on systematic cultural and historical modifications of the body, sometimes nature seemed to intervene in mysterious and unpredictable ways, producing human marvels that defied description. Nearly everyone was familiar with these kinds of stories; they had the sort of currency that urban myths—those apocryphal tales that involve such things as people putting French poodles in the microwave to dry them off after a bath—enjoy today. In the seventeenth and eighteenth centuries, these stories centered around the inexplicably bizarre monsters that sometimes simply occurred with no apparent reason. For example, J. G. Grevenbroek reports that Africans "who live near our Cape [Good Hope] are of middle height; but the inhabitants of the remote parts of this region are shaggy fellows, with taller and sturdier frames, and with frizzy hair. Among them has been seen a king, Longurio, twelve foot high, with hair all over his body thicker than a water spaniel's."[69] Among the most common of these sorts of tales were those containing reports of human beings sporting tails. These stories were so popular that even the generally sober and judicious Buffon—one of the eighteenth century's greatest naturalists, admitted to France's prestigious Académie des Sciences—could not resist passing them on, even though his use of the passive voice does relegate the tale to the domain of rumor: "Several of them [blacks from the Philippines] have been spotted with tails four or five inches long."[70] Another commonly occurring inexplicable phenomenon was the mysterious appearance of a white child from African parents. In 1559, for example, João dos Sanctos reported the following: "In Mocaranga some Parents as blacke as Pitch, have white Goldi-locked children like Flemmings. Whiles I was in the Countrey, the Quiteve [a royal title] nourished one white childe in the Court, as a strange Prodigie. The Manamotapa kept two other white Cafres with like admiration. The Cafres say such are the Children of the Devill, begotten of blacke women by him when they are asleep."[71] The concurrent deviant and hackneyed nature of these tales established the human oddities they narrated as a sort of external limit of variation. In other words, they allowed the parameters of human physiognomy—however strange they might be—to become fixed for a given culture.[72]

In many respects, the two sets of examples delineating the causes of morphological variation that seventeenth- and eighteenth-century observers noted help establish the boundaries of a hegemonic narrative of European identity. On the one hand we have the outlandish reports of human prodigies, reports that seem to set nature's frontiers for human diversity. On the other hand we have the more mundane accounts of far less spectacular, far more common morphological and cultural difference. The accounts of freakish variation complement the more mundane stories of difference, because it is in those latter that we see the attempt to locate a cause for difference, an attempt that would be vain in the stories of inexplicable human prodigies. The search for a cause of difference is significant here because the search for such cause acknowledges the need for a reasoned, symbolic appropriation of the natural world, one that binds cultural difference to physical variation. Reports of people with tails or other similar unlikely appurtenances may appear unbelievable, but since they are inexplicable occurrences they require no sustained symbolic intervention in the form of an explanatory narrative, and furthermore in their very outlandishness they make the explanation of the more common sorts of variation seem logical, or at the very least justified. Like lightening blasts or earthquakes, they may be uncommon but nevertheless real, and they readily assert themselves all the more forcefully precisely because they require no explanation—they simply are, a state Kant would call natural necessity.

This is not the case, however, with the far more common reports of human variation that seemed to require an explanation. Removed from the category of freakish single occurrence, repeated variations following a similar pattern appeared to require a reason for diverging; the establishment of an explanation or cause for human variation locates such variations squarely in the domain of the symbolic and of the ideological. Outside of the register of what simply is, the different people whom early modern observers described required a reason to be the way they were. On the one hand one could argue that Europeans' apparent need to explain morphological difference simply betrays the somewhat obvious fact that they considered themselves the original or natural form from which other varieties distinguished themselves, and as we will see in chapter 3, this is certainly the case. On the other hand, however, and far more significant is the fact that by producing an explanation of difference, early modern observers actually articulated—in both senses of that word that I have already noted—the differences they registered. That is, in line with the philosophical and epistemological prevalence of the late seventeenth century, they established parameters for what would count as different and how that difference would matter, and they simultaneously and in the same gesture created the features of their own bodies they found critical.[73] In effect, by explaining morphological difference, generally focusing on skin color, hair, and certain other characteristics made visible by such analyses and observations, these early modern travelers, philosophers, and anthropologists not only produced the differences they tried to explain, they also politicized them. In this way, observers writing of their adventures produced an encounter with the real: the disarticulation of the body isolates significant parts, particularly when the delineation of those parts may be a phenomenon contingent on bodily functions either only recently discovered or newly valued. The partitioning of the body into component parts recognizes the body's social existence, particularly when causal structures are summoned from cultural practices to explain human difference. Body and culture map one another in difficult to catalog ways, and it becomes ever more difficult to determine the extent to which differing bodies determine cultural activities, and that to which social existence alters morphology.

To posit cause is to narrate and produce difference, not as something natural or given, but as an element of cultural production. Jacques Lacan puts the problem this way: "Cause is to be distinguished from that which is determinate in a chain, in other words, the *law*. By way of example, think of what is pictured in the law of action and reaction."[74] Lacan illustrates his point by arguing that when a body crashes on the ground there is, strictly speaking, no causal relation, but rather one of immediacy and determinacy, because, he says, the body's "mass is integrated in this force that comes back to it in order to dissolve its coherence by a return effect."[75] It is clear here that no one is going to accuse Lacan of bewildering his readers with obscure scientific jargon, but his point is that in the action-reaction chain, "there is no gap."[76] That is, there is a direct, immediate, and indivisible relationship uniting the two moments of action and reaction. No symbolic or cognitive period interposes between these two moments.

This is not the case with causality, however. Causality requires a gap, but that gap has nothing to do with the way the real operates; it has to do with the way we perceive, understand, and order it. Thus, Lacan argues, "The phases of the moon are the cause of tides—we know this from experience."[77] Slavoj Žižek glosses this passage by observing that "the Cause *qua* the Real intervenes where symbolic determination stumbles, misfires—that is, where a signifier falls out."[78] Žižek and Lacan are referring to the inconsistencies in the symbolic order that appear to be produced—caused—by some intervention emanating from an external, nonsymbolic or real source. In other words, what we take to be causal, in contradistinction to the absolute determinism of the law of the real, or that which cannot be contradicted, are those things that disrupt the smooth and apparently seamless flow of signifiers.[79] Elements of causality, in other words, are things that do not make sense—and cannot be made to make sense—in the current symbolic arrangement; they are excluded from the domain of meaning as it is produced and consumed in a given culture. Causality requires a rethinking of the system it explains or orders. If one thinks of the often-noted fact that people frequently search for the cause of homosexuality, but never search for the cause of heterosexuality, one can quickly see how causality intervenes to keep a determinate ideological system on track.

It is not the case, of course, that Lacan and Žižek merely offer us philosophically anachronistic accounts of causality with little bearing on the texts I have been considering. Philosophers roughly contemporary to those observers trying to establish the causes of human variation viewed the problem in much the same way. One of the most famous philosophers of causality, David Hume, argues that because of repeated conjunctions of objects, we learn to draw connections between and among them; the idea of cause and effect derives from human experience, which tells us that particular entities have in the past been related to one another.[80] In this fashion, causality as a link of contiguity exists only as a function of human signification. However, reason does not suffice to explain the connections between and among the objects in question. That is because "reason can never shew us the connexion of one object with another, tho' aided by experience, and the observation of their constant conjunction in all past instances. When the mind, therefore, passes from the idea or impression of one object to the idea or belief of another, it is not determin'd by reason, but by certain principles, which associate together the ideas of these objects, and unite them in the imagination."[81] Reason and causality enter into a difficult relationship; the conjunction does nothing to establish reason, nor does reason illuminate the conjunction: "We only observe the thing itself, and always find that from the constant conjunction the objects acquire an union in the imagination."[82]

Immanuel Kant, of course, may have had the most to say of any philosopher from this period on the subject of causality. What seems particularly useful for the purposes at hand are his remarks from the *Prolegomena to Any Future Metaphysics*. Here Kant interrogates objects of the sensible world and their relationship to natural law; he asks what an effect is, and how effect relates to natural law and to reason.

> What, then, is required for natural necessity? Nothing more than
> the determinability of every event in the sensible world according
> to constant laws, and therefore a relation to a cause within ap-

pearance; whereby the underlying thing in itself and its causality remain unknown. But I say: *the law of nature remains,* whether the rational being be a cause of effects in the sensible world through reason and hence through freedom, or whether that being does not determine such effects through rational grounds.[83]

From this we deduce that true causality only applies in cases divorced from natural necessity, which is another way of referring to the impenetrably hard kernel of the real. Strictly speaking, the real lies outside of the domain of causality because it is not disarticulated; it has no "parts." What is subject to cause are only those elements in which human signification comes into play, or, as Lacan puts it, "There is cause only in something that doesn't work."[84] What is subject to cause, in other words, are those elements of a system that appeared natural or unvarying until some sort of crisis or other event exposed the system's contingent nature.

Hume's and Kant's arguments are long and complex.[85] The point I want to draw from them, however, as well as from the examples from Lacan and Žižek, is that causality, like the definitions of narrative and hegemony that I have been employing, is a sort of retroactive establishment of significance. Causality normally establishes a necessary, generally temporal relation between and among things, such that one thing seems not only to have preceded another, but to have been the agent or producer of that later thing.[86] But what our recourse to narrative and hegemony can help show is that it is only by knowing in advance the whole story—or at least the significance one is expected to draw from it—that one can discern the elements that will later prove to have been prerequisite in the first place. That is, and in the baldest possible terms, one can only look for a cause when the effect one is interested in is firmly established. That is why I argued above that early modern observers who tried to locate the cause of human variation actually articulated differences on the body by *disarticulating* the body into component parts or features that could then be shown to diverge from the European idea of beauty, perfection, or ideality. In seeking out reasons for variation, they needed to do two things: first, they had to produce an implicit notion of the integral and indivisible European body; and second, they needed to articulate in the process the morphological features to which they could later seem simply to be referring.[87]

Several critics have made this point when dealing with sexual difference, emphasizing that hegemonic positions work in part by covering over their own construction. Judith Butler, for example, points out in *Bodies That Matter* that we generally feel comfortable with "sex" (as opposed to gender) as something that is at least partially *un*constructed, with, that is, a real referent on the physical body. She argues that matters of "construction" and "reference" are remarkably complicated, such that we always need to be aware of "demarcating and delimiting that to which we then 'refer,' such that our 'references' always presuppose—and often conceal—this prior delimitation."[88] Furthermore, she emphasizes that "insofar as the extra-discursive is delimited it is formed by the very discourse from which it seeks to free itself."[89] In his *Making Sex*, Thomas Laqueur makes a similar point when he reminds us that "the metaphorical and the corporeal are so bound up with one another that the difference between the two is really one of emphasis rather than kind."[90] I would argue, in fact, that one cannot accurately separate the two at all, since what we have been seeing in these examples of European attempts to understand difference is that the corporeal *is* the metaphorical. That is, the way one experiences the body, including how one identifies its parts or characteristics, has everything to do with how one's culture defines and valorizes it. The issue becomes, in other words, the extent to which culture maps itself onto the body, and whether we can isolate a pre-existing, "natural" corporality preceding or somehow otherwise removed from social meaning.

From these observations on the pliancy of human morphology and the causes of its variation we discern two things: The first is that Europeans considered their own complexions to be the originary state of human complexion, from which others may have been "discolored" or otherwise modified, an implicit assumption that would be rendered explicit and would form the basis for many anthropological assumptions in the eighteenth and nineteenth centuries, most notably in the works of Buffon and Blumenbach. The second thing we note is that naturalists and others generally presumed that specific historical and cultural practices—predictable or not—caused the variations Europeans observed in other peoples, and that consequently not only did a shared corporality describe all human beings, but one could trace the connection between human morphological and cultural difference.[91] Samuel Stanhope Smith may have epitomized the early modern belief that human morphological differences were the effect, and not the cause of cultural difference when he wrote that "the greater part of the varieties in the appearance of the human species may just be denominated habits of the body." Leaving absolutely no doubt that such "habits of the body" could be responsible for systemic, and not just individual variation, Smith specifies that "of habits, both of mind, and of body, nations are susceptible as well as individuals."[92]

In relating "habits of the body," some of which would later be recognized as "racial" difference, with the question of nationhood, Stanhope Smith implicitly theorized what both Lacan and Homi K. Bhabha explicitly articulated more than two centuries later: cultural groups— nations—formulate themselves on the basis of perceived difference.[93] It is not necessarily the case, however, that distinct cultural groups perceive and gauge difference in the same way, nor is it the case that distinct groups identify the same difference—that is, given the complexity of human physical and psychological features, it seems fairly clear that the way groups segment the body into organs and how they divide the mind into capacities will depend on how they live. More powerful groups generally have the resources to define the less powerful, which is to some extent how power is defined.[94] If different human groups identify difference differently, each group's identity depends to a large extent on the metaphors it uses to establish difference. Just as forms of language contribute to the formation of community, as Anderson has argued, at an even more fundamental level shared metaphors serve as economies of signification, regulating not only what can be signified, but also how.

We might take stock here of precisely where the issue of causality, particularly as it implicates the zone where things don't work or where a signifier falls out, resonates with the issue of knowledge, the body, and white racial thinking. European traditions of knowledge produced culturally and politically charged parts of the body because observers, in seeking a cause for difference, constituted those parts as excessive, peripheral, or in some other fashion unincorporable into the ideas of human morphology that had made sense to them. Philosophically predisposed to find order and symmetry in the world, seventeenth-century Europeans needed to articulate a cause for variation, and their articulation of a theory simultaneously constituted an articulation of the body into significant parts. Body parts disarticulated from the integral person assumed in their specific materiality the capacity to express meaning about the body to which they belonged, and it is surely worth noting that the integral European body correlated the integrity of whiteness: as we will see in a moment, Europeans recognized only one shade of whiteness, but varying degrees of nonwhiteness. It is in this way that specific forms of European thinking created not only the exotic body of the culturally different, but, as we will see, the European "white" body as well, since for all intents and purposes Europeans' engagements with "believing is seeing" consolidated ideological systems into their own and others' bodies. The problem at hand, then, is this: what social systems bind modes of thinking to bodies?

The problem is particularly difficult because modes of thinking about the body rapidly came to stand in for the body itself. This is nowhere more evident than in the descriptions that seventeenth- and eighteenth-century Europeans and Americans made of peoples they found to be unlike themselves. But even modern commentators sometimes fail to see how deeply our metaphors quite literally color what we see. We sometimes forget, that is, that the words we conventionally use to describe human variation reveal far more about the political history behind the choice of such words than they do about the people or objects to which they ostensibly refer. For example, Winthrop Jordan reveals the complexity of this issue when he states that we are destined to remain baffled

> as to whether white men originally responded adversely to the Negro's color because of strictly accidental prior cultural valuation of blackness *per se,* instinctual repulsion founded on physiological processes or perhaps fear of the night which may have had adaptive value in human evolution, the association of dirt and darkened complexion with the lower classes in Europe, or association of blackness with Negroes who were inferior in culture or status.[95]

In a similar vein, Alden T. Vaughan reports the litany of terms for Africans in various European languages. Pointing out that "Africans were almost invariably labeled by color," he goes on to remark that "in each language the word for 'black' carried a host of disparaging connotations. In Spanish, for example, *negro* also meant gloomy, dismal, unfit, and wretched; in French, *noir* also connoted foul, dirty, base, and wicked."[96]

The first and most obvious issue that arises is that the color designation "white" with which Jordan begins his description of blackness is a convention: it is surely obvious to everyone that Europeans' skin is not white at all. Similarly, "black" as a skin color descriptor follows a convention—albeit a long-standing one—applied to Africans, but it has no real descriptive value when applied to the color of human skin. What appears to be less obvious is that there is a tremendous cultural leap involved in the association of the "blackness" of the night with the "blackness" of the Africans' skin, or in that of the "blackness" of dirt with the "blackness" of human complexion. There is, of course, absolutely no connection except the one forged in the Western mind already predisposed to see things that way. The associations that Jordan and Vaughan propose as possible reasons for the adverse reaction "white" people have had to "black" people tell us little except that cultures need metaphors bridging the gaping chasm separating sense from nonsense. They need, in other words, ways to forge links to make the world fit into the systems they have established to understand it. Thus, people can be "black" or "white," especially—perhaps only—to the extent that those colors link with a series of cultural associations already laden with social meaning.[97] The social correlates the biological such that what appears to be ineluctably "natural" turns out to be part of a larger ideological complex, and political configurations of identity influence what people can see, creating what I call an ideological trajectory of perception.

This ideological trajectory of perception consists of the social, political, and psychological inflection of the visual field that structures what subjects can apprehend and internalize in the form of knowledge. Whatever does not lie within the confines of the ideological trajectory of perception will in general not be grasped by subjects as a significant object of contemplation—in fact, strictly speaking it will not be grasped at all, since nothing in its constitution would be able to hook the subject's attention.[98] Narrative theory has provided a model for understanding this somewhat difficult concept by theorizing the issue of how we know, in fiction, when something "happens." An accepted background of stasis provides the field into which significant—because different—

elements inscribe themselves, and in that act become "events."[99] Elements that seem neither to differ from the norm nor have a discernable connection to it are ignored. In a similar manner the ideological trajectory of perception restricts subjects' sensitivity to specific fields and simultaneously regulates the field of metaphors they can use to understand and order what they perceive.

The first group of narratives of human variation that I have focused on highlight the production of difference. The second group of accounts of human variation, which developed toward the very end of the seventeenth century, and in which difference seemed to have no particular cause, belongs instead to the realm of what Kant called natural necessity. What we need to investigate is precisely how Europeans conscripted the domain of the natural to markedly ideological ends. Furthermore, we need to analyze how construing something as ineluctably natural removed it from the realm of causality, and consequently from the domain of what can be narrated. We saw in *Oedipus the King* that the eponymous hero constructs a narrative to cover over an original absence. What we will now see is that the evolution of the concept of humankind's "natural" state in the eighteenth century constructed a narrative not to cover over an original absence, but rather to produce the sort of fundamental absence Oedipus originally shunned. That absence, I will show, is the absence whiteness strives to assume.

If early modern observers, typically those up until the last quarter of the seventeenth century, produced descriptions of the people they visited that construed the world as adhering to a more or less unified, discernable set of rules, we see new phenomena beginning toward the end of the seventeenth century. First, the discourse of causality focuses less on human intervention and more on natural sources; and second, the more specific and pervasive Enlightenment discourse of reason begins to correlate European discussions of bodies and cultures. We move, in other words, from the geometric formality of seventeenth-century notions of reason, in which order and precision, the hallmarks of Cartesian rationality, seemed to inhere in certain innate ideas, to the logical empiricism of Locke and his eighteenth-century followers, in which discovery of truth and meaning hinged on observation of the world at large.[100] Contributing factors to these new ways of understanding human difference are the influence of the philosophical notions of natural order and natural law; the Great Chain of Being; and the implicit assumption, shared by most but not all eighteenth-century thinkers, that reason was a transcendent human characteristic that could be used to overcome prejudice, emotion, and authority. An unexpected problem arose, however, when Europeans confronted the universality they cherished in reason with what they found in other cultures.

I have already argued that early reports of human difference that found a cause for such difference illustrate a non-antagonistic relationship toward that difference. When on occasion early observers cataloged morphological variation alongside moral difference, they generally found relative equality.[101] One observer who explicitly compared physiological and moral worth was J. G. Grevenbroek, who traveled to the Cape of Good Hope toward the end of the seventeenth century. Grevenbroek's report of the people he encountered is unusual for its time because it correlates culture with biology while nevertheless remaining within the confines of a relatively non-antagonistic notion of difference. Unlike later observers who allied morphology and moral worth, Grevenbroek made the comparison between Africans and Europeans and found the latter wanting in character. "In whiteness of soul they [the Hottentots] are superior to many of our countrymen, and in whiteness of body they are equal to some, and, in my judgment, would perhaps be so to all, if they cared for cleanliness. But as things are, what with fat and the scorching heat of the sun and the sharp pigment they put on their faces, they have grown dark and are of a swarthy brown colour."[102] Grevenbroek accomplishes what I have identified as the standard gesture for a late seventeenth-century observer of attributing human variation to cultural practices, but unlike many if not most of his contemporaries he addresses moral worth and connects it, even if only obliquely, to physiognomy. Oddly enough, according to Grevenbroek the Hottentots are more righteous than the Europeans from whom they presumably diverged physically, but one cannot fail to notice that good character is nevertheless defined in terms of whiteness.

At about the same time that the European discourse of causality for morphological variation was ceding to one of natural necessity in human variation, philosophers began theorizing about the natural laws specifying human relationships and cultural dynamics. By observing how people lived in the world, and by analyzing the connections among diverse manners of living, they began to theorize a relationship between human beings and nature, between, that is, material bodies and the abstract systems governing and regulating them. We find notions of a natural law in such writers as Hugo Grotius and Samuel Pufendorf, but it was Thomas Hobbes who perhaps most forcefully articulated the idea that human beings share a radical form of equality.[103] In his *Leviathan* (1651), Hobbes argued that equality must be conceptualized not through individuals, but through entire groups.[104] Hobbes maintained that because human beings are so fundamentally equal they will desire the same things; scarcity of resources leads almost inevitably to war. It is humankind's natural condition, Hobbes argued, to be at war

> of every one against every one; in which case every one is governed by his own Reason; and there is nothing he can make use of, that may not be a help unto him, in preserving his life against his enemyes; It followeth, that in such a condition, every man has a Right to every thing; even to one anothers body. And therefore, as long as this naturall Right of every man to every thing endureth, there can be no security to any man . . . of living out the time, which Nature ordinarily alloweth men to live. And consequently it is a precept, or generall rule of Reason, *That every man, ought to endeavour Peace.*[105]

Hobbes identified the endeavor for peace as a "Fundamentall Law of Nature"; he defined such a law *(Lex Naturalis)* as a "Precept, or generall Rule, found out by Reason, by which a man is forbidden to do, that, which is destructive of his life, or taketh away the means of preserving the same; and to omit, that, by which he thinketh it may be best preserved."[106] As Althusser noted, Hobbes conceptualized the law of nature as an unchanging set of organizing principles, which human beings can discover—but not, of course, change—through the application of reason. Such laws describe not only the physical arrangement of the earth, but that of human beings and their relationships as well.

This is not the place to rehearse all of the debates concerning the history of natural law, but it is important to underscore the extent to which most philosophers who treated the issue incorporated the notion of universality into their treatises and the importance of reason for recognizing and systematizing natural law.[107] Hobbes's early supposition that the state of nature was one of war ceded in the eighteenth century to visions of a state of original community. Rousseau's *Discourse on Inequality*, Diderot's *Supplément au voyage de Bougainville*, Locke's *Essay*

84 White Men Aren't

Concerning Human Understanding, particularly Book I, on the possibility of innate ideas, and Thomas Paine's *Rights of Man* enjoined readers to consider a naturally occurring and fundamental equality. More and more philosophers joined juridical concerns to rational ones. It was Montesquieu, however, who no doubt most explicitly articulated fundamental notions of law and nature: "There is a primal reason, and laws are the relationships existing between reason and different beings, and the relationships of these different beings among themselves."[108] Furthermore, he specifies that "law, in general, is human reason in its capacity to govern the peoples of the earth."[109]

The conjunction of natural law and reason in the eighteenth century correlates the shift away from a discourse of causality to explain morphological variation. That is, as European observers began to consign human difference to the realm of natural necessity, or the domain of the real without cause, they required a means to *think* themselves different from those they found to *be* different. So, the discourse of reason and the emphasis on empiricism led philosophers, travelers, and other observers to abandon the idea that innate ideas—the sorts that led people to theorize causes for human difference—could lead to an understanding of the world. They turned instead to observing the world and its people in order to articulate nature's structure and purpose. This juncture in the seventeenth century has traditionally been viewed as a crucial epistemological turning point because it represents the move from a mechanistic view of the universe to an empirical one. In fact, Bernard le Bovier de Fontenelle, author of the 1687 *Histoire des oracles,* characterized the two different kinds of thinkers separated by this juncture as follows: "The one begins with what he understands distinctly in order to find a cause of what he sees. The other begins with what he sees in order to find its cause."[110] In fact, in the article "Philosophe" in the eighteenth century's tremendous literary monument the *Encyclopédie* we read that "the philosopher *[philosophe]* disentangles causes as much as it is in him."[111] More and more, naturalists, philosophers, and travelers began to consider the differences in morphology they noted to be not so much produced by the world's different people, but part of a natural order of things that, as Hobbes suggests is the case with natural law, can be discovered through the deployment of human reason. Paul Hazard writes, in fact, that "it was understood: Nature and Reason were linked in a constant relationship; and nothing was simpler, surer, more often repeated by the learned: nature was rational, reason was natural; there was a perfect harmony."[112]

Descriptions of other peoples became more obsessively detailed and more implicitly indicative of what observers believed to be the world's natural order. Rather than seeking the cause for human variation, eighteenth-century observers sought the conclusions to be drawn from their discovery of difference. The comte de Buffon, for example, was one of the century's most famous and most prolific writers on human variation. In his massive *Histoire naturelle,* a forty-four volume opus charting the earth, its plants, animals, and people, Buffon begins the chapter on "Varieties in the Human Species" by noting that "The first and most remarkable of these varieties is that of color."[113] Buffon attempted to classify the people whom he observed according to physical type and to custom, and he endeavored to unearth deep structures implicated by his observation of human difference. Thus, he would write that even though at first blush they might appear quite different, "The savages to the north of the Eskimos are thus all men of the same species, since they resemble one another in form, size, color, morals, and even in the bizarreness of their customs."[114] And, although Buffon submitted that custom and manner of living contributed to morphological variation (at least as far as skin color was concerned), he also held that the most significant factor in determining complexion was the climate,[115] thus relegating to the domain of natural necessity differences in human morphology. One extended explanation of color reads as follows:

If the elevation of that country [Peru], and the snows found there, did not chill the air and remove from the east wind all the heat that it might have acquired while crossing the land, it still retains enough of it to influence the inhabitants' color, for those who, according to their situation are most exposed to it are the most yellow; and those who live in the valleys between the mountains and are thus sheltered from this wind are much whiter than the others.[116]

The wind affects skin color in Buffon's analysis of human morphological variation, and it is important to underscore that nature, and not cultural activity, plays a more significant role in producing human variety the further into the eighteenth and nineteenth centuries we proceed.

In the following chapter I will look more closely at Buffon's work in order to determine the extent to which he allowed the poles of dominant identity—in this case whiteness and maleness—to influence one another and even to blur their own distinctions. But by way of concluding this chapter I would like to show how a significant component of white racial thinking developed precisely in the shift from considering human variation to be the result of determined cultural practice to thinking such difference in the domain of natural necessity. I have already investigated the manner in which whiteness as a form of knowing inhered in versions of statutory law designed to specify who was white, and I have also examined how the discourse of human causality disarticulated the body into significant parts derived from determinate political practices, thus creating a sort of ideology of the body. These procedures have in common the tuché, the encounter with the real, in that each anchors an abstract and immaterial sense of identity into a real, material object, but they do so in an indeterminate zone, in a space that remains undefinable precisely because it is the spot where referent and signifier meet. It is, in fact, the domain of the signified, that oddly immaterial thing that provides consistent substance to subjects' worlds. When eighteenth-century naturalists, philosophers, and other observers turned to empiricism and its attendant rationality, they, too, quilted signifiers to materiality, of course, but in erecting a taxonomy of the world, a system of knowledge empowered to discover universal law, they divided that world up in such a way that not only was whiteness a matter of knowing, but the very systems of reason these thinkers valued were premised on the body as well. In order to see how this was the case, we need to look briefly at how human reason and knowledge ordered the Enlightenment universe.

No doubt the best-known manifestation of Enlightenment order and reason is the celebrated Great Chain of Being, that conceptual scaffolding that facilitated the contemplation of the entire natural world as a continuous and unbroken existential unit. The Great Chain of Being provided a way of thinking about the world and about humankind's condition in it. Less a positive collection of ideas than a rubric or framework for thinking, the Great Chain structured thought according to specific taxonomic beliefs. A prime example of "believing is seeing," the Great Chain was a way of making the universe conform to scientific categories already in place. The Great Chain of Being, which Arthur O.

Lovejoy has defined as a gradation of creatures, "every one of them differing from that immediately above and that immediately below it by the 'least possible' degree of difference,"[117] is perhaps best exemplified in Leibniz's attempt to cause the natural world to conform to the dominant but nevertheless speculative order that late seventeenth-century science had established. Leibniz, who along with many of his contemporaries believed in an inherent and natural continuity uniting all things material and metaphysical, affirmed a belief in plant-animals. These "zoophytes" were creatures whose irresolute properties would cause them to straddle existing biological categories.

> And so great is the principle of continuity, to my thinking, that not only should I not be surprised to hear that such beings had been discovered . . . but, in fact, I am convinced that there must be such creatures, and that natural history will perhaps some day become acquainted with them, when it has further studied that infinity of living things whose small size conceals them from ordinary observation and which are hidden in the bowels of the earth and the depths of the sea.[118]

Leibniz's zoophytes have properties that would enable them to pass equally well for plants or animals; as missing links they would call into question existing taxonomies, since systems of classification already in place left gaps in what many naturalists were coming to believe was a seamless continuity. In Leibniz's theory an abstract and culturally contingent philosophy provides the ground for scientific research, as observers set out to find things that their socially encoded beliefs told them would be there. As eighteenth-century naturalists saw it, once the taxonomy was finally complete it would be difficult if not impossible to determine the differences between hierarchically contiguous creatures, since one would blend so neatly into the other.

Leibniz's belief in an intermediate species underscores his concern that human reason should be able to uncover, if not to dictate nature's systems. The "principle of continuity" correlates natural occurrences in the world Leibniz imagines; he posits a reality of nature based on an idealized belief of what it ought to be, and he has faith in the correlation of his desire with its ultimate manifestation in the real world. Like the subject's relationship to the law that Montesquieu theorized a hundred years later, belief, and not empirical verification, regulates what subjects know and what the world seems to be, but the crucial element here is that belief is located not in the subject, but in the system that governs it (Montesquieu wrote, we recall, that "the law believes for him, and it relieves him from examination and from doubt"). In other words, Leibniz created a natural world in the image of human knowledge.[119]

A continuous gradation of physical features, each nearly imperceptibly different from those surrounding it, proved an attractive idea for a great many seventeenth- and eighteenth-century naturalists who were attempting to classify human beings. They used that gradation not only to predict new species, but to determine both where human beings fit in the Chain and how they diverged among themselves. These two projects sometimes overlapped when naturalists speculated about the position in the Chain occupied by those from less familiar cultures. Early on, however, the Chain simply served to position human beings in an overarching rational schema of existence. For example, in the late seventeenth century, Sir William Petty established a hierarchy between God, man, and the "holy Angells, Created Intelligences, and subtile materiall beings,"[120] and he elaborated two scales of animate beings, one with humans at the top, reigning over the animal world, and the other with humans at the bottom, beneath the celestial minds. In a similar manner, Richard Blackmore, writing in 1714, mused on the specific place in the Chain of Being that human beings occupied. A physician, Blackmore located humans in the natural order previously reserved strictly for animals. The result was to create a contiguity between people and animals that would later characterize most eighteenth-century anthropology:

> As Man, who approaches nearest to the lowest Class of Celestial Spirits (for we may justly suppose a Subordination in that excellent Order) being half Body and half Spirit, becomes the *Æquator*, that divides in the Middle the whole Creation, and distinguishes the corporeal from the Invisible Intellectual World, so the Ape or Monkey, that bears the greatest Similitude to Man, is the next Order of Animals below him.[121]

Further examples include James Burnett, who in his *Origin and Progress of Language* maintained that man is "rational, and he is irrational; he has intellect, and he has not intellect; he is a biped, and he is not a biped; he is a land-animal, and he is a water-animal. . . . In short, he appears to be placed on the confines betwixt different kinds of beings."[122] Then, explicitly evoking Leibniz's belief in plant-animals, he writes, "As the *Zoöphyte* is in the middle betwixt the vegetable and animal, so *man* appears to occupy the space betwixt the several classes of animals."[123] Linnaeus cataloged the animate world in his *Systema Naturae*, arranging at the top of the hierarchy the mammals; first among them were the simians, sloths, and the "homo."[124] Finally, Alexander Pope committed this continuity of being to verse in his *Essay on Man*, in which he notes the irresolute manner in which human beings take their place in the Chain of Being:

> Plac'd on this isthmus of a middle state,
> A Being darkly wise, and rudely great:
> With too much knowledge for the Sceptic side,
> With too much weakness for the Stoic's pride,
> He hangs between; in doubt to act, or rest:
> In doubt to deem himself a God, or Beast.[125]

If the Great Chain of Being unites the most debased with the infinitely powerful and wise, and does so without gaps or schism, most of these thinkers reasoned, then it must also follow that human beings adhere to a similarly structured hierarchical system. Locke argued that "in all the visible corporeal world we see no chasms or gaps," and he applied these general observations to the specific case of human beings: "There are some brutes that seem to have as much reason and knowledge as some that are called men."[126] Not everyone agreed with Locke that reason was parceled out equitably along the Great Chain of Being, as we will see; most observers used morphological characteristics to classify people into different social and cultural groups, however, and one of the differences in human constitution most commonly observed was skin color. In his *Essay on the Causes of the Variety of Complexion and Figure in the Human Species*, for example, Samuel Stanhope Smith showed how skin color lay among the subtle gradations established by the Great Chain of Being, and he mapped—literally—those gradations geographically: "Each parallel of latitude is, among them, distinctly marked with its characteristic complexion. In no other country is there such a regular gradation of colour as is traced from the fair natives of Pekin to the inhabitants of Canton, who are of a dark copper; or from the dark olive or swarthy colour of the Desert Arabia, to the black of the province of Yemen."[127] Smith reasoned that skin color was "habitual," a term he used to explain the "influence of the state of society in multiplying the varieties of mankind."[128] Human morphological variety, he maintained, resulted from "habits of the body" that apply both to individuals and to nations, and they arise "by continual, and almost imperceptible touches."[129] Buffon placed human beings on a spectrum of skin color roughly corresponding to latitude and longitude, arguing not only that "white seems to be the primal color of nature"[130] and that "heat of climate is the principal cause of the color black."[131]

If dark skin varied by geography, however, the same was not true of so-called white skin; European observers did not catalog varieties or shades of whiteness. The European body, which according to Buffon and most other observers from the period differed primarily because of its white color, suffered no divisional gradations such as those we see in the Great Chain of Being. That is, while travelers and naturalists noted gradations of dark skin that they correlated to cultural practice and to changes in latitude, white European skin underwent no such division. Buffon identified white skin with the most beautiful populations[132] and, as we will see in chapter 3, he described white as nature's primal skin color from which other colors degenerated. He went so far as to argue that "nature as perfect as it can be made men white."[133] Whiteness for Buffon and his contemporaries constituted an absolute; gradations of the color simply were not recognized. Divergences from pure whiteness were seen as degenerations, imperfections, or mutations. White was white, at least until the threat of "contamination" posed itself in the American slave-holding south toward the end of the eighteenth century.[134] White skin, at bottom, seemed not to come in shades.[135] By way of demonstrating the unchangeability of white skin and its priority over other social indicators, Stanhope Smith argued that "the white population of America affords us less conspicuous instances, than many other nations, of that variety of countenance, and of personal beauty or defect arising from diversity of rank, and refinement in society."[136]

It is particularly striking, however, that when a non-European body happened to bear a resemblance to the European variety, particularly in terms of those features articulated as significant, that body required an explanation. That seemed especially urgent when non-European bodies exhibited the crucial mark of European distinction: whiteness. João dos Sanctos was one of the earliest explorers to observe this phenomenon,

as we noted above in his description of the "white Goldi-locked children" that sometimes issued forth from "Parents as blacke as Pitch."
Dos Sanctos's successor Manoel de Almeida reported similar occurrences in Ethiopia, but he felt the need to qualify the phenomenon: Of
the Ethiopians' complexion he writes that "the majority of them are
black. . . . There are some who are whitish, but it is a bloodless white."[137]
Almeida's qualification of unexpected or illegitimate whiteness as one
that is somehow also unnatural finds echo in Andrew Battell's description of unusual white complexions among the residents of Loango.
"There be certain persons called *Dunda [ndundu]*, which are born by
negro parents, and yet are, by some unknown cause, white. They are
very rare, and when such happen to be born, they are brought to the
king, and become great witches: they are his councillors, and advise
him of lucky and unlucky days for execution of his enterprises."[138] Like
the human prodigies we noted earlier, these individuals inexplicably
appear where Europeans do not anticipate them. Each time an explorer
or adventurer reports such an occurrence, however, we note either that
the unexpected white person is either presumed to have unusual powers, as in Almeida's account, or that the person's skin, although white,
somehow lacked an unidentifiable essence, a sort of *je ne sais quoi* that
instead of allying the body more tightly with the European, made that
person all the more uncannily other.[139]

There are, nevertheless, reports from naturalists who situated specific human groups somewhere between white and nonwhite. Buffon,
for example, described the Hottentots as "men who, in the race of
blacks, are beginning to approach the white,"[140] and in chapter 3 I will
address the significance of Buffon's very unusual characterization of
this group as a link between black and white.[141] The reports of unfore-
seen white complexions in cultures or geographic locales where Europeans did not expect them offer the only causes or explanations we have
for white complexion.[142] They are significant because they demonstrate
the manner in which whiteness encodes far more than a simple color.
Were whiteness to represent nothing more than one possible shade that
human skin color might have—and we have already considered the fact
that it is not even a possible skin color, but already situated squarely in
the metaphoric domain of "believing is seeing"—there would be no
reason to explain it in other cultures. Furthermore, there would be no
need to ally a mere color with a debased, insane, or otherwise troubling

character. Clearly whiteness encodes a way of being and a way of thinking that Europeans needed to preserve in the face of a potentially illegitimate claim to humanity that the freakish appearance of white skin in a person lacking whiteness's other crucial qualities might make.

In the following chapter I will devote considerable attention to how Europeans addressed the question of skin color; what I want to emphasize now is that Buffon's and Smith's most significant contributions to the study of human variation centered on how difference occurs, but more important, they wondered what difference meant. To this end, they recognized the staggering variety of possible forms the body can take, and in a more or less characteristic Enlightenment move, Stanhope Smith wonders, "If human nature actually embraces different species of men, by what criterion shall we distinguish them? . . . Where do they now exist pure and unmixed?"[143]

Smith's question proved to be a loaded one, and throughout the eighteenth century there were, of course, many attempts to synthesize the natural human being from the apparently corrupted, civilized one. For however attractive the Great Chain of Being may have proved as a heuristic device to conceptualize the universe according to a single line of development, it nevertheless struck contemporaries as necessary to disrupt that Chain with a line, a radical break distinguishing the human from its nearest nonhuman neighbor on the Chain. Blackmore shows to what extent contemporaries believed such a demarcation necessary: "The most perfect of this Order of Beings [Apes], the *Orang Outang,* as he is called by the Natives of *Angola,* that is, the Wild Man, or Man of the Woods, has the Honor of bearing the nearest Resemblance to human Nature."[144] Likewise, in an observation similar to Grevenbroek's and Pope's, Blackmore also worried about the collateral distance and proximity of cultures that Europeans generally deemed inferior: "Nor is the Disagreement between the basest Individuals of our Species and the Ape or Monkey so great, but that were the latter endow'd with the faculty of Speech, they might perhaps as justly claim the Rank and Dignity of the human Race, as the Salvage *Hotentot,* or stupid Native of *Nova Zembla.*"[145] Finally, Linnaeus, who was one early taxonomist who decided to rank human beings among all the animals in nature, wrote that "there is something in us, which cannot be seen, whence our knowledge of ourselves depends—that is, *reason,* the most noble thing of all, in which man excels to a most surprising extent all other animals."[146] If it seemed relatively simple to demarcate mortals from divinities, naturalists found it extremely problematic to determine how far down the Chain one could go and still find humans; many frequently wondered, in fact, whether those they observed were of the same species as themselves, but most seemed convinced that they could draw a line separating human from animal.

As Blackmore and others argued, it was comparatively simple to break up the Great Chain of Being by drawing a line separating speaking from nonspeaking beings. That line distinguished beings that possessed reason from those that did not. As the eighteenth century's most famous naturalist, Buffon puzzled over the same problem that Blackmore had encountered, and by way of differentiating humans from beasts, he proposed his own quite similar solution to this taxonomic dilemma:

> Man is a reasonable being; animals are beings without reason. And just as there is no middle point between positive and negative, just as there are no intermediary beings between the reasonable being and the being without reason, it is evident that the nature of man is entirely different from that of the animal, who only resembles him externally, and that to judge him according to this material resemblance is to allow oneself to be fooled by appearances and voluntarily to close one's eyes to the light that must cause it to be distinguished from reality.[147]

Similarly, John Locke held that a line may be drawn separating human from beast, in spite of the fact that the rest of the Great Chain of Being seemed so utterly devoid of such explicit divisions: "If it may be doubted whether beasts compound and enlarge their ideas that way to any degree; this, I think, I may be positive in,—that the power of abstracting is not at all in them; and that the having of general ideas is that which puts a perfect distinction betwixt man and brutes, and is an excellency which the faculties of brutes do by no means attain to."[148] Reason clearly separated humans from beasts in Buffon's and Locke's schemas; generally speaking, one cannot possess reason partitively.[149] Where we might expect to find varying degrees of reason, as we did with skin pigmentation, parceled out along the Great Chain of Being, we discover instead a unique binary logic that stands out in this linear array of minute gradations. Reason stands to measure and gauge all things, yet by virtue of its unparalleled form and function in the continuum of Being, it stands outside, like any sort of general equivalent, of that which it is called on to measure.[150]

Two sorts of binary logic thus interrupt the ostensible seamless continuity of the Great Chain of Being: whiteness/nonwhiteness, and reason/lack of reason. But it is not the case that these two binaries form a simple, coincidental disruption of the Great Chain. As Sir William Petty's writing demonstrates, by the end of the seventeenth century, and certainly well into the eighteenth century, most observers associated whiteness with reason. Petty was a disciple of Hobbes, an original member of the Royal Society, and author of an unpublished work called the *Scale of Creatures* (ca. 1677). A subscriber to the heuristic device of the Great Chain of Being, Petty joined intellectual and morphological features as a way of articulating the links or steps in the Chain. Petty found that "between God and man, there are holy Angells, Created Intelligences, and subtile materiall beings; as there are between man and the lowest animall a multitude of intermediate natures."[151] Explicitly evoking his Scale of Creatures to situate people in a taxonomic abstraction, like Stanhope Smith he also uses the heuristic device to create a hierarchy describing his fellow human beings. Also like most of his contemporaries, he finds reason to be the crucial separator. After listing the different sorts of human beings that he finds significant, he writes:

> Besides those differences between Man & man, there bee others more considerable, that is, between the Guiny Negros & the Middle Europeans: & of Negros between those of Guiny and those who live about the Cape of Good Hope, which last are the Most beastlike of all the Souls of Men with whom our Travellers are well acquainted. I say that the Europeans do not onely differ from the aforementioned Africans in Collour, which is as much as white differs from black, but also in their Haire which differs as much as a straight line differs from a Circle. . . . They differ also in their Naturall Manners, & in the internall Qualities of their Minds.[152]

Petty expressly articulates morphology to intellect, skin color to reason, whiteness to the mind. Furthermore, he sets up the European as actively differentiating itself from the African, in marked contradistinction to most earlier writings in this vein that, through the discourse of human causality, found the non-European to have differentiated itself. The point is subtle, yet crucial: because of the discourse of natural necessity, which in an era of rational and empirical observation presumed to catalog the world as it was, Europeans could describe themselves as actively distinctive by exercising their reason. In fact, the deployment of reason as a predominantly European characteristic in the late seventeenth and eighteenth centuries meant that unlike other living creatures on the Great Chain of Being, white people could alter their condition, thus making them unique. Historically evolving, white people possessed a form of reason that identified them and that they in turn defined. The point here is not simply that a hegemonic narrative directed Europeans to consider people from other cultures—and in particular from African cultures—as somehow inferior both physically and intellectually, although that such narratives existed is of course certainly the case. The point is, rather, that the hegemonic narrative that does the work of allowing the articulation of morphology and intellect in the first place is the one that stealthily articulates as a fundamental gesture reason with whiteness.

We have already seen that the narrative in question is the one that begins with the early reports of different kinds of people and then attempts to explain the reasons why their bodies differed from what Europeans might have expected. In the production of such a cause, I maintained, lies the work of articulating socially significant difference that operates by isolating specific body parts as crucially discrepant from their European counterparts. Thus, as the body's differences began to require explanation—which, it should be noted, rarely occurred previously in European physiological treatises except as a function of gender—the body and its varieties became subject to a discursive articulation that situated it squarely in a political register. The hegemonic narrative responsible for producing white racial thinking, however, is part of the same discourse that promotes reason not only as an indivisible human faculty uniquely dissociated from the Great Chain of Being's gradations, but also as a transparent vehicle, lacking in content, for delivering analytical access to other epistemological domains. Whiteness and reason have in common the fiction that they are transparent and contentless; they also share the premise that they are without history and, like the real, simply there, with no cause or ground.[153]

What we note is that there is only one form of whiteness, just as there is only one form of reason, and that whiteness and reason— at least the European variety, which passed and in many respects continues to pass as the only kind—formed an indissoluble bond in the minds of European naturalists, philosophers, and other social and cultural observers.[154] Europeans looked at the continuity of the Great Chain of Being, and drew a single stroke to divide themselves from the "brutes" they determined to be beneath them. That defining stroke consisted of the nonquantifiable, indissoluble bedrock of reason, a bedrock that happened to apply also to the indivisibility of whiteness.[155] In fact, Stanhope Smith makes explicit the connection uniting bodies and minds:

> The body and mind have such reciprocal influence upon each other, that we often see certain peculiar powers or tendencies of the rational faculty intimately connected with certain corporeal forms. And whenever the moral, not less than the physical causes, under the influence of which any people exist, have produced any visible effect on the form and expression of the countenance, they will also be found proportionally to affect the operations of the mind.[156]

But in the simple act of drawing that stroke, Europeans constituted white humanity and reason as organically linked: both escaped the graded calibrations of the Great Chain of Being, both seemed utterly devoid of content, serving instead as markers or standards of other forms of content, and both appeared to be outside the discourses of either history or causality as the two social identifiers somehow inhering naturally in the real. By identifying various missing links in the Great Chain of Being, from Leibniz's hydra to Buffon's white-black Hottentots, practitioners of white racial thinking constituted a social and natural continuity in which whiteness was not only privileged, but part of the discourse of an ostensibly transparent and timeless vehicle of logic. That logic appeared to have no positive substance of its own yet it was nevertheless endowed with the capacity to characterize and organize other forms of thought.[157]

But the missing link in the Great Chain of Being that Europeans tried to find in the people whom they visited is only the incarnation— the reification or physical manifestation—of the more fundamental link in thinking and in representing that allied whiteness with other social institutions.[158] That link, which functions as a sort of trace, or condition of possibility of other links, is the one that caused what is ostensibly a simple, albeit impossible skin color to inform and affect other social identifiers that strictly speaking have little or nothing to do with the body. The missing link that I am here identifying functions as a *point de capiton,* a key signifier that provides stability and substance to other signifiers by arranging and modulating them. Meaning arises from the movement and play of signifiers in relation to a key signifier that seems essential or fundamental largely as a result of such play.[159] The missing link that I am attempting to identify here is the one that works by casting inchoate thought into meaning, but more important, it does so while simultaneously effacing as much as possible the traces of its own labor. As part of what I have been calling a hegemonic narrative, whiteness erects the visible and knowable part of itself—that is, the ostensible self-evidence of an originary skin color from which other colors degenerated and, to a lesser extent, a specific form of thinking about other cultures—in the place occupied by the far more fundamental epistemological operation of articulating a kind of thinking with a kind of body and then predicating that thinking as universal, natural, and eminent.

The missing link, the largely invisible, structurally unconscious link that performs the structuring of meaning also produces whiteness as an encounter with the real because it maps the production of signification onto the apparently indelible materiality of the human body. It is crucial to consider whiteness as this sort of link because whiteness only exists as a dynamic, meaning-producing endeavor, even if it functions as part of a hegemonic identity precisely by obscuring that component of its identity. So much of whiteness's power derives from a largely effaced history of overlaying one form of discourse on top of another, perhaps unrelated one. That overlaying not only produces a formal similarity, but it causes formal similarity to produce or at least imply contextual similarity. In the travel narratives and anthropological accounts explored here considerations of causality allied the body with cultural practices and consequently with the division of the body into significant parts or characteristics. The seventeenth-century scientific discourse of causality blended in nearly seamlessly with the later discourse of empirical observation that considered bodies that differed from the European variety to be expressions of nature's intent to create higher and lower forms of life distributed along the links of a Great Chain. Thus, the forms of whiteness produced by pre-Enlightenment narratives assumed the status of natural necessity, and they served as a point de capiton or anchor for the strand of reason that ultimately served to legitimate whiteness as natural and itself as transparent.

In the cases we have considered in this chapter, pre-Enlightenment narratives of causality and Enlightenment discourses of rational natural systems construe whiteness and the reason that it engenders as inexplicable and, simultaneously, the source of all explanation. That is, whiteness either has no cause, but simply is; or it is coupled with logic and reason and serves as a transparent vehicle of comparison with no substance of its own, providing in its indissolubility the means to make equivalences or becoming in its integrity the instrument of thought. Seventeenth- and eighteenth-century Europeans construed their identities as necessary offshoots of their own very particular ways of viewing the world, and they linked ways of thinking with ways of being. In that gesture they articulated a set of positive characteristics for whiteness that because of their particular features have generally escaped attention, primarily because that is how those characteristics are implicitly designed: for whiteness's defining features consist of functioning as a hard kernel resisting symbolization in the real, and as an empty space, a hole, in the symbolic.

But it is important to bear in mind that what I am claiming here about the positive features of whiteness differs substantially from previous arguments, some of which I cited at the beginning of this chapter, that whiteness is empty or somehow absent. I am not arguing that whiteness is any of those things, but rather that, in the particular encounter with the real forged in the struggle to map ideological beliefs onto the materiality of the body, Europeans implicitly forged whiteness as an emptiness, the same way that they construed reason as transparently without content. Put another way, whiteness is only absent or empty when considered from within most contemporary paradigms of critical discourse, since those paradigms are heir to Enlightenment logic and reason, the same way that reason seems transparent until we consider it historically as in part the bourgeois rejection of absolutist authority and religious received tradition.[160] Put yet another way, to think of whiteness as colorless or featureless is already to be located smack in the middle of white racial thinking.

Max Horkheimer and Theodor Adorno provided one of the first and most rigorous criticisms of Enlightenment thought, arguing, among other things, that Enlightenment thinking constructs itself as a universal much like the universals it rejected, and that Enlightenment concerned itself only with entities that could be apprehended as unities.[161] Recognizing that modes of thought are historical products, every bit as much as the content that thought would produce, Horkheimer and Adorno demonstrate the extent to which Enlightenment thought, which tried to break free of oppressive political and epistemological systems, remained tied, as any form of thought, to its own past:

> Factuality wins the day; cognition is restricted to its repetition; and thought becomes mere tautology. The more the machinery of thought subjects existence to itself, the more blind its resignation in reproducing existence. Hence enlightenment returns to mythology, which it never really knew how to elude. . . . The world as a gigantic analytic judgment, the only one left over from all the dreams of science, is of the same mold as the cosmic myth which associated the cycle of spring and autumn with the kidnapping of Persephone. The uniqueness of the mythic process, which tends to legitimize factuality, is deception.[162]

As I have been trying to demonstrate, the development of Enlightenment thought—in particular but not limited to what it considered logic and reason—correlated, but by no means was absolutely tied to, seventeenth- and eighteenth-century discourses of the body, its causal development, and its relationship to social practice. Whiteness developed as the bodily incarnation of a specific mode of thought, and as we have seen, whiteness itself is less a kind of bodily being than it is a mode of thought. Thus, I would argue, the same kinds of political gestures that produce Enlightenment thought's effacement of its own genesis and politics operate in whiteness's struggle to obfuscate its own production of an absence or emptiness at the core of its identity.

In this chapter I have been primarily interested in looking at a historical moment and a geographical space in which both the term and the identity "whiteness" came to have meaning for a specific group of people. My concern has been to demonstrate that if the thinking I identified as Oedipal in chapter 1 overflowed the boundaries of gender normally assigned to it (particularly by contemporary psychoanalysis), the thinking we call "racial" overruns characteristics normally attributed to the body and inflects as well—and in fundamental ways—philosophy, logic, and reason. Again, I am not pretending to do a linear history of the white male, but I have chosen to emphasize particular points as crucial in the development of the hegemonic narrative supporting the white male identity. Horkheimer and Adorno might provide suitable egress for this chapter when they write that "he who calls himself Nobody for his own sake and manipulates approximation to the state of nature as a means of mastering nature, falls victim to *hubris*."[163] When seventeenth- and eighteenth-century thinkers constructed their own encounter with the real in the form of a bodily identity that incarnated a way of thinking, they may well have been victims of hubris. But, when we remember that hubris is generally reserved for those who would be gods, we can see that approximating and mastering nature in the form of an ostensibly empty subjective identity nevertheless remains a powerful political enterprise.

3. THE FAIR SEX:

IT'S NOT WHAT YOU THINK

> Who in the rainbow can draw the line where the
> violet tint ends and the orange tint begins? Dis-
> tinctly we see the difference of the colors, but
> where exactly does the one first blendingly enter
> into the other?—Herman Melville, "Billy Budd"

I noted toward the end of the previous chapter that the comte de Buffon, the eighteenth century's most renowned naturalist, considered the wind to be at least partially responsible for variations in human complexion. Buffon observed that the inhabitants of Peru who were least exposed to the wind had the whitest skin; the more people undergo the wind's action, he theorized, the darker their complexion develops. While such a theory might strike twentieth-century readers as unusual, Buffon in fact reports far more bizarre "proof" that the wind causes dark skin when he observes different skin tones on a single individual. Summarizing the findings of Alexis Littré, a highly respected member of the Académie des Sciences, he writes:

> Monsieur Littré, who in 1702 performed a dissection on a Negro, observed that the tip of the glans of the penis which was not covered by the prepuce was black like the rest of his skin, and that the rest, which was covered, was perfectly white. This observation proves that the action of the air is necessary to produce the blackness of Negroes' skin. Their children are born white, or rather red, like the children of other men, but two or three days after their birth, their color changes.[1]

Neither Buffon nor Littré was alone in his curiosity about the genitals of African men. Winthrop Jordan notes that "by the final quarter of the eighteenth century the idea that the Negro's penis was larger than the white man's had become something of a commonplace in European scientific circles."[2] But in Buffon's claim we are not dealing with the size of these men's genitals, we are dealing with their color. And despite what Buffon says concerning the color of children's skin at birth, he still holds to the wind theory of adult complexion, as his report about the whiteness of that portion of the male genitals not exposed to the modifying effects of the air reveals.[3] This strange conjunction of observations leads to a single, somewhat startling conclusion: according to Buffon (and to the other men of his coterie), if you have a penis, it must somehow be intrinsically white.[4]

Buffon's unusual theory articulates the tensions resulting from different kinds of taxonomic contradiction, and in this chapter I will show how in the eighteenth century white masculinity constituted itself by negotiating those tensions. Specifically, eighteenth-century white masculinity consolidated itself as the compromise in a logical impasse involving competing classificatory systems, in particular the systems for organizing people according to gender and morphological features that could be shown to correlate other, intangible human indicators. Reducing a variety of forms of difference to a basic opposition by applying brutal interpretive force, the identity in the process of imposing its hegemony as white and male did so in part through the complex—and contradictory—position of enunciation it occupies.

The pronounced discomfort that Buffon and other naturalists in the eighteenth and nineteenth centuries manifested when they confronted the difficult conjunction of conflicting systems for classifying people reveals the amount of intellectual and ideological work involved in sustaining the idea of a given signifying system's natural dominance. In particular, European men implicitly endeavored to show that all men, from whatever culture, were engendered as male in fundamentally the same way, an operation that would install as primary and foundational the signifying system based on their particular ways of experiencing their bodies in history. In fact, Buffon's implicit assumption that penises have to be white simply literalizes that fantasy. As more or less enthusiastic subscribers to the idea of the Great Chain of Being, these men maintained a belief that all creatures occupied a discrete position on the same scale; they thus needed to find a way to discern sameness in difference, and difference in sameness, since the very act of classifying caused observers to consider the ways in which the people they visited were simultaneously like and unlike themselves. And, when taxonomists faced multiple sorts of difference—in the cases to be considered here, what we now think of as racial and sexual—it was not immediately clear to them how to classify them, since the Great Chain provided merely a linear perspective and could consequently only account for a single variable at a time.

When European men encountered and attempted to classify other *males*, they lacked a paradigm for inserting them into the Chain of Being. They often confronted that lack by attempting either to ascribe to all males the same experience of gender—including desire, sexuality, and their relationships to women, to other men, to their bodies, and to the body's constituent parts—or to make them so radically other that they could not even be considered men at all. As Londa Schiebinger has observed regarding the sometimes conflicting taxonomic systems of race and gender that different cultural venues produced, "Racial science interrogated males and male physiology, while sexual science scrutinized European subjects."[5] When paths of investigation crossed and naturalists needed to prove a theory of human difference through recourse to what people have in common, tensions developed in classificatory systems and in the men who deployed them. It is important to emphasize, however, that the observers we will be dealing with in this chapter had agendas ranging from the blatantly racist to the most benignly egalitarian, and yet we still find similar discursive constructions of white masculinity. What this suggests is the pervasiveness of white racial thinking, even in (or perhaps particularly in) areas of thought not generally recognized as having such a content.[6] As Kenan Malik bluntly puts it, "The discourse of race lies at the very heart of modern society."[7] It remains to be seen how European and American men used whiteness to gauge masculinity.

We saw in the preceding chapters some of the manners in which the social identifiers of masculinity and whiteness necessarily incorporate other descriptors with which they have not been traditionally associated, and that those identifiers themselves are far more complex than often appears at first blush. In this chapter I will return to the claim I made in the introduction that whiteness and masculinity—at least the European and American varieties—are discursively constructed according to the logic of hysteria, and I will also show how that form of hysteria combines with another discursive register—mastery—to produce a formidable ideological unit. By looking at anthropological, philosophical, and political writings concerning the conjunction of masculinity and nonwhite identity, I will show that white men in the eighteenth century constructed an implicit supplement to the Great Chain of Being, one that specified that to be really male, you must be white. When these two identities could not be brought into alignment, nonwhite maleness produced easily identifiable anxieties in the white men of the period, primarily, it seems, because one of the pillars of a hegemonic identity—in this case, masculinity—existed in forms other than those that Europeans and Americans valorized. Consequently, the white men of the time went through logical and rhetorical contortions to produce unified narratives legitimizing specific traits as fundamentally masculine, consolidating into a single variety many ways of being male.

In the discussion to follow I am striving to gain some insight into how early modern men identified as men, and hence to the greatest extent possible I am trying to avoid the phenomenon in which a white man (myself) once again looks at women or people of color as objects of study. While it might be argued that despite my efforts I am nevertheless engaging in precisely what I claim to be trying to avoid, if perhaps only in slightly mediated fashion, I want to direct our attentions to how European men looked at others to see what we can determine about the lookers. That is, looking at what they thought they saw will tell us something about those who were doing the looking. Deborah McDowell has cautioned that when we look at the bodies shaping our discussions of race, gender and/or sexuality, our work "is implicated in the reproduction of the very racialized subject/object relations" that we would attempt to critique.[8] Keeping that caution in mind is an essential part of our efforts.

As we have seen, whiteness produces itself as an apparently empty category, a putatively transparent vehicle that, like the ostensibly transparent vehicle of Enlightenment reason, gauges other forms without nevertheless appearing to have any positive content of its own. In this chapter I will pursue the issue of gender and racial identity as forms of knowledge, particularly as that knowledge is not only the product of gendered and racial thinking, but also its organizing principle, one that is anchored by the white male.[9] The first step to take in this pursuit is to delineate the manner in which the concept "knowledge" will be useful here, and to begin I refer back to the concepts of "missing link" and "articulation" developed earlier. Whiteness (and to a lesser extent masculinity) achieve consistency through discursive action and manipulation, particularly as the latter grafts behaviors and beliefs onto bodies and especially as they both engage power dynamics. Furthermore, they become concepts and hence achieve a certain density of meaning through their articulation with other concepts and objects. Thus, when eighteenth-century naturalists and philosophers associated a specific kind of thinking with a particular form of body, they implicitly contributed to the formation of whiteness not as something that a person is or has, but as something he or she knows or does. In addition, by ascribing particular features and attributes to bodies that they presumed must exist because of the linear epistemological construction of the Great Chain of Being, these Europeans constituted whiteness as a real surface or site onto which they could inscribe a network of ideological values. They fashioned what amounted to a new human characteristic by construing a formal similarity among a nexus of already existing concepts—moral goodness, logic as an ahistorical and transparent vehicle for thought, natural necessity as endower of unquestioned empirical reality—and then by causing that formal similarity to inflect the philosophical, epistemological, and political domains on which they brought it to bear. The formal similarity that early modern Europeans gleaned in the structures of these diverse systems contributed to the constitution of what would later turn out to be gender and racial knowledge.[10]

The production of whiteness as a form of knowledge during the specific historical moment in which the discourse of reason became culturally predominant depended on the promulgation of particular master signifiers applied to the human body and on the putting into play of those signifiers in regularized fashion.[11] In short, a genuine production of knowledge demands that those who receive its fundamental building blocks not simply accept them as given, but internalize them, manipulate them, and refashion them to construct a workable system that is personally meaningful. The production and the reception of discursive elements partially constitute, in fact, what Lacan theorizes as the four forms of discourse. Lacan considers the determining and determinant other in enunciation, and he identifies the obfuscated or underlying

truth of the agent of enunciation as well as the product of that enunciation as crucial factors in discursive analysis. Each of these factors operates in all discourse, he maintains, and different kinds of discourse
result when a different executor occupies those agencies or positions.[12]
The four principal types of discourse that Lacan specifies are those of the
university, the master, the hysteric, and the analyst; the four principal
factors in discourse, he maintains, are knowledge, master signifiers, the
divided subject, and *jouissance,* or surplus enjoyment, the object-cause
of desire.[13] By determining which of the four principal discursive factors
functions as agent or other of enunciation, and product or obfuscated
truth of enunciation, Lacan derives his four discourses.

The algebra Lacan developed using his infamous "mathemes" to
illustrate the discourses can seem somewhat hermetic.[14] It is important
to bear in mind that Lacan's discourses are structural, however, and not
essential. They produce effects; they do not necessarily define people.
As Bruce Fink puts it, "While Lacan terms one of his discourses the
'hysteric's discourse,' he does not mean thereby that a given hysteric
always and inescapably adopts or functions within the hysteric's discourse. As an analyst, the hysteric may function within the analyst's
discourse; as an academic, the hysteric may function within the discourse of the university."[15] It is not the case, in other words, that someone diagnosed as hysterical simply and unproblematically produces the
discourse of the hysteric. We should not expect the Lacanian discourses
merely to reconfirm what we think we already know—which is what we
criticized in some forms of scientific discourse above—merely because
we seem to know something about the identity of the person speaking.

In fact, to some extent, the form of scientific discourse we saw in the
introduction—the kind restricted to finding what is sought—succinctly
encapsulates the discourses of the university and of the master. In
chapters 1 and 2 I analyzed the manner in which a dominant identity
carves out its position by concealing an original absence and thus by
causing a resolutely ideological position to appear historically and culturally universal and hence neutral. These two operations epitomize the
first two discourses related above. In the discourse of the university,
which also accommodates the discourse of science in its quest for objective, external truth, the various signifiers available through systems of
received knowledge craft identity positions for subjects to accede to.[16]
Such a discourse affects for itself the status of neutral or disengaged

knowledge; it construes itself as the objective, self-effacing reporter of objective laws or events. As Lacan puts it, "The myth of the ideal I, of the I that masters, of the I through which some thing at least is identical to itself—namely the enunciator—is quite precisely what the discourse of the University cannot eliminate from the place where its truth is found."[17] What the discourse of the university conceals is its reliance on paradigms or master signifiers, which Lacan defines as those whose function is to "represent a subject for all other signifiers."[18] Mark Bracher glosses this definition as follows:

> A master signifier is any signifier that a subject has invested his or her identity in—any signifier that the subject has identified with (or against) and which thus constitutes a powerful positive or negative value. Master signifiers are thus the factors that give the articulated system of signifiers (S_2)—i.e., knowledge, belief, language—purchase on a subject: they are what make a message meaningful, what make it have an impact rather than being like a foreign language that one can't understand.[19]

In other words, the discourse of the university, which incorporates science and the ostensibly direct and uncontaminated representation of the world, both relies on and—crucially—masks its reliance on the investment of particular signifiers. Signifiers invested with particular social, historical, political, or economic value acquire the capacity to structure and organize entire domains of meaning. Claude Lévi-Strauss has demonstrated, for example, how kinship relations serve as fundamental organizing principles for entire social structures, extending into and governing relations that have no apparent connection to the rules that stipulate which pair bonds may be formed.[20] The discourse of the university correlates the Enlightenment discourse of reason that I examined in chapter 2: eighteenth-century thinkers construed that faculty as a more or less transparent standard able to gauge the quality and rigors of various forms of thought and the conclusions that resulted from them. That form of reason appeared to stand outside of history and culture, and it is precisely owing to the obfuscation of the hegemonic agendas underpinning it that reason could appear to be universal.[21]

The discourse of the university with its emphasis on stable, transmissible truths evokes the discourse of the master, which is characterized by an investment in the myth of the ideal "I," or of the subject that would be exactly equivalent to what it can say about itself, or, as Lacan puts it, "to be identical to one's own signifier."[22] The discourse of the master differs from that of the university in that in the position of enunciation one finds a predominance not of knowledge, but of master signifiers. The discourse of the master orders knowledge according to specific paradigms such as truth, reason, gender, race—any of the social moorings that hold sway in the way a culture understands itself. Those signifiers order our understanding of the world by furnishing stable points of reference—quilting points—that provide consistency, coherence, and priorities to the various components that together constitute a world view. Nancy Leys Stepan and Sander L. Gilman write of the discourse of science in the following terms, which evoke the Lacanian discourses of the master and of the university:

> As science acquired status as the preeminently empirical, value-free, and objective type of knowledge, its power to settle political issues concerning "nature" was increased. Theological, ethical, and political approaches to what scientists now presented as problems of mere empirical nature were reduced in their authority. Thus scientists effectively removed from science the most powerful defense against scientific racism and sexism—namely, the assertion that individual and group variation made no difference to issues of justice and rights.[23]

The discourses in question here are those that admit no division and no contradiction. Both the discourses of the master and of the university obfuscate their dependence on paradigms that they, in part, establish and sustain. Furthermore, the discourse of the master is constituted in part by the repression of the divided subject, and thus eschews self-division. Such a discourse forecloses desire, anxiety, or any other emotional state characterized by lack or by a failure of adequation between a thing and its name. The master deludes himself into thinking that the performance of the fictional or idealized domain in which name and thing coincide constitutes the achievement of that state. Ellie Ragland-Sullivan writes of the master that "in his own eyes he is the perfect individual, an autonomous, whole subject one might liken to God. What the master fails to see, however, is that one can only command another by putting that other to work to validate him (or her)."[24] The master is characterized, Lacan writes, by the fact that "he doesn't know what he wants."[25] One might even add, in fact, that the master doesn't know *that* he wants. The repressed truth of the master's division keeps the master ignorant of his desire, and Lacan calls castration the radical separation from desire and fantasy: "The essence of the position of the master is to be castrated."[26]

If the divided subject as hidden truth characterizes the master's discourse, it rises to the level of preeminence in the discourse of the hysteric. Where the master performs the adequation of signifier and thing, attempting to embody that one-to-one correspondence, the hysteric eschews identification with any master signifier, while simultaneously and perhaps paradoxically craving someone invested with knowledge to provide a stable identity. "What the hysteric wants," Lacan writes, " . . . is a master."[27] The hysteric searches for significance in the form of a name or identity that can fill the disjunction constituting its subjectivity and bring to a halt the slippage of signification that engages the search in the first place. Continually enthralled by a search for a signifier that would name it definitively, the hysteric seeks and simultaneously avoids the master signifier that would pin down identity.[28] The hysteric's fundamental question—"Am I a man or a woman?"—is not sex-specific. That is, Lacan emphasizes that it emanates from both men and women, even though empirically speaking more women than men are clinically hysterical. Hysteria is not about one's real-world physical capacities, but about how one relates to them subjectively and socially. "Paternity, like maternity, has a problematic essence—these are terms that are not situated purely and simply on the level of experience. The symbolic provides a form in which the subject inserts itself on the level of its being. It is from the signifier that the subject recognizes itself as being this or that."[29]

The discourse of the hysteric—and I again emphasize structure, and not essential identity—privileges symptomatic expression and highlights the repression of that part of being not addressed by master signifiers. The hysteric addresses another in hopes of finding self-knowledge, and that address causes a form of identification with the other. The hysteric's invocation to the other as master demands that he know, but when he expresses his knowledge, as knowledge it fails. The master so invoked must formulate his knowledge in the form of speech, and in that very formulation he falls from mastery.[30] The hysteric's symptomatic question—"What am I?"—not only demands of the other a response that is doomed to fail to satisfy; it also and in that very gesture causes the hysteric to desire as the other. In short, the hysteric brings out the lack in the other and identifies with it.[31]

White masculinity is comprised of the two discourses I have been focusing on: that of the master and that of the hysteric. I have already elaborated on some of the manners in which white masculinity deploys the discourse of the master in my discussion of Enlightenment reason, and I will continue that discussion below when I turn to taxonomic concerns expressed by early modern naturalists and anthropologists. I will also show, in this and the following chapters, that white masculinity also situates itself along a lack that it identifies and identifies with in the other, and that it consequently adopts, in addition to the discourse of the master, that of the hysteric. But it is important to note that I am not arguing that white men are hysterical (nor, by the way, am I arguing that they are necessarily *not* hysterical). I am concerned here only with the structural similarities in the discourse of the hysteric and in one of two principal components of white masculinity. Since as far back as the late nineteenth century, beginning with the work of Charcot and with that of Breuer and Freud, hysteria has been considered in its relationship to feminine sexuality, and as already noted it is commonplace in clinical theory and practice to underscore that although both men and women can be hysteric, more women than men are hysterical. A great deal of feminist scholarship has focused on the ideological suppositions inherent in the labeling of women as hysterical, and a considerable amount of work has also focused on the politically transformative possibilities that hysteria, particularly in its relationship to feminism and feminine sexuality, can bring about. Such possibilities for transformation involve recognizing the portion of being excluded from speech—in this case, specifically feminine desire—and reintegrating desire into the social and political domains.[32]

Lacan maintained that one can never achieve revolutionary ends through traditional revolutionary means.[33] To avoid reinscription of master signifiers one needs in part to give recognition to that portion of being that is excluded from speech, just as in the analytic situation the analyst must effect on the part of the analysand a "hysterisation of discourse."[34] Discursive positions, in other words, adapt to fit particular situations; they can be learned and manipulated. If more women than men are clinically hysterical, it is surely not because of any organic predisposition: it is more likely because of prohibitions and frustrations directed to specific kinds of people. There is thus nothing ineradicably female about hysteria, and no particular reason why white masculinity might not adopt that discourse, especially when it can be politically expedient to do so. While adopting a given discourse may well contribute to gendering the agent of that discourse, the discourse itself in its structure and its form has no gender.

It is commonplace, perhaps even fundamental, in contemporary psychoanalysis to subscribe to the premise that gender constitutes the foundational inscription of difference, an inscription which on occurrence inaugurates subjectivity, initiates symbolic access, and divorces the newly formed subject from the inchoate realm of being that it ostensibly inhabited previously. However, some recent scholarship has begun to question that assumption. For example, in her work on psychoanalysis, gender, and race, Ann Pellegrini expresses her frustration that "feminist theory may seem to have taken over psychoanalysis's virtual fetishization of sexual difference as its point of every return."[35] Similarly, Kalpana Seshadri-Crooks pointedly maintains, against some of the fundamental tenets of psychoanalysis, that "if we are to understand the reality of race, it must be granted coevality with sex; not to do so trivializes the effects of racial identification."[36] And Hortense Spillers, Gwen Bergner, and Jean Walton, each in different ways, demonstrate that kinship systems, family structure, and the concomitant exchange of women produce subjects that are gendered differently in white and black households. That does not mean simply that race adds a new dimension to how psychoanalysis has traditionally conceived of sexual difference, nor does it mean that race provides a supplement to sexual difference that we ignore at our peril if we want to fully understand gender and the manner in which people perform it.

It means instead that fundamental features of subjectivity that form on the installation in the individual of elementary arrangements of difference that are themselves responsible for the passage from, in Lacan's formulation, being to meaning (*l'être* to *lettre*) cannot be simply attributed to one formal opposition—in this case, that opposing male and female. As the rest of this chapter will show, the ostensibly rudimentary difference we refer to as sexual encodes far more than what we can call gender without actually doing violence to the concept. Furthermore, to argue that psychoanalysis cannot be historicized because it takes a universally occurring set of prohibitions formalized into a law that expresses the regulation of desire is only to mystify the highly specific articulations of those prohibitions. Even if we accept the transcultural validity of those claims, we can still assert that sexual difference gets articulated in and through other forms of difference that in a given culture are more fundamental than the notions of gender through which they present themselves. In this vein, Judith Butler has argued that "the symbolic—that register of regulatory ideality—is also and always a racial industry" and that we must "rethink the scenes of reproduction and, hence, of sexing practices not only as ones through which a heterosexual imperative is inculcated, but as one through which boundaries of racial distinction are secured as well as contested."[37]

Butler's project aligns the discourse theory of poststructuralism with theories of subjectivization in an attempt to retheorize how fantasmatic identifications—by definition excluded from discourse—might be more fluid than psychoanalytic theory has traditionally allowed. She agrees with Slavoj Žižek, for example, that theories of the subject must consider foreclosure, or what the subject must reject or repudiate in order to emerge as subject.[38] But she distrusts a set of invariant structural laws that comprise the transcultural process of foreclosure giving rise to any and all subjects, arguing:

That there is always an "outside" and, indeed, a "constitutive antagonism" seems right, but to supply the character and content to a law that secures borders between the "inside" and the "outside" of symbolic intelligibility is to preempt the specific social and historical analysis that is required, to conflate into "one" law the effect of a convergence of many, and to preclude the very possibility of a future rearticulation of that boundary.[39]

It is in this context that we need to understand the idea that sexual difference belongs to the order of the real. Like the constitutive outside, the real is exterior to discourse. Sexual difference belongs to the real not because it is preordained or natural, but because it is excluded from discourse. Hence, subjects' manners of negotiating it will always be symptomatic, partial, and part of a fantasmatic identification. At issue here is the extent to which a constitutive outside—that nondiscursive and hence extra-logical medium that shapes psychic constitution—can sustain the distinction male/female as not only fundamental, but free from other forms of subjective identification no more or less culturally determined.

That leaves us with two interrelated considerations: the historical determinacy of the categories "race" and "gender"; and the mutual inflections those two categories perform on one another, including the indivisible interpenetration that goes on between them. If white males have enjoyed a position of social and political dominance for as long as the identity has had any meaning (and potentially even before that), it is not the *same* dominance and it does not have the same meaning, nor does it work in the same way. Not to interrogate the specificity of that dominance at a given historical moment is to give in to the myth—the myth of mastery—that white masculinity is simply the seamless and apodictic force of plenitude and stability that it has traditionally claimed for itself. Furthermore, not only is there an *intersection* between race and gender, these terms are almost completely meaningless except in conjunction with one another and with other key elements of social identification.[40]

But if the master signifiers "gender" and "race" are simultaneously historically and culturally determined as well as mutually dependent, that means not only that they might inflect one another differently in various circumstances, but also that in some circumstances they might not exist at all, at least not as we have traditionally viewed them. Consequently, the specific configurations of race and gender that European and North American men mobilized when observing the males from other national or cultural groups reveal nothing so much as the implicitly, no doubt largely unconscious ways they experienced their own bodies and identities. In other words, by observing the observers, we can analyze how they understood themselves by examining the tools they deployed to understand others. The white male hegemonic position consists of the very particular amalgamation of social identifiers that it assembles together with the imposition of the established configuration on different cultural and historical groups.

To demonstrate that the hegemonic position crafted by the European and North American male depends on fusing contingent bodily and social identifiers, let us look at some instances in which we can observe master signifiers charged with delivering and securing gender and racial meaning in the process of evolving. The examples at hand will show that white male hegemony sustains its force not only by causing forms of knowledge to masquerade as modes of being, a process whose roots we excavated in the previous chapter, but also by transfiguring the discursive positions from which it speaks. Such a transfiguring affects the establishment or the support of the master signifiers that anchor white male identity. White masculinity shares with Sophocles' Oedipus the characteristic of speaking simultaneously as sovereign and as supplicant, as master and as hysteric, provided we bear in mind that the positions of master and hysteric are structural and not essential. However, there is nothing contradictory about that particular configuration. Hallmark of stability and standard of identity, white masculinity strives to equate saying and being, signifier and signified. At the same time, however, by interrogating its presumed others about the nature of its being and by remaining blissfully ignorant of its own division, white masculinity also repeatedly asks for confirmation of its own identity. In the eighteenth and nineteenth centuries, in both Europe and North America, white masculinity interrogated its others, and more often than not found that those others lacked morphological integrity. While ostensibly unstable in both gender and racial characteristics, nonwhite, nonmale people provided a paradoxical consistency that buttressed the white male hegemonic position, but that very stability became the site of a significant ideological weakness.

The middle years of the eighteenth century, during which Enlightenment conceptions of reason mapped the human body, also marked a time during which that same body seemed pointedly unstable. And while it has become something of a critical commonplace in eighteenth-century studies to chart the progression from a mechanistic view of the universe to a more fluid understanding able to account for the subtle variations and evolutions that escape the routines of kinetics, neither mechanistic nor biological views of humanity can account for the unusual morphological variations that observers often found on a single individual.[41] In fact, the somewhat grotesque theory that Buffon and Littré developed concerning the cause of difference in human complexion based on their observations of an African man's penis is not really all that unusual. The move from a mechanistic universalism to a fluid morphological variety correlates what I identified above as white racial thinking. White racial thinking mapped abstract philosophical concepts onto specifically European bodies while obfuscating the racial component involved, in effect performing the distinctions it purported merely to describe. Nancy Stepan looks at racial science in a similar light, noting that its evolution

> involved a change from an emphasis on the fundamental physical and moral homogeneity of man, despite superficial differences, to an emphasis on the essential heterogeneity of mankind, despite superficial similarities. It was a shift from a sense of man as primarily a social being, governed by social laws and standing apart from nature, to a sense of man as primarily a biological being, embedded in nature and governed by biological laws. It was a move away from an eighteenth-century optimism about man, and faith in the adaptability of man's universal "nature," towards a nineteenth-century biological pessimism, and a belief in the unchangeability of racial "natures."[42]

The move Stepan charts from humans as social beings to humans as biological beings depends no less on the ideological move we saw earlier, in which the initial articulation of morphology—how people identified and spoke about body parts—was already steeped in a way of thinking we can identify as white. The shift Stepan identifies from similarity to difference marks a crucial point in the evolution of modern hegemonic thinking because the fact of the shift itself not only uncovers a search for a master discourse, it also stamps the contingency of point of view with a paradigmatic focus that organizes fields of vision according to specific ideological imperatives, thus underwriting the work of master signifiers.

In fact, the changes in racial science that Stepan describes and the Enlightenment taxonomy that performs the distinctions it purports to describe situate us squarely within the bounds of the discourse of the master. In addition to the master's characteristic gesture of assuming adequation of identity and signifier, the master is distinguished by a repression of self-division and of fantasy. That is, in the discourse of the master any sort of self-division is denied so that in addition to identifying absolutely with his own signifier, the speaker also and as a consequence actively disregards the objects and causes of his own desire. Thus, in the discourse of the master the enunciator is completely detached not only from desire, but from the reasons he might have for propagating his paradigms in the first place. In the context we have been considering, a discursive agent in the form of white racial science and reason promulgates a series of truths about itself and its others, and it does so in a fashion that, because of its discursive and political power, equates what it says with what it is, thus creating its own truth. What remains to be seen is the mechanism it puts in place to sustain that myth.

Despite whatever claims to mastery any powerful individual or group might make, and despite any evidence that could demonstrate an adequation of signifier and referent, the position of master is untenable.[43] Although it seems gratuitous to demonstrate why a completely apodictic, seamless ideological figure cannot preserve itself from resistance, the reasons divide into two concerns: On the one hand, and most obviously, there is the nature of language, which can only ever fragment the dimension of being, against which it lies in stark opposition. But on the other hand, it is also impossible to occupy the position of master because the position itself forecloses any and all nonlinguistic entities— or, perhaps more accurately, it radically excludes anything that escapes or extends beyond the signifiable. Desire and anything belonging to the affective register, things for which there is, properly speaking, no signifier, have no place in the discourse of the master. Yet, foreclosing or refusing to recognize those things does not mean they do not exist and exert their influence on the subject—they simply become another's purview.

Both Enlightenment reason and what Stepan calls racial science constitute discourses of the master to the extent that each relies on a series of unacknowledged master signifiers to concoct an apodictic truth about human identity. But white masculinity is perhaps unlike other socially powerful identities in that it supplements coercion with an extraordinarily powerful ideological grip. Specifically, white masculinity produces racialized subjects, but it does so in part by constraining its others to know the truth of its desire and to accept its fragmentation as their own. Furthermore—and this is a point that will require a great deal more explanation and illustration later on—white masculinity is caught and implicated in its own production.[44] That is, none of the real people who fall into the category "white male" can actually sustain the extraordinary linguistic prowess required in the discourse of the master, and that is not only because the discourse qua discourse is unsustainable, but also because the particular hegemonic position in question is contradictory in nature. That is, white masculinity functions by adopting simultaneously the discourses of the master, the university, and the hysteric. Because the position or category of white masculinity transcends any of the real individuals embraced by it, those individuals are produced by the larger ideological structure, just as the others of white males are so produced. And, one of the ways in which individuals who identify as white males can participate in the performance of the discourse of the master is to foreclose division, that which expressly characterizes the discourse of the hysteric. In manifestos of personal identity and in cultural artifacts from the eighteenth through the twentieth centuries, the two principal means by which white men perform the discourse of the master consist either of abjecting onto their presumed others specific forms of fragmentation, or of making those others responsible for knowing what it is the master wants and lacks.[45]

The first strategy of performing the hegemonic discourse of the master is the projection of fragmentation, best characterized by the infamous "one drop of blood" rule. The superordinate group, which primarily regulates the rules of racial designation in the first place, shuns the fragmentation accompanying association with mongrelization, and because members of that group can never prove that their lineage is pure, they convert their own anxiety into another's problem.[46] But there are other, perhaps more subtle forms of the projection of fragmentation in the interests of assuming individual bodily and subjective integrity, and many of these forms extend beyond the issue of race for which the rule appears to have been originally devised.

For example, a perhaps surprising but nevertheless not infrequent European and American observation is that of cross-gendered behavior as a sign of unstable racial identity. By the middle years of the eighteenth century we find remarks, generally offhand ones, in which explorers note clashing cultural values that express themselves by referencing corporeal instabilities in non-European bodies. We have already seen that early reports of human marvels focus on unlikely morphological features such as tails, and they suggest some kind of affinity with the animal kingdom. But we also find unusual accounts of people in other lands who bear the same features that Europeans and Americans boast, although not necessarily in the same combinations. Thus, João dos Sanctos could report of

one Peter a Christian Cafar at Sofala, his Wife dying after tra-
vell of a Daughter, nourished the same with Milke of his own
brests. . . . Persons of credit in India told me the like of a poore
Jew of Ormus, which nourished his Sonne with his brests. . . . A
Cafar in the River Quilimane had brests great, and bearing out
like a woman which gives suck, but had no Milke therein. After
my returne to Portugall, I heard by eye-witnesses of a poore man
in Moura, which being sixtie yeares old, had as much Milke as a
woman Nurse, and gave sucke to two children.[47]

Cross-gendered characteristics were not limited strictly to males displaying feminine traits, and they were by no means restricted to the
less trustworthy writers: even John Locke passes on stories of human
groups "where the males have no beards, and others where the females
have."[48] Although cross-gendered characteristics appeared to plague
both the women and men of other cultures, the net effect was generally
the same: to render less masculine the males of the group in question.

Unexpected differences in gendered identity extended beyond unusual bodily configurations, and often involved encoded social practice, particularly as that practice concerned sexual difference. As noted
above, a perhaps surprising maladroitness marred white observers' capacities for making any kind of subtle distinctions concerning the de-
meanor or practices of nonwhite peoples, particularly when they found
it difficult or impossible to lay the template of their own behavior and
appearances on top of those of another human group. Comments about
sex-specific behavior ranged from the apparently disinterested objective
observation to a discussion of the significance of the practices noted.
J. G. Grevenbroek, whose remarks on the Hottentots' "whiteness of
soul" occupied us in the previous chapter, perceived the following unusual differences in gendered bodily function: "The women stand up
and part their legs to make water; the men bend their knees and almost touch their ankles with their hams. Neither sex breaks wind or
belches."[49] However, Andrew Battell, in "A voyage to Benguella, province of Dombe," reported the following situation: "The men of this
place wear skins about their middles and beads about their necks. They
carry darts of iron, and bow and arrows in their hands. They are beastly
in their living, for they have men in women's apparel, whom they keep
among their wives" (Battell, incidentally, was among those who re-

The Fair Sex   119

ported white children mysteriously born of black parents).[50] One cannot fail to notice the causal construction in his report of cross-gendered behavior here—the folks of Benguella appear to be "beastly" precisely because there are men who look and act as Battell would expect women to do. The lines are drawn quite cleanly: if a group of people behave in a manner incongruent with European expectations, regardless of the culturally specific consistency of that behavior, then that behavior falls from the category of "cultural" to land squarely in the domain of animal naturalism.[51]

Europeans traveling eastward were not alone in finding examples of cultures in which gender-specific morphology or behavior appeared either random or significantly destabilized. In North America, Thomas Jefferson found the native men there disappointingly asexual. Furthermore, he noted a generalized lack in sexual dimorphism: "The savage is feeble, and has small organs of generation; he has neither hair nor beard, and no ardor whatever for his female."[52] It seems that Europeans in general found North America's natives similarly undersexed. Johann Friederich Blumenbach, whose anthropological treatise *De Generis Humani Varietate Nativa* influenced nearly as many people as Buffon's *Histoire naturelle,* believed that "on the first discovery of . . . the beardless inhabitants of America, it was much easier to pronounce them different species than to inquire into the structure of the human body."[53] Blumenbach supposed that his predecessors were so disturbed by the discovery of differing—indeed, perhaps lesser—expressions of masculinity that they would classify as a different species any group whose menfolk did not share the secondary sexual characteristics that they valued.

Destabilized gender expectations almost always caused nonwhite men to seem less masculine than the Europeans reporting on them, and Blumenbach not only followed a host of anthropologists fascinated with beardlessness, he preceded a good many others in making such leaps in cultural and gendered logic. Beginning roughly in the early years of the nineteenth century, anti-abolition writers commonly debated the significance of what they deemed to be the absence of African men's beards. In fact, European and American men commenting on the appearance of men from other locales seemed positively obsessed with the forms of their beards. For the most part white men found the beards of men of color to be lacking and hence somehow indicative of a less than fully masculine presence. In one of the stranger European descriptions of the relative presence or absence of men's beards, the anonymous author of the *Relation des costes d'Afrique appellées Guinée* (1669) writes of the men of the gold coast: "Although they get their beards rather late, they are nevertheless quite amateurish, and their officers and captains wear it quite large on the chin, some of them even wearing it like Capucins."[54] Beardless men were a veritable fixation among European and American observers—who, we presume, had professional beards—and whether they lived in China, Africa, or the Americas, the lack of this particular secondary sex characteristic appeared to somehow unman them in European and American eyes. The anonymous author of *Six Species of Men* (1866), however, neatly recapitulates Blumenbach's claim that different sexual characteristics seemed to signal different taxonomic types when he writes:

> Another peculiarity of the negro is absence of beard. The Caucasion is really the only bearded race, and this is the most striking mark of its supremacy over all others. All other races approximate to it in this respect, but the typical, woolly-headed negro, except a little tuft on the chin, and sometimes on the upper lip, has nothing that can be confounded with a beard. Negroes are sometimes seen with considerable beard on their faces, but it should be remembered that it is common to call all who are not pure Caucasians, negroes. Bearded negroes have a large infusion of white blood. A negro with the flowing, dignified, and majestic beard of the Caucasian, would indeed be a curiosity, and about as amusing a specimen of humanity as it is possible to conceive of.[55]

Strangely enough, this writer failed to see how easy it would be to counter his argument simply by claiming that the hairier people are, the closer they are to beasts. But the latter part of the above citation reveals the circular logic underlying this author's claim, and the gender logic operating in the conjunction of whiteness and masculinity: any African man or man of African descent who displays the white man's secondary sexual characteristics must, in fact, not be African at all.

Although most examples of cross- or counter-gender characteristics seem to concern men, significant cases involving women also arise, but these cases also illustrate the taxonomic difficulties just addressed. Londa Schiebinger has provided a very extensive account of the manner in which early modern (primarily eighteenth-century) observers dealt with the issue of competing cultural variables when they tried to arrange all living creatures in the hierarchically ascending Chain. Noting that the great apes seemed to be the missing links connecting humans and animals, she goes on to identify reports from mystified European explorers who tried to force their culturally different brethren into that category. Some naturalists claimed that neither African women nor female apes menstruate, which they took to be evidence of a fundamental similarity; others, most notably Charles White, arrived at the opposite conclusion when they "proved" that the higher up the Chain one goes, the less copious menstrual flow one finds.[56] Further interest was aroused when European naturalists considered whether female apes have clitorises, and by way of demonstrating that brute pleasure was, indeed, brutish and not human, these observers speculated about how various female animals were constructed. Schiebinger reports: "Tyson, who never dissected a female ape, reported that clitorises were extremely brutelike in apes, being larger and more visible than in women. Blumenbach, who devoted many years to this question, found that in mammals clitorises were frequently quite large, especially in certain types of lemurs."[57] Apparently still in the thrall of "believing is seeing" and of Leibniz's invention of intermediary species based on what his paradigms indicated, early modern observers construed physiology according to their own perceptions of what human beings ought to be.[58]

Eighteenth-century observers seemed particularly interested in the clitoris because it was, as Blumenbach so deftly put it, "the obscene organ of brute pleasure," and could thus appear to gauge a culture's proximity to animalistic behavior.[59] Yet, for all that interest, no one appears to have considered removing one for examination or for collection.[60] The same is not the case, however, for men's genitals. Blumenbach, reporting on the then already commonplace idea that African men's penises were particularly large, makes the following offhand yet disturbing comment: "It is generally said that the penis in the Negro is very large. And this assertion is so far borne out by the remarkable genitory apparatus of an Æthiopian which I have in my anatomical collection."[61] Charles White, the English physician whose *Account of the Regular Gradation in Man* was, as its title suggests, a paean to the Great Chain of Being, wrote, "That the *Penis* of an African is larger than that of an European, has, I believe, been shown in every anatomical school in London. Preparations of them are preserved in most anatomical museums; and I have one in mine. I have examined several living negroes, and found it invariably to be the case."[62] The immediate impulse, based perhaps on vulgar psychoanalytic notions, might be to assume that castration is a male anxiety, that the penis, unlike the clitoris, seems particularly detachable because of its greater size and variability, and that penises were more collectible because men as a sex were more valuable than women.[63] All of these things are, in fact, to some extent true—but only to the extent that we recognize the conditions supporting their truth. That is, penises are only more detachable than clitorises if, as we noted in the previous chapter, we understand the ideology of the medical and other social discourses that articulated the body into specific parts in the first place.

Furthermore, castration is a male anxiety only if we take care to define the manner in which the gender identity "male" is contextually circumscribed within other social identifiers.[64] That is, the above examples of what Europeans considered cross-gender behavior seem to activate a series of anxieties of insufficiency, particularly as such insufficiency presented itself in the form of fragmentation. As we saw in chapter 1, Sophocles' Oedipus eschews self-division or fragmentation because his particular psycho-social circumstances require him to embrace a single identity despite valorized cultural examples, the Sphinx foremost among them, of the possibility of multiple identity. What most forms of psychoanalysis take to be a story about the anguish of gender indeterminacy and the ubiquitous nature of that anguish in fact mask a far richer, dramatically more complex network of social identifiers that, taken together merely present as a question of gender, or, perhaps more accurately, are allowed to present simply as a question of gender. What I am arguing here is not simply that people are gendered differently in different historical and cultural contexts, but that we cannot even imagine the category "gender" without simultaneously invoking a host of other social identifiers, a phenomenon analogous to the structuralist postulate that signifiers only signify in relation to all other signifiers. Correlatively, I am arguing that not only do social identifiers inflect and express one another, but the specific way they interact might remain latent, and that way of interacting in point of fact defines those identifiers in the first place. Every one of those identifiers shares with all the others the impossibility of being reduced to the oneness that its conceptual and indexical imprints would suggest. And all of that goes to say that castration as a form of fragmentation clearly says almost as much about race as it does about gender. The anxiety over castration, it might just turn out, is not exclusively, nor even perhaps mostly, about a narcissistic injury to a man's gender identity, at least not if we understand gender in its traditional sense.[65]

To begin to understand gender in this context as having everything to do with race, it is useful to remember that castration, especially in the form of lynching, was a not at all uncommon way for North American whites to manage their fears of African American men's sexuality. But in its connection to race, castration either as a punishment or as an act of violent aggression has a very particular history. Winthrop Jordan points out that castration as a weapon of angry mobs was not an antebellum phenomenon, and that its juridical and penal uses were very specific: reserved almost exclusively as a punishment for African American and Indian men, it was nearly always restricted to serious sexual offenses. Pennsylvania was the only colony that authorized castration of white men, but significantly, Jordan's research shows not a single incident of castration of a white man. What is most revealing, however, is the fact that castration as a punishment for particular crimes is a specifically American phenomenon. Jordan writes: "As a legal punishment castration was a peculiarly American experiment, for there was no basis in English law. . . . [Castration] was a measure of the gulf between Americans and Englishmen created by America's racial slavery that such laws should be passed in America and vehemently disallowed in England."[66] Robyn Wiegman has analyzed in detail the phenomenon of lynching, and she maintains that such a form of mutilation focuses on separating the privileges of masculinity, which occurs across racial lines, from those of whiteness in order to preserve hegemonic privilege. She writes that "in the disciplinary fusion of castration with lynching, the mob severs the black male from the masculine, interrupting the privilege of the phallus, and thereby reclaiming, through the perversity of dismemberment, his (masculine) potentiality for citizenship."[67]

By way of understanding how the phenomenon of castration as aggression or punishment can help disarticulate masculinity from whiteness, it is important to look at the sort of thinking that allowed white

European naturalists to consider actually removing or collecting African penises in the first place. What conditions made penises—foreign penises—the sort of thing one could remove and take home as souvenirs or objects of study? The brief anecdote with which I opened this chapter relating the different shades of skin on an African man's penis can help answer that question because it illustrates the manner in which whiteness and maleness are expressions of one another, at least for those who qualify as both white and male, and it also shows how white European and American men attempted to maintain an integrity of identity partially represented by an intact body. By way of representing the white male body as integral and whole, they projected the body of their others as fragmented. However, fragmentation does not necessarily imply dismemberment—as I have been arguing, the body is articulated into parts primarily through discursive means, and while white European and North American men strived to achieve a stabilizing discourse of the master, they also employed strategies to disinvest other men of the potential for mastery. Just as whiteness attempted to mark itself as an absolute—susceptible, to be sure, to corruption but not malleable enough to admit for degrees or shades—maleness, particularly or even exclusively as white men understood the phenomenon, could allow no varieties or division. By way of explaining that fact, I will look at several instances in which white men theorized about other men's genitals. These white men found ways to divide what had heretofore seemed indivisible—masculinity. I hope to make it abundantly clear that the terrorism and violence that whites visited on black men in the nineteenth century followed a discursive path established in the eighteenth century which, while not as materially violent, certainly laid the ideological and epistemological foundations for the brutal fragmentation of the nonwhite male body.

There is something of a contradiction at work in white men's descriptions of Africans in the seventeenth and eighteenth centuries; while it had already become commonplace to remark or speculate about the size of black men's penises, at the same time there were broad attempts to make those men appear less masculine. I noted above the stories in which men performed tasks either normally the exclusive province of women, such as breast feeding, or in the manner of women, such as squatting to urinate. But there are far more complex stories that we begin to see in the late seventeenth century and which continue well on into the nineteenth century that perform a discursive fragmentation of the black male body and a correlative reinforcement of the white male body. These stories, like the theory of the wind as agent of skin coloration on the African penis, generally involve unusual speculations about the nature and meaning of nonwhite men's reproductive apparatuses. In chapter 2 I cited John Rawlins's distress, narrated in his *Wonderful Recovery of the Exchange of Bristow,* over the forcible circumcision of a group of British seamen. There I analyzed the manner in which Europeans considered the modification of the human body to be deliberately practiced by specific cultural groups in order to distinguish themselves. Later European descriptions of the practice of male genital alteration stress not only the bizarre nature of the practice, but also its implicit and explicit links with other aspects of the culture that engages in it.

William Ten Rhyne (1686) was one early reporter of the Hottentot practice of male genital alteration, and he provides a fairly flat description of such rituals that purportedly took place at birth: "All the males that are born are immediately at birth deprived of one testicle, so that their barren land may not receive more inhabitants than it can nourish, and, as they add by way of further explanation, so that they may be able to run the more quickly."[68] This fairly sober description of a perhaps unusual ritualistic practice, however, was nevertheless reasonably controversial. Many early writers on the Hottentots were interested in that group's genitals; most often we have read about the famous "apron" of skin hanging down from the women's pudenda, and there was general agreement about what it looked like, even if not everyone was sure what it was. Ten Rhyne referred to that part of the Hottentot woman's anatomy as a "dactyloform appendage,"[69] while Olfert Dapper believed that the body's lining simply dangled out.[70] The observations concerning men's genitals, however, seemed to provoke considerable more disagreement and debate. Although a great many writers mentioned the practice of removing a testicle, opinion generally differed about whether the procedure was performed in early childhood, at puberty, or just before marriage; experts disagreed as well over why the operation was performed, and over how it was carried out. One early writer, J. Maxwell, offers literally firsthand evidence of the practice and tries to put an end to the controversy:

Being inquisitive to know the truth of this I had the curiosity to search several of 'em (who will readily suffer you for a double stiver to do it), in two of which I could find but one testicle, they I suppose being married, as the rest who had two were not; which however shows the mistake of Nieuhoff and others who assert that the Hottentots cut out one of the testicles of all their male children as soon as they are born.[71]

On the one hand these late seventeenth-century observations square completely with what we noted in chapter 2 concerning Europeans' beliefs in other cultural groups' deliberate modification of the human body in order to provide distinguishing characteristics. On the other hand, however, and perhaps somewhat more troubling, there is a fascination with the male genitals that goes beyond the question of size that we have read so much about.

In fact, this fascination with the male genitals seems to derive from an assumption that those parts of the body, particularly as they are deliberately modified and especially when they belong to nonwhite people, can express specific cultural values as well as inborn natural truths. Allowing formal similarities in morphology to animate theories of cultural affiliation, European observers made unlikely taxonomic alignments that allowed them to map existing cultural prejudices onto recently discovered groups. Thus, J. G. Grevenbroek prefaces his description of the Hottentot practice of depriving males of a testicle with the following explanation: "It must be supposed that it is from the Jews that the inhabitants of the remoter parts have learned the practice of circumcision, although it is a more serious operation with the Africans, involving the cutting away not only of the prepuce but of the skin right up to the base of the abdomen. From the Jews also the natives near us must have acquired the practice of removing the left testicle, if you will excuse the mention of it."[72] It is highly improbable that the Africans whom Grevenbroek describes learned their circumcision practices from people of the Jewish Diaspora, particularly since the two circumcision rituals are so markedly different.[73] It is also unlikely that any Jews who made it to southern Africa would have instructed the native inhabitants on the practice of removing testicles.[74] It is far more likely that, given the prevailing negative attitudes in Europe toward both Jews and Muslims during this time, Grevenbroek and other observers were performing a cultural rapprochement in which one unfamiliar or alien group could appear to explain another.

For as much as Grevenbroek and his coterie amalgamated multiple forms of difference into a somewhat comforting sameness, however, they also cinched their own identities by ventriloquizing what they took to be the irrational racialized others in their absurd practices. Speaking as a member of the observed group, Grevenbroek speculates about the dire consequences and their attendant emotions arising should any man refuse to participate in the ritual of genital mutilation:

> Should any of our Hottentots refuse to subject his male-members to the sacrificial blade or lancet or operating knife of the priest, preferring to preserve his genital organs perfect in the shape and number provided by nature rather than submit himself to agonies of pain and a partial castration, this enemy of all amputation is insulted by the name of "ram," shut out from all fellowship and inheritance, and shunned as if blasted by the lightning of heaven.[75]

It would be hard to miss the condescension and sarcasm in Grevenbroek's tone when he refers to "our Hottentots" and "this enemy of all amputation." What seems most striking in these accounts, however, is the manner in which the production of difference seems designed not, as we saw in the previous chapter, to distinguish all members of one cultural group from outsiders or from those who do not belong, but members of the group among themselves. There is nothing unusual at all, of course, about ritual practices of initiation in which initiates become full-fledged members of the community. What is unusual in these accounts of male genital alteration, however, is the manner in which European observers present such practices. Not only do they appear to exaggerate or otherwise misstate the importance attributed to these rituals; they often devote disproportionate amounts of space to the descriptions of these rituals. Furthermore, in the repetition of specific practices as well as in the manner in which observers align these practices with other marks of the cultures in question, European observers seemed to be attempting to demonstrate the second-class masculinity of nonwhite men. Such a debased masculinity, located as it is in a culture ostensibly more savage than the European one observing and describing it, paradoxically appears tamer or gentler because of its practices of genital mutilation. In other words, European men could con-

strue themselves as more manly, despite that characteristic's association with the untamed or the wild, precisely because the Hottentot men
who submit to genital mutilation seem more domesticated and consequently less masculine.

Direct observation of particular cultural rituals and customs might
lead to specific conclusions concerning that culture's fundamental
structures, of course, and one would certainly expect different observers
to report on the things that most interested them. However, what is
particularly striking about the reports of Hottentot circumcision practices is how much they seem to derive from a relatively restricted number of sources. In fact, the wording of the different reports is so similar
that in some cases it suggests direct appropriation. One of the earliest
accounts seems to be Ten Rhyne's (1686), cited above, followed by
Grevenbroek's (1695), which simply states that they "make an incision
in the scrotum, cut away a little skin from the right testicle, send the
young man home, and when the wound is cured regard him as his own
master."[76]

But when we find similar reports in the eighteenth century, they
become far more protracted, somewhat more astonished and astonish-
ing, and sometimes much more dramatic in their manner of reporting.
In 1719 Peter Kolb described the ceremonial removal of a testicle in
tremendous detail. Because the detail of Kolb's eyewitness report will be
significant, it is worth citing his narrative at length:

> The Patient being first besmear'd all over with the Fat of the
> Entrails of a Sheep newly kill'd, lies on his Back, at full Length, on
> the Ground. His Hands are tied together; as are his Feet. On each
> Leg and Arm kneels a Friend, and on his Breast lies another, to
> keep him down and deprive him of all Motion. Then advances the
> Operator, with a common Cafe- or Table-Knife, well sharpen'd,
> (They have no better Instrument,) and laying Hold of the left
> Testicle, makes an Orifice in the *Scrotum* of an Inch and a Half
> long, and squeezes out the Testicle and cuts and ties up the Ves-
> sels in a Trice. . . . Then taking a little Ball, which he has at Hand,
> of Sheep's Fat, mix'd with the Powders of salutary Herbs, par-
> ticularly of *Buchu,* and of the Bigness of the outed Testicle, he
> crams it into the *Scrotum* to fill up the Vacancy. . . . He then sews
> up the Wound. . . . The Wound being sew'd up, the Friends of the

Patient, who were severally planted on his Legs, his Arms, and his Breast, rise; and his Bands are loos'd. But before he offers to crawl away, Mr. Operator, with the still warm and smoaking Fat of the Kidney and Entrails of the Sheep . . . anoints him again . . . adding fresh Flame to the already raging Torments of his Patient, who drops and smoaks under it like a Pig a roasting.

But we have not done yet. The Glory of the Ceremony is still behind. When the Patient is sufficiently besmear'd at this Second Unction, the Operator makes Furrows with his long Nails in the Fat upon him, and administers the last Comfort by Pissing all over him. This he does with a plentiful Stream. He lays up for the Occasion. When he has dribbled the last Drop, he rubs his Patient again all over with his Hand, closing the Furrows in the Fat. The Ceremony being now at an End, the Patient, trembling and sprawling on the Ground, as in the Agony, is abandon'd of every one, and left, without farther Remedy, to perish or recover by himself. Near the Place where the Operation is perform'd they previously erect a little Hut, as a Sort of Infirmary. Into this he crawls as soon as he can; and There remains for a Couple of Days or so; all the while alone, and without any Refreshment besides the Fat upon his Body, which he may lick if he pleases.[77]

Here we are a long way from the first report we considered ("make an incision in the scrotum, cut away a little skin from the right testicle . . ."). Although I would not suggest that the richness of Kolb's description, which he claims is an eyewitness account, is a matter of pure fabrication, I would argue that Kolb's choice of detail is significant. It is difficult not to find the last phrase in the citation above just a little bit outrageous, for example, and the details of urination and sheep's fat contribute to the overall sense of the ritual's strangeness or even absurdity.[78] It is precisely the air of strangeness that Kolb achieves in this description that interests me here, because it appears that what he is doing is defamiliarizing as male the men he is describing.[79]

It seems fairly obvious that Kolb's manner of emphasizing the unusual aspects of this ritual in his report not only presents the rite as somewhat ridiculous, but also portrays the men in this culture as somehow less than men. Members, perhaps, of a second-string masculinity, these men appear debased as a result of undergoing a ritual in which part of their genital apparatus is forcibly removed and they are urinated on by another man. In fact, the masculinity generally associated with this particular culture is highly problematic since in order to be admitted fully as men, these men have to be partially unmanned, at least from a European perspective, and that is what makes them the object of considerable derision. Like Grevenbroek before him, Kolb can barely contain the scorn he feels for the practice, referring condescendingly to the officiant as "Mr. Operator," and comparing the inductee to "a Pig a roasting." Kolb's ironic final comment, that the initiate can lick if he likes the urine-soaked fat caked on his body, coupled with the singular lack of analysis in the description of the entire process, seems designed not only to make the entire process as radically distant as possible from anything a Westerner might imagine, but to make the culturally masculine ideal associated with that process equally distant, absurd, and debased.

It may well be that Grevenbroek's account of a circumcision ritual practiced in the province of Natal in what is now South Africa influenced Kolb. In Grevenbroek's account of 1695 (that is, some twenty years earlier), he discusses the surgical procedure, and then he writes:

[The priest] then anoints the wound with fat, and applies to it a wrapping of some bulb with coats not very different from those of an onion. Only when they are cured may [the youths] leave the booth; only then are they permitted to talk with parents, friends, and girls, whose business it is to secure that food and drink and other necessaries, to be dealt out by the priest, should not fail the poor sufferers for the space of three months. When this compulsory inactivity of twice forty days has gone by, each returns dancing home, and being now adult is numbered among the men.[80]

The similarities in the two rituals are striking. What interests me here, however, is not whether the rituals themselves actually bore such a resemblance; rather, I am concerned with what appear to be attempts to form similarities on a conceptual or narrative level among cultural practices that may have no particular affinity with one another. What results is a master discourse of culture and meaning, by which I mean a method of describing and hence understanding one group in the terms and conditions of another. Such a process relies on paradigms established exclusively by the narrating culture, paradigms anchored by specific valorized signifiers that we noted above in the discussion of the four discourses of psychoanalysis. Furthermore, by looking at some of the descriptions of male genital alteration involving specific turns of phrase borrowed from earlier writers, we should be able to discern the development of a generalized narrative tradition surrounding a specific gender/racial practice, a narrative tradition that may have little to do with the events ostensibly instigating it, and everything to do with establishing a discursive construction of a racialized body and a racialized, nonwhite version of masculinity. In fact, Grevenbroek's and Kolb's descriptions of male genital mutilation seem to have served as a basis for later reports, and in an era singularly devoted to direct and objective observation and the annihilation of the prejudices imposed by tradition it seems particularly significant that men of science would drop the pretense of detachment specifically when discussing race and masculinity.

The phrases and expressions that previous writers had used to describe the Hottentots crop up with a certain regularity in later reports, especially those of the eighteenth century. Accounts of exotic peoples featured certain formal conventions that served the purposes of establishing the generic conventions both of travel literature in general and of the Hottentots—or any sufficiently foreign group—in particular.[81] In other words, early reports on the Hottentot morphology and way of life influenced succeeding ones, giving rise to a "believing is seeing" arrangement of relaying information that tended to confirm what Europeans already thought they knew about their racial others. Thus, most accounts corroborated preceding ones in style and substance. Perhaps surprisingly, succeeding generations of writers used the same turns of phrase their precursors had employed. Even the iconoclastic contributors to the *Encyclopédie* seemed unable to resist direct appropriation of earlier writers' observations and insights. In the article "Hottentots," for example, a simple description of Hottentot appearance refers to their "very flat and very broad noses" (les Hottentots ont le nez fort plat & fort large),[82] repeating word for word Buffon's earlier description ("Tous les Hottentots ont le nez fort plat et fort large . . ." [286–87]). Also like Buffon, the author of the article on the Hottentots refers to the men as "half-eunuchs" (*demi-eunuques* in the *Encyclopédie*, as opposed to Buffon's virtually identical *demi eunuques*).

But the linguistic and stylistic parallels among these various writers concerning the Hottentots' physiology and culture go well beyond these comparatively simple phrases. In the area of ritual male genital mutila-tion, which is what principally concerns me here, Buffon appropriates word for word Kolb's report on the Hottentot's unusual practice of removing a testicle, and his 350-word account is for all intents and purposes identical to Kolb's.[83] The only differences lie in Buffon's insis-tence on the religious nature of the ceremony, which Kolb had not emphasized, and in his changing of Kolb's phrase "like a pig a roasting" to describe the unfortunate initiate to "roasted capon," which is, ironi-cally enough, a castrated rooster. Despite Buffon's claims to have based his work on observation, he resorts to another's words to situate a phenomenon delicately balanced in racial and sexual taxonomies, pro-ducing in the process what amounts to nothing more than hearsay.

The compulsion to repeat stories about ritual male genital alteration and to construe the men participating in these rituals as not only muti-lated, but also by that very fact as somehow not really male accom-plishes the articulation of white masculinity. Such an articulation is principally discursive, even though it appears irreducibly bodily, be-cause on the one hand it depends on a narrative tradition of what nonwhite men look like and what they do, despite superficial claims to objective empirical observation; and on the other hand because the fragmentation projected onto exoticized others depends on a notion of bodily integrity—in this case the fear of castration—that may not apply in non-Western cultures. What makes this discursive construction of white males so compelling from the perspective of the white men them-selves is first of all the presumption of bodily integrity it allows them, and what is almost equally important, the definition of both nonwhite and differently-maled people as poor approximations of the white men themselves. That is, by describing males from other cultures as having undergone a partial castration *(demi-eunuques),* white observers con-strued those men as male the way European men are male.[84] Yet, at the same time, European and North American males went to great discur-sive lengths to keep those other men from being completely male the way they themselves were male.

The principal method by which white men attempted to anchor their own identities as males evoked anxiety of ambiguous or indeterminate identity. Damaged or otherwise not completely intact genitalia marked other males as not entirely masculine in the European observation of Hottentots, and, tellingly enough, those same observers found the Hottentots to occupy a similarly indeterminate zone of racial identity. If Hottentot men were *demi-eunuques*, that is, they also appeared to be, at least according to Buffon, almost white.

> It is easy to see that the Hottentots are not true Negroes *[Nègres]*, but men who, in the race of blacks, are beginning to approach white. . . . These Hottentots are, furthermore, a species of quite extraordinary savages: the women especially, who are much smaller than the men, have a sort of growth or hard skin which grows from above the pubic bone, and which falls down to the middle of the thighs in the form of an apron (286).

Corroborating my claim that discursive tradition, and not necessarily empirical observation, was principally responsible for the construction of racialized others, the *Encyclopédie* cites Buffon in stating that "Hottentots are not Negroes,"[85] but no further explanation or qualification is provided. What is truly unprecedented here, however, is Buffon's claim that the Hottentots are "beginning to approach white" *(commencent à se rapprocher du blanc)*, particularly in light of his claim, noted above, that "white appears to be the originary color of nature, which climate, food and lifestyle *(mœurs)* alter and change into yellow, brown or black" (304).[86] Surprisingly, Buffon charts the movement of the human complexion's evolution in two directions: from white to black, since white was "the originary color of nature," and also from black to white, since the Hottentots are "beginning to approach white." It is rare in any of Buffon's discussions to see such a reversal. This one seems to indicate an attempt to reintegrate into established taxonomic patterns human data that at first blush does not make sense. Thus, when Buffon addresses the question of the famous white-black men—Africans, presumably albino, who appear to be white—he writes that "what proves that these white men are only in effect individuals who have degenerated from their species *(dégénéré de leur espèce)* is the fact that they are all much less strong and vigorous than the others, and that their eyes are extremely weak" (304). Like the anonymous author of *Six Species of Men*, cited above, who deemed that any men of color sporting a beard must by that very fact be partially white (a category that in most circumstances would have been inadmissible), here Buffon requires a cause or rationale in order to make white Africans somehow less masculine.

The fascination with Hottentot men, and in particular with the ritual mutilation of their genitals, provides dramatic support of my early claim that both whiteness and maleness do not so much mark taxonomic realities as they signal a form of hysteria, a concern with fragmentation premised both on the anxiety of never being able to embody completely the identifiers associated with Western hegemony and on maintaining the other as fragmented and hence desirous in a manner that is possible to manage. Consequently, white men's fear of not measuring up, which they could never make manifest without risk of revealing internal division or schism, emerges elsewhere: on the bodies of the men they take to be their others. Indeed, it would seem impossible to appear more fragmented, at least from the point of view of someone for whom integrity is a crucial issue, than the Hottentots whom Buffon describes: at once people who are "not true Negroes," and folks who are merely "beginning to approach white," this race of half white, half black people are also—and this is what caused all the excitement to begin with—half eunuchs.

Now we can see why Buffon might have believed the wind to be at least partially the cause of variation in complexion of the African man whose penis he examined. In light of the veritable obsession Europeans seem to have had with African male genital alteration, the presumption that the penises of those men that had not been exposed to the wind were actually white is stunning indeed. It suggests that unadulterated, fully masculine penises are, fundamentally, white. Thus, early modern European men carefully examined the genitals—the sex—of the men and women they visited, and from among the "obscene clitorises" and "dactyloform appendages" it was clear to them that when you get right down to it, it is the fundamental, originary, and genuine white penis that is truly the "fair sex."

It is difficult to imagine more compelling support for the theory that hegemonic gender or racial positions depend absolutely on the complex social nexus of identity interaction. Masculinity that is not also white fails to achieve ascendancy, and whiteness that is not also fully male generally misses the mark as well. But the elaboration of criteria requisite for hegemonic identity did not respect the boundaries of the physical body. Buffon may well have presented his argument as a series of rational deductions, but we can observe in his argument a discourse of desire that might not appear at first blush. He strives to maintain a strict detachment from passionate or otherwise emotionally invested forms of observations, pointing out that "nature has neither classes nor categories; it only comprehends individuals [and] these categories and classes are the work of our minds" (43). Nevertheless, a significant portion of Buffon's observations derive their organizing principles from anything but objective criteria or physical proof. Indeed, some of his putatively dispassionate efforts to investigate and classify people derive not from objectivity, but from passion. In their most disengaged forms his remarks simply include offhand comments about how attractive some of the people he observes are: "The most temperate climate is between the fortieth and fiftieth degree of latitude . . . and it is also in this zone that we find the most beautiful and most handsomely built men; it is in this climate that one must derive the idea of the true natural color of man" (it is worth noting that Paris is at 48° latitude).[87]

But the significance of Buffon's remarks here ranges well beyond the simple pretension of objective standards of beauty: his own systems for classifying people, systems which he well admits "are the work of our minds," depend to a very great extent on his own desires. In fact, I would even argue that Buffon's taxonomy depends to a large extent on a form of white male desire that positions both men and women, at home and abroad, in quite specific ways. On the one hand he needs to direct his male compatriots to appreciate the charms of non-European females when they are sufficiently familiar in appearance, and on the other hand he also construes foreign men as desiring not only like European men, but sometimes in their place. Thus, according to this logic, there is nothing particularly odd when he compares peoples as disparate as Greenlanders and Ethiopians, since in both countries he finds "the women as ugly as the men, and [that] they resemble them so much as to be barely distinguishable from them" (224). In similar fashion he argues that "the savages to the north of the Eskimos resemble one another through their ugliness, their smallness of size" and other physical characteristics (225).

Buffon does not balk at passing judgment on physical attractiveness based on his own sets of criteria: He finds the women of the kingdoms of Pégu to be "passably white" (239), and furthermore he enthusiastically includes as attractive all women whose skin color is white enough. He believes, for example, that the "Arab princesses and ladies" are "very beautiful and nicely built. . . . They are white, because they remain out of the sun" (258). Finally, in perhaps the most explicit declaration of his own cultural prejudices, he writes that "if we examine now those who inhabit a more temperate climate, we will find that the inhabitants of the northern provinces of Mogol and of Persians, the Armenians, the Turks, the Georgians, the Mingreliens, the Circassians, the Greeks, and all the people of Europe, are the most beautiful, the whitest, and the best built people of the earth" (262).

But Buffon's classifications of people and his observations of their cultural mechanisms extend beyond his opinions of their physical charms. When he describes the native inhabitants of some cultures, he seems unable to resist inserting himself or people like him into the picture as a sort of foil or, in keeping with the terminology established earlier for this chapter, a master signifier for understanding and gauging relations between and among cultures. The same "savages to the north of the Eskimos" who apparently form a cultural group because Buffon finds them singularly unattractive also seem to consider it quite an honor if men from other lands deign to sleep with their wives (226). Furthermore, that honor appears to derive from the fact that their own capacities for discernment require validation from Europeans: "[The custom] of offering to foreigners their women, and to be quite flattered that one might want to make use of them, might derive from the fact that they are aware of their own deformity and of the ugliness of their wives. They apparently find those whom foreigners do not spurn less ugly" (227).[88] Positioning nonwhite males as lesser versions of itself, white masculinity here finds its self-definition by construing all forms of desire as imperfect expressions of itself.

There is nothing paradoxical or contradictory in Buffon's amalgamating subjective and objective observations, despite the dissidence such a rapprochement evokes in anyone whose thinking is structured by Enlightenment paradigms of logic and reason. The real paradox arises precisely in the attempt to separate the subjective perception of structures of thought from the equally biased articulation of body parts and characteristics whose particular crystallization reifies the ideological values inherent in the identification of those parts, a process we noted in chapter 2. Buffon's consolidation of the ostensibly disparate realms of objective and subjective judgments reveals the fundamental logic of hegemonic masculinity that differentiates it from many if not most other forms of domination: by linking to a single, valorized morphology, one especially esteemed through the privileging of a linear taxonomic system and a univocal form of desire, white masculinity sustains itself in the position of the stable and stabilizing master, eschewing any problematic indeterminacies by construing all males as engendered through precisely the same means and culturally valorized forms and institutions.

European reports of other cultures implicitly structure a great deal of their accounts on white masculine desire as well as on the morphology and, indeed, the meaning of the ostensible integrity of the male genitals. They do so in order to privilege as intact or complete their own culturally informed image of the body, and then to suture to that body a form of desire that borders on the solipsistic. That is, because of the fear of lacking, from both a racial and a gendered point of view, white masculinity projects that lack onto the bodies, and indeed, the desires, of the men it takes as its others. Incomplete or deficient genitalia marked those men as insufficiently masculine from a morphological perspective. But as we saw in chapter 2, morphological variation as such has historically signified domination or subalternity far more dramatically when it adjoins and simultaneously obfuscates—that is, when it articulates—moral and/or intellectual qualities. Thus, if in the previous chapter we observed the articulation of a specific kind of thinking through a particular bodily form—eighteenth-century logic and reason as an expression of whiteness—here we are seeing the mutual articulation of race and gender and the concomitant imputation of a form of desire on men who quite likely in no way at all experience their bodies and the world in the manner imputed to them.

The articulation of a specific form of desire and a particular morphological arrangement allowed white observers to fabricate an other who was simultaneously like and unlike them, and furthermore, it allowed them to produce a white identity, one that appeared transparent and without its own identifying features. Crucially, the elaboration of such an other functions only when that other is simultaneously the same as and different from the perspective of the defining observer. That is why from a morphological point of view the definition of body parts took place from within the context of how Europeans used their bodies. Thus, while people who engage in ritual alteration of their bodies perceive a determined cultural meaning and function to that practice, outsiders might well view it as pointless mutilation. Likewise, since different groups put the body to use in different ways, it is by no means inconceivable that they would delimit the body's parts differently. Furthermore, imputing a form of desire on an entire culture, a desire that coincides with that of the observing civilization, not only positions the observed group as coincident with the observers, but more explicitly it casts them as expressions of the defining authorities. It obviates the need for the overlapping taxonomic systems that arose when classifiers confronted what appeared to be multiple sets of difference inhering in the same individuals because it naturalizes the terms of classification—race, gender—as invariant human qualities residing in determinate morphological features.[89] White European men of the eighteenth century alternately employed race to define masculinity and masculinity to define race with an overarching goal of always assuming themselves at the top of whatever hierarchy resulted.[90]

To put the claims I am making about the mutual inflection of masculinity and race into context, we might recall some of the other studies that have illustrated that interaction. A considerable body of work has already developed concerning the "racing" of gender and the gendering of race in the nineteenth centuries, particularly as these processes concerned Jewish identity and African American identity. Perhaps most notably, Sander Gilman argues in his *Freud, Race, and Gender* that a discourse of race surreptitiously informs the lion's share of Freud's thinking about gender. He argues that "the language Freud used about the scientific unknowability of the core of what makes a Jewish male a male Jew was parallel to that which he used concerning the essence of the feminine."[91] He also posits that the famous "dark continent" metaphor for femininity correlates the fact that Jews were often considered to be black, particularly by Europeans. In fact, Gilman argues that the specific differences separating the white male and the ostensibly dark, Jewish male formed a repressed subtext of difference that was written onto the body of "the woman" as the mark of the principal, most fundamental difference inaugurating human subjectivity. Finally, and perhaps most important for the discussion of differently gendered males and the disposition of their genitals that we have been considering here, Gilman stresses the fact that in Freud's time one of the slang terms for the clitoris was *der Jude;* according to Gilman such a slang term encoded the anti-Semitic and misogynist hypotheses that the circumcised Jewish penis and the clitoris were fundamentally cropped or otherwise abbreviated versions of the genuine article: the white, Aryan penis.[92]

The eighteenth century provided a particularly fertile ground for unstable or fluid identities, as the numerous studies devoted to changing or emerging class identities have amply demonstrated. Thus, it is crucial to note that at roughly the same time that explorers and naturalists were attempting to catalog human beings according to a hierarchy that would later be called "race," scientists were attempting to systematize the manners in which the sexes differed from one another. Thomas Laqueur has argued that despite anatomical discoveries concerning the physical nature of sexed human bodies, the popular imagination still held tightly to the one-sex model of humanity, in which women were fundamentally inverted or otherwise imperfect versions of men.[93] As knowledge of morphological difference increased, people began to view the sexes as radically different from one another, but ideologically invested perceptions still kept women defined in opposition to men. Laqueur writes:

> Organs that had shared a name—ovaries and testicles—were now linguistically distinguished. Organs that had not been distinguished by a name of their own—the vagina, for example—were given one. Structures that had been thought common to man and woman—the skeleton and the nervous system—were differentiated so as to correspond to the cultural male and female. As the natural body itself became the gold standard of social discourse, the bodies of women—the perennial other—thus became the battleground for redefining the ancient, intimate, fundamental social relation: that of woman to man.[94]

Although the two-sex model of human morphology emerged as observers identified and named the organs peculiar to each sex, the one-sex model continued to hold people in thrall. The identification of real physical features that differentiated male and female did not immediately revoke the tremendous power that historical and cultural truths had exerted for centuries. Ideologies of gender existed and continue to exist independent of scientific observation; in a strictly logical world, however—if by that we understand one adhering to a rigid indexical adequation of signifier and referent and one devoid of affect, desire, and ambiguity—they could not sustain themselves.

In the two-sex model of human morphology an ideological lag separated what people believed about sex and gender and what scientists and other observers could demonstrably prove. That ideological lag expanded with the introduction after about 1700 of a third gender role, one that Randolph Trumbach and others have identified as the province of the sodomite or molly, terms used to refer to men who engage in sex with other men. According to Trumbach, "In the public mind, all men in the molly-houses—as well as those who used the public latrines, the parks, or the cruising streets and arcades to find sexual partners— belonged to the same category, no matter what their behavior in the public sphere. All were members of a third gender that deserved to be treated with contempt."[95] The introduction of this third gender role considerably altered the manner in which males identifying as "mas- culine" could behave, since it dramatically restricted the range of their sexual behavior and desires that could be considered legitimate. Prior to this time and especially during the Restoration, Trumbach argues, an older sexual culture accommodated men who engaged in sexual rela- tions with adolescent males as well as with women. Such men fell within the parameters of manhood, and their behavior did not neces- sarily constitute a revocation of their masculine privilege.

The introduction of a third gender had the effect of reorganizing the manner in which men and women related to each other within and across gender lines. Specifically, men defined themselves to a consider- able extent by recalculating their relations with other men; women also defined themselves through their sexual and other relations with men. During the eighteenth century, there seem not to have been large, socially visible avenues through which women could derive signifi- cant portions of their identities through relations with other women.[96] George Haggerty complements Trumbach's claims by arguing that in addition to "sodomite," which implied a specific form of sexual be- havior, "pederasty," another common and similar term deployed during this same period, referred to specific forms of erotic desire or love.[97] William Edmiston has shown that by the end of the eighteenth century we can find evidence not simply of a third gender, but also of belief in a third sex, which refers both to an androgynous as well as to a bisexual person, even though no specific congenital condition is necessarily implied.[98]

These investigations into the evolving nature of the way people could identify as gendered subjects demonstrate the extent to which the components in the category of gender are neither static nor irreducible, and furthermore that what "gender" is called on to describe and contain varies as well. How the descriptor changes is largely a function of the ideological lag mentioned above—that is, the discrepancy between competing truths that comes about through some combination of historical change and political antagonism. Consequently, regardless of the facts that seem to focus interpretation of particular natural or social phenomena, perceptions of those phenomena continue to be directed by attitudes and beliefs historically connected to them but perhaps no longer directly obtaining. Furthermore, because some of the forces implicated in producing ideological lag remain unconscious, the metonymic links among them operate outside of our direct gaze, and can thus produce unexpected results.[99]

Some of those unexpected metonymic links occur when different methods for classifying human beings collide, often producing bizarre results. Schiebinger illustrates, for example, the serious problems that arose in the attempt to classify human beings when naturalists tried to accommodate women into the linear structure they had devised:

> Scientific racism and scientific sexism both taught that proper social relations between the races and the sexes existed in nature. Many theorists failed to see, however, that their notions of racial and sexual relations rested on contradictory visions of nature. Scientific racism depended on a chain of being or hierarchy of species in nature that was inherently unilinear and absolute. Scientific sexism, by contrast, depended on radical biological divergence.[100]

A critical juncture had arisen: the two principal systems responsible for sustaining the hegemony of the upper-class European male—racism and sexism, both newly founded on a burgeoning scientism that claimed for itself detached objectivity—were becoming taxonomically incompatible. Scientists and naturalists had come to view nature as having produced on the one hand an array of creatures seamlessly related to one another in a linear hierarchy, and on the other hand a discontinuous jumble of living creatures perhaps metonymically associated but sharing no necessarily organic link. Paradoxically, it was precisely owing to the incompatibility of these two indexical systems, both of which aimed to keep whiteness and maleness at the top of their respective hierarchies, that defined modern white masculinity and also prevented it from being the apodictic master that it claimed to be, and that paradox, which is one of mastery and hysteria, is what we find at the heart of modern white masculinity.

Throughout this chapter I have been pointing to examples in which other sexes, other races, other bodies, and other forms of desire not only failed to match or attain the ostensible integrity of the white male, but also, when taken together, uncovered startling incompatibilities in the epistemological and taxonomic structures of the times. What I now want to suggest is that the white male emerged during this time not necessarily as the agent of these incompatibilities—or in any event not exclusively as their agent—but as the effect of the contradictions enumerated above. At a time when different methods for organizing and identifying components of the human body nullified one another in the forms of what Laqueur and Schiebinger have more generally called scientific sex and scientific race, it was not merely the case that this new identity formed simply to cap off each of the two principal strands for delineating morphology and its attendant cultural meanings. Rather, while both components of this new identity—whiteness and maleness—represented the dominant and paradoxically unmarked position in two different schemas for categorizing people, the dominance so represented functioned in entirely different ways. The white masculinity we find during this time was not simply the sum of whiteness and maleness, but instead a sort of whole greater than the sum of its parts, and that was precisely owing to the manner in which it negotiated the contradictions just noted in classificatory systems.

In the examples discussed above, the projection of fragmentation onto the body of nonwhite men, and the imputation of specific forms of desire onto those same men represent two fundamental ways of dealing with the problem of organic unity competing with radical discontinuity, and both involved construction of a specific identity for white European males. The first manner of dealing with the issue involved simply not classifying nonwhite people as people at all—or, perhaps more accurately, positing radically different origins at different places and times for the human species. Arising toward the end of the eighteenth century and becoming very popular throughout the nineteenth century, polygenesis held that we could identify specific human difference and trace it back to diversity of origin. Josiah Clark Nott and George R. Glidden, two of the nineteenth century's most prominent proponents of this theory, maintained that "if the teachings of science be true, there must have been many centres of creation, even for *Caucasian* races, instead of one centre for *all* the types of humanity."[101] Charles White, who, incidentally, was one of the penis collectors we saw above, staunchly defended the principles of polygenesis, primarily by attacking the notion, popularized by Buffon and others, that the climate was at least partially responsible for human variation.[102] On the popularity of theories of polygenesis, particularly in North America, Stephen Jay Gould wryly comments: "It is obviously not accidental that a nation still practicing slavery and expelling its aboriginal inhabitants from their homelands should have provided a base for theories that blacks and Indians are separate species, inferior to whites."[103]

The voluminous material dedicated to the question of humankind's multiple origins generally reduces to a single question: to what extent can one identify a distinct human group and posit a genetic or otherwise empirical affinity based on selected valorized traits? That such a question depended ultimately not on the human groups in question but on the terms used to describe them became the battling cry of the vast majority of monogenists, among whom was James Cowles Prichard. Prichard maintained that the issue boiled down to a matter of language.

> Races are properly successions of individuals propagated from any given stock; and the term should be used without any involved meaning that such a progeny or stock has always possessed a particular character. The real import of the term has often been overlooked, and the word race has been used as if it implied a distinction in the physical character of the whole series of individuals. By writers on anthropology, who adopt this term, it is often tacitly assumed that such distinctions were primordial, and that their successive transmission has been unbroken. If such were the fact, a race so characterized would be a species in the strict meaning of the word, and it ought to be so termed.[104]

The theory of polygenesis could help sustain an organic view of humanity that risked contradiction with the taxonomic system meant to uphold it primarily by summoning traditional ways of knowing—logic and reason—and deploying them to "prove" what polygenesists already believed. As Prichard's comments demonstrate—and he was by no means the only one to recognize language's capacity to create that which it appears simply to name—those who advanced the theory that humanity had multiple origins and who based their belief on a primordial inequality among the different human groups did so less through empirical observation than by establishing in advance the criteria that they would look for to prove their nonwhite others inferior.

If the first solution to the problem of contradiction between humankind's organic unity and the multiple taxonomic systems designed to measure it was simply to declare indexically problematic groups subhuman, the second solution was far more diffuse even if it did produce very similar results. That second solution involved, as we have seen, the many ways in which early modern white males attempted to project onto their differently raced—and hence differently gendered—others a fragmentation of morphology, character, or desire that seemed to disqualify them as truly male. Rather than assert through an ever more restricted and specialized use of language the identity of the defining group, this solution involved white masculinity's implicitly asking its others for definition or confirmation of what it was. While the first solution deploys a body of culturally specific signifiers to direct and organize thinking about morphology and its significance, even in cultures that do not share those signifiers, the second solution hinged on desire and the anxiety that some forms of maleness might be inferior to others.

The rhetorical composition of these two solutions diametrically oppose one another, but taken together they constitute the remarkable ideological power of white masculinity. By way of concluding this chapter on the development of white masculinity as an early modern hegemonic identity, I want to return to the discursive models elaborated at the beginning of this chapter in order to help understand that ideological force. In the four discursive positions that Lacanian psychoanalysis postulates, identities depend on the subject's relationship both to knowledge in the form of master signifiers and to desire and its causes. I have argued that whiteness functions doubly, on the one hand by mapping the ostensibly neutral discourse of reason onto a particular kind of (white) body, thus simultaneously obfuscating its own identity and actively producing itself as an empty category; and on the other hand by mobilizing a collection of signifiers in the form of scientific knowledge, signifiers largely derived from culturally specific notions of how the body works, and applying them unilaterally to people who may not use or understand their bodies the way the defining culture does. That is why, for example, the sorts of taxonomic contradictions enumerated above could arise, in which theories of race conflicted with postulates about gender, and that is also why white observers remarking on cultures that practiced various forms of male genital alteration seemed compelled to make the men so altered appear somehow less manly. Because they were contending with beings whose genitals constituted them as male, considering them not of the same species allowed them to avoid treating them as equals. In other words, the inhabitants of the cultures in question might certainly be male, but because of the modifications made to the sign of their maleness, they seemed less male than the white observers. Requiring other males to exhibit the same signs of maleness that the white classifiers valued established a paradigm of knowledge in the form of particular master signifiers that would have appeared to justify polygenesis: the differently gendered males from other cultures could only be considered male if they did not belong to the same species as the observing classifiers.

By the same token, white observers appear to have felt compelled to characterize masculine desire from other cultures as functioning as their own desire did, but in a somewhat diminished or otherwise debilitated capacity. The examples we saw, in which European travelers speculated that the men of color whom they visited would prefer a white woman, or that they would find their own women more attractive if a white man deigned to sleep with them, demonstrate that early modern white males fixed their own identities by mapping a unified theory of desire onto a circumscribed construction of the male body. In that gesture they applied to the image of an empirically observable and stable human body produced through Enlightenment forms of thought the notion of a single form of masculine desire directed toward privileged Western objects. That combination of accepted knowledge and projected desire—knowledge that bodies demonstrably have the same functions and hence articulations in all cultures, and desire for the same objects and for the same reasons—forms the basis of early modern white masculinity as a discursively produced human identity. In fact, white masculinity's particular ideological strength appears to derive in large part from the contradictory nature of its complex composition. Anchored on the one hand by a host of master signifiers that create a stable form of knowledge concerning the nature of whiteness, the white male identity consists, on the other hand, in large part of a kind of hysterical desire continually interrogating the parameters of what it itself appears to define.

Having established some part of the extent to which social identifiers such as race and gender commonly overlapped one another to the point of inflecting portions of identity not normally associated with their own purviews, we can now interrogate how such inflection contributed to the ideological strength of white masculinity. As mentioned above, this is an identity that mobilizes diametrically opposed subjective identities in the psychoanalytic framework that privileges knowledge and desire as significant components of discursive positions. We have also confirmed that part of Enlightenment philosophy depended on a stable notion of the European body and its place in a natural hierarchy, which produced an array of master signifiers whose promulgation constructed rather than described the white male European body and identity in question. The discourse of the master, we observed, is characterized by the illusion that, as Lacan puts it, its purveyor is "identique à son propre signifiant," that is to say, identical to his own signifier.[105] The structure of the master's discourse puts knowledge in the form of master signifiers in the place of the agent, and the divided subject and surplus enjoyment in repressed or subordinate positions. The master orders knowledge in such a way that it conforms to his standards, and we have seen numerous examples in which the attribution of taxonomic characteristics completely disregards the history and cultures of the folks being indexed. The master, in short, through a deft manipulation of "believing is seeing," arranges the world such that the way he perceives it becomes ensconced in the very possibilities for symbolically representing it.[106] Other methods or modes for depicting reality either fall outside of the domain of logic and reason or, worse yet, fail to achieve sufficient density and consistency of meaning to attain discursive coherence, deteriorating instead into what the master deems to be nonsense.

But it is important to understand that white masculinity as it developed in the early modern period achieved an ideological strength far greater than that which would result merely from the forceful imposition on hapless others of a particular way of thinking. It was not simply the forefather of an Orwellian newspeak, for example, resistance to which provoked harsh punishment, nor was it merely some sort of lingua franca one needed to speak in official circumstances. Rather, it was the embodiment of a way of knowing and a way of representing. In this vein, Kimberlé Crenshaw and Gary Peller have argued persuasively that the apparent dominance of brute force frequently masks the ideological struggle over narrative and meaning. They write that "at stake at each axis of conflict is a contest over which, and whose, narrative structure will prevail in the interpretation of events in the social world."[107] However, a great part of white masculinity's ideological strength derived from the hold on knowledge and signification inhering in the position of the master combined with the components peculiar to the position diametrically opposed to the master's: the hysteric's. Where the master's province is knowledge, certainty, and the repression of desire and self-division, the hysteric functions in a world of questioning, fundamental doubt, and foregrounded desire. The hysteric's refusal to incarnate or otherwise comprise that which paradigms of knowledge have made available to it produces a never-ending quest for an answer to the question of what it is. As John Forrester puts it, "The world of the hysteric is a world of the desires of other people, in which the subject is submerged and lost in the theatre of other people's demands, desires, and reproofs."[108]

White masculinity in the early modern period clung as much to hysteria as it did to mastery, as much to a search for meaning as it did to providing meaning's answers. What this means is that those for whom the identity became available in the early modern period did not simply lay down the law and reap the benefits of placing themselves at the top of the social order and of the knowledge underpinning it. It seems almost pointless to mention, but if that had been possible, no critique, this one included, could ever have arisen, not because of censorship, but because the idea itself could never have occurred in the first place. Instead, they found themselves subjected to the same scrutiny to which they subjected their others, mainly because, as I have been maintaining, no one could ever occupy the position of master. The hysteric's position privileges the divided subject; symptoms that exemplify the subject's lack of conformance with its representations arise to prominence.[109] The hysteric is racked by an uncertainty of identity, continually testing its relationship to the master signifiers—the paradigms of knowledge—that give rise to valorized and legitimized modes of being. As Slavoj Žižek writes, the hysteric's archtypical question is, "Why am I what you [the big Other] say that I am?"[110] Thus, although separated from any agency involved in the production of master signifiers, the hysteric nevertheless remains enthralled by those signifiers, since its interrogation of its own identity repeatedly assesses its coincidence with its own ideal type and simultaneously repudiates the value of that type.[111]

In this chapter's many examples of European males constructing a unified narrative of their own social and natural ascendancy based on ascription of morphological, intellectual, and libidinal insufficiency or fragmentation, we have encountered the foreclosure of discontinuity in favor of discursive regularity.[112] But while the discursive mastery characteristic of early modern philosophical and anthropological systems led to a certain kind of stability in the domain of knowledge and law, that same mastery highlighted the hysteria at its heart and to which it owed its very existence. To wit, European males required the participation of their nonmale, nonwhite others to buttress their positions, to be sure, but such participation extended well beyond a simple process of unilateral negating. Thus, in addition to allying a mode of knowing with a disposition of the body and tendering that decidedly color-based knowledge as the transparent determinant of all modes of knowledge, early modern white males also retained control by implicitly causing their others to affirm their identity and reflect it back to them (as Ragland-Sullivan remarked, "One can only command another by putting that other to work to validate him").[113] Whether through bizarre presumptions that men from other cultures desired the women that white men possessed, or through equally outlandish beliefs that those same men required validation of their own desires through European sexual conquests of native women, early modern white men sought and continually found gaps in the constitutions of those they deemed to be unlike them. The equation of knowledge and being not only solidified European males' identification with the color white; it also circumscribed males whose cultures engendered them as male differently, thus ascribing to them specific masculine deficiencies.

The white male's ideological strength hinged precisely on the assertion of mastery that required the other's participation, since making that other dependent on particular master signifiers that bolstered the white male's identity involved the other in a specific mode of thinking. Crucially, however, the subjective identity of white masculinity in the early modern period was constituted in part as a failure. The introduction of the numerous contingencies designed to explain why bodies from other cultures and sexualities from other lands failed to attain the integrity and stability necessary for white male ascendancy made it impossible for anyone to identify as a white male without experiencing the hysterical anxiety of insufficiency.

4. IN DEFENSE OF THE PHALLUS

> Given the power to contemplate the Au-
> thentic, who would run, of choice, after
> its image?—Plotinus, *The Enneads*

The phallus is not a penis. That is a pronouncement we have heard repeatedly, and yet many of us still struggle in an apparently vain attempt to pin down once and for all precisely what this most notori-ously difficult concept/body part/imaginary effect really is. In fact, both Jane Gallop and Judith Butler have gone so far as to suggest that those who would even try to define "phallus" situate themselves squarely within a discourse that is, well, phallic; such people seem to engage in a form of posturing that would purportedly situate them at language's origin. Gallop writes that "the Lacanians' desire clearly to separate *phal-lus* from *penis,* to control the meaning of the signifier *phallus,* is pre-cisely symptomatic of their desire to have the phallus, that is, their desire to be at the center of language, at its origin."[1] Similarly, Butler writes that "the phallus . . . is considered the privileged signifier by Lacan, that which originates or generates significations, but is not itself the signifying effect of a prior signifying chain. To offer a definition of the phallus—indeed, to attempt denotatively to fix its meaning—is to posture as if one *has* the phallus and, hence, to presume and enact precisely what remains to be explained."[2] Both Gallop and Butler ex-plicitly question the phallus's originary relationship to signification, and each implicitly assigns to the phallus and those who would pre-sume to possess it a sort of delusionary mastery.

A number of questions arise from any warnings to those who would believe in the phallus's power: How does the delusion associated with phallic pretensions relate to that devolving from the pretension to mas-tery as seen in the last chapter? Why do so many of Lacan's critics (and there are quite a few[3]) go to such rhetorical complexities to convince us that the phallus is somehow really a penis—or, phrased another way, what is the concern that some of us might get it wrong? And, finally, if it seems advisable to avoid the phallic error of attempting to define the phallus, how can we ever know it? Surely it cannot be the case that any attempt to convince others of the validity of one's argument amounts to phallic posturing. Nor does it seem likely that only under certain circumstances—say, attempting to define the phallus—does trying to get it right amount to such posturing. And is one any less phallic in one's attempt to be correct when one calls someone else phallic?[4] From critiques of the Lacanian notion of the phallus, it also appears that words such as "symptomatic" and "posturing" are often attached to "phallic" in such a way as to render that latter thing undesirable, or at the very least ridiculous. But is the phallus necessarily ridiculous or pathetic when finally laid bare (if such laying bare is, in fact, even possible)? And to what extent is the desire to expose the phallus as a pathetic failure coextensive with an attempt to demonstrate that real individuals who occupy a society's dominant position—in general, white men—aren't somehow all they have traditionally been cracked up to be?

Perhaps all of these questions betray my own concern about appearing to engage in phallic posturing, since in this chapter I fully intend to get the phallus right. It seems important, therefore, to distinguish between all things associated with the phallus on the one hand, and posturing on the other. If the phallus is a signifier that is more properly the effect, rather than the cause, of a specific signifying mode, then we only know it retroactively and obliquely as implicated in the conditions of representation.[5] In other words, the essence of a signifier is to delineate an epistemological dimension from an ontological one (or, in the formulation that Lacan often used, to cause people to exchange *la lettre* for *l'être*); the phallus thus denotes—or more properly arises as—the condition or the possibility of that separation. It stands in for the gesture of demarcating the continuous realm of absolute being into relational units that evoke one another because of symbolic taxonomic operations arising through the work of politics, history, and culture. That the function denoted by the signifier "phallus" must exist seems to me beyond doubt; why the signifier in question is called *phallus* is another matter.[6] Investigating the reasons behind the latter quandary might help establish parameters for answering the question of whether all phallic activity is posturing; how and why getting it right—the phallus, or any-thing else for that matter—is itself phallic; and what might be ridiculous either about attacking the phallus or trying to defend it, two activities that might just turn out to be the same thing.[7]

One of the principal goals of this chapter is to demonstrate that the phrase "phallic posturing" is, in fact, redundant, and also to explore possible subjective identities not phallically determined, or at least not so determined in the traditional sense of the phallus as hyperbolically masculine. (The word "posture," incidentally, is etymologically related to the words "to place" and "to posit," affinities that I will make appar-ent later on.) I take it as given—and this is one of the fundamentals of my argument—that all knowledge is to a certain extent based on mis-recognition, since it comes to us through the symbolic, which neces-sarily imposes culturally based form on its object. Since I will be argu-ing that the phallus is the condition or possibility of signification in the first place (or at least of any signification that I am aware of—but I leave open the question of whether other forms are possible), it is always and as a necessary condition wrong, at least to the extent that all symbolic representation both adds to and deletes from what it would purport to depict. I would thus argue that "phallic posturing" is redundant in the same way that Marjorie Garber has labeled the term "male subjectivity" redundant. Garber expresses frustration with much work on male sub-jectivity, and she wonders whether such work represents "anything more than a wishful logic of equality, which springs from a feminist desire to make 'man' part rather than whole."[8] Further elaborating, she maintains that "male subjectivity" is a "phallic redundancy" since "to be a subject is to have a phallus, to be male literally or empowered 'as' male in culture and society."[9]

Unless we are prepared to admit that masculinity and its close asso-ciations are necessarily and exclusively associated with males, a pros-pect that has been rejected by theorists such as Eve Kosofsky Sedgwick and Judith Halberstam, or that there is something irreducibly pathetic or ridiculous about masculinity, a supposition that some may, in fact, support, then we need to understand the phallus and its coercively organizing capacities as extending beyond the parameters normally associated with gender as traditionally conceived. We need to consider it first and foremost as a product of signification, and then we can ask how and why the specific label attached to this thing evokes not only males, but a specific male part; and, furthermore, why it evokes a specific male part in a sort of venerated, almost religious fashion.

The Oedipus of Sophocles' very particular handling of the ancient myth is perhaps the first and most exemplary manifestation of the phallic function in Western society. That rendition of the tale, originally staged for an audience in the process of consolidating political and cultural divergences, explicitly erects a key signifier in the form of the title character to stand in for and amalgamate a host of disparate discursive positions, making them compatible or mutually coherent in the process. That amalgamation can serve as the hallmark of the phallic function as I will be using and developing the term here, since it provides for metaphoric exchange, not only within similar registers, such as poetic language or economic exchange, but across those registers as well. The work of the phallus is what allows us to organize complex networks of signification with reference to one another, such that a new mode of thinking—say, philosophy in the Greek *polis*—can be seen to express and be expressed by a new kind of dramatic representation, such as tragedy.

While Oedipus stands in for the phallic function, he is not the phallus, nor does he have it; he merely represents it. Despite its ontological status as signifier and despite its implicit association with masculinity, no one, male or female, can possess the phallus.[10] Lacan makes clear the distinction between being or having the phallus and representing it when he posits that the real father in the intersubjective unit of the family is not the person who possesses the phallus—he merely represents its possessor:

> Now, if affective, imaginary exchanges become established between the mother and the child around the imaginary lack of the phallus, which makes of it the essential element in the intersubjective coaptation, the father, in the Freudian dialectic, has his, and that's all; he neither exchanges it nor gives it up. There is no circulation. The father has no function in the trio *if not to represent the bearer,* the possessor of the phallus. The father *as* father *[le père, en tant que père]* has the phallus—one point, and that is all (my emphases).[11]

In Lacan's treatment of the phallus and its manipulation of signification and imaginary relationships, the male in the intersubjective trio stands in for the real possessor of the phallus, but what is particularly poignant in his rendition is that the *real* possessor of the phallus is, of course, a fiction. Such a figure necessarily arises as the child accedes to the symbolic order and must recognize that the mother's desire is elsewhere, and that her desire is the desire of the other. However, that figure remains real to the extent that it models the tenor and availability of culturally determined signifiers. That is, since the child coming into its culture's signifying system must and as a consequence of that fact recognize that it is neither part of its mother nor a supplement to or completion of her, it concomitantly apprehends an outside agency that causes or reflects her desire.[12] It does not matter whether there are real persons or things to which one could point as the origin of her desire; what matters is that for the child acceding to language, the potential for satisfaction of that desire lies somewhere else. The father as other is the site of the power to satisfy, and like Oedipus, he does so by amalgamating a series of various elements—by causing, that is, elements to find common denominators, and hence the potential for translation and comprehension from among disparate, otherwise incompatible substances. In fact, it is because the father represents the possessor of the phallus that unlike elements can be compared in the first place. As Lacan writes in the fourth seminar, "In order for there to be the three terms of the trio, you need a closed space, an organization of the symbolic world, which we call the father."[13]

Why should we call the organization of the symbolic world the father? In traditional heterosexual family structures consisting of a male and female parental unit, the female—mother—provides the tremendous majority of child care *and* represents the only member of the parental dyad whose direct, material link to offspring has been observable. Not only does the infant develop with an attachment to its mother that is so profound that the child does not distinguish itself as a separate entity, but as it matures and gains access to language, symbolic links supersede earlier, imaginary ones. Separation from the mother, the rupture of the earlier, seemingly organic dyad, accompanies the access to desire and its satisfaction only through the alienated and alienating substitutional structures of language. Because that operation occurs simultaneously with the realization that the mother's desire is elsewhere, the father becomes the site of satisfaction through symbolic—that is mediated or metaphoric—means, which complements the purely inferential nature of his material link to off-spring. That is why the symbolic world has traditionally taken the side of the father.

The organization of the symbolic world is necessarily unconscious because the structures governing symbolic activity fall outside of that classification.[14] But we know from Freud that things that are not conscious fall into more than one category: material that is dynamically repressed, and that which has not yet become conscious. Such forms of nonconsciousness often involve dropped links formerly connecting conscious thought processes. In two different contexts, Maria Torok and Jean-Joseph Goux have argued for the necessity of recognizing lost or displaced unconscious links operating in our understanding of particular social phenomena. In an extended discussion of so-called "penis envy" in women, Torok stresses the metaphoric dimension of the phenomenon, underscoring that it is not a real penis that women wish to possess, but "the acts and enjoyments attached to it" (34).[15] Referring to the "envious desire for the male member" as a wish for "its symbolic equivalents" (3), Torok also comments on the biblical myth of Adam and Eve, in which the latter represents a detached part of the former; the myth, she argues, illustrates Eve's assumption not only of her own guilt, but that of Adam as well, and it projects Eve as a part of Adam's body, "at once his thing (his servant) and his attribute" (37). The myth, like the penis, contains a metaphoric link to or substitution for knowledge of an equivalent social structure, even if that knowledge is felt rather than understood—in short, unconscious. The power that such unconscious links can hold lies in their scope: the signs of unconscious desires (what Torok calls "object-things") have social dimensions, and consequently "their being the same for everyone makes them apt for exchange, but also for disguising desires" (5).[16] Similarly, in his analysis of the ancient story of Osiris, the Egyptian god who was dismembered and reassembled with a simulacrum erected in the place of his irrecoverable penis, Goux argues that a once explicit link connecting the phallic emblem and a culturally valorized form of reason no longer obtains for moderns. In fact, Goux goes so far as to claim that the unconscious consists precisely in the unintelligible continuance of a connection that we fail to understand: "The unconscious is this: that persistence on another scene, contrary to our clear and distinct reflections, of a link which can no longer be conceptualized."[17]

The unconscious links to be investigated here involve those uniting the phallus as the condition or possibility of representation—that is, as the convertibility of object-things that allows for symbolic exchange—and the unmistakably masculine dimension that the word "phallus" itself seems necessarily to invoke. We can address the first issue by referring to the work of Jacques Lacan and to that of some of his commentators; we will need to refer to the material in the preceding chapters, as well as to some other contemporary phenomena, to address the remaining questions. By way of opening the debate, I would like to refer to a passage from the introductory pages of Lacan's second seminar, in which he evokes the historical legacy of the subject's *moi*. Recalling Socrates as the person who inaugurated in human subjectivity the idea of a form of knowledge *(savoir)* dependent on demands for coherence, Lacan points out that once specific models for thinking and representing become installed in human consciousness, we cannot *not* think through them.

> Think about the origins of language. We imagine that there must have been a time when people on this earth began to speak. So we admit of an emergence. But from the moment that the specific structure of this emergence is grasped, we find it absolutely impossible to speculate on what preceded it other than by symbols which were always applicable. What appears to be new thus always seems to extend itself indefinitely into perpetuity, prior to itself. We cannot, through thought, abolish a new order. This applies to anything whatsoever, including the origin of the world.[18]

Language acts as a sort of barrier through which we cannot proceed backwards in epistemological history to conceptualize whatever human instrument of consciousness might have preceded it. Even if we were able to unearth such an institution, we would only be able to understand it in terms of the significatory tools we currently employ, thus stripping it of whatever specificity it may have enjoyed. The only way available to us of understanding the phallus parallels the manner just described of understanding a pre-linguistic world. That is, whatever the phallus *is* is inaccessible to us because on the one hand its form and function lie outside of language, and on the other hand its paradoxical nature as signifier of desire means that the moment it becomes visible it simultaneously undoes itself. Significantly, all attempts to define or understand the phallus translate into inappropriate discursive terms its pre- or extra-linguistic aspects. Yet, as indescribable as the phallus may be, it remains an indispensable component of signification, if not as an agent, then at least as a heuristic device enabling us to conceptualize that difficult-to-fathom space at which the symbolic universe joins the material or bodily domain. In other words, the phallus is the converter that allows the otherwise incompatible domains of materiality and ideality to come together in the peculiar domain of signification.[19]

As a component of signification, the phallus is fundamental in the establishment of difference. It signifies a break or a cut in the realm of indifferentiation, but more important, it establishes the parameters of what difference is "about." But what concerns me here is the phallus as original mark or cut in an otherwise unformed realm of indifferentiation. The phallus marks the possibility of difference; it guarantees that once difference occurs and registers, other differences will align according to the difference first established. In short, it causes difference to be "about" something. The guarantor of difference and of the ordering of signification that such a fixing entails is fundamental to the inception of subjectivity. To accede to subjectivity is to abandon the realm of inchoate mental activity unattached to any particular cultural or historical forms. It is to recognize and accept a very specific way of dividing up the world into discrete and organizable units whose taxonomic logic turns on place, moment, and configurations of prohibitions and desire. Finally, it is to acknowledge oneself not only as signifiable by those units, but ultimately dependent on them for coherence and cohesion. The phallus is that signifier that provides the consistency necessary to ensure that sense can quite literally be made from a diverse collection of differences.

Lacan maintains that the phallus plays a dialectical role in the formation of the subject. Not only does it register difference, but because difference has to engage multiplicity in order to initiate contrastive relations, the phallus as fundamental signifier orders that difference, most often hierarchically. Lacan writes: "The constituting function of the phallus in the dialectic of the introduction of the subject to its pure and simple existence and to its sexual position is impossible to deduce if we do not make of it the fundamental signifier by which the subject's desire has to make itself recognized as such, whether it's a matter of a man or a woman."[20] At first blush the above definition appears nearly circular in its logic: the phallus cannot be constituting if it is not the fundamental signifier of the subject's desire. However, we need to lay particular emphasis on Lacan's restrictive prepositional phrase: "by which the subject's desire has to make itself recognized as such." The phallus as signifier—again, we are not yet considering the perhaps bizarre name for that signifier—registers the movement from being to meaning. That is, the phallus marks the fundamental inscription of difference through which a subject comes to recognize a discernible, socially encoded signifying order from an inchoate realm of undifferentiated being, or that which is literally non-sense. The phallus as a signifier signifies that realm of being that cannot be signified, and, paradoxically, the moment it is called on to perform that signification is also the moment at which it fails. The signifier "phallus" stakes out the parameters of the signifiable, attesting in its very premise to signification's limits, since its function is to stand in as a human construction marking the place of an impossible articulation: that point where abstract meets material.

But it is also crucial to emphasize that the phallus signifies the subject's desire, or, more properly, allows desire to be recognized. Lacan is explicit: "It is the desire of the subject . . . but in so far as the subject itself has received its power as subject from a sign."[21] The fundamental signifier simultaneously marks the possibility for the inscription of difference and, in its very differentiation of an inchoate realm, causes other inscriptions to refer their meaning to it. One way to think about this is to imagine a chalk stroke on a freshly scrubbed blackboard. Once the stroke appears, a form of difference arises where previously there had been none. Other marks, be they words, pictures, or scribbling, refer themselves to that first, defining mark, the mark that gives rise to all other marks; new marks can be thought in terms of the original mark. What makes the fundamental signifier particularly compelling is its dual existence as a material thing and as an abstract organizing principle. Requiring a corporeality to allow information to be transmitted, this fundamental signifier nevertheless has a purely ideal nature responsible for the convertibility of other signifiers through the differential play of signification.

The principal function of the phallus is thus to represent the subject's desire and to allow that desire some mitigated form of expression in a culturally contingent and coherent system of signification that achieves its consistency through a fundamental founding gesture. That gesture functions like the mark of chalk on the fresh blackboard in that it establishes a simultaneously material and abstract dimension in a symbolic system; in the case to be considered here, however, it also involves an ideological component absent in the example. It is the recognition of the function of the father that performs all of those charges: as noted above, the father abstracts the mother's desire, making of that desire for the nascent subject something only available in the other in symbolic form. But in addition, the father derives his symbolic function from the fact that, until very recently, proving paternity—that is, a direct empirical link uniting father and child—has been impossible. The father could only ever assert his connection to his offspring symbolically and inferentially; his tie to the family is thus ideological, not biological. As Lacan writes: "That the father . . . might be the true agent of procreation is not in any case a truth of experience."[22]

The father has the phallus, then, to the extent that it is he who marks the fundamental signifier of symbolic difference as the child learns that it is not all for the mother, and to the extent that it is he who stands in for the way the culture deploys the differential play of material signifiers in its symbolic communication. In fact, Lacan goes so far as to claim that the figure of the father was the central obsession guiding Freud in his work on the unconscious:

> Freud's entire investigation—not only theoretical but in Freud's subjective experience as well, which we can find traced throughout the confidences he makes to us, in his dreams, in the evolution of his thought, in all that we now know about his life, his habits, and even in his attitudes toward his family that Jones reports more or less completely but accurately—Freud's entire investigation boils down to this: What is it to be a father? . . . That was for him the central problem, the fertile ground from which all of his research is truly oriented.[23]

Reiterating a similar idea four years later in the seminar on transference, Lacan argued that "the most hidden relationship, and as Freud says the least natural, the most purely symbolic, is the relationship between father and son."[24] The interest in the father that Lacan explicitly manifests and that Freud, at least according to Lacan, implicitly shared does not concern the biological male and his relationship to his offspring, but rather the manner in which intimate and ideological relationships forge bonds among people based on their relationships to sexual difference.[25] The interest in the father marks a concern with the alienating and metaphoric capacities of culturally contingent representation. Lacan expressly specifies the symbolic dimension of paternity when he shifts focus away from real men and onto the social dimensions that paternity regulates: "To ask *what is a father?* is entirely different from being oneself a father, from acceding to the paternal position. Let's examine it closely: for as much as for each man the accession to the paternal position is a quest, it is not unthinkable to say that, finally, no one has ever completely been it."[26] Fully occupying the position of the father is an impossible quest.

It seems clear that for Lacan—and presumably for Freud as well—the interest in paternity lies not in real biological males who sire children, but in the cultural processes that formed a political institution around an unsubstantiated material link. In fact, one could arguably maintain that the institution of paternity might have arisen precisely to compensate for the lack of such a link, as if to relegate to the realm of the symbolic what was missing in the real. In short, we are dealing here not with fathers, but with the father. We are not concerned with how a man or men relate to their families, but with a more fundamental consideration: the abstract link standing in for the material one, the symbolic recompense that privileges idealized and immaterial substitutions over the matter whose lack occasioned them in the first place. "The father *as* the father has the phallus," Lacan claimed, as we noted above. That would appear to mean, then, not that the man who sired children has the phallus, but rather that the possessor of the phallus is, in fact, the father.

The phallus embodies ideality and abstracts materiality, providing a necessary and culturally contingent manner for the transmission of bodily realities onto the ineluctably ideological mode of symbolic expression. That is, even though any experience of our bodies is filtered through the politics—highly complex though they may be—of our means of signification, we still need a way to theorize the relative consistency with which most people understand the social existence of this most apparently natural of all our possessions. What causes us to accept as transparently given the political prohibitions and conscriptions ordering not only what we can do with our bodies, but how we understand and, indeed, experience the use we make of them?[27] The phallus as a signifier not only guarantees a fit between cultural abstractions and material forces, it applies a social consistency to that fit. Furthermore, since any adequation of non-identical things demands a conjunction to provide the possibility of coherence, the phallus bridges the chasm separating the material and the ideal, thus providing a mode and a manner for substitution to occur.[28]

No wonder, then, that the phallus should be situated on the side of the father, since both phallus and father are sheer constructions, figures that mark the possibility of difference in the way that a culture understands and organizes that difference. But the father himself need not appear to ensure the proper transmission of his order: his name will suffice. Lacan devoted significant attention to the *nom-du-père*, the name-of-the-father, throughout his teachings, but in the seminar on psychosis he maintains that a subject's failure to incorporate the fundamental cultural signifiers based on the paternal metaphor leads to psychosis.[29] The paternal metaphor structures and organizes our symbolic systems, giving them coherence and convertibility. The father's function in organizing the symbolic world is so important, in fact, that Jacques-Alain Miller refers to the foreclosure of the name-of-the-father as "the absence of the fundamental element in the locus of the Other,"[30] which leads to the subject's not finding his or her proper place in the symbolic order.

While it might be the case that other symbolic realms not based on the name-of-the-father could be possible, we cannot currently think them except through that agency. In the order we are dealing with here, the name-of-the-father provides coherence and consistency to the symbolic order because it represents the primary nonmaterial link establishing identity in the intersubjective unit of the family. "The first relationship of reality is drawn between the mother and the child," Lacan writes. "But let us not forget that [the father] is only real for us in so far as institutions confer onto him, I won't say his role or function as father—it's not a sociological question—but his name of father."[31] Because the father's role in procreation as an unverifiable inference provides him a purely symbolic dimension, the name-of-the-father "is a necessity of the signifying chain." Lacan continues: "From the fact alone that you institute a symbolic order, something responds or not to the function defined by the Name-of-the-Father, and in the interior of that function you place signification that can be different according to circumstances but which in no case depends on any other necessity than the necessity of the function of the father, to which responds the Name-of-the-Father in the signifying chain."[32] The interiorization of the name-of-the-father as hallmark of the symbolic order caps off the Oedipus complex in Lacanian psychoanalysis: the father's principal function is to deprive the child of the mother by interfering with that intersubjective duality, and he does so in the imposition of symbolic mediation, thus laying down the framework and the blueprint for future avenues of signification.

It thus does not seem exaggerated to claim, as François Regnault does, that "the Name-of-the-Father . . . is substitution as such."[33] The father's function, in fact, is precisely to govern and to order the kinds of substitution that can be made and the manner in which they can transpire. Often referred to as the paternal metaphor, the function of the father I have been discussing regulates an economy of symbolic exchanges the same way that any other denominator manages expression.[34] Just as the denominator in a fraction stipulates in which terms—thirds, say, or twenty-fourths—a numerical value can be expressed, or just as a unit of currency limits the expression of price to what can be expressed in a given specie, the paternal metaphor opens up a signifying system based on the forging of symbolic and ideological links to stand in for the ostensibly material or natural ones that defined a subject's pre-social dynamics.[35] The problem now at hand is to determine how the paradoxical nature of the signifier—that it must be both material and ideal—also characterizes the phallus and the father who possesses it, and how such features enter into the question of why the signifier that marks the zone of cultural differentiation bears the sexually loaded label "phallus."

On several occasions throughout the course of his seminars Lacan characterized the difference between penis and phallus.[36] While some of those characterizations might appear ambiguous, particularly when they seem to suggest a corporeal dimension to the phallus, on the comparatively few occasions when Lacan explicitly distinguished penis from phallus he remained adamant about the difference. In the seminar on the formations of the unconscious, for example, he poses the following questions on that difference:

Why do we speak of phallus, and not purely and simply of penis? Why do we actually see that something else is the mode through which we make the phallus intervene, that something else is the manner in which the penis comes in a more or less satisfactory way to supplement it, both for the masculine and for the feminine subject? To what extent is the clitoris involved *(interessé)* on this occasion in what we can call the economic functions of the phallus?[37]

In the "Signification of the Phallus" essay in his *Ecrits,* Lacan writes that "the phallus in Freudian doctrine is not a fantasy. . . . Nor is it as such an object. . . . It is even less the organ, penis or clitoris, which it symbolizes."[38] It would seem particularly perverse to deny any affiliation between the phallus and the male genitals here, especially in light of the oddly formulated definitions specifying the body parts that the phallus is not. But I am arguing here not simply that the phallus is not a body part, but that, strictly speaking, it *is not* anything at all, at least not in the usual sense of how we conceptualize objects or things. I am arguing that as a marker or placeholder that designates an impossibly demarcated realm of being—but one that a symbolic system based on desire or lack necessarily insinuates—the phallus as an effect operates precisely at the interstices between the material and the abstract, such that the phallus becomes responsible for how we think of objects as the signifier born from the capacity to differentiate. It is the entity that gauges and regulates the division of objects, and that is why it inhabits the intermediate zone between the material and the ideal. That is a zone that Butler identifies in her analysis of the phallus as the "radical difference between *referent* and *signified,*" a "site where the materiality of language and that of the world which it seeks to signify are perpetually negotiated."[39] While Butler is concerned with demonstrating that the phallus as Lacan describes it must have some affiliation with an imaginary body part, that it must, in fact, be implicated in the ideological idealizations of specific gendered organs that produce subjects as male or female, I am less interested in its status as body part than in its function as organ, a distinction I will clarify later on. The phallus has more to do with maleness and masculinity than it does with whatever anatomical parts we may traditionally associate with those characteristics. The phallus is not penile, in other words, but the penis may well be phallic, to the extent that that characteristic represents a purely culturally contingent phenomenon.

In her influential piece on the "Lesbian Phallus" Butler begins her critique of the phallus as a privileged signifier by citing a passage from Lacan's second seminar: "The issue is knowing which organs come into play in the narcissistic imaginary relation to the other whereby the ego is formed, *bildet*. The imaginary structuration of the ego forms around the specular image of the body itself, of the image of the Other."[40] She further cites that "certain organs are caught up in *[sont intéressés dans]* the narcissistic relation, insofar as it structures both the relation of the ego to the other and the constitution of the world of objects" (bracketed French citation in Butler's original).[41] Then she makes the following move in her argument: "Although these organs are not named, it seems that they are, first of all, organs *[les organes]* and that they enter into play in the narcissistic relation; they are that which act as the token or conjectured basis for narcissism. If these organs are the male genitals, they function as both the site and token of a specifically masculine narcissism."[42] The conclusion Butler draws here concerning the ego's imaginary bodily dimension and its relationship to masculine narcissism, based as it is on the premise that the male genitals structure identification, seems to me beyond reproach. However, it is not entirely clear that the organs in question do, in fact, refer to the male genitals: immediately following the passage in Lacan concerning the "specular image of the body itself" in a section that Butler does not cite, Lacan comments further on the imaginary structures, saying that "the relation of looking and being looked at does concern an organ, the eye, to call it by its name."[43] The male genitals are not discussed in this session of the seminar, nor is any organ other than the eye.

Butler goes on to argue that the manner in which Lacan's phallogocentrism produces the phallus is not so much as a privileged signifier, but as an imaginary body part fashioned after the male genitals. Citing Lacan from the seminar on the ego that "all the objects of [man's] world are always structured around the wandering shadow of his own ego,"[44] she writes that "this extrapolating function of narcissism becomes phallogocentrism at the moment in which the aforementioned organs, engaged by the narcissistic relation, become the *model* or principle by which any other object or Other is known" (my emphasis).[45] A curious slippage arises here, and it is significant not because Butler "got it wrong," but because in this discussion of phallogocentrism the male genitals have somehow slipped in where they were never originally present. As we have seen, Butler's argument focuses on the supposition that the organs in question are the male genitals ("If these organs are the male genitals, they function as both the site and token of a specifically masculine narcissism"). But that postulate is not proven, since the only organ Lacan explicitly mentions here is the eye. Furthermore, as Butler advances her argument to demonstrate phallogocentrism, the organs that were originally merely "caught up in [sont intéressés dans] the narcissistic relation" in Lacan's words have in Butler's language become the "model" by which the other is known.

Like some others', Butler's rapprochement of the male genitals and the phallic signifier strives to uncover psychoanalysis's implicit anatomical and ideological investments in an ostensibly neutral signifier that in reality sustains masculine and heterosexist privilege. However, the techniques deployed to accomplish that uncovering sometimes reproduce the forms of dominance in question.[46] In the example just cited, for instance, Butler implicitly assigns a greater role and importance to the male genitals on occasions in which to do so seems counter to the argument Lacan puts forth. Furthermore, citing a passage from the "Signification of the Phallus" in which Lacan argues that the phallus "est encore moins l'organe, pénis ou clitoris, qu'il symbolise" [even less the organ, penis or clitoris, which it symbolizes], she dismisses all but out of hand the importance of the clitoris in Lacan's formulation. Although Lacan argues that the phallus symbolizes both the penis and the clitoris, Butler maintains that in its assertion of ontological difference through symbolization, "the phallus *must* negate the penis in order to symbolize and signify in its privileged way," which would make the phallus "bound to the penis, not through simple identity, but through determinate negation."[47] The argument that the phallus symbolizes only the penis and that it is completely bound to it derives from the premise that the symbolization in which the phallus engages necessarily makes it not what it symbolizes ("To the extent that the phallus symbolizes the penis, it is not that which it symbolizes").[48] That is because to be symbolized is not to be symbolizing ("To be the object of symbolization is precisely not to be that which symbolizes").[49]

While Butler and I concur that the phallus is not the (a?) penis, we arrive at that conclusion from diverging perspectives that take the functioning of signification as their focus. While Butler finds an inadequation between symbolizing and being symbolized, I would argue that there is no paradox or logical impasse in the premise that something can simultaneously signify and be signified. In fact, the entire notion of the signifying chain depends precisely on a signifier's capacity to be signified by another signifier.[50] Butler maintains that the phallus's symbolization of the penis works in constant negation of any direct connection, such that "the phallus would be nothing without the penis" and "the phallus requires the penis for its own constitution."[51] I am maintaining the contrary, however. Without the phallus the penis would be nothing, since body parts, having no necessary natural articulation, require an imaginary projection in order to be delineated as parts in the first place. That imaginary projection depends heavily if not absolutely on the ideological investments in the social morphology that categorize people into races and genders and then value and privilege them accordingly. The issue the urgency of which concerns me most is not why the Lacanian phallus seems to reproduce male privilege, for that amounts to accepting the terms of phallic discourse itself—or, to put it another way, to argue that the Lacanian phallus is phallic in the traditional sense that it enables male dominance is to exclude its other functions and consequently to fail to grasp other cultural forms of domination that reside in language and in other apparently benign types of signification. Rather, the issue that concerns me involves investigating that portion of the phallic function tied to matters more or less traditionally associated with gender politics in order to see other phallic functions unrelated to gender or sexual difference but no less politically charged.

My discussion so far of the phallus as a fundamental signifier that marks the inception of difference and orders and regulates all other difference lacks specific historical or cultural depth. Such a signifier possesses a certain theoretical elegance, perhaps, in its paradoxical figuring of the unfigurable—that is, in its fragmentation for the purposes of translating into a symbolic system that which is, strictly speaking, nonfragmentable, functioning something like a zero whose presence holds the place for an absence to be registered. Yet, if the phallus provides a common denominator of meaning to give difference a structure and a center—in other words, to make it "about" something—then it must have a historical and cultural specificity heretofore unmentioned.

In short, we need to consider how and why the designation "phallus," which unavoidably evokes the male genitals, has become attached to the signifier of an impossible signified that we have investigated thus far.

I have already cited Freud, Maria Torok, and Jean-Joseph Goux concerning the persistence of psychic or unconscious links operating in human mental activity even when the conscious thought processes that initially occasioned them have disappeared. Such a link might in fact be operating in the characterization of the phallus as the signifier joining the material to the abstract, thus providing materiality to the ideal and ideality to the corporeal. That link involves the sharp distinction Western philosophy has traditionally made between the object and the idea, and it is one that reaches at least as far back as early Platonic philosophy: we can trace it through the works of Plato, Aristotle, Plotinus and others. Early Greek mythology posits an earth goddess called Gaia, who teamed up with a sky god named Ouranos; their offspring engendered the gods and mortals of ancient Greece.[52] The gendered separation cleaving inert matter and productive spirit underpins a great deal of Greek literature and philosophy, and while the separation between materiality and spirituality did not depend absolutely on a specifically gendered dynamic, the stark opposition between object and idea certainly persisted. For example, Platonic philosophy investigated the deceptive nature of appearances and their derivative relationship to being or reality. Aristotelian metaphysics postulated being and unity as constituent of primary being, and that branch of philosophy concerned itself with eternal modes of being; Aristotle's epistemology construed different ways of knowing depending on the materiality or abstraction of the object, an abstraction often viewed as the distinction between male animating principles and female raw material.[53]

It is hardly worth mentioning that Platonic and Aristotelian conceptions of materiality and ideality harbor a complexity far too vast to be considered here. Of interest to the current argument are the gendered dynamics of those conceptions and, in Goux's words, the "persistence on another scene, contrary to our clear and distinct reflections, of a link which can no longer be conceptualized."[54] In fact, Goux combines the two issues just elaborated to offer a historical and culturally nuanced analysis of the phallus that accounts on the one hand for that signifier's role as mediator between the material and the ideal, and for the masculine hegemony of that mediation operating in the signifier's explicit evocation of the male genitals on the other. Goux finds evidence of that signifier's origins as far back as classical antiquity, and he also argues that we can see its operation in a wide array of ancient and modern philosophy, including that of Hegel. But he begins his analysis of the phallus with the Egyptian myth of Isis and Osiris. Osiris was a highly cultivated king of Egypt who was murdered; his body was cut into fourteen pieces, and Isis, his sister and wife, reassembled the pieces— all but the missing "virile member"—and together with her son Horus avenged Osiris's death.

The Egyptian god Osiris represented male reproductive capacities, and according to Plutarch, who in his treatment of mythology frequently compared Egyptian and Greek legends, Osiris figured a sort of animating originary principle akin to a portion of the right triangle. In the *Moralia* Plutarch writes that the upright in such a triangle "may be likened to the male, the base to the female, and the hypotenuse to the child of both, and so Osiris may be regarded as the origin, Isis as the recipient, and Horus as perfected result" (*Moralia* 5:135).[55] Plutarch conjectures that like the Greeks the Egyptians held that triangle in high esteem; in Plato's *Republic*, he says, the right triangle represents the form through which one might most closely figure the nature of the universe (5:135). That the Greeks might use such an abstraction to figure the world and the principles motivating it is not unique: the Egyptians used their mythology, and perhaps especially the story of Isis and Osiris, to illustrate that material objects expressed fundamental abstractions. For example, an Egyptian legend had it that Osiris's resurrection led to repeated dismemberment and reassembly, and that cycle communicated a fundamental truth about the world. Of that legend Plutarch writes, "It is not . . . out of keeping that they have a legend that the soul of Osiris is everlasting and imperishable, but that his body Typhon oftentimes dismembers and causes to disappear" (5:131).[56] That is because

> that which really is and is perceptible and good is superior to destruction and change. The images from it with which the sensible and corporeal is impressed, and the relations, forms, and likenesses which this takes upon itself, like impressions of seals in wax, are not permanently lasting, but disorder and disturbance overtakes them, being driven hither from the upper reaches, and

fighting against Horus, whom Isis brings forth, beholden of all, as the image of the perceptible world (5:131).

Osiris's unchanging and animating soul counters Isis's materiality. She represents "the female principle of Nature, and is receptive of every form of generation" (5:129) and "because of the force of Reason, she turns herself to this thing or that and is receptive of all manner of shapes and forms" (5:129).

The story of Isis and Osiris offers more than a simple reconfirmation that the feminine represented inert matter and the masculine figured productive intellectual force, however. Through its recounting of Osiris's fragmentation and the reassembly of his body it provides a means to conjoin the ancient but nevertheless still operative formula of the masculine idealized animating principle with two other concerns implicated in psychoanalytic notions of the phallus: the impossible injunction to emulate the figure of the father that boys in Western culture are faced with, and the unconscious nature of the link articulating ideal signified to material signifier. The significant elements of the story—and Goux's commentary will be of decisive significance—involve the manner in which Osiris's body was fragmented and what resulted from the attack. As the myth goes, Osiris "was to deliver the Egyptians from their destitute and brutish manner of living" (5:35), but Typhon, representative of evil, particularly as such evil is a corruption of the good, devised a scheme to encase him in a chest and seal it with molten lead; Isis discovered the crime, and later removed the body to mourn her dead brother and consort.[57] Typhon, who was hunting by night, came across the dead Osiris, and "recognizing the body he divided it into fourteen parts and scattered them, each in a different place" (5:45). Isis learned of the deed and "sought for them again, sailing through the swamps in a boat of papyrus. . . . The traditional result of Osiris's dismemberment is that there are many so-called tombs of Osiris in Egypt; for Isis held a funeral for each part when she had found it" (5:45). Nevertheless, "of all the parts of Osiris's body the only one which Isis did not find was the male member, for the reason that this had been at once tossed into the river, and the lepidotus, the sea-bream, and the pike had fed upon it. . . . But Isis made a replica of the member to take its place, and consecrated the phallus, in honour of which the Egyptians even at the present day celebrate a festival" (5:45–47).[58] Strikingly for us as moderns, Plutarch believes that the symbolic significance of the dismembering and reassembly in the Isis and Osiris myth is completely obvious. Specifically, he writes that Isis's having fashioned a replica of the missing male member "plainly comes round to this doctrine, that the creative and germinal power of the god, at the very first, acquired moisture as its substance, and through moisture combined with whatever was by nature capable of participating in generation" (5:89).

What may have been obvious to Plutarch and his contemporaries, however, as well as to the generations of Greeks and Egyptians that preceded them, may not at all be obvious to us. In his extraordinarily penetrating analysis of the phallus's historical dimensions, Goux argues that what gives us as moderns so much difficulty understanding this most notoriously puzzling of signifiers is precisely the fact that something has been lost, that a connection in other circumstances quite explicit only persists now for us moderns in unconscious dimensions. What has been lost in the myth for us, in short, is twofold: on the one hand the comparatively simple mutilation of a body part that is replaced with a quite explicitly constructed representation; and on the other hand the particular nature of the articulation joining material and ideal, signifier and signified. But the other, far more difficult to conceptualize loss is the form of knowledge represented by myth that speaks more or less directly to members of the culture in which such knowledge is active. The components of loss and its constructed replacement in the myth of Isis and Osiris are what constitutes the present-day, mainly psychoanalytic notion of the phallus.

Goux emphasizes the patent constructedness of the phallus that replaced Osiris's missing penis, underscoring that "the phallus is a fabrication. It is a constructed model. It is an artifact that simulates what is missing, at the same time rendering it sacred and larger than life to make it a cult object."[59] Similarly, Lacan writes that "we see first of all that the phallus is in no way identical to the organ in belonging to the body, length, member, organ with a function. The use of the word which by far dominates is its use with respect to a simulacrum, a sign, in whatever mode it presents itself."[60] But why would anyone form a cult around the representation of a missing penis?[61] Would such a cult have formed if the irretrievable part of Osiris's body had been, say, his elbow? It would seem unlikely: the phallus as a prosthesis or as a manufactured substitute replaces the missing penis because it is that part of the human anatomy that is irreducibly male; it thus countervails dismembering and the concomitant reduction to materiality that that would imply. To that end a human construction supersedes natural integrity, by which I mean a state of affairs preceding the notion of divisibility only apparent after division has occurred. The phallus simultaneously signifies a lost integrity—an integrity that is only apparent or even, perhaps, existent once it is lost—as well as that integrity's relationship to animating spirit immune from destruction and change.

A cult object thus seems to have formed around the artificial construction that displaced the unsalvageable penis in order to venerate the conjunction of human artifice and the animating principles of reason and ideality figured by the male. Goux writes that "if the phallus fills in for the absent, destroyed, and lost penis (due to a savage and sub-human aggression), this supplement is also valorized, but on a higher plane (it is elevation itself) in exchange for the sacrifice and the loss."[62] Privileging form-giving power over inert matter, the phallus represented for Egyptians and Greeks the portion of ideal maleness dedicated to creation and reason, but in its very presence in religious festivals and rituals it simultaneously signaled the limits of such masculine power: real men have material, and hence corruptible, changeable bodies, and consequently can only ever approximate the power of which the phallus is an unfulfilled promise. Furthermore, the phallus's material presence in initiation rituals and religious festivals contaminated the signifier's ideal integrity in the very act of invocation that its presence accomplishes.

All of which should go to show that the phallus is less about any sort of visual or material echo of a penis, and more about a pure articulation, one not so much based on anything biological, but providing a link conjoining the biological and the cultural. Nevertheless, the idea that the phallus is some sort of super penis persists. A cliché of contemporary cultural criticism, especially as that criticism focuses on gender politics, is that the penis cannot measure up to the phallus, and that is supposed to explain why male nudity is a relatively rare cultural phenomenon. In what is no doubt the most exhaustive treatment of the material, Peter Lehman writes that "the awe we attribute to the striking visibility of the penis is best served by keeping it covered up."[63] Lehman maintains that keeping the penis invisible is the most efficacious way to preserve patriarchal power,[64] and that as we see in mainstream cinema "the important point is precisely that all penises are inadequate to the phallus, that none of them can measure up to it."[65] In a similar formulation, he writes that "penis size relates to castration anxiety because it evidences that the mere possession of a penis may not fulfill the function of adequately marking the male body."[66] Lehman's speculation concerning penis-size jokes and the comparatively few instances of male frontal nudity occurring in mainstream cinema focuses on the penis's inability to achieve phallic dimensions, a postulate that implicitly suggests that the phallus not only has penile shape and scope, but that it is some sort of disembodied organ, one whose immense and incomparable magnitude severs it from any material body, save perhaps that of Paul Bunyon. But how did it come to pass that modern audiences apparently find large penises most desirable—at least from the standpoint of the visual pleasure afforded in film and photography— when ancient audiences clearly prized small penises? In her exhaustive study of ancient Athenian culture, Eva C. Keuls maintains that "dainty" penises afforded Athenian consumers of pottery and other visual media the most pleasure. "Large sex organs were considered coarse and ugly," she writes, "and were banished to the domains of abstraction, of caricature, of satyrs, and of barbarians."[67] Yet, while vase paintings' culturally "realistic" depictions of Athenian men emphasized delicate male genitals, the ritualistic display of the phallus consisted of a massively disproportionate male member, often abstracted completely from any body, paraded through the streets or revealed in initiation rituals.[68] Clearly those most intimately associated with the construction of the phallus perceived little resonance between that object and the exemplary penis. As if to drive the point home with an almost absurd specificity, Lacan points out that although males in various species have penises, "relationships between fish are not phallic relationships."[69]

Given the disjunction the ancient Greeks maintained between ideal penis and venerated and constructed phallus, it seems appropriate to stress once again that the phallus is a fabrication and an articulation, and I want to emphasize anew the polysemantic richness of that latter word. The phallus articulates the material and the ideal in that it allows them access to one another, thus making signification possible, and it articulates—joins *and* expresses—the cultural values making such a conjunction practicable in the first place. In short, the phallus is the missing link, the pure construction that initiates difference and in

that very gesture founds difference as "about" something. That is because we cannot conceptualize a socially significant "pure" difference,
one that grounds the possibility for further difference and hence coherent signification, without the simultaneous recognition of an ideologically regulating system that privileges specific forms. The phallus is
the signifier of how fundamental or primal—perhaps even originary—
difference is founded in our culture: not necessarily as sexual difference, but as intersubjective affiliation that may have a great deal to do
with sexual difference, but which, like kinship relations, is not necessarily exhausted by such difference. The phallus signifies the unit or
measure of abstracted subjective difference as that difference finds material expression in real historical and cultural contexts. As soon as
idealized difference attains material expression, the abstraction is lost,
of course: the phallus is pure difference expressible only in material,
culturally available form.

Like some others, Goux finds that the culturally available form that
provides the phallus with a means of expression is the regulation of
reproduction. Much like the position of the father I described above,
which can only ever be inferred and symbolic because of the lack of any
visible, direct connection to the matter of reproduction, the phallus
remains a signifier of culture's attempts to regulate nature. Goux writes
that in its relationship to the penis

> what emerges is the radical connection which the phallus would
> have the privilege of ensuring between nature and culture, be-
> tween the biological and the signifying. Because if the phallus is a
> signifier, distinct from the organ which it represents, it is because
> reproductive *(génésique)* activity is subject to prohibitions, to pre-
> scriptions: it is inscribed in the structures of kinship. It is finally
> the constraints felt by man to have the vital operation of genera-
> tion pass through the ways of the signifier, or the ordered ex-
> change, which imposes the substitution of a phallic dialectic in
> place of the animal drives or sexuality.[70]

The phallus signifies male participation in reproduction, but because
it is constructed and symbolic and hence of a delineated and consequently regulated order, masculine animating reason—logos—maps the
otherwise undifferentiated realm of being that in reproduction osten-

sibly consists of pure, unmarked feminine matter. Regulation of reproduction and of kinship presuppose the phallus because such regulation
establishes fundamental cultural metaphors on a community's apparently natural bodies, allowing laws of the body and bodies of laws to
appear to express one another. But the phallus as explicitly constructed
substitute asseverates that the penis can never suffice: not because it
isn't big enough, but because it isn't immaterial enough to express the
cultural lineage whose relationship to reproduction and to the law
aligned itself on the side of the purely ideational. Lacan calls such lineage
the heritage of the male ancestors; he writes: "In the end, man is only
ever virile through an indefinite series of proxies which come to him
from all his male ancestors, passing through the direct ancestor."[71]

As we saw above, Butler argued that the penis and the phallus enter-
tain a negative dialectical relationship, such that the phallus negates the
penis "in order to symbolize and signify in its privileged way." While I
obviously agree with Butler that the phallus differentiates itself from
the penis, my reasons differ somewhat from hers. Following Goux, I
would like to suggest that a real penis cannot approach phallic dimensions not because of its size, but because of its very nature: it is flesh
and blood. Therein lies the paradoxical relationship of masculinity to
the phallus, at least—and perhaps only—to the extent that masculinity
and the male genitals evoke one another: while the male principle has
traditionally consisted of form, idea, and spirit, real males embody per-
ishable matter, and thus share with traditionally feminine principles the
traits of variability and corruptibility. Goux writes:

> The mother, matter, nature, the immediate, the sensible—all of
> this is on the side of the corruptible, the variable, and the mortal
> (like the body and the penis itself), while the father, the idea, the
> spirit, the represented—and also the phallus—are on the side of
> the invariable and the eternal. From this it is clear that the penis is
> the natural organ that "belongs" to the mother (joins with her,
> attaches to her realm) and that it must be abolished in order for
> this juncture to be destroyed and replaced by the spiritual junc-
> ture that phallic simulacrum ensures.[72]

What the myth of Isis and Osiris teaches us, Goux has demonstrated, is
that castration encodes far more than a physical and narcissistic wound

to the male body and psyche, and that is a position perfectly consistent with Lacanian psychoanalysis: in the fourth seminar (*La Relation d'objet*), Lacan concisely stated that "castration can only be classified in the category of symbolic debt."[73] Castration is always counteracted by prosthetic replacement, whether such replacement consists of an artificial body part, as in the case of Osiris, or symbolic recompense, as in the case of the Lacanian subject renouncing imaginary plenitude and accepting satisfaction through the symbolic.

Such a conclusion brings us around to one of the perhaps more paradoxical consequences of the phallic theory I have just been examining. If castration as symbolic debt always involves prosthetic replacement, then the real penis takes on its value as something to be envied not by being a natural appendage on the male body, but by becoming phallic—that is, by being constructed and by having meaning conferred on it from elsewhere. That should follow directly from the observation noted earlier that so-called penis envy has little to do with male flesh and everything to do with the power and privilege metaphorically associated with that flesh.[74] It also follows from what we observed in chapter 3 concerning the male genitals: only white penises can perform the cultural work of endowing their possessors with the power and privilege generally associated with masculine ascendancy. To receive its stamp of cultural approval, however, that male flesh must receive its value from another, culturally valorized source; otherwise, male dominance would be a natural part of culture that, lacking any outside, simply and unproblematically reproduces itself. Lacan asserts that assuming the heterosexual male position entails accepting castration and hence acceptance of a particular order, both in the sense of an arrangement and an injunction. That order derives from a very particular source:

> The assumption of the very sign of the virile position, of masculine heterosexuality, implies castration from the very beginning. That is what the Freudian notion of the Oedipal teaches us. Precisely because the male, exactly opposite to the feminine position, perfectly possesses a natural appendage, because he holds the penis as belonging *(appartenance)*, it's necessary that he have it from someone else, in this relation to what is the real in the symbolic—he who is really the father.[75]

The penis supplemented by cultural or symbolic weight achieves phallic proportions because of the lineage that masculine privilege and abstract principles bestow on it. However, the phallic proportions so acquired extend beyond what can be simply mapped onto a body part—as we saw in the preceding chapter, for example, penises that were not white or that were circumcised lacked the cultural force to accede to phallic pretensions. Because the phallus as signifier of the link between biology and culture regulates the social use of metaphor and substitution, it must do so in all domains of biological and cultural intersection, and that would implicate any and all body parts as well as bodily attributes not generally reducible to "parts."[76] To argue that the phallus is really only a cleverly and densely concealed penis substitute in the service of reproducing masculine hegemony is to overlook the phallus's function as installer of fundamental cultural metaphors regulating exchange, both symbolic and economic, and guarantor of the kinds of significatory consistency we generally associate with diverse forms of human identity.

So why bother, really, with the penis/phallus distinction? Since we know we live in a male-dominated culture, isn't it simply splitting hairs to insist on a distinction between the forms of cultural domination and a symbol of those forms? What harm could there be in not maintaining a strict separation between penis and phallus? I would like to suggest that to argue that the phallus is a disguised penis is in many ways to reproduce the very form of hegemony that most critiques of the phallus purport to undermine. Denunciations of the phallus that attempt to align it with the penis, particularly by trying to show either that those who theorize about it deliberately promote a masculinist agenda or that they do so unwittingly, assign to the phallic signifier a unified focus and a specificity that cast complex cultural negotiations as unified expressions of strictly male dominance. Shunted aside are all ideologically invested bodily expressions that exceed the gendered specificity rendered by the penis. In other words, to argue for a confluence between penis and phallus in the attempt to identify a sexist or otherwise masculinist agenda at work in this fundamental signifier (or, indeed, in its description) is to overlook the other, vastly more complex work that the phallus performs.[77] But to what extent are these two positions—that the phallus is really a penis, or that the phallus is more complex than it may perhaps at first appear—simply arcane philosophical ones that amount to little more than so much academic hair-splitting? Or, to reprise two questions considered at the beginning of this chapter, what is at stake in the debate over what the phallus really signifies, and why would it matter if someone got it wrong?

The answer depends on the extent to which one finds troubling or politically problematic the great globalizing narratives generally associated with modernism and frequently lambasted for their repressive, homogenizing effects. As I argued in chapter 1 in my discussion of the Oedipus myth, psychoanalysis has provided a circumscribing narrative of human difference and identity by containing a nexus of social classifiers, including age, civic identity, and status as a cultural initiate within the comparatively unified category of sex. Freudian and Lacanian psychoanalysis traditionally cast fundamental difference as primarily sexual with little regard for the kind of cultural work required to disarticulate sex as a phenomenon separate from the nexus of social identifiers based on signification to which we attribute an identifiable integrity. Not only is it the case that we disrupt both the subtleties and the intricacies of human identifiers by artificially isolating a handful of characteristics that seem in current epistemological and ideological conditions to form a unit—and oftentimes in other locales or periods those units lose their apparent integrities—but we also reproduce certain forms of hegemony in the process. The social identifier "masculine," for instance, simultaneously describes more than simply those people with biologically male bodies, as Judith Halberstam demonstrated, and less than those people, as the previous chapter's discussion of white penises showed. By isolating sex as fundamental or somehow originary, we not only artificially isolate it from other forms of difference, but we also and in that very process factitiously create a unified field of meaning responsible in the first instance for governing most if not all other forms of meaning. In short, critiques of the phallus that fail to consider how the phallic signifier comprehends other human identifiers—and thus how masculinity is as much the product of culture as any other human identifier—reproduce the form of masculine hegemony they would purport to undo by casting masculinity either as seamless and apodictic or as something that needs to be exposed or undone. Such critiques are in fact themselves phallic, at least as that attribute has been traditionally understood. They inadvertently or otherwise produce their own defense of the phallus as a monologic and monolithic signifier not only somehow unilaterally invested in gender; they also leave out of the operation through which bodies and means of signification become articulated any other ideologically invested morphological characteristics that have been conscripted in the service of domination.

It is nevertheless useful to interrogate the phallus as a signifier in order to determine not only how we might be inadvertently sustaining hegemonic positions by buttressing their claims to natural ascendancy, but also how the oddly-named signifier might function outside of areas traditionally reserved for sex. If "phallus" appropriately named for Egyptians and Greeks the cultural construction that explicitly articulated male animating powers to female bodily matter, it does not necessarily follow that an analogous operation of quilting symbolic and ideological abstractions to material bodies needs to be restricted to constructions of masculinity. We have packed into the identifier "sex" social relations that, for as morphologically informed as they may appear to be, nevertheless do not always pertain, strictly speaking, to that category. Furthermore, sexual difference is largely inseparable from other forms of difference. Thus, although the modern notions of white masculinity are heir to the Egyptian and Greek conceptions of phallic construction in their dependence on ideological bodily relations, their different histories and cultural arrangements stipulate divergence from the gender-only parameter of ancient phallicism.

By looking at the work of Lacan, Goux, Butler, Silverman, Gallop, and others, I have argued that the modern phallic function performs a double articulation. On the one hand it allies the materiality of the physical vehicle necessary to convey information to the ideality of the acoustic image invoked in signification. On the other hand, and structurally homologous, the phallus conjoins to the seemingly incontrovertible naturalism of the body a specific and immaterial signifying effect, one based on the regulation of kinship and reproduction, and by extension of many if not most other forms of exchange that require an abstraction in order to unite two unlike things.[78] But that double articulation of material to abstract and of body to language surpasses the frontiers of gender for the obvious reason that such an articulation applies to a host of other social identifiers, and in each of the previous chapters I have sketched out it obfuscated social operations functioning under the auspices of another, perhaps more apparent operation.

That the word "phallus" is used to describe the tremendously complex operation of articulating the material to the abstract, especially as that operation concerns the interconnection between body and ideologically based signification, is simultaneously appropriate and misleading. Appropriate, because masculine hegemony inflects most domains of signification, and especially those domains involving bodily matters such as kinship and reproduction: thus, phallogocentrism, which describes the manner in which our language is permeated with both subtle and explicit advancing of male interests, names a fundamental metaphor—that is, that which provides the foundation of sense or meaning to other metaphors—for Western culture. Misleading, because although the phallic function as I have described it in this chapter accomplishes the task of articulating a link between materiality and ideality in large part through sexual difference, its operation is not exhausted by such difference. Thus, critiques of the phallus need to focus not simply on the gendered bias that this complex signifier's name insinuates, but on the entire operation through which bodies and signification merge.

And that is why phallic posturing, to return to one of the frequent critical phrases we saw at the beginning of this chapter, is redundant: whatever articulates the material and the ideal can only ever function through a process of placing or positing, which as we have seen lies at the heart of posturing. The phallus in its material manifestation deriving from the myth of Isis and Osiris as well as in its philosophical and psychoanalytic dimensions has always been the work of construction to substitute for something missing. Whether that construction involves an artificial penis or an abstraction capable of synthesizing inconsonant expressive systems, the entity so produced necessarily bears the bias inherent in any construction that carves something out of the inchoate realm of being. The phallus as a construction is the effect and the cause of positing; it is the effect and the cause of the pact of language by which particular human beings recognize the same objects and consider themselves as similar kinds of subjects.

However much the phallus as a bodily and ideological signifier articulates the material and the abstract in ideologically, historically, and culturally specific ways, because we can never exhaust the specificity of all those particulars, the phallic function will always exceed our capacity to name it. That is why any attempt to define what the phallus is, as opposed to what it does, can never succeed, and that is also why such an attempt produces the discourse of the master that we saw in chapter 3. The discourse of the master is characterized by the illusion of adequation between signifier and referent; such a discourse eschews desire and self-division, and its most salient structural feature is its dependency on master signifiers, which it produces and deploys as a means to restrict the other's interpretation to within the parameters of its own moral, political, and economic systems.[79] Any attempt to define the phallus, including the move to equate it to a penis, reproduces the discourse of the master because it excludes what is repressed from the master's speech. That is, those elements—be they human identities, forms of knowledge, ways of being, or simply objects—that have no place in the master's system cannot be represented in that system. Critiques of or attacks on the phallus that attempt to reduce its function strictly along the lines of gender or sexual difference consequently and ironically reinforce the hegemonic discourse they would attempt to undo.

And that is why, to return to one of the questions posed at the beginning of this chapter, it matters if someone gets the phallus wrong. To get the phallus wrong, provided such error comes down on the side of an indexical inaccuracy that would attempt to fix its meaning, is to foreclose fantasy, desire, and the relational nature of truth effects whereby closure is eschewed for what Lacan referred to as "mythic" knowledge, a form of knowing and understanding that privileges the disconnected over the hegemonic, the partial over the absolute, and the relational over the unvarying. To get the phallus wrong, in other words, is to leave out the other ideologically charged bodily functions that participate along with sexual difference to graft signification onto the body. It is to reproduce and sustain masculine and white hegemony because it is to unify and fortify those entities as monologic and first-instance causes—masculinity because of its long-standing status as logical animator of inert matter, and whiteness because of its putative invisibility. In short, to ascribe to the phallus a penile dimension or to proceed as though it is only concerned with sexual difference is to work in the service of white masculine hegemony because on the one hand it sustains the mystique of male power by reducing a complex network of difference to the single identifier "masculinity," and on the other hand it maintains whiteness in its position of invisibility, from which it can accomplish its most invidious tasks.[80] To get the phallus wrong, finally, can wind up as an implicit defense of the phallus, at least insofar as that term has traditionally indexed masculine power and privilege.

To complement the inadvertent defense of the phallus I have been outlining I offer my own defense of the phallic function, as well as a proposal, in the following chapter, for how one might conceive of a way to eschew the hegemonic discourses of whiteness and masculinity that we have looked at up to this point. I am suggesting that we extend our interests in and critiques of the phallic function to all those domains, once restricted to the realm of gender as Goux's and others' work have shown, now involved in the sorts of body-based signification we have looked at in this and the preceding chapters. Although I do not believe, as some have suggested, that we can "unveil" the phallus, I do think it possible to bring to the fore some of those things excluded from the master discourse that makes sexual difference the site of all difference in analysis of bodies and signification.[81] As I suggested in chapter 3, hysteria figures significantly, if not necessarily conspicuously, as the underside of white masculinity as a hegemonic discourse. In the next chapter, I will look closely at hysteria, as well as at some other elements of white masculinity not traditionally associated with that identity, in order to see what we exclude from the position most often called dominant.

5. WHITE MEN AREN'T

Reverend Sykes's voice was as distant as Judge
Taylor's: 'Miss Jean Louise, stand up. Your father's
passin'.'—Harper Lee, *To Kill a Mockingbird*

Robyn Wiegman begins her *American Anatomies,* a provocative study
of race and gender in nineteenth-century America, with an assess-
ment of the analytic inadequacies for cultural analysis of binary oppositions. Specifically, she analyzes the complex of cultural meanings that
gets packed into the comparatively simple terms we have traditionally
used to designate race:

> Making the African "black" reduces the racial meanings attached to
> flesh to a binary structure of vision, and it is this structure that pre-
> cedes the disciplinary emergence of the humanities and its method-
> ological pursuits of knowledge and truth. This does not mean that
> imperialism was not well served by the negative equation between
> "blackness" and an ontological difference, but that the framework
> for such an equation must be approached in terms broader and
> more historically and culturally comprehensive than the slave
> trade and its necessity for ideological and economic justification.[1]

Wiegman wonders how and why vast numbers of individuals from a
variety of geographic and cultural locales became consolidated under
the standardizing term "black," and she also interrogates the visual
logic that consigns individuals to one or the other pole of a binary
opposition.[2] Such an opposition, she notes, apparently depends on another, perhaps more pervasive one: "In formulating an analysis of the
powerful array of prescriptions and practices that have accompanied
this society's investment in race, it becomes apparent that the binary
construction of race reiterates the logic of our culture's other, often
competing visual paradigm: sexual difference."[3]

At the close of the preceding chapter I argued that the phallic function, which articulates signifying processes and the human morphologies implicated in and by them, overruns sexual difference, which has traditionally been viewed as its unique prerogative. In this chapter I will look more closely at some specific examples of the failure of sexual difference to account adequately for the formation and maintenance of human subjectivity, in particular those unconscious or otherwise disavowed processes that exceed our capacities to name and to know them completely. Specifically, I will look at more recent examples of the phenomena we observed in chapter 3, in which early modern white masculinity secured its own identity as morphologically intact, and sustained the ideological force of that integrity by proffering a discourse of the master, one that required the participation of its others for conferral of an identity that construes itself as having no outside.

Early modern white masculinity coalesced its identity in large part first by obfuscating the morphological connections that associated whiteness with reason, and then by constructing a discourse anchored by a host of master signifiers that order knowledge in a way that best serves its agent. Furthermore, because the particular master discourse of white masculinity in the early modern period also incorporated the discourse of the hysteric, one that refuses to incarnate or otherwise comprise what paradigms of knowledge have made available to it, what resulted was a never-ending quest for an answer to the question of what it itself is. In this chapter I will concentrate more fully on the hysterical components of white masculinity, with an eye toward understanding how that hysteria has contributed to the strength of white masculinity's dominance, particularly in American contexts. The kinds of violence inflicted on black men in the United States during Reconstruction and the years that followed expressed white male hysteria, especially as it reproduced the concerns over bodily integrity, discursive unity, and the production of master signifiers. As I will show, however, traditional investigations of white masculinity that focus on the violence perpetrated against women and minorities in order to gain a sense of identity do not reveal the entire story. What complements the violence and coercion intrinsic to white masculine subjectivity is a form of hysteria, a concomitant assignation of self-division or non-integrity to the white male himself. Such internal incoherence obtains, we will see, on the morphological as well as the epistemological fronts.

Most of us have probably come to accept as given that the way we experience our bodies depends to a very great extent on the valuations and regulations our culture places on them and the parts that comprise them. As we have seen, Londa Schiebinger, Thomas Laqueur, Marjorie Garber, Stephen Greenblatt, and others have demonstrated the manner in which the ostensibly natural presence of the body has evolved according to historical and cultural logics that privilege specific morphological configurations over others, and I have shown how such putatively neutral cultural components as logic and reason encode highly charged racial agendas. At the same time, the phallic dimension of signification—that is, the material component of signification that is also and simultaneously the abstract component of the body—is the guarantor of meaning's stability for a particular cultural group. My investigations have led to the conclusion that we need to recognize the fact that cultures create morphological difference of all sorts, just as they create sexual difference by regulating reproduction and pair bonding and by defining kinship relations.

In previous chapters we saw that the "believing is seeing" phenomenon caused European observers visiting faraway locales to write ostensibly empirical reports that reproduced their culture's morphological— and hence political—values. In this chapter we will investigate the morphological constructions of whiteness and maleness in later centuries and in other locales that betray a form of hysteria on the part of those who manifest both of those characteristics. Understanding white masculinity as a form of hysteria is crucial to the disarticulation of identity and discourse—of, that is, the way real individuals inhabit that identity and the culture's construction of the impossible ideals that comprise it. That forms the crux of white masculinity's ideological grip, both on the culture and on the individuals who would aspire to that identity, because no one can ever inhabit the cultural ideals espoused, which makes failure inevitable and hence those fleeting ideals consistently valued and pursued. (And, as I will show below, that formula lies behind the mythology Freud established in his *Totem and Taboo*.) The hysteria in question here typically manifests itself in one of two ways: either individuals who identify with the dominant position implicitly or explicitly so identify by inquiring of their others who they are; or they find in those others a morphological instability, a physical and psychic lack with which they identify.

As we saw in chapter 3, one very prevalent manifestation of white male morphological hysteria concerned the presumed deliberate modification of the subaltern body. Later occasions of the apparent modification of the nonwhite body seemed less the result of deliberation. For example, Samuel Stanhope Smith, whose late eighteenth-century theories of "denominated habits of the body" we observed earlier, reports the following bizarre phenomenon: "Henry Moss, a negro in the state of Maryland, began, upwards of twenty years ago to undergo a change in the colour of his skin, from a deep black, to a clear and healthy white. . . . He was a vigorous and active man; and had never suffered any disease either at the commencement, or during the progress of the change."[4] While such a dramatic alteration in appearance seems unusual enough in itself, what is particularly striking about this transformation is the reaction of those who witnessed it: "The extraordinary nature of this phenomenon strongly attracted the attention and benevolence of the public; and the man obtained, from the liberality of those who visited him, a sum sufficient to purchase his freedom."[5] So great was the hold that "believing is seeing" had on people that it appears they could not bear the thought of a white man held in slavery; at the same time, however, the fact that he was allowed to purchase his freedom, and not liberated directly, demonstrates that people held equally firmly to the belief that some people were "really" white, while others were only formally white—the very cultural phenomenon responsible for the failure of Virginia's 1785 law specifying that a legally "white" person could be as much as one quarter "black."

Fears and anxieties concerning morphological difference were not limited to markers of race, however, and they extended well into the nineteenth century. One J. H. Van Evrie (1868), for example, neatly demonstrates how sexual difference combines and competes with other forms of morphological variation. Reconsidering the question of beardlessness that so fascinated earlier anthropological observers, particularly its relationship to other, generally abstract human qualities, he writes:

> [In our own race] the youth is beardless, and pari passu as he approaches to the maturity of manhood there is a corresponding development of beard. The intellect—the mental strength—the moral beauty, all the qualities of the inner being, as well as those

outward attributes tangible to the senses harmonize perfectly with the growth of the beard, and when that has reached its full development, it is both the signal and the proof of mature manhood. . . . The Caucasian is the only bearded race.[6]

As pointed out above, some early descriptions of people from geographic locales outside of Europe or North America highlighted gender instability, as characteristics Europeans took for granted to be singly possessed by one sex or the other seemed to occur randomly on men and women of color. Nineteenth-century American writers continued that tradition. Quoting one Winwood Reade, James Hunt dissertates in his *Negro's Place in Nature* (1868):

The men of Africa are feminine. Their faces are smooth, their breasts are frequently as full as those of European women; their voices are never gruff or deep. Their fingers are long; and they can be very proud of their rosy nails. While the women are nearly always ill-shaped after their girlhood, the men have gracefully moulded limbs, and always are after a feminine type—the arms rounded, the legs elegantly formed, without too much muscular development, and the feet delicate and small.[7]

In chapter 3 we saw examples of white men ascribing forms of fragmentation to their presumed others in a move that seemed designed to diminish the difference between the ideals of masculinity and masculinity's manifestations in those real individuals. A good portion of the distance separating the ideal from the actual specimens arose when existing taxonomies could not successfully negotiate the multiple human variables of sex and race.

We also saw situations in which white men sought implicit confirmation of their identities from the very men whom they had determined to be less male than they. In a process structurally analogous to hysteria, they identified with the lack in the other, sought knowledge from it, and then found that knowledge insufficient for confirmation. The question at hand concerns the manner in which race, a human identifier with a cultural and historical specificity both far more specific and far more recent than those of sex, can nevertheless inflect subjectivity in unconscious and highly determining ways. Our avenues of investigation will continue to lead to the mutual inflection of body and knowledge, and I will focus once again on psychoanalysis and the raced and gendered body.

Lacan's celebrated mirror stage, which theorizes the human subject's entry into language, postulates that "the image of [man's] body is the principle of every unity he perceives in objects."[8] Because the image of our bodies is an imaginary construction, however, it is consequently "maintained by a succession of momentary experiences, and this experience either alienates man from himself, or else ends in a destruction, a negation of the object."[9] Lacan is seeking a way to understand not only the process through which we can recognize objects by finding ourselves in them, but also and correlatively the process of displacement itself, particularly as that operation depends on the stability of the naming world. That is, if the subject maintained a purely narcissistic relationship to objects—an extremely radical form of perceiving the unity of those objects—then the objects would be only as momentary for the perceiver as his or her fleeting experience of self at that particular time. The stability of objects and thus of perception that we actually experience derives from the symbolic order and from the pact on naming whereby individuals agree on an arbitrary sign and assign it to a specific object.[10] The imaginary and symbolic domains consequently come together at this point: where the fluid experience of narcissism as it derives from the experience of objects finds a more fixed dimension as the symbolic order provides more permanence through the enduring contract of language.

We have already seen that when some European men visited other locales and found that the men they observed there were lacking in some crucial way, they arrived at the unusual implicit conclusion that all penises must somehow really be white. The operation we observed in chapter 3 concerning the fragmentation of the nonwhite male body contributed to the argument I made in the succeeding chapter, namely that the phallus as a cultural construction maintains little if any reference to the male genitals, and focuses instead on the complex processes through which particular social identifiers—not necessarily relating to sexual difference—become master signifiers and hence help to gauge the value of other signifiers. The convergence of imaginary and symbolic in a narcissistic recognition of objects as described in Lacan's mirror stage joins with the phallic establishment of master signifiers to create a hierarchy of human identity, and in the particular case we are addressing here we observe a striking paradox: when identifying as a white male means ordering the world according to systems of knowledge founded on the white male morphology and the rational systems to which it gave rise, the external coherence that the world appears to have destabilizes the white male sense of self; when the aforementioned white male grasps his sense of identity and fixes it firmly, not as an ongoing reaction or response to the world but as a thing in itself, the world at large seems to fragment and lose its coherence.

That is perfectly consonant with psychoanalytic theories concerning the human subject and its relationship to the world and its objects.[11] Here I want to focus on specifically American manifestations in more contemporary contexts in which white males not only project fragmentation or other insufficiencies onto other men, but explicitly engage in the process of building a discourse of the master, which we noted above consists in part of repudiating self-division and fantasy. Furthermore, the white males under consideration base that discourse on the paradox just noted, in which to identify as an integral unity causes a loss of external meaning, while to identify with an external object leads to a sense of internal disconnectedness.

The most striking examples of this phenomenon occur in the years immediately following the American Civil War, and they extend in a slightly modified form up to the present time. Much if not most of the historical and cultural studies surrounding the violence done to African American men in the nineteenth century and onward focuses on how practices of lynching were carried out in the name of protecting Southern white women. The first incarnation of the Ku Klux Klan, which formed shortly after emancipation, encoded the end of legalized white male domination over chattel slaves as an assault on the sexual purity of white women, an assault that according to the racial logic of the time would have devastating contaminating effects on the white race as a whole. The ritualistic violence inflicted on black men displayed white masculine violence acting in the service of threatened white femininity. Although the Ku Klux Klan has often publicly repudiated acts of violence,[12] what is particularly striking is that official Klan documents explicitly associate feminine chastity and household integrity with the form of racial purity that gave rise to the white male anxiety underpinning the belief that all penises are fundamentally white.[13] In the *Papers Read at the Meeting of Grand Dragons at their First Annual Meeting held at*

Asheville, North Carolina, July 1923, "Klankraft," a word standing for the KKK's beliefs and the practices necessary to uphold them, is defined as follows:

It is the spirit of pure patriotism toward this, our glorious country, and the preservation of American ideals and institutions, it is the exemplification of the noble ideals of chivalry, wherein the chastity of our women, the protection of our homes, the relief of the weak and unfortunate, the unqualified allegiance to our flag and government, the sublime reverence for our Lord and Savior, Jesus Christ; the maintenance of the supremacy of that race of men whose blood is not tainted with the colorful pigments of the universe, and the observance of that rule of all rules: honor and justice in all things pertaining to our fellow man. These are but living definitions of the golden word "Klankraft."[14]

A certain anxiety emanates from writings such as these and the ones we saw in previous chapters, an anxiety that surrounded the white male capacity to assert dominance and to demonstrate self-evident superiority over women and nonwhite men. In the citation above, we note a curious identification with the "weak and unfortunate," an identification that is even more explicit in other passages from this official KKK document.[15] For example, the Grand Dragon of Georgia laments not only the carpetbaggers who swept "like vultures" over the South, but also and more important the fact that "the ignorant negro rode into power, and the black heel was placed upon the neck of the proudest race the sun ever shone upon."[16]

The anxieties manifested in documents such as these express not simply a rhetorical move to justify illegal and brutal violence perpetrated against mainly black men in the years following enfranchisement and beyond, but also a genuine concern over the integrity of the white male body and the identity it appeared to guarantee. White men in post–Civil War American culture seemed to experience as a threat to their manhood the collapse of an entire social and economic regime, but as I argued in the previous chapter, what culture oftentimes encodes as gender or sexual difference merely assigns a stable, culturally recognized signification to transversing strands of social meaning that simply may not be readily containable in a single category.[17] Thus, white masculinity in the years following the American Civil War attempted to fit what amounted to the round peg of sex into the square hole of an enormously complex shifting culture: the fit could be forced, but sex had to take on a tremendously overdetermined set of other forms of difference in the process. Sexual difference, particularly as it appeared to be an issue for white men, became more than ever something to defend, to the death if need be. But what made the defense of sexual difference distinct during Reconstruction from what it may have been in other times or places was the fact that difference itself, and not necessarily the "fair sex," appeared to be under attack.

As if to protect themselves from the charge of sexual or racial in-differentiation, authors of travel writing and anti-abolition expository prose often focused on indistinction between the sexes in people of color. White masculinity had to guard against all potential breaches, and as a consequence had to stand out as the most sharply delineated identity, that which was least contaminated by other forms of subjec-tivity precisely because it had to gauge those other forms of subjectivity. Thus, with respect to white masculinity's relative distinction from other social identifiers, James Hunt, in his *Negro's Place in Nature* imagined: "There seems to be, generally, less difference between the Negro and Negress, than between the European male and female."[18] Hunt and many of his contemporaries saw white men as wholly apart from other kinds of people, and the more refined sexual difference they attributed to whites correlates what we observed in chapter 3 concerning the rela-tive morphological integrity of white masculinity. And, as in the defini-tion of Klankraft above, we can see how the integrity of the white male stood in for a host of ideological components in traditional Klan rheto-ric, which generally opposed the vulnerable white female body to such masculine ideals as morphological and national integrity. Illustrating the manner in which sexual difference stood in for other social iden-tifiers, William Joseph Simmons, the Klan's "Imperial Wizard," ad-dressed his fellow Klansmen in 1914 by listing the physical, social, moral, and vocational aspects of klannishness. Strikingly, the complex-ity of all of those dimensions boiled down to one thing: "Oh, Klansmen, minimize not the importance of your sacred mission in life and dis-count not your most laudable achievement that is—to attain to the high standard of klannish character—Matchless Manhood!"[19] Similarly, dur-ing the 1867 reorganization of the Ku Klux Klan, a prescript under-scores the tight relation between Klan behavior and ideals of white masculinity as defined through traditional models: "This is an institution of Chivalry, Humanity, mercy, and Patriotism; embodying in its genius and its principles all that is chivalric in conduct, noble in sentiment, generous in manhood, and patriotic in purpose."[20]

Sexual difference had encoded a complex of other forms of difference long before the establishment of the second Ku Klux Klan in the 1920s. And if a potential insufficiency of sexual distinction obsessed white men, they seemed to enact that obsession on the black men and white women around them as far back as Reconstruction. Perhaps the manifestation of white men's fixation most often observed was the fear that black men would rape white women as a means of revenge against the white man. Both Alex King and Clifton Breckinridge, participants in the First Annual Conference Held Under the Auspices of the Southern Society for the Promotion of the Study of Race Conditions and Problems in the South (1900), argued that during the time of slavery black men never raped white women, but that after emancipation that problem exploded.[21] Modern historians have made the same claim: Trudier Harris reports that "during the years of the Civil War, when white men left their wives, daughters, and homes in the hands of black men, not a single instance of rape was reported."[22] Regardless of the truth value of such a claim, what is significant is that white men understood the rape of white women as a form of protest or revenge for their treatment of black men. That is, it made sense to them (in that it did not astonish them) that such might be a logical response on the part of the men they had enslaved. Thus, if white men at the close of the Civil War and in the years to follow distinguished themselves through their "matchless manhood" and chivalric behavior, the potential that those things might no longer be the exclusive province of white masculinity seemed to loom forth. Creating difference appeared to be a convenient solution.

One of the principal strategies in the creation of difference focused on spotlighting the white woman as a pivot around which male difference could maneuver. The white woman thus stood both as the racial source from which issued either uncontaminated white children or racial mongrels; and, more important, as the more complex guarantor of the integrity of the white male, the object that he alone could possess, or, what Robyn Wiegman calls "the ultimate symbol of white civilization."[23] The striking thing about this symbol of the ostensibly superior white civilization, however, is its apparent fragility, which should give us some pause when we consider the sorts of contemporary rhetoric that identified white culture as the natural world dominator—in his *Tempter of Eve*, for example, Charles Carroll cites his contemporary Haeckel, who refers to "the cultured, progressive white, whose flashing intellect, restless energy, and indomitable courage discovers, conquers, and develops continents."[24] It seems, in fact, that the white woman's vulnerability contributed to her worth as moral touchstone, much as a delicately wrought piece of crystal accrues value in part by surviving the passage of time intact. On the one hand the white woman represented the incomparable pinnacle of virtue, as J. H. Van Evrie found when he compared the moral constitutions of white and black women and found the latter lacking because he believed they were unable to blush: "It is not intended to say," he concluded, "that the negress has not a moral nature; it is only intended to demonstrate the fact that she has not *the* moral nature of the white woman."[25] On the other hand, white men saw the white woman as a frequent target for assault, perhaps precisely because she represented for them the privileged possession guaranteeing their distinction. In an article defending lynching, Alex C. King underscored the aggression he perceived in assaults on white women when he wrote that "no crime strikes at the integrity of race or so insults its purity as the crime against women."[26]

But in order for the sense of imperiled white civilization to achieve its full emotional force, the vulnerability of white women had to be combined with the contrite powerlessness of the white Southern man. In the prescripts of the KKK, for example, we read the following: "We note the smile of helpless masculinity gives but feebly assuring answer to its mate's frown of distressful inquiry, as the sullen roll of the drum and the beastly roar of the savage rasp the chords of racial instinct. As we watch the noble countenance of modest, innocent Southern maidenhood pale into death-defying scorn, as she contemplates the hellish design of the black brute in human form."[27] Endangered white womanhood could only deliver its full emotional impact when accompanied by a self-reproaching masculinity. This suggests, in fact, that it was actually white masculinity experiencing the cultural threat. In her *Women of the Klan*, Kathleen M. Blee corroborates that point when she shows that while the image of threatened white Southern womanhood and the virtue it stood for strongly motivated white men in the years immediately following emancipation, that strategy was less successful for the second Klan: "The second Klan, too, tried at first to use white woman-hood to symbolize threatened religious, national, and racial supremacy. But newly won female enfranchisement and women's political experi-ence complicated this strategy."[28] White women no longer adequately symbolized imperiled Southern civilization when they began to take on for themselves political agency, which underscores the extent to which white masculinity continued to require the participation of instrumen-talities external to it to provide its shape and dimensions.

But Blee also points out that endangered white womanhood encoded not a threat to specific women, but a menace to white men's property. The hierarchical division of male and female and of white and black, she argues, "kept white women within a role that was exalted in prose but sharply divided from and inferior to the privileged social role of white men. White men monopolized rights to property and the fran-chise and dictated the rules by which their wives, children, slaves, ser-vants, and hired labor would live."[29] In the years following the Civil War, white men had to renegotiate their relationship to human property, since they no longer had legal rights over chattel slaves. They did, nev-ertheless, retain coercive ideological control, which they deployed in part by underscoring erotic access to the white woman as a mark of masculine privilege. Black men forbidden access to the white woman lacked the means to express the only culturally approved outlet for masculine desire, and hence fell short of the male ideal. Thus, the white woman endowed the full form of masculine distinction on the white man. Implicitly, she was a form of property and, as Cheryl I. Harris has observed so was whiteness itself, a phenomenon we will investigate below.

In his *Hooded Americanism,* David Chalmers cogently analyzes the sexual dynamic operating in the selection of the white woman as the symbol of a culture. Analyzing her relationship to the white male, he writes: "[White womanhood] not only stood at the core of his sense of property and chivalry, she represented the heart of his culture. By the fact that she was not accessible to the Negro, she marked the ultimate line of difference between white and black. . . . It was impossible to assault either the Southern woman or the South without having im-plicitly levied carnal attacks on the other."[30] That property might form a material base for culture has been a fundamental tenet of Marxism for generations, and the concept of women or blacks as implicit or explicit property of white men has been a historical reality for centuries. But as we have repeatedly observed, looking to white women or people of color to define white men simply recapitulates the problem of white masculinity's apparent lack of properties and its implicit identification with the lack in the other. That is, to continue to rely on women and people of color to define the white male not only perpetuates the notion that whiteness and masculinity serve as standards of subjectivity but are themselves empty categories; it also performs the gesture we have identified as fundamental to white masculinity's preservation of mastery in demanding of others validation of its identity. One way to demystify the apparent emptiness of whiteness as a category is to look at it as a thing to possess, or a form of property, as Cheryl I. Harris has done, in order to determine not only how white masculinity relied on women and people of color for its self-definition, but also how white men implicitly encoded themselves during Reconstruction and afterwards in direct opposition to their explicit claims of cultural, economic, and political mastery.

In her groundbreaking article "Whiteness as Property," Harris maintains that whiteness as a physical descriptor of people conforms to most definitions of property as that latter has traditionally been related to objects, whether material or abstract. Thus, she points out, since property can consist in a privileged relation to an object that is intangible, property is a right, and not a thing. Reviewing such matters as the manner in which federal and local laws in the U.S. have determined who is white and what privileges and entitlements accrue to a legally defined racial status, Harris writes: "According whiteness actual legal status converted an aspect of identity into an external object of property, moving whiteness from privileged identity to a vested interest."[31] By way of example, Harris cites the Supreme Court decision in *Plessy v Ferguson* in 1896. In that case, the Supreme Court upheld a Louisiana law dating from 1890 that obligated railroads to maintain "equal but separate accommodations for the white and colored races" and made it illegal for people to be in cars not designated for their race. The law was not deemed unconstitutional because the Court held "the underlying fallacy of the plaintiff's argument to consist in the assumption that the enforced separation of the two races stamps the colored race with a badge of inferiority. If this be so, it is not by reason of anything found in the act, but solely because the colored race chooses to put that construction upon it."[32] The Court's further reasoning in that case demonstrates the extent to which racial logic does not proceed along isomorphically equivalent lines, and furthermore it shows that if a white man is thought of as nonwhite, that amounts to a loss of property: "If he be a white man and assigned to a colored coach, he may have his action for damages against the company for being deprived of his so-called property. Upon the other hand, if he be a colored man and be so assigned, he has been deprived of no property, since he is not lawfully entitled to the reputation of being a white man."[33] Harris glosses the Court's logic by noting that "the reputation of being white was treated as a species of property, or something in which property interest could be asserted"[34] and furthermore that "as it emerged, the concept of whiteness was premised on white supremacy rather than mere difference. 'White' was defined and constructed in ways that increased its value by reinforcing its exclusivity."[35] It thus follows that as the courts and the popular imagination converted difference into antagonism, whiteness not only defined itself as the hierarchically valorized component of a complex network of identities, but externalized itself as a possession, and hence an entity with economic and social value meriting legal protection.

Harris's argument concerning the sharp parallels between classical theories of property and the functioning of whiteness seems hard to refute, but I believe that some of the potential rebuttals to her arguments that she projects serve, in fact, to illustrate white masculinity's hysterical components. For example, Harris establishes that being white equates to having property: "It was solely through being white that property could be acquired and secured under law. Only whites possessed whiteness, a highly valued and exclusive form of property."[36] Cases such as Plessy all but prohibit refutation of that claim. But when Harris investigates the philosophical nature of property a subtle but significant dissimilarity arises.

> Classical theories of property identified alienability as a requisite aspect of property; thus, that which is inalienable cannot be property. As the major exponent of this view, Mill argued that the public offices, monopoly privileges, and human beings—all of which were or should have been inalienable—should not be considered property at all. Under this account, if inalienability in-

heres in the concept of property, then whiteness, incapable of being transferred or alienated either inside or outside the market, would fail to meet a criterion of property.[37]

Classical theories of property do not contradict Harris's observation that whiteness has functioned in constitutional and legal discourse as a form of property because, as I have been arguing, whiteness is as alienable a human characteristic as any other, and in many respects perhaps more so. In fact, one of the fundamental definitions of whiteness—and of masculinity as well, it must be noted—is precisely its uninhabitability. Harris is right to argue that in the abstract and as far as collectivities are concerned whiteness appears stable and inalienable, but that is true only insofar as the existence of the category itself is concerned. That is, since its inception in the seventeenth century, whiteness has persisted as a social identifier even if the individuals or groups who classify as white have been notoriously unstable. Because of that instability, individuals who identify as white may not experience their own whiteness as an inalienable characteristic.

The examples of white masculine hysteria I have offered so far hinge both on an anxiety of insufficiency, one that arises over individuals' fear of not coinciding with cultural ideals, and on the projection of and consequent identification with a lack in the other. Since the fullness of white masculinity is not available to be inhabited by individual men, it remains an alienated identity, both in the abstract sense I have been elaborating, in which white men project fragmentation onto other males, and in the ideological sense we have just observed, in which the identity is articulated with a nexus of other social concerns, in this case economic and political property. White masculinity, then, as an identity ostensibly derived from morphology achieves the phallic dimension we observed in chapter 4: A human materiality in the form of culturally defined "parts" takes on the role of expressing abstract ideological concerns, and the ostensible naturalism of the human body evinces an immaterial signifying ideological effect. As the preceding analysis of whiteness as property shows, it is in large part because of whiteness's alienability that the identity achieves such a profoundly ambivalent nature for those who would inhabit it: on the one hand because whiteness can be alienated as property it acquires a more privileged socioeconomic status in the form of property rights, which must be firmly guarded; and on the other hand the potential alienation of whiteness (and of masculinity, as we have seen) contributes to the anxiety of insufficiency that leads white men to continually seek out proof that they are who they would aspire to be.

The experience of whiteness and masculinity as unstable illustrates the particular conjunction of the discourses of the master and the hysteric I elaborated earlier. In the preceding chapters we saw examples from the early modern period in which an anxiety of insufficiency led to the concern of not being white enough or male enough. We can see similar concerns in the nineteenth and twentieth centuries, this time in the U.S. White masculinity constituted itself as simultaneously coincidental with its own signifiers and dependent on its others for self-knowledge during this period; it thus became more ideologically powerful through that apparent contradiction, a contradiction that evinces the tremendous dimension race occupies in subjective determination.

One of the principal examples occurred in the years immediately following the American Civil War, notably in a very particular Ku Klux Klan activity that consisted of attempts to frighten recently enfranchised African Americans. I am using the term "frighten" advisedly here, even though it may perhaps seem inappropriately understated, given the KKK's violent history. A great deal of the current research on how white men negotiated racial and gender difference during Reconstruction and beyond has focused on ritual mutilation of black men, but I will be looking at one of the unusual subtexts of the KKK's terrorism and violence. Critics and historians such as Robyn Wiegman and Trudier Harris have focused their attention on lynching and castration as the two principally significant components of KKK violence; the explanation for the perpetration of such ritual violence on black men generally involves an attempt to impose femininity on them during a time in which white males were jealously guarding access to their culture's dominant position. In stark opposition to the implicit meanings we can discern in much KKK behavior, those who have focused on Klan violence note a tacit attempt on the part of the perpetrators to remove black men from the domain of masculinity. Wiegman writes that "by figuring blackness as a feminine racial formation, the possibility of the African (–American) male assuming an equal position with the crusader for advanced civilization, the white male, was thwarted and racial hierarchies became further entrenched according to the corporeal inequalities inscribed by sexual difference."[38] Trudier Harris concurs, and points out that through lynching and castration "the black man became the harmless eunuch who could be tolerated if he accepted that role, or the raging beast who could be killed without conscience if he did not."[39]

Both Harris and Wiegman base their arguments on implicit Freudian assumptions that the detachability of the male's penis makes him subject to feminization, and they conclude that by castrating black men the white men who brutalized them not only attempted to remove them from the order of masculinity, but to place them squarely within the feminine.[40] While the logic behind these assumptions is perhaps impeccable, it does not necessarily tell the whole story, since while it accounts for the white male's attempt to feminize the black man, it does not tell us specifically why he would attempt to do so. That is, this story relies on a "binary structure of vision," the structure that Wiegman critiqued in the opening pages of her book, one that makes black and white racial opposites, just as it construes male and female as similar gendered opposites. Freudian accounts of children's passage through the Oedipal phase propose that humans adopt their gendered identities based on their relationship to castration: those who have been castrated versus those who might potentially be castrated. Thus, while according to that logic it makes sense to conclude that someone who is castrated is in the feminine position, such a conclusion relies on an imaginary identification of penis as phallus and establishes a binary relation that lacks sufficient subtlety to account for more elaborate negotiations of phallic relations involving more complex social identifiers. In other words, if we consider the Lacanian proposal that the phallus is not a penis, and that the phallus is not for anyone to possess—we recall that he argues in the seminar on psychosis that the father represents the bearer of the phallus—we conclude that people take their gendered identity not simply as a binary opposition, but also and at the same time in relation to a third term.[41] Thus, while it makes sense on one level to argue that white men's ritual castration of black men served to feminize the latter by denying them possession of the phallus, such an argument fails to account for a nonbinary manner of conceptualizing gender, and hence cannot theorize how to explain white men's experience of their own noncoincidence with the bearer of the phallus.

In fact, however, we see numerous examples of white men's interrogation of their own relationship to the phallic signifier in Ku Klux

Klan activities from that group's very inception, and in many of those interrogations the men implicitly display anxiety over their failure to coincide with that signifier. While on the one hand Klan activities terrorized recently enfranchised African Americans, on the other hand the nature of the Klan's activities themselves almost seemed designed to work through white men's anxieties, both those explicitly stated concerning the fear of organized companies of blacks taking political and sexual control of the nation, and the implicit fears that white men themselves could not sustain the image of integrated masculinity their group had promulgated. In fact, even the very structure of the group signals an affiliation with concerns reaching much further back in history than the immediate concerns caused by the Civil War, or even, for that matter, slavery in the United States. That is, the Klan is a secret fraternal organization, one whose very name, which derives from the Greek word for "circle," helps to perpetuate exclusion based not only on gender, but on access to specific forms of cultural capital. In fact, J. C. Lester and D. L. Wilson, two members of the first Ku Klux Klan, write: "Looking back over the history of the Klan, and at the causes under which it developed, it is difficult to resist the conclusion that the order would never have grown to the proportions which it afterwards assumed, or wielded the power it did, had it not borne this name or some other equally as meaningless and mysterious—mysterious because meaningless."[42]

Members of the Ku Klux Klan appear to have been extremely fond of juvenile behavior, both internally in initiation and other official ceremonies within the group, as well as externally, in their dealings with outsiders. According to internal histories roughly contemporary with the Klan's rise to prominence, the principal aim of the original Klan formed in Pulaski, Tennessee in 1865 or 1866 was hilarity and mirth.[43] In his account of the first Klan's origins, J. A. Rogers specifies that not only was the name itself chosen to increase the air of mystery surrounding the group, but that "the main idea was to create a society, different from those in vogue—one whose aim was solely fun and frolic."[44] Even the attorney general of Mississippi declared in 1871 that Klan members got involved with the group out of the innocent desire for fraternal association: "I believe that very frequently young men—boys and youth—are deluded into this thing by its novelty and mystery and secrecy; there is a sort of a charm in this respect to young men, and they go into it frequently without realizing the extent of their wrong-doing."[45] The putative merrymaking associated with the first Klan also apparently involved scaring passersby, and many accounts of the first Klan give the impression that night riding, and especially Klan parades, were not aimed at any particular group. Furthermore, early accounts from both Klan members and outsiders characterized the group's nighttime activities as harmless pranks perpetrated on recently freed people: the Klan's characteristic garb was ostensibly meant to suggest that the night riders were the spirits of slain Confederate soldiers rising from the dead to take their vengeance, and that is why, despite the fact that the color of Klan members' robes was never officially specified, white was said to be the preferred color.[46]

In 1914, one Mrs. S. E. F. Rose published *The Ku Klux Klan, or Invisible Empire,* in which she subscribed to the belief that Klan attire was meant to frighten victims by conjuring up images of the spirit world. Then she added, without any apparent irony: "Of course, beneath these robes they carried pistols strapped to their waists."[47] Nevertheless, Klansmen persisted in maintaining that their power derived solely from the superstitiousness of the ignorant. Thus, according to Lester and Wilson, as a result of the Klan's nighttime pranks, "it was noticed that the nocturnal perambulation of the colored population diminished, or entirely ceased."[48]

> In this way the Klan gradually realized that the most powerful devices ever constructed for controlling the ignorant and superstitious were in their hands. Even the most highly cultured were not able wholly to resist the weird and peculiar feeling which pervaded every community where the Ku Klux appeared. Each week some new incident occurred to illustrate the amazing power of the unknown over the minds of men of all classes.[49]

One might wonder about the extent to which disavowal was operating in Klansmen's supposition that it was their antics that terrified people in the countryside: In most of the descriptions of Klan activities that we read, none of the tricks Klansmen favored seems particularly terrifying, and none seems all that hard to demystify. In fact, many of them date back hundreds of years prior to the nineteenth century; some of the more mundane seem positively silly. Klan members' descriptions of their parades, for example, nearly always focused on two things: they were held in almost complete silence, and the number of horsemen riding must have seemed astonishingly large to observers. Rogers explains the low-tech manner in which the illusion was achieved: "For more than two hours the hooded horsemen rode in deathly silence. They numbered only four hundred, but arriving at a lonely spot they would wheel and march back, giving the impression that they were tens of thousands."[50]

Interestingly enough, witnesses' reports of these parades focus not on the overwhelming numbers of riders, but on the bizarre dress of the participants, which I take to mean either that no one was fooled by the trick, or that no one even noticed that an illusion of great numbers was being attempted. In fact, on one occasion, one witness who did notice the number of riders reported only twelve.[51] So unusual was the dress of the parade participants that in most accounts of these marches witnesses liken the men's attire to dresses or gowns, even though the Klansmen themselves almost always refer to their garments as robes.[52] A Mr. C. C. Hughes, witness to KKK behavior, reports that the riders of the Georgia Ku Klux Klan wore "something over their bodies similar to gowns,"[53] and a Joseph Gill, who was whipped by the KKK for not giving up his horse, said that "they had on gowns just like your overcoat, that came down to the toes; and some would be red and some black, like a lady's dress."[54] To judge from contemporary witnesses' accounts of what they saw during KKK parades or raids, it was the bizarre appearance of the KKK, and not so much their attempts to make themselves appear ghostly or otherworldly, that was frightening.

Other favorite KKK pranks highlighted not the Klansman's multiplicity, but his divisibility. Stunts suggesting the infinite expansion or the minute fragmentation of the night rider's body ostensibly frightened victims who were supposed to take such marks as indications of a ghostly presence. In one familiar routine robed horsemen would surreptitiously store rubber sacks underneath their garments, and then approach a victim, explaining that they hadn't had a drink of water since the battle of Manassas, Shiloh, or some other significant skirmish. When the victim handed up a bucket of water, the horseman would feign to drink it, but covertly empty it into the rubber sack, and then ask for another bucket. In another ploy, disguised men would carry artificial limbs underneath their robes and approach their victim, asking to shake his hand. When the latter grasped the false hand, the Klansmen would release it, thus ostensibly giving the impression that his body could decompose and recompose itself at will. Another similar trick was to use the ubiquitous hood to cover a pumpkin or other object roughly the size of a human head, and at a given point during the ride to "decapitate" oneself. Lester and Wilson believed that "such tricks gave rise to the belief—still prevalent among the negroes—that the Ku Klux could take themselves all to pieces whenever they wanted to,"[55] and that such a belief constituted the terror Klan victims felt as a result of night-time raids.

While KKK members persistently maintained that it was the frightening content of their pranks that terrorized their victims, it seems far more likely, given the context in which they were operating, that it was the fact of the nighttime visitations, combined with the threats and acts of violence, that intimidated. One wonders, in fact, how Klansmen could persist in the belief—or even in the posture—that victims were frightened primarily by the threat of ghosts when one reads reports such as that of J. A. Rogers: "Negroes would now and then shoot a ghost to learn its identity" during a given nighttime visit.[56] Of course, anyone receiving such a "visit" might well have cause for alarm, in fact: various laws enacted in Southern states immediately after the Civil War contained the behavior and the rights to work, to vote, and to possess arms of recently enfranchised African Americans under what is known as the Black Code. Furthermore, one of the first gestures the KKK made either immediately preceding a raid or as the raid's principal function was to disarm its victims. Finally, according to dozens of contemporary witnesses, for however peaceful Klan members claim their raids to have been, acts of violence, most often whippings, frequently punctuated their frightening "pranks."

Contemporary reports reveal that Klan disguises and pranks that meant to suggest a connection to the spiritual world did little if anything to frighten their victims. What frightened them were the death threats and whippings deployed to keep them under control. KKK victims rarely mention anything particular abut Klan dress other than to remark on the fact that the robes kept Klansmen from being identified, and they almost never mention the juvenile pranks that KKK members seemed to believe frightened the superstitious liberated men and women. One witness interrogated before the Senate Joint Select Committee appointed to investigate conditions in the Southern states following the Civil War reported an exchange between a freed man and

Klansmen claiming to have come back from the dead: "They asked him who he belonged to before the war. He told them he belonged to Barton Thrasher, but that Barton Thrasher was dead now. One of them men said, 'Oh, yes; he is dead; I saw him the other day; I am just from hell; I saw Barton Thrasher there. I was killed at Manassas. I just came out of the grave to-night. I see Barton Thrasher every day or two.'"[57] The intended victim reports only fearing death or bodily harm, however ("they intended to kill me or make me leave, one or the other").[58] On the one occasion in which he makes offhand reference to the Klansmen's dress, it is incidental to the threats of violence that men in such dress posed: the witness refers to others he has known who were "whipped off—whipped off by these men in disguise. If they do not whip a man, they come and knock his door down and run him out, and he gets scared."[59]

As I mentioned above, however, it is not the violence that primarily concerns me here, but the mode in which it was perpetrated. Klan members' dress and the particular pranks they pulled in order to frighten their victims betray an uneasy relationship to the integrity of the identities they felt they ought to possess. Much Klan recruiting and insider literature specifies that to join their ranks one must be a "100 per cent" or "real" or "true" man; it seems hard to reconcile such an image with the fragmented body created in the very common missing limb or decapitation prank, or, indeed, with the mode of dress adopted early on that a disproportionate number of contemporary observers likened to women's gowns.[60] Many observers have in fact pointed out that since full-length robes are a less than practical way of covering oneself when on horseback in wooded areas, we need to seek out ways of explaining the peculiarity of KKK garb. Charles Flynn associates Klan behavior and dress with the charivaris popular in medieval and Renaissance France. Such events, which consisted of "noisy masked demonstrations,"[61] were associated with religious festivals in which participants simultaneously mocked and affirmed their culture's values, and just as the Klan did, they claimed to be protecting the sexual purity and innocence of their women.[62] So similar was Klan behavior to that found in these masked demonstrations of early modern Europe, in fact, that Flynn compares them to the White Caps, who engaged in similar practices concerning similar punishable offenses.

Natalie Zemon Davis has pointed out that in early modern Europe men found occasion to dress as women to draw upon the "sexual power and energy of unruly woman and on her license . . . to tell the truth about unjust rule."[63] Flynn concurs, and suggests that "the long, impractical gowns were a stylized anachronism, a symbol of fraternal, festival justice sapped of its former cultural significance. It is even possible that not all the symbolism had been lost for under the chivalric code of white southerners women remained the repository of moral values."[64] I am not suggesting that members of the KKK went out in high drag on their missions of terror, or that they had anything more in mind when they devised their disguises than making sure that they would not be readily identifiable. However, when we note witnesses' observations that the men who terrorized them were dressed in "gowns" in conjunction with the fact that the most popular Klan pranks consisted of losing parts of their bodies, it is difficult not to detect a certain symptomatic common denominator operating. What I am thus suggesting is that the Klan's determinate control of bodies, both of the recently enfranchised and of the white women who represented the purity of their race, together with its resolute intent to direct the meaning of those bodies directly contradicted the way it represented itself when engaged in clandestine Klan activities.

In Klan behavior the apparent paradox of a discourse of hysteria opposing a discourse of mastery turns out to be, in fact, only an apparent paradox. In fact, mastery and hysteria complement one another in modern white masculinity to the extent that what is excluded from the discourse of mastery reappears in the hysterical discourse in the form of a radical interrogation requiring from the other a stabilizing answer. Thus, where fragmentation, discontinuity, or other kinds of self-division are banished from the discourse of the master, the divided sense of self characteristically motivates and gives voice to hysterical discourse. The master believes himself univocal, but belies his certainty with gestures that reveal his repressed truth: he doesn't know what he wants, and requires that his other supply him with that information. KKK members who apprehended themselves as "100 per cent" men and as uncontaminated whites owed that apprehension in large part to the white woman, since they projected onto her body anxieties of gendered insufficiency or the possibility for racial contamination.[65] From black males members of the KKK strived to differentiate themselves, but the symptoms of difference they had located on the black male body—in particular, morphological fragmentation, which white males symbolically produced in the early modern period and the KKK actually inflicted on that body in the form of whipping, burning, or castration—reappeared on the body of the Klansmen in the unusual pranks they played.[66]

Members of the KKK consequently simultaneously enacted the discourse of the master and that of the hysteric, a dual performance whose early manifestations we observed in chapter 3 when we noted a resolute uncertainty of identity in early modern white masculinities. Modern manifestations of the identity explicitly locate themselves between mastery and hysteria, on the border delineating the power to name and its attendant hold on knowledge and identity, from the simultaneous search for and flight from master signifiers that might provide secure meaning and identity. Members of the KKK thus explicitly enact the contradictions that I have been arguing provide white masculinity with the ideological force to contain most forms of knowledge and stabilize or gauge senses of identity, while at the same time remaining a culturally separate product that prohibits individual men from coinciding with it directly.[67] We need to recognize, however, that it is precisely the contradiction between ideological force and individual aspiration that drives white masculinity's urge to classify and to interrogate, and that fuels the lack of coincidence between the stability of the world as object and that of the white male as a coherent and stable thing. That is, as early KKK behavior demonstrates in the most explicit fashion, when the world order disintegrates—and in this case that order refers to the specific hierarchically arranged racial and gender order engineered according to white and male logic and reasoning—the identity of the white male takes on its most urgent order and stability as that agency responsible for reconstituting the missing meaning. When that world order is forcibly reestablished, it is the white male himself who symbolically disintegrates, as Klan pranks aptly showed. That phenomenon continues to be prevalent in twentieth-century American culture, as we will now see, and it continues to involve not only the implicit projection of fragmentation onto the nonwhite male body, but also the negotiation of hysteria and mastery that characterized earlier discourses of white masculinity.

There is a memorable passage in James Baldwin's novel *Just Above My Head* in which Hall Montana, a young African American who manages the gospel singing career of his brother, Arthur, speculates about what it means to be white. In this passage, Hall describes the stops he and his brother make on their tour through the Southern states; he observes the racial tension opposing the black people who come to hear his brother and the white people who gather in numbers for the express purpose of intimidating—and sometimes of harming—Arthur's audience. Hall beholds the black people watching the white people watching them. The eyes of the black people convey both scorn and pity as they survey the gaze of the white people, and Hall translates their look into these words:

> Do you now suppose that this density of passionate connection has turned me into nothing more than a peculiar mirror, reflecting only what you want to see? What do I care, if you are white. *Be* white: I do not have to prove my color. I wouldn't be compelled to see *your* color, if you were not so anxious to prove it. Why? And to me, of all people.—But I know why. You are afraid that you have been here with me too long, and are not really white anymore. That's probably true, but you were never really white in the first place. Nobody is. Nobody has, even, ever *wanted* to be white, unless they are afraid of being black. But being black is nothing to be afraid of. I knew that before I met you, and I have learned it again, through you.[68]

Hall registers the black observers' recognition of the white gaze, as well as their simultaneous refusal to accept that gaze's definitional objectification. More significant for my purposes here, however, is Hall Montana's assertion that whiteness is an assumed, constructed identity. Hall recognizes that whiteness does not constitute a stable essence in relation to which various ancillary and consequently "racialized" others align themselves. It is instead a complex response to, among other things, the threat of ethnic, class, and cultural indifferentiation. Whiteness, Hall recognizes, is an absurd and impossible abstraction that nevertheless has very real effects. Corroborating the gravity of those effects is the fact that it is Hall, the black man, who is forced by situation to understand the white people better than they understand themselves.[69]

Extrapolating from the citation of *Just Above My Head,* I turn now to other means that reveal that modern white masculinity is not the seamless, naturally dominant social agency many have come to imagine, but, again, a dialectically constituted identity marked for both gender and race.[70] My earlier depictions of white masculinity highlighted either adventurous naturalists who traveled halfway around the world, or frightening terrorists who threatened the people around them. Yet another approach depicts white men as completely average, unextraordinary characters. Neither heroic champions bravely saving the day, nor bumblingly pathetic wretches ironically buttressing idealized, masculine integrity, the white men in the films I will deal with here are unspectacular, nonheroic protagonists who don't really do anything significant at all. Lawrence Kasdan's *Grand Canyon* and Ron Shelton's *White Men Can't Jump* both portray a white guy who plays basketball with his black friend and attempts to understand his wife and/or girlfriend. Of particular interest is the manner in which, uncharacteristically for most mainstream cinema, it is the white man who, in a reversal of conventional narrative paradigm, has to learn to play by someone else's rules.[71] A great deal of contemporary work on masculinity has centered on its marginal or otherwise unconventional varieties; the more routine strains, that is, average white guys, have typically gone unremarked.[72] While characterizing specific types of masculinity as conventional or routine further normalizes them, and consequently runs the risk of further mystifying them, nevertheless, it seems beneficial to attempt to uncover what it is about white masculinity that we commonly accept as normal or average, since the work that goes into obfuscating white men's gender and racial characteristics, as we have seen, is also that responsible for sustaining their political, cultural, and economic dominance.[73]

The principal characters in both *White Men Can't Jump* and *Grand Canyon* exhibit the "nice guy" effect. That is, both display a sort of bovine, avuncular good nature toward the women in their lives, a nature characterized by nothing so much as a grinning, often condescending tolerance of their partners' "irrational" behavior. Both films derive a comedic effect from the scatterbrained manner in which these nice guys deal with the chaos in their lives, as well as from the relative powerlessness, at least with respect to their domestic situations, these men seem to exhibit. Furthermore, both these white men have a particular fascination with black men, a fascination that might appear to stem from the American liberal tradition, but which seems, in fact, to border on fetishism. The protagonists in *Grand Canyon* and *White Men Can't Jump* are men of the '90s who visibly make the effort—and this, as we will see, is part of the problem—to accommodate the women and black men in their lives.

White Men Can't Jump portrays Billy Hoyle (Woody Harrelson), a white basketball hustler, in never-ending attempts to negotiate his relationships with his Puerto Rican girlfriend and his black basketball partner. As part of his multicultural education, the often bewildered Billy learns from his girlfriend Gloria (Rosie Perez) that, in her words, "Sometimes when you win, you really lose, and sometimes when you lose you really win. And sometimes when you win or lose you actually tie, and sometimes when you tie, you actually win or lose." Billy, the only character explicitly coded as white in the movie—a fact that will be significant later on—continually contests and negotiates meaning with Gloria in conversations that only Roseanne Rosannadanna or perhaps Deborah Tannen could fully appreciate. When Gloria wakes up and says she's thirsty, for example, Billy gets her a glass of water. "When I say I'm thirsty, it doesn't mean I want you to get me a glass of water," Gloria castigates. "When I have a problem you're not supposed solve it . . . you're supposed to sympathize!"

White Men Can't Jump focuses on Billy and Gloria's relationship by portraying Billy's good-natured attempts to understand and conform to Gloria's principles and beliefs. Primarily ingenuously, and with varying degrees of success, Billy endeavors to relinquish his belief in a world informed by binary opposites (winning versus losing) and causal linear structures (thirst causes a demand for water) in favor of a more fluid, more complicated universe in which terms both mutually implicate and exclude one another. What he fails to achieve, however, is a way of balancing his relationship with his lover and his partner. Gloria's aphorism that "sometimes when you win you really lose" hits home when, at the end of the movie, Billy and his basketball partner defeat a legendary duo: When he returns home he finds that Gloria has left him.

Billy's relationship with Gloria is in many ways complemented by his relationship with Sidney Deane (Wesley Snipes), an African American with whom he teams up to hustle street basketball. Billy and Sidney meet when the former hustles the latter on the courts at Venice Beach—Sidney and his friends refuse to believe that a white man can play basketball. Billy and Sidney's hustling in Los Angeles street pick-up games works for the same reason. The film flirts with the stock racialist assumption that black men are naturally superior athletes; its title derives from the fact that Billy, a white man, is the only character who appears constitutionally unable to stuff the ball.

Everyone who's seen the movie, and probably even anyone who hasn't, knows or can guess that the climatic basketball scene in the movie belies its title. In this scene, Sidney passes the ball to Billy at point game. He passes it so high, in fact, that the only way Billy can retrieve it is by jumping up and jamming it. What makes this scene significant is the fact that Billy had just lost $2,500 to Sidney in a bet precisely over Billy's inability to stuff the ball. Sidney, however, seems to have known all along and better than Billy what, in fact, the latter was really capable of, and it is Sidney who is, in effect, charged with empowering his white partner.

What I want to derive from this brief look at *White Men Can't Jump* is first of all the fact that Billy Hoyle, the white guy, has to abide by rules that are uncharacteristically slanted against him. Not only is it the case that Billy has no special privilege in his social group, but no one, except perhaps Sidney, knows who he really is: at various points in the film he's compared to Cathy Rigby, Jane Fonda, Martha Graham, and even Cindy Brady. It is precisely the apparent instability of Billy's racial and gender identities that keeps him in power in this movie, but what is more significant still is that it would seem to be black men's misrecognition of Billy's identity that gives him such a competitive edge. Strikingly, the first words we hear in the film, occurring in the opening musical piece, are "You keep asking me what I am."

The other feature that interests me here is the fact that there are at least two possible conclusions about race, at least as far as it concerns white men, that the film leaves us with. The first is that if the sententious claim that white men can't jump is true, perhaps Billy isn't white at all, but merely thinks he is or passes for such. The second is that, regardless of the truth value of the film's title, it is Sidney Deane, Billy's African American hustling partner, who bears the responsibility of knowing and understanding his white partner's truth, his identity, abilities, and limitations, and then of communicating them to him.[74] In fact, contemporary American cinema has developed an apparent obsession with the formula in which people of color not only convey back to white men (and often women) their true identities, but also selflessly support those whites in their daily activities and their more noble ventures. In the late 1980s, for example, we discovered in *Mississippi Burning* and *The Long Walk Home* that although occasionally assisted by African Americans, white people—including the FBI—were fundamentally responsible for the Civil Rights movement. Other films have showcased noble African Americans who appear to have nothing to do but improve the lives of the white people around them, sometimes to the point of making them nearly immortal. In this vein we find *Driving Miss Daisy, The Legend of Bagger Vance,* and *Unbreakable,* a spectacular year 2000 release in which Elijah (Samuel L. Jackson), an infirm art dealer, stages a series of horrible accidents to prove to David Dunn (Bruce Willis) that the latter, is, in fact, an immortal superhero, a revelation that David shares with his son, but which he withholds, strikingly enough, from his wife.

The late twentieth-century manifestation of white masculinity receiving confirmation of its identity from projected others structurally recapitulates the phenomena we noted in the early modern period in Europe and in the years following the American Civil War. As I noted in chapter 3, however, the confirmation is structurally engineered by white masculinity; often it occurs only on the level of representation, such as in the above cinematic examples. But this kind of representation, in which a dominant discursive and political practice reproduces itself in large part through control of signification, is not restricted to fictional works such as literature or film. We find the same attempt at mastery in theoretical interventions, and perhaps most notably in the discourse of psychoanalysis. The brief theoretical discussion of sexual difference that follows looks at another aspect of the apparatus of psychoanalytic theory that appears to produce some of the effects that by implication it has simply discovered. Theory can often generate what it purports to characterize, and the socially meaningful difference we identify as "sexual" may actually contain information conscripted to perform work in other social arenas. The separation of "sexual difference" from other forms of difference not only adumbrates these other forms, but further participates in the construction of a (white) norm, even when the subject at hand seems only to be male.

As I noted briefly in chapter 1, in his attempt to uncover what lies behind the prohibition of murder and incest, the only two crimes that ostensibly concerned primitive society and which contributed to the formation of group identity, Sigmund Freud postulated along with Charles Darwin and Robertson Smith a primogenital crime responsible for virtually all subsequent social organization. Freud's myth of the primal horde and of the murder of the father by a band of brothers represents an attempt to account for the ambivalent admixture of fear, love, and envy characterizing the son's relationship to the paternal figure. The well-known myth, in which a "violent and jealous father who keeps all the females for himself and drives away his sons as they grow up," relates the sons' rebellion against the father: "One day, the brothers who had been driven out came together, killed and devoured their fa- ther and so made an end of the patriarchal horde. United, they had the courage to do and succeeded in doing what would have been impossible for them individually. (Some cultural advance, perhaps, command over some new weapon, had given them a sense of superior strength)."[75] This "memorable and criminal deed" constitutes the origin of "social organization, moral restrictions and of religion."[76]

The principal aim of Freud's story is to account for the strength that the idealized image of the father exerts in most cultures. As in *The Ego and the Id,* in which Freud describes the ego ideal as a "substitute for a longing for the father" and consequently the "germ from which all religions have evolved,"[77] *Totem and Taboo* seems fundamentally con- cerned with the mechanism through which patriarchal authority ex- tends over most aspects of a given society. The principal mechanisms responsible for the spread of this authority are guilt and fear; the broth- ers who killed the primal father identified with him both because of their love for him and because of their fear of each other: "Though the brothers had banded together in order to overcome their father, they were all one another's rivals in regard to the women."[78] Because of their guilt for the crime they had committed, the brothers instituted the sanctity of the blood tie, which effectively outlawed murder. "In thus guaranteeing one another's lives, the brothers were declaring that no one of them must be treated by another as their father was treated by them all jointly."[79] It is for that reason that Freud stipulates that "the dead father became stronger than the living one had been"[80]—because the sons invested in him their senses of guilt, remorse, and affection, the dead father came to represent an impossible ideal of masculine authority that none of the sons individually could ever hope to achieve.

Freud's fable of the primal horde, particularly as it relates the cooperation and organization of the brothers both in their murder of the father and in their legislating against a repetition of the crime, establishes a heuristic metaphor of the origins of patriarchal control. It is a way, in Freud's own words, of accounting for the existence of "bands of males . . . composed of members with equal rights and . . . subject to the restrictions of the totemic system."[81] In other words, it allows us to speculate about the sorts of events that led to the establishment of a patriarchal society in which the prohibition of murder and incest seems inevitably to have led to a culture centered around sexual difference and the concomitant domination of women by men. Yet, not only does this myth posit masculine identity as resolutely hysterical, since no one can ever identify with the figure of the father as the ideal man, but, more important, it depends on the very sort of social organization—male cooperation in the oppression of women—that it claims to account for. In other words, the story of the brothers' banding together to arrogate to themselves the father's once exclusive possession of the women ostensibly explains the origins of moral and religious thought as well as the organization of contemporary culture. Nevertheless, the organization whose origins the story attempts to chronicle must be in place for that story ever to be told in the first place.[82]

The crucial element in the myth of the primal horde—the narrative moment from which the psychoanalytic interpretation underpinning the ideological analysis of gender relations in our culture derives—is the brothers' decision to murder and consume the father. Freud dismisses the circumstances behind the decision with a brief parenthetical phrase: "Some cultural advance, perhaps, command over some new weapon, had given them a sense of superior strength." I recognize that Freud's use of the term "cultural" is a speculation about the anthropological development of new tools, for example, capable of effecting a change in the material reality of the horde. Nevertheless, it seems important to point out that Freud describes a cultural change that acted as a catalyst in a story that would purport to portray what is, in effect, the origins of culture. In other words, in the event that Freud describes, the brothers of a clan recognize a bond that unites them in the common cause of doing away with what amounts to an enemy; the coalition of male domination that expresses itself in the control of female sexuality must have existed prior to the murder of the father, despite the fact that *Totem and Taboo* situates this form of social organization as the result of that murder. Owing to the very specific manner in which their sexuality is governed by a highly powerful figure and to the concomitant regulation of their desire, the brothers are already united in a relationship that is the cause—and not the result—of their murder of the father ("United, they had the courage to do and succeeded in doing what would have been impossible for them individually"). Consequently, our current psychoanalytic understanding of the myth of the primal horde relies on an event that for all practical purposes had to have always already happened for it ever to happen in the first place.

Freud uses the myth of the primal horde in *Totem and Taboo* to account for the prohibition of both murder and incest, the two principal components in the Oedipal complex. The resolution of the Oedipal complex, of course, is in this schema fundamentally responsible for engendering the individual as either male or female. The relatively restricted but significant consequence we can derive from this brief reading of the myth of the primal horde concerns the way in which the father relates to gender as well as the use of sexual difference as the fundamental key to identity in our culture. If we accept the more or less traditional reading of the myth of the primal horde, in which the crucial moment in the narrative is the brothers' murder of the father, then the prohibition of murder and incest that results is the act that engenders the brothers as Oedipally male and that initiates religion, morality, and most other aspects of our culture. Because the brothers are so highly ambivalent toward the father—they both love and fear him—they implicitly establish the sanctity of the blood tie and the prohibition of incest, and they form the foundation of a culture based on the exchange of women. The brothers, consequently, are the first fully Oedipalized males.

What this means is that the father is not masculine, at least not in the culturally defined way we have come to think and theorize about masculinity. The father, through no agency of his own but because of his sons' ambivalence toward him, becomes after his death the powerful and fearsome patriarch principally responsible for the retroactive establishment of the taboos against murder and incest.[83] Since, however, the father only attains this tremendous control over his sons after his death, he is not culturally engendered as masculine, because never having been in the cultural role of brother or son, he remained outside of Oedipalization. In addition, if the brothers were united by an intense emotional bond before they killed the father, a bond that expressed a consimilarity only recognizable after the murder of the father, then that means that something other than the Oedipal complex was responsible for giving the brothers a common identity or social organization to begin with. In other words, some form of social or cultural organization existed prior to the moment of the Oedipal complex's inception that caused the brothers to band together to commit the fundamental act of Western culture, and we should resist the temptation to consider that bond in terms of the culture that such a bond, together with the violent act it facilitated, ultimately produced. The pre-murder bond, in other words, formed what amounts to a prehistorical condition or possibility of an act that would indelibly mark all acculturated males from that point on: Everything we take masculinity to be in Western culture is in some sense informed by the violent act that Freud narrates, and consequently we do not have access to the cultural expressions of maleness that would have existed prior to that act.

What I am describing here in many ways recapitulates the claims I made in chapter 1 concerning Oedipus's repudiation of traditional knowledge in favor of deploying his own reason and wherewithal to solve a civic problem. In the case at hand, if the sociocultural organization to which the father belongs and from which the Oedipal engendering of his sons derives forms the prehistory of what has come to be called Western culture, and is, as such, inaccessible to us, it is because our system of language is based on the symbolic order initiated by the Oedipal moment. If they remain as unconscious traces in our culture, the prehistoric social organization and the father who characterizes it can only be evoked or understood in terms of our existing cultural practices. Because our social symbolic, at least as it appears in the discourse of psychoanalysis, is largely articulated around the concept of sexual difference, that means that the form of social organization underpinning sexual difference is substantially inaccessible to us, and can only be understood in terms of sexual difference. It is thus difficult to escape the conclusion that the primal father who organizes our culture is not a male in any traditional sense, but that we have no other way of thinking about that figure. That might therefore suggest that the fundamental identity difference in our culture is based on something that extends well beyond what we have traditionally thought of as sexual difference.

There is a very simple reason why I want to stress the fact that the father in Freud's account of the primal horde cannot be a male in the traditional Oedipal sense. If we fail to exclude the father from the social structures that engender men as culturally male, then we face the taxonomically impossible task of trying to use masculinity to define masculinity. In other words, by refusing to recognize the primal father's external position in the engendering of his sons as culturally male, we inevitably revert to a biological essentialism, and we further mystify masculinity by construing it as mastery—that is, as a seamless and self-engendering entity with no outside. Furthermore, by recognizing the contingency of masculinity's cultural domination, we can also begin to understand how other forms of difference, no less contingent, can be culturally eroticized in ways similar to sexual difference. In short, what we are doing when we identify the historical and cultural contingency of masculinity by considering its prehistory in the stories we tell about it is erecting the sorts of master signifiers discussed in previous chapters. Differences not generally associated with gender can be mapped on a similar paradigm and according to similar master signifiers, and subjects' relationships to identity positions might be seen to be similarly based on a form of hysteria. What has come to be referred to as the law of the father, therefore, derives its authority from social structures that are not limited to sexual difference. In addition, because it governs the social symbolic, this law specifies the parameters of thought and language, controlling to a large but by no means absolute extent the way we understand culture.

There are an infinite number of ways of organizing a given culture, and our inability to account for the specific choices made in such areas as the mode of production, the arrangement of the family, or the disposition of sexual desire attests to the function of the law. That is, not only is it the case that to all appearances these things simply are what they are, as in the discussions of natural necessity and human morphological difference that we noted in chapter 2; it is also the case that we are largely unable to identify as cultural variables most of the potentially mutable institutions, including language, that we think of as meaningful. Anything and everything could be different, and there are generally no identifiable reasons why they are not. The apparent consistency of social existence is a function of the irrational but nevertheless very real ideological field of the law of the father. The law of the father *is* the ideological disposition of our culture because of the collection of master signifiers that such a law puts into place and reproduces through manipulation and supervision of language; to identify with the symbolic domain of a culture is to associate oneself with its moral, ethical, and social underpinnings.[84] The law of the father, in short, is little more than a disguised form of the law of the brothers, but what is significant is that the father as source of the law is culturally inaccessible, and thus the law he governs appears simultaneously natural and apodictic.[85]

If psychoanalysis has traditionally conceived of sexual difference as culture's fundamental difference, it can nevertheless help us articulate the function of differences not based on gender. We have been accustomed to think of the "dominant position" in our culture as being first and foremost male, and references to men's phallic privilege are frequently invoked in such a way as to eradicate the differences among men of different ethnic, racial, sexual, and national identities. Concomitantly, the similarities between men and women who share corresponding racial or class identities tend to disappear, as do forms of power and domination based on those identities. Jane Gaines makes a similar observation when she writes, "By taking gender as its starting point in the analysis of oppression, feminist theory helps to reinforce white middle-class values, and to the extent that it works to keep women from seeing other structures of oppression, it functions ideologically."[86] I would simply amend Gaines's formulation by noting that men as well as women are vulnerable to this sort of theoretical blinding. With the symmetry of a purely gender-based system of identification thus destabilized, I would like to make the simple, unastonishing suggestion that not only men fill the paternal function, and that not all men have equal access to that function.

Hortense J. Spillers has made the point that the paternal function is neither universal nor racially blind in an article on maternity and paternity in the African American enslaved family. Spillers analyzes the captive body, in particular the status of enslaved women's offspring. She notes that, because notions of kinship did not accord legal recognition to the children of the enslaved, a tension arose between the concepts of family and property, particularly in instances in which a white "owner" fathered the child. This meant that the mother had no rights with respect to her child, and the man who fathered the child did not

recognize it as his relative. Spillers writes: "In effect, under conditions of captivity, the offspring of the female does not 'belong' to the
Mother, nor is s/he 'related' to the 'owner,' though the latter 'possesses'
it, and in the African American instance, often fathered it, *and,* as often,
without whatever benefit of patrimony."[87] This is an extremely powerful
insight because it forces us to confront the manners in which "family,"
particularly in its legal dimensions, can be invoked to support specific
kinds of racial supremacy. During a large part of American history—
to say nothing of the history of other cultures—vertical family structures were the privilege of the free, largely white community. What that
means, then, is that we cannot count on psychoanalytic explanations of
identity that take sexual difference as their sole significant underlying
feature to help us understand the paternal function because a significant portion of the male population has traditionally been barred, by
virtue of skin pigmentation, from ever filling that function. We have
seen, in fact, that part of the paternal function is precisely to preclude
specific contenders from acceding to it. As Spillers writes, "Legal enslavement removed the African American male not so much from sight
as from *mimetic* view as a partner in the prevailing social fiction of the
Father's name, the Father's law."[88]

The remainder of this chapter illustrates how the "believing is seeing" model correlates the phenomenon I just described, in which apparently fundamental differences encode far more complex social operations. By looking at Lawrence Kasdan's *Grand Canyon,* I will show both
how contemporary versions of white masculinity exhibit the hysterical
structure identified earlier, and how white masculinity attempts to constrain its gendered and racial others to reproduce for and reflect back to
it the elements of its specific form of identity.

In Kasdan's *Grand Canyon,* a series of small catastrophes intervenes
in the lives of a dozen or so citizens of Los Angeles, and brings them
together in unexpected ways. Shootings, an earthquake and a heart
attack, love affairs, and the discovery of an abandoned baby bring together what are represented as unlikely associates; depicted as fundamentally responsible for their incongruity is the admixture of race and
gender, and, to a lesser extent, class. That is, the characters in *Grand
Canyon* seem to be thrust together despite what the film suggests are
unbridgeable social chasms resulting from their identities as male or
female, white or black, professional or working class. The film relies on

some bald cuts to suggest insipid racial differences—the white teenager gets in a bus to go off to summer camp, for example, and the black teenager gets in a car to go off with a street gang. Although *Grand Canyon* would purport to depict the social enlightenment of an upper middle-class, suburban white man, it actually insists on the breakdown of knowledge and meaning that it would apparently have us believe are relatively easily surmountable obstacles in the road toward social understanding.

The first ostensibly improbable association is between Mack (Kevin Kline), a white immigration lawyer, and Simon (Danny Glover), a black tow-truck driver. Mack's car breaks down in a predominantly black neighborhood; a group of young men drives up behind him, and they force him out of his car at gun point; Simon arrives in his tow truck and for all intents and purposes rescues Mack. Despite the fact that Simon and Mack are brought together in a purely professional association, the encounter causes Mack to pursue a friendship with Simon, the terms of which are dictated to a very great extent by Mack's desire to know precisely who and what Simon is. At one point, in fact, he even wonders whether Simon is for real.[89]

Although the question of race is never explicitly addressed in this sequence, the soundtrack articulates the racial tension at play, with the car stereos in the two vehicles proclaiming the drivers' relationships to symbolic authority. As Mack pulls out of the crowded Los Angeles traffic, he sings along with Warren Zevon the words to "Lawyers, Guns, and Money." As Mack sings out, "Send lawyers, guns, and money, fuck! the shit has hit the fan," his car sputters and dies. The car with the five young men pulls up behind him, its car stereo blaring N.W.A.'s "F*** the Police."

Encoded in this initial encounter are the different kinds of access to symbolic power and the law that will characterize nearly all of the subsequent encounters the film will chronicle. As an immigration lawyer—who, incidentally, ridicules the names of his clients that he is unable to pronounce—Mack both represents and has access to the culture's symbolic authority in the form of the law and the economic interests backing it up. The complex of "lawyers, guns, and money" ironically stipulates how a dominant ideology can assert and maintain its hegemony—juridical and economic coercion are the superstructural elements sustained by the implicit threat of real force. The network of symbolic authority to which Mack has access, however, is not only largely unavailable to the men whom he encounters, but it appears, in fact, to be barely recognized.[90] The five black men who accost Mack disregard his claim that he called the police on his cellular phone, and they mock him and his possessions ("Aw, he's nervous." "Did you call your Mama on that telephone?"). These young men embody white anxiety about race to the extent that they seem not to recognize any of the rules governing, among other things, property. Black men here represent lawlessness. *Grand Canyon* thus immediately establishes a dichotomous relationship to the recognition and preservation of symbolic authority, a relationship that divides neatly along racial lines. White men line up on the side of representation and symbolic authority; black men seem to take their places on the side of the real. One of the young men threatening Mack points out, in fact, that for him, "no gun, no respect."

Back at the service station, Mack and Simon's conversation continues to align the former on the side of meaning and the latter on the side of the nonsymbolic real. Mack obsesses about how "many ways to buy it" there are. Simon responds by noting that the young men Mack encountered were just traveling along, and Mack crossed their path. They are like a shark, he says, who sees something to eat. "He don't hate you. He got no feeling at all for you. To him, you just look like a piece of food. You don't hate a hamburger, do you?" To illustrate his point, Simon tells Mack about his trip to the Grand Canyon. It was pretty enough, he admits, but its real impact on him derived from its sublimity. Immeasurable both in time and space, the Grand Canyon confirmed to Simon the insignificance of human problems. When Mack continues to lament the destruction of meaning in his life, Simon, who by the way is the first to articulate Mack's question about whether or not Simon is for real, tells him, "Man, get yourself to the Grand Canyon."

Simon's use of the Grand Canyon as part of the nonsymbolic real is countered toward the end of the film by Davis (Steve Martin), Mack's friend who produces raunchy, violent movies. Davis is shot in the leg by a man trying to steal his Rolex. The event causes him to reconsider his life and his work, but he eventually returns to his job making movies. Davis explains to Mack that the reason for the apparent breakdown in society is the gap separating "the people who have stuff and the people who don't have shit." That gap is like the Grand Canyon, he claims, and it explains everything about how we behave.

Simon's and Davis's competing interpretations of the Grand Canyon underlie the struggle for meaning that the entire film is concerned with depicting. Simon uses the Grand Canyon as a sort of limit of meaning, the point at which human understanding reaches its capacity to confront and understand an object. For Simon, the Grand Canyon as a sort of unknowable thing returns to the human who contemplates it nothing more than the knowledge of his or her insufficiency in its presence. Davis, on the other hand, construes the thing as one more metaphor in a symbolic system which, by his own admission, people like him largely control.

The struggle over meaning and the concern for its destruction are shared by each of the principal white characters, who articulate in turn their fear that their world is crumbling. Strikingly, each of them (and only them) is the object of a bizarre, random event, all but one involving violent crime. Each of the unusual events that happen to the white people causes a disruption in the way they perceive themselves in the world. In general, that disruption involves an element of brute reality— physical violence—obtruding into the order of their lives. What is continually put into question is the law, whether as the guarantor of general societal order or as bestower of filial identity. The breakdown in meaning that *Grand Canyon*'s white characters repeatedly lament is thus the anxiety over the dissolution of a monolithic master code of symbolic authority according to which they can organize and understand their lives.

Mack would seem to be the film's representative of symbolic authority, but his association with it extends beyond his purely professional relationship to the law: he is also identified with the scopic regime of authority the film establishes in the form of an obtrusive ubiquity of helicopters. As in John Singleton's *Boyz N the Hood*, the sight and sound of police helicopters intrude into a great deal of the shots, and they often serve as thematic links tying together many of the film's narrative sequences. In fact, even before the film's first image illuminates the screen, the sound of a helicopter fades in and then out, as though to situate everything that follows under the watchful control of legitimate authority. Mack becomes intimately connected to the vigilant and controlling scopic regime of authority when, in the first of the film's dream sequences, he flies over the city of Los Angeles in imitation of the police helicopter. The sequence begins with a high aerial shot of the city of Los Angeles; a helicopter swoops down from the left of the frame and disappears out the bottom. Then from the right Mack enters, flying high above the city. He effortlessly swoops past buildings, and dives and climbs over the city; suddenly, however, he loses his power of flight and begins to plunge to the ground. Regaining at the last moment his gift of flight, he flies over to an apartment building and hovers outside a bedroom window, gazing in. Lying in bed, nude and in a sexual pose, is his secretary, with whom he had a brief affair. He peers at her displayed body when suddenly, as though it had been projected on glass, the image of the young woman shatters and what appears behind it is Mack's own bedroom.

This dream sequence is striking first of all because it explicitly connects Mack's gaze with that of the police. More important, however, is the manner in which the gaze associated with the law is also coupled with erotics. That is, Mack adopts the regulatory surveillance of the police helicopters in his dream; he seems empowered to oversee civic activity, but in addition he assumes the disposition of the principal subject of sexuality in his dominating, obtrusive voyeurism upon the carefully exhibited woman's body. Although in his dream Mack appears to stand in for the controlling and penetrating gaze of legitimate authority, his association with that authority nevertheless remains incomplete. Since Mack can neither sustain himself in flight nor retain control of the image of the woman, he identifies with the law without, however, managing to become it.

Mack is a lawyer, a husband, a lover, a boss, a teacher, and a father. Strikingly, the one significant male role we do not see him fill or attempt to fill is that of son. Despite filling the white male, patriarchal position in such an overdetermined fashion, however, Mack continually questions the security of his situation. The dream sequence underscores his hysteria with respect to his gender position, and it is his encounter with Simon in the streets of Los Angeles that seems fundamentally responsible for bringing to light his racial hysteria. When he gets in the tow truck with Simon, a brief flashback of a bus whizzing by his face connects the events that have just transpired with an earlier episode; the sense of that episode will only be revealed later on when, in the first of his attempts to forge a more intimate relationship with Simon, Mack shows up at his garage and offers to buy him breakfast. During their breakfast, Mack tells Simon of an event that happened three years earlier while he was walking down Wilshire Boulevard on his way to an important meeting. Preoccupied with business details, he carelessly stepped off the curb; a hand reached up and grabbed him by the collar, pulling him back a split second before he would have been crushed by the speeding city bus. Mack turned around to see who was responsible for saving his life, and was startled to see a young woman wearing a Pittsburgh Pirates baseball cap. Because the Pittsburgh Pirates had been Mack's favorite baseball team since he was a child, and also because Mack's son, Roberto, was named after Roberto Clemente, his favorite player on the team, Mack searches to make the event meaningful. "I just wondered later on," Mack tells Simon, "was she for real?"

Like Hall Montana in Baldwin's novel, Simon feels compelled to respond to the question the white man implicitly poses him. "Is that what you wonder about me?" he returns. Mack and Simon's breakfast conversation, which began with the two comparing their respective experiences playing high school basketball, thus turns into a mock psychoanalytic session. Simon completes his assumption of the role of the subject presumed to know—that is, the analyst—when he tells Mack, "You got a right to try to figure out what confuses you." He assumes the position of the analyst for Mack, becoming the figure of stable and secure knowledge, much like what Hall Montana called a "peculiar mirror." Furthermore, the flashback to the scene in the street, in which Mack was rescued from the city bus, serves here as a sort of primal scene: the meaning of the situation in which the unknown woman stepped in from out of the blue to save Mack's life only surged forth after he was rescued by Simon, once again in the street, and once again completely unexpectedly. Casting his racial and gender others as analogous agents of his own preservation, Mack can only think of them as allied mystical agents whose sole function seems to be to sustain him. Mack locates the meaning of these two random occurrences at the level of his own identity. He strives to cast these two incidents of more or less pure contingency into a form that will have significance for his life.

The film's diegesis sustains Mack's effort to cast other people as characters in his own life, and that is how it continues to pose the issue of the struggle over meaning. First, it establishes the fear of the randomness and nonsense of the world on the side of the white people, and then it portrays something significant happening to each character in the film except Mack. Most of them find long awaited lovers (Simon and Jane get one another, an arrangement Mack set up; Roberto finds a girlfriend at summer camp; Mack's secretary, Dee, we are led to believe, will date the policeman who rescues her when she is attacked in her car), Claire finds a baby, and Davis finds the meaning of life after he is shot in the leg by a robber. Despite the fact, however, that the other characters do not obsess over the random events in which they are involved—Simon never once mentions his rescue of Mack to anyone else, for example—each such event is reinscribed as somehow significant for or dependent on Mack. Nothing in *Grand Canyon* happens to Mack, but nearly everything happens because of him or for him. It's hard to think of a film, in fact, that is less "about" its main character.

I would argue, in fact, that Mack occupies in nearly paradigmatic fashion the position of the father. His only function is to hold the whole ensemble together, to provide it with the interpretive key that gives the totality a meaning. It is only because we perceive the individual narratives through Mack—because, that is, they are inscribed in the film as having a global significance only in relationship to him—that the film can sustain some sort of narrative point. Furthermore, the film continually interrogates Mack's adequacy as an organizing, structuring presence by highlighting his gender and racial hysteria on the one hand, and by bringing all the film's characters together in the end to confront the figure of their symbolic variance on the other.[91] After Mack fixes Simon up with Jane, his secretary's friend, Simon thanks him by taking him and his family out to the Grand Canyon, and the film's final sequence finds all the principal characters lined up at the edge of the abyss.

I'm going to leave aside the irony implicit in the fact that when Mack fixes up a man he barely knows with a woman he doesn't know at all he is, in fact, engaging in an exchange of women that might ideally characterize the patriarch. What is striking about the film's final sequence is that Simon's act of gratitude undoes the apparently apodictic nature of white masculine hegemony in the control and definition of meaning. That is, although the film casts Mack as the organizing center of narrative coherence, that coherence and its association with particular configurations of meaning is destabilized when all of the film's principal characters peer into the abyss. The two competing interpretations of the Grand Canyon—Simon's and Davis's—vie with at least four others as all of the characters are individually shot in close-up as they catch their first glimpse of the site. Because they all have such radically different relationships to the law and symbolic authority, and especially because Mack's privileged position as a white male has been so severely undermined, the Grand Canyon simply lies there as a thing, no longer functioning either as the limit to understanding and thus as a sign of human insignificance, or as the metaphor of social fragmentation (which may come down to the same thing). It would seem to become instead simply another contested site of meaning, an element of the real that, depending on the contingencies of social interaction, can get appropriated as another signifier in a complex symbolic order.

Perhaps paradoxically, *Grand Canyon* seems to be culturally honest with respect to the position most white men inhabit. That position, one of constant negotiation with and differentiation from specific racial and gender identities, is resolutely hysterical because it can never coincide with the cultural ideal it is enjoined to become. It either refuses or is unable to embody the master signifiers responsible for naming it. The film's final shot correlates the irresolution of that hysterical identity by briefly grafting viewers' gazes onto Mack's. That shot begins with the two principal families—Mack's and Simon's—lined up along the edge of the canyon. A crane shot swings around from a medium-long, oblique frontal view of the characters, back behind them, and then zooms over their heads into the canyon. When it dissolves into a helicopter shot soaring through the canyon, viewers, like Mack in the dream sequence, are placed in the scopic position reserved for the representatives of the law. Yet, as our gaze is directed into the huge chasm, past rock outcroppings and into fathomless fissures, it is effectively prevented from capturing anything because of the vast, overwhelming spectacle before it. No longer does association with the gaze represent control of erotics and the supervisory penetration of the law. Liberated from any controlling agency, the gaze scans the awesome abyss, now detached from the various contested meanings the film had earlier attached to it. The power of the gaze is in fact subverted by the vast expanse it would purport to apprehend.

I don't mean to imply by my readings of gender and racial hysteria in the white male protagonists of these films that *White Men Can't Jump* and *Grand Canyon* are necessarily progressive movies. Both, in fact, are somewhat vicious because in their comedic depiction of confused masculinity they seem to endorse the position that white men are justified in asking others to determine their identity. The smarmy Mack, in fact, seems so self-righteous in his obsequious treatment of the people around him that when one sees him standing at the edge of the Grand Canyon one almost finds oneself wishing that at least *some* white men could jump. I also want to underscore the fact that when I refer to hysteria in racial and gender identification, I am not invoking a free-floating void of specific characteristics, but a problematic response to the realization that whiteness and maleness, frequently summoned as *standards,* are actually historically and culturally determined racial and gender *identities.* Rethinking not the fact of white masculine hegemony, but its genealogy might help us view it dialectically and consequently understand what network of discourses produces it. I use the term "network of discourses" in order to disarticulate white masculinity from the structure referred to as the law, since it seems to me that only by admitting a lack of coincidence between the identity and the discourse can we escape the sort of essentialism inherent in reference to a univocal symbolic order prohibiting individual agency. White masculinity is what Judith Butler has called a "performance constituted by the expressions that are said to be its results";[92] it thus has traditionally established its point in space as the one with which all subjects have to situate themselves.

By way of wrapping up, I want to turn to James Baldwin once again, this time from *The Fire Next Time:* "It is now absolutely clear that white people are a minority in the world—so severe a minority that they now look rather more like an invention."[93] I would like to suggest that if whiteness is an invention, a hysterical identity response arising in a specific historical context, it surely is an invention by and of white people that is foisted off on others. Whiteness has this in common with masculinity, that it constructs for itself its own internal inconsistency— the brothers in Freud's myth of the primal horde, who invented a patriarchal figure more complete than any of them could ever become, defined ideal masculinity as impossible to achieve, consequently reserving for others the possibility of theorizing precisely what it is and where it fails. I now find myself in a paradoxical situation: I cannot attempt too deft a conclusion, one that would suggest that I have the final truth about white men or how we work, yet I nevertheless cannot force the last word on someone else. It seems, then, that white masculinity's ideological strength and weakness, which might in fact coincide almost completely, inhere in the simultaneous privilege and responsibility that identity grants its others of defining what it is.

AFTERWORD

In an article dedicated to understanding the links between consciousness and the unconscious, Sigmund Freud compared what he called the derivatives of unconscious instinctual impulses to specific kinds of human beings: "We may compare them with those human half-breeds who, taken all round, resemble white men, but betray their coloured descent by some striking feature or other, on account of which they are excluded from society and enjoy none of the privileges of white people."[1] Freud's goal in that essay is to demonstrate that although these mental activities are qualitatively preconscious, they are factually unconscious, and consequently that "their origin remains decisive for the fate they will undergo."[2] Whatever the point of his metapsychological observations, however, Freud's comparison is telling: in his analysis, the nature of mixed race people, like that of unconscious instinctual impulses, depends on their origins. Without access to their genealogies, one cannot fully understand either, since they are never quite what they appear. Furthermore, since their origins determine their fate, their identities hinge not on who they appear to be or on what they do, but on a specific, historically contingent form of knowledge: both the essence and the fate of unconscious instinctual impulses and of mixed race people turn on what people already know them to be.

What interests me most in Freud's comparison of "human half-breeds" with unconscious instinctual impulses, however, is the liminal space that both seem to occupy. Fitting squarely into none of the categories designed to receive them, neither the mental activity that Freud describes nor the sorts of people to whom he compares it has a proper identity; both need to be understood in terms of something else. Both unconscious instinctual impulses and the mixed race person, that is, can only be understood through expressions and definitions designed for some other purpose—in short, never precisely on their own terms, because they have no terms explicitly their own. But, given that the classic example Freud provides of these unconscious instinctual impulses is fantasy-formation, what is more arresting still about his comparison to the "human half-breed" is the fact that this human identity is, precisely, a fantasy. On the one hand it is built on the notion that there are people who, although they outwardly resemble one particular variety of human being, have an entirely different nature only discernible through some unspecified "striking"—yet, somehow, invisible—feature. Furthermore, the essential difference that half-breeds manifest is a difference from "white people," and it is a difference that only matters if one knows that they are different (they "betray their coloured descent"). And it is worth noting that it is the "half-breed" who is analogous to unconscious mental activity, while the "white people" simply are what they seem to be. On the other hand, however, what is particularly gripping about Freud's comparison with the "human half-breed" is the fantasy that "white people" comprise a pure, uncontaminated racial stock, one whose origins reveal no corruption by other "breeds."

In this book, I have examined the complex human identity generally referred to as the white male. One of my principal concerns has been the fantasmal nature of the pure categories of maleness and whiteness, and I have been equally concerned with the consequences facing men who seem not to be able to live up to what it means to be a white man. Whiteness and masculinity are not merely like the fantasies that Freud describes—they are themselves complex cultural fantasies, and they operate largely on the principal of exclusion characterizing the half-breeds mentioned above. That is, whiteness and masculinity function as negations of their presumed counterparts, as we saw in the example of the famous one drop of blood rule that developed in colonial America. White masculinity sustains an identity by excluding other positions, positions that are largely the invention of white masculinity itself. Two significant consequences arise from that fact: First, the threat of contamination or corruption that encumbers white masculinity casts that identity as hysterical, since not only is there little internal corroboration for what it is, but also there is always the nagging fear that one is not white or male enough. Second, white masculinity has come to be understood as a set of alienable properties that constitute the individual possessing them.

My investigation of white masculinity has necessitated detailed analysis of the categories that make it up, categories relating expressly to gender, race, and, to a lesser extent, class and national origin. Furthermore, the investigation has also required taking a close look at theories of hegemony, since by virtually any account it is the straight white male who occupies what is generally referred to as the "dominant" position in contemporary American culture. What I have tried to show is that white masculinity is less a thing, an entity, or even a position, than it is a response or a function. Just as with Freud's "human half-breeds," in which seeing is not always believing since a detailed knowledge of origins is in order, white masculinity depends on astonishingly complex networks of knowledge in order to sustain its identity. But its hegemonic position only lasts as long as the illusion of adequation between signifier and signified sustains itself, and as we have seen, the discourse of the master that characterizes such an adequation relies on a privileging of specific master signifiers and forms of knowledge. No less crucial to the maintenance of that discourse, however, is the rejection or repression of forms of knowledge, and those two operations work in tandem to produce the effect I have been referring to as "believing is seeing." Such an effect ideally suits the phallic function that we defined in chapter 4, since the paradoxical relationship of white masculinity to the phallic function specifies that what is most purely phallic is that which is least material, most ideal; real men approximate with difficulty that function since their own corruptible corporality distances them from the ideal lineage of masculine, ideational ancestry that animated feminine raw material. White masculinity thus encodes complex cultural phenomena, such as legitimizing the unequal transmission of property rights, treating as cross-cultural specific forms of logic and reason, or naturalizing as scientific or biological specific forms of historical inequality. In overdetermined fashion it stands in for and represents a host of social, political, personal, and ideological principles.

But what we have seen is that white masculinity isn't always simply about race and gender, at least not explicitly. As we saw in the case of Oedipus's determined effort to insert himself into a cogent social order regardless of the criminal identity he needed to assume in order to do so, maintaining a coherent and unified social identity has depended on

causing tremendously complex and internally contradictory social identifiers to cast themselves as expressions of far more restricted markers
of identity. Hence, Freud and most other proponents of psychoanalysis
could read the Oedipal scenario as a more or less circumscribed story
about gender—specifically masculinity—and all but ignore the fact that
the social work it takes to disregard the instances of civic status, national origin, generational position, and social legitimacy that the tale
also evokes is the same social work that constitutes masculinity as what
we defined as phallic in the first place. That same act of disregarding
was also responsible for codifying a racially scripted form of thinking as
a transcultural and transparent mode of reason ostensibly able to gauge
the viability of most if not all other forms of thought.

The different historical moments I have visited in this analysis of
white masculinity range from the early modern European to the contemporary American, and we pass from Sigmund Freud's incestuous
Oedipal dreams to Mack's highly overdetermined patriarchal authority
dreams. So where do these dreams, each of which articulates a specific
symbolic system derived from particular psychological, economic, morphological, and desiring systems, leave us? We set out in a critique of
meaning's stability and the political conditions giving rise to a discourse
of the master, noting that in the case of Oedipus a complex of social and
political oppositions consolidated in the form of a single difference
constructed as sexual. Finding that gender has a genealogy consisting
in large part of obfuscated social identifiers subtended in the overarching category of human reproductive dimorphism, we also noted that
even our attempts to understand or analyze the social identifiers we
deploy perform the social work those categories were designed to accomplish. We moved on to discover that our most basic and ostensibly
neutral forms of evaluative thought—Enlightenment logic and reason—
are rooted in morphology, specifically in the white male body, and that
the male genitalia, which in many accounts of psychoanalytic thought
serve as the model for the intact human body, need to be white to rise to
their full power. Defending the Lacanian notion of the phallus as that
which articulates the material and the abstract—both the materiality of
the body and the abstraction of signification, as well as the ideality of the
body and the physicality required for signifiers' transmission—we observed that those who mistake that concept for the penis inadvertently
reproduce the structures of domination because they sustain the mys-

tique of male power by reducing a complex network of difference to a single identifier for masculinity; they also maintain whiteness in its position of invisibility, from which it can accomplish its most invidious tasks.

Throughout this book I have opted to think about white masculinity through what may well appear to be unorthodox views of psychoanalytic terms and theories. I have shown that modes of conceptualizing postulated by psychoanalysis—in particular those that locate the juncture of the material and the abstract, especially in relation to human morphology—serve especially well to illuminate an identity that for so long has passed itself off as empty or transparent, but more important, I have demonstrated that hysteria as a critical response to conflicting demands encodes the problems and issues associated with white men especially well. That is because psychoanalysis can help us see into the obfuscated realms of social existence, not by lifting a veil to uncover the truth underpinning false consciousness, but by allowing us to look at thought processes themselves as culturally determined objects whose historical and cultural specificities provide each of us with the illusion of our bodies' fundamental naturalness. Yet, if psychoanalysis, particularly the Lacanian strands I have emphasized here, gives us the tools to discern the ideological dimensions of what has traditionally passed as purely personal and intimately idiosyncratic ways of conceptualizing the world, it has also generally remained tethered to a single form of difference through which to form those concepts. As I have been arguing throughout this book, we need to rethink the notion of a fundamental or initializing difference with respect to human identity, because remaining tied to a single paradigm produces the phallic blindness to the workings of other kinds of difference elaborated in chapter 4.

Rethinking that fundamental form of difference is both a theoretical and a political correlate of the basic claim I have been advancing throughout this book, namely that white masculinity constitutes a hysterical response to competing and contradicting cultural demands. Unless we recognize white masculinity as the product of culture, and not as culture's apodictic spokesman, we will continue to seek out ways—just as Oedipus did—of producing unified meaning. We will eschew the productive dialog or even conflict that might give voice to those forms of identity that lack language or even form in the discursive registers we have been using to critique hegemonic identities. Can we dismantle the master's house with the master's tools? Maybe. But why even try? To continue to combat the master on his own turf by using his key signifiers bolsters the strength of the system that produces those terms, and it further disenfranchises those who either have no access to them or who are not articulated by them. It seems especially prudent in an era repeatedly defined as postmodern to recall that when Oedipus avoided conflict, that's when all the trouble began. Ironically, in a culture that defines reason, morphological integrity, and subjective legitimacy according to the impossibly fleeting definitions of what is white and what is male, it's important to remember that white men aren't.

NOTES

INTRODUCTION

1 Susan Jeffords has looked at the manner in which both war and the conservative economics and politics of the Reagan era brought about changes in contemporary American masculinities. See her *Remasculinization of America* (Bloomington: University of Indiana Press, 1989) and *Hard Bodies: Hollywood Masculinity in the Reagan Era* (New Brunswick, N.J.: Rutgers University Press, 1994).

2 See also David Savran, who argues that "a gendered identity, on account of its contingency, is of all identifications the one most subject to intensive social pressures, the most anxiety-ridden, the most consistently imbricated in social, political, and economic negotiations, and thus the most sensitive barometer of culture" (Savran, *Taking It Like a Man* [Princeton: Princeton University Press, 1998], 8). Victor J. Seidler discusses this side of masculinity by noting that "it is always something you have to be ready to defend and prove. You have to prove that you are as much a man as everyone else" (Seidler, *Recreating Sexual Politics* [London: Routledge, 1991], 132).

3 There is a large and growing body of study surrounding masculinity, and it is interesting to note that as of this writing, the Library of Congress subject headings lists 411 titles for "masculinity" and 283 for "femininity," and 1130 under "feminism."

4 Peter Hutchings phrases the problem thus: "Inasmuch as a man is the subject of patriarchy, then he has power. However, this power is not his personal property, it does not emerge from within his own unique being. Rather it appertains to those institutional and ideological positions which the male individual occupies and through which he finds an identity. In this respect, power takes on an alienating quality: it can be used but it can never be owned" (Hutchings, "Masculinity and the Horror Film," in *You Tarzan: Masculinity, Movies, and Men,* eds. Pat Kirkham and Janet Thumin [New York: St. Martin's Press, 1993], 92).

5 See in particular T. W. Adorno, E. Frenkel-Brunswick, D. J. Levinson, and R. N.

Sanford, *The Authoritarian Personality* (New York: Wiley, 1950) and W. Miller, "Lower-Class Culture as a Generating Milieu for Gang Delinquency," *Journal of Social Issues* 14 (1958): 5–19.

6   Sigmund Freud, *The Ego and the Id*, trans. Joan Riviere (New York: Norton, 1960), 24.

7   Michael Kimmel has investigated many of the conflicting cultural cues directed to men in the 1960s and later. He defines a "masculine mystique"—an ironic echo of Betty Friedan's "feminine mystique"—which consisted of an "impossible synthesis of sober responsible breadwinner, imperviously stoic master of his fate, and swashbuckling hero," and he also argues that such a mystique was exposed as fraudulent (Kimmel, *Manhood in America* [New York: Free Press, 1997], 262).

8   A complex series of exchanges with Hans and his father makes this clear. Hans tells his father that "every one has a widdler. And my widdler will get bigger as I get bigger, because it does grow on to me" (Sigmund Freud, "Analysis of Phobia in a Five-Year-Old Boy," in *The Sexual Enlightenment of Children* [New York: Macmillan, 1963], 74); and another with his father, in which the little boy projects a moment when he will have a mature masculine body. Hans dreams that a plumber came and removed his behind and his widdler. Then:

> FATHER: He gave you a *bigger* widdler and a *bigger* behind.
> HANS: Yes.
> FATHER: Like Daddy's; because you'd like to be Daddy.
> HANS: Yes, and I'd like to have a moustache and hairs like yours (136).

9   Sigmund Freud, "Contributions to the Psychology of Love," in *Sexuality and the Psychology of Love* (New York: Macmillan, 1963), 81.

10 Many have called for a self-critical examination of the stakes of discussing whiteness, or of making whiteness an object of study in the first place. See in particular Mike Hill, "Vipers in Shangri-la: Whiteness, Writing, and Other Ordinary Terrors," in *Whiteness*, ed. Mike Hill (New York: New York University Press, 1997), 1–18; Robyn Wiegman, "Whiteness Studies and the Paradox of Particularity," *Boundary 2* (26), no. 3 (fall 1999): 115–50; Ruth Frankenberg, "Local Whitenesses, Localizing Whiteness," in *Displacing Whiteness*, ed. Ruth Frankenberg (Durham, N.C.: Duke University Press, 1997), 1–33; Deborah E. McDowell, "Pecs and Reps," in *Race and the Subject of Masculinities*, eds. Harry Stecopoulos and Michael Uebel (Durham, N.C.: Duke University Press, 1997: 361–85); and Mason Stokes, *The Color of Sex* (Durham, N.C.: Duke University Press, 2001), especially 11–14.

11 A notable early work on psychoanalysis and masculinity is Stephen Frosh, *Sexual Difference: Masculinity and Psychoanalysis* (New York: Routledge, 1994).

12 John Brenkman makes a similar argument, but not with the same object in mind. He writes that "it is indeed my view that Freud's fashioning of Oedipal

theory was itself a strategic response to the many-sided *and* largely unsolvable problems of his own social, political, sexual world. Distilled to a triangular, familial, ultimately intrapsychic conflict, these problems were made to appear curable" (Brenkman, *Straight Male Modern: A Cultural Critique of Psychoanalysis* [New York: Routledge, 1993], 233).

13 Thomas Laqueur raises similar questions in his *Making Sex:* "The history of the representation of the anatomical differences between man and woman is thus extraordinarily independent of the actual structures of these organs or of what was known about them. Ideology, not accuracy of observation, determined how they were seen and which differences would matter" (Laqueur, *Making Sex* [Cambridge, Mass.: Harvard University Press, 1990], 88).

14 Ernesto Laclau and Chantal Mouffe point out, calling *paradigm* what I am referring to as "cultural metaphors," that "the paradigm reduces the number of pertinent structural differences, but . . . it fixes them through the attribution to each of a *single meaning*, understood as a precise location within a totality" (Laclau and Mouffe, *Hegemony and Socialist Strategy* [New York: Verso, 1985], 15).

15 Arthur de Gobineau, *The Moral and Intellectual Diversity of Races,* trans. H. Hotz (Philadelphia: J. B. Lippincott and Co., 1856), 380–81.

16 Simon LeVay, *The Sexual Brain* (Cambridge, Mass.: MIT Press, 1993), 127.

17 There is, of course, a vast amount of material dealing with the scientific dimension of race. See in particular Anthony Appiah on W. E. B. Du Bois and the use of science to determine race (Appiah, "The Uncompleted Argument: Du Bois and the Illusion of Race," in *Race, Writing, and Difference,* ed. Henry Louis Gates Jr. [Chicago: University of Chicago Press, 1989], 21–37); Benno Muller-Hill, on Nazi Germany's attempts to apply scientific theory to practices of genocide (Muller-Hill, *Murderous Science* [New York: Oxford University Press, 1988]); Michael Omi and Howard Winant, *Racial Formation in the United States* (New York: Routledge and Kegan Paul, 1986); Londa Schiebinger, *Nature's Body* (Boston: Beacon Press, 1993); Nancy Stepan, *The Idea of Race in Science: Great Britain 1800–1960* (Hamden, Conn.: Archon, 1982); Ann Thomson, "From *L'Histoire naturelle de l'homme* to the Natural History of Mankind," *British Journal for Eighteenth-Century Studies* 9, no. 1 (spring 1986): 73–80; and Sandra Harding, ed., *The Racial Economy of Science* (Bloomington: Indiana University Press, 1993).

18 Margaret Homans, "'Racial Composition': Metaphor and the Body in the Writing of Race," in *Female Subjects in Black and White,* eds. Elizabeth Abel, Barbara Christian, and Helene Moglen (Berkeley: University of California Press, 1997), 77.

19 Mason Stokes writes that "whiteness exists simultaneously as anxiety and uncertainty *and* as a normative and disciplinary social structure" (Stokes, *Color of Sex,* 24).

20 Anne Fausto-Sterling, "How to Build a Man," in *Constructing Masculinity*, eds. Maurice Berger, Brian Wallis, and Simon Watson (New York: Routledge, 1995), 131.

Similarly, writing of the phallus, that standard of masculinity, Stephen Frosh remarks that "it becomes a burden to the man; living up to it becomes the necessary condition of masculinity, which is therefore always in danger of being betrayed and undermined" (Frosh, *Sexual Difference*, 78); Drucilla Cornell writes of a "phantasmatic masculinity haunted by its inability to realize its fantasy persona" (Cornell, *The Imaginary Domain* [New York: Routledge, 1995], 140).

21 James R. Barrett and David Roediger point to organized labor activity as one of the reasons why previously "nonwhite" groups became white. Greeks and Italians, they maintain, participated in a tense strike of the Western Federation of Miners in 1912, and the category of white worker expanded after that event (Barrett and Roediger, "How White People Became White," in *Critical White Studies*, eds. Richard Delgado and Jean Stefancic [Philadelphia: Temple University Press, 1992], 404).

22 *United States v Thind*, 261 US 204, 209 (1922).

23 Doug Daniels has in fact suggested that the white race is shrinking. He argues that the range of ethnicities considered to be "white" is becoming ever smaller, and speculates that to be labelled a "white" nation it is at least as important as being a member of NATO or another pro-Western alliance, politically stable, wealthy, and industrialized. Anti-Western, poor, politically unstable (especially revolutionary), and nonindustrial countries tend to be excluded from the white race of the 1980s (D. Daniels, "The White Race Is Shrinking: Perceptions of Race in Canada and Some Speculations on the Political Economy of Race Classification," in *Critical White Studies*, eds. Richard Delgado and Jean Stefancic [Philadelphia: Temple University Press, 1997], 53). *United States v Thind* was not the only case, nor was it the most recent, in which the Supreme Court had to pronounce on the variability of race. In *St. Francis College v Al-Khazraji* (481 US 604, 606–13 [1987]) and *Shaare Tefila Congregation v Cobb* (481 US 615, 617–18 [1987]) the Court had to contend with whether Arabs and Jews were distinct races.

24 Or, as Ira Gollobin writes, "Science would be superfluous if all aspects of things, their inner and outer nature, were accessible to simple inspection" (Gollobin, *Dialectical Materialism* [New York: Petras, 1986], 91). In *Sunseri v Cassagne* (196 So. 7 [La. 1940]), which involved a white man seeking annulment of his marriage because his wife was legally a Negro (and Louisiana prohibited such marriages), the court had to decide what racial classification to apply to a woman who looked like a white person and identified herself as one, yet who was not legally such a person. See Katherine M. Franke, "What Does a White Woman Look Like? Racing and Erasing in Law," in *Critical White Studies*,

eds. Richard Delgado and Jean Stefancic [Philadelphia: Temple University Press, 1997], especially 467–69.

25 Homi K. Bhabha makes a similar argument: "To speak of masculinity in general, sui generis, must be avoided at all costs. It is a discourse of self-generation, reproduced over the generations in patrilineal perpetuity, that masculinity seeks to make a name for itself" (Bhabha, "Are You a Man or a Mouse?," in *Constructing Masculinity*, eds. Maurice Berger, Brian Wallis, and Simon Watson [New York: Routledge, 1995], 57).

26 David Hillman and Carla Mazzio have recently argued that bodily partitioning was particularly fluid during the Enlightenment, but that sometimes the partitioning recognized seemed natural. They write that "influential philosophers like Paracelsus and Van Helmont went so far as to argue that parts were individuated not only lexically and physiologically but also ontologically: to the isolated organs belonged what were termed *ideae singularum partium*—so that, for instance, there existed an *idea ocularis* in the eye, or an *idea sanguinis* in the heart—imparting integrity and spiritual significance to each part of the body" (Hillman and Mazzio, introduction to *The Body in Parts*, eds. David Hillman and Carla Mazzio [New York: Routledge, 1997], xviii).

27 Luce Irigaray, *Speculum of the Other Woman*, trans. Gillian C. Gill (Ithaca, N.Y.: Cornell University Press, 1985), 133.

28 Toni Morrison, *Playing in the Dark: Whiteness and the Literary Imagination* (Cambridge, Mass.: Harvard University Press, 1992), 47.

29 See also Victor J. Seidler, who writes, "For heterosexual men, the particularity of our experience has remained invisible" (Seidler, *Rediscovering Masculinity: Reason, Language, and Sexuality* [London: Routledge, 1989], 18). Ellie Ragland-Sullivan takes a deconstructive view of masculinity, arguing that "indeed, the male *qua* male might be called the cultural lie which maintains that sexual identity can be personified by making difference itself a position" (Ragland-Sullivan, "The Sexual Masquerade," in *Lacan and the Subject of Language*, eds. Ellie Ragland-Sullivan and Mark Bracher [New York: Routledge, 1991], 50–51).

30 Benedict Anderson, *Imagined Communities* (New York: Verso, 1991), 37–46.

31 Ernesto Laclau and Chantal Mouffe have provided perhaps the most useful definition of articulation when they refer to "any practice establishing a relation among elements such that their identity is modified as a result of the articulatory practice" (Laclau and Mouffe, *Hegemony*, 105). Marjorie Garber points out that syntax is a system of conjoined parts forming complex structures: "*Syntax*, in modern usage most frequently considered as an aspect of grammar, and *articulation*, frequently regarded as an aspect of speech, thus each inhabit, in their early modern forms, an intellectual and conceptual space modeled on the body, and, quite specifically, on its 'connexions' or joints" (Garber, "Out of Joint," in *The Body in Parts*, eds. David Hillman and Carla Mazzio [New York: Routledge, 1997], 35).

32 Here I am following Winthrop Jordan, who argues that the term "white" began
to appear consistently as an identifier for human beings toward the end of the
seventeenth century: "There seems to have been something of a shift during
the seventeenth century in the terminology which Englishmen in the colonies
applied to themselves. From the initially most common term *Christian*, at mid-
century there was a marked drift toward *English* and *free*. After about 1680,
taking the colonies as a whole, a new term appeared—*white*" (Jordan, *White
Over Black: American Attitudes Toward the Negro, 1550–1812* [Chapel Hill: University of North Carolina Press, 1968], 95).

33 I am not so naive as to suggest, of course, that all of the features traditionally
associated with the concept of "race" can be distilled to the question of skin
color. I will discuss in chapter 2 the physical, moral, linguistic, and sexual distinctions, in addition to the morphological ones, that have traditionally marked
the differences between groups of people deemed to belong to separate "races."

34 Garber wonders whether theoretical constructions of masculinity have not
gone so far as to make "masculine" absolutely synonymous with "subject," and
whether some theories of gender have not constructed masculinity as completely apodictic. Asking whether some theoretical discussions of masculinity
do not reflect the urge to chip away at the monolith they have inadvertently
built, she writes: "Does 'male subjectivity,' conceptualized, represent anything
more than a wishful logic of equality, which springs from a feminist desire to
make 'man' part rather than whole? Is 'male subjectivity' not, in fact, like
'female fetishism,' a theoretical tit-for-tat which finally demonstrates the limits
of theorization when it comes to matters of gender construction?" (Marjorie
Garber, "Spare Parts: The Surgical Construction of Gender." Differences 1,
no. 3 [fall 1989]: 137).

35 Kaja Silverman, *Male Subjectivity at the Margins* (New York: Routledge, 1992),
61.

36 Ibid., 34.

37 Ibid., 30. It is also important to mention at this juncture that another recent
book on white masculinity, David Savran's *Taking It Like a Man*, posits narrative as one of the dominant modes for understanding cultural change and
differences in identity. In his Introduction, Savran writes, "I hope to demonstrate that social, political, and economic initiatives are always constructed as
narratives and that cultural texts simultaneously shape, consolidate, and reflect
diverse subjectivities and social practices" (6).

38 Laclau and Mouffe, *Hegemony*, 7.

39 Ibid., 96.

40 Ibid., 112. Raymond Williams, whose writings on hegemony no doubt influenced Laclau and Mouffe, argues that "Hegemony is . . . not only the articulate
upper level of 'ideology,' nor are its forms of control only those ordinarily seen
as 'manipulation' or 'indoctrination.' It is a whole body of practices and expec-

tations, over the whole of living. . . . It is a lived system of meaning and values—constitutive and constituting—which as they are experienced as practices appear as reciprocally confirming. . . . It is, that is to say, in the strongest sense a 'culture,' but a culture which has also to be seen as the lived dominance and subordination of particular classes" (Williams, *Marxism and Literature* [Oxford: Oxford University Press, 1977], 111).

41 Similarly, in her "Terror of Consensus," Françoise Gaillard writes that "to deny conflicts . . . means eliminating from the consensual community all those who are not party to this consensus, in other words, all those to whom the provisions of the consensus do irremediable harm" (Gaillard, "Terror of Consensus," in *Terror and Consensus,* eds. Jean-Joseph Goux and Philip R. Wood [Stanford, Calif.: Stanford University Press, 1998], 68).

42 Benedetto Fontana, *Hegemony and Power* (Minneapolis: University of Minnesota Press, 1993), 160.

43 Alenka Zupančič poses this concern as a question, and makes the stake of that question's answer seem almost dire: "What happens if this other is really the Other, if his/her difference is not only a 'cultural,' 'folkloric' difference, but a fundamental difference? Are we still to respect him/her, to love him/her?" (Zupančič, "The Subject of the Law," in *Cogito and the Unconscious,* ed. Slavoj Žižek [Durham, N.C.: Duke University Press, 1998], 43).

44 Žižek's formulation seems clear and concise: "The fact that the Real operates and is accessible only through the Symbolic does not authorize us to conceive of it as a factor immanent to the Symbolic: the Real is precisely that which resists and eludes the grasp of the Symbolic and, consequently, that which is detectable within the Symbolic only under the guise of its disturbances" (Žižek, *The Metastases of Enjoyment* [London: Verso, 1994], 30).

45 Kalpana Seshadri-Crooks also contests the belief that sexual difference is *the* fundamental difference, and in an extended critique of Silverman's reading of Althusser, she writes: "That sex must be understood as phantasmatic belief is unquestionable; what is questionable is Silverman's assumption that sexual identity precedes racial identity because the former emerges in the family" (Seshadri-Crooks, "The Comedy of Domination: Psychoanalysis and the Conceit of Whiteness," in *The Psychoanalysis of Race,* ed. Christopher Lane [New York: Columbia University Press, 1998], 356).

46 Judith Butler, *Bodies That Matter* (New York: Routledge, 1993), 5.

47 I will have occasion throughout this study to refer to a body of literature dealing with the question of race and psychoanalysis. At this juncture, however, I would simply like to note Sander Gilman's work, in particular his *Freud, Race, and Gender.* Gilman explores how the concepts of race and gender were mixed in the medical literature of Freud's time, and he examines concepts concerning ideological presuppositions that influence what people think they see. On Freud's famous pronouncements on castration, Gilman writes, for example:

"What marks the Jew as only marginally different, but as so visible? Is it not the salient sign of Judaism, the marking of the male body through circumcision? By the end of the nineteenth century the body of the Jew came to be the body of the male Jew, and it was the immutability of this sign of masculine difference that was inscribed on the psyche of the Jew. The fantasy of the difference of the male genitalia was displaced upward—onto the visible parts of the body, onto the face and the hands where it marked the skin with its blackness" (Gilman, *Freud, Race, and Gender* [Princeton: Princeton University Press, 1993], 21). European observers travelling to other cultures frequently wondered about the deliberate modifications to their bodies that people of other cultures made, and circumcision was one of the modifications that interested them most. The appearance and integrity of the male genitalia became a signifier not only for gender, I will demonstrate, but also for race.

48 Joseph Breuer and Sigmund Freud, *Studies on Hysteria* (New York: Penguin, 1988), 58.

49 Catherine Clément and Hélène Cixous, *La jeune née* (Paris: Union générale d'éditions, 1975), 289.

50 Ibid., 283–84. My translation.

51 Ibid., 258–64.

52 Charles Bernheimer, "Introduction: Part One," 6.

53 See Claire Kahane, "Introduction: Part Two," in *In Dora's Case*, eds. Charles Bernheimer and Claire Kahane (New York: Columbia University Press, 1985), 19–31. Kahane follows Clément's lead in identifying narrative structure as implicitly conservative, especially with respect to its uses in hysterical discourse. Clément writes: "The stories stolen from this or that couch take, with a few variants, the form of the nineteenth-century novel, as far as sentences, structures, and development are concerned. . . . No trace of the experiments of Guyotat, Nathalie Sarraute, or Claude Ollier; no trace of the efforts of the avant-garde, or so-called avant-garde, that strives so valiantly to take Freud's discoveries into account. . . . No, nothing but traditional story-telling, with all the loose ends tied up, at best slickly arranged. Old style" (Catherine Clément, *The Weary Sons of Freud*, trans. Nicole Ball [New York: Verso, 1987], 39).

54 Dianne F. Sadoff, *Sciences of the Flesh* (Stanford, Calif.: Stanford University Press, 1998), 16.

55 Dianne Hunter, "Hysteria, Psychoanalysis, and Feminism," in *Writing on the Body*, eds. Katie Conboy, Nadia Medina, and Sarah Stanbury (New York: Columbia University Press, 1997), 272.

56 Ibid.

57 Joel Kovel, "On Racism and Psychoanalysis," in *Psychoanalysis in Contexts*, eds. Anthony Elliott and Stephen Frosh (New York: Routledge, 1995), 206.

58 Jane Gallop, "Keys to Dora," in *In Dora's Case*, eds. Charles Bernheimer and Claire Kahane, (New York: Columbia University Press, 1985), 201.

59 See Jacqueline Rose, "Dora: Fragment of an Analysis," in *In Dora's Case*, eds. Charles Bernheimer and Claire Kahane (New York: Columbia University Press, 1985). Rose argues that in the study of Dora what "feminine sexuality reveals . . . is the persistence of the question of desire *as* a question" (145–46).

60 Ibid., 146.

61 Toril Moi, "Representation of Patriarchy: Sexuality and Epistemology in Freud's Dora," in *In Dora's Case*, eds. Charles Bernheimer and Claire Kahane (New York: Columbia University Press, 1985), 192.

62 The literature on hysteria, particularly as it relates to subjective identity and representational systems, is vast. In addition to the titles already mentioned, see in particular Monique David-Ménard, *Hysteria from Freud to Lacan* (Ithaca, N.Y.: Cornell University Press, 1989); Juliet Mitchell, *Mad Men and Medusas* (New York: Basic Books, 2000); Janet Beizer, *Ventriloquized Bodies* (Ithaca, N.Y.: Cornell University Press, 1994); Claire Kahane, *Passions of the Voice* (Baltimore: Johns Hopkins University Press, 1995); and Charles Bernheimer, *Figures of Ill Repute* (Durham, N.C.: Duke University Press, 1997).

63 I stress the word "mainstream" in this formulation, since much of the best early work on masculinity emphasized hysterical or otherwise incapacitated men. See in particular Kaja Silverman, *Male Subjectivity*; Lynn Kirby, "Male Hysteria and Early Cinema," *Camera Obscura* 17 (May 1988): 67–85; Klaus Theweleit, *Male Fantasies*, vol. 1, trans. Stephen Conway (Minneapolis: University of Minnesota Press, 1987); Christopher Lane, *Burdens of Intimacy* (Chicago: University of Chicago Press, 1999); Scott Derrick, *Monumental Anxieties* (New Brunswick, N.J.: Rutgers University Press, 1997); Mark Breitenberg, *Anxious Masculinity in Early Modern England* (Cambridge: Cambridge University Press, 1996); and Jan Goldstein, "The Uses of Male Hysteria: Medical and Literary Discourse in Nineteenth-Century France," *Representations* 34 (spring 1991): 134–65.

64 I will have occasion in chapter 3 to elaborate more fully the hysterical question and its relationship to other forms of discourse.

65 In *New Reflections on the Revolution of Our Time* Ernesto Laclau identifies "the central character of negativity" as well as "the ideological nature of collective representations—which establishes a permanent gap between the real and the manifest senses of individual and social group actions" as fundamental points where Marxism breaks from Enlightenment traditions and can establish a dialog with psychoanalysis ([New York: Verso, 1990], 94).

1. COMPLEX OEDIPUS

1 Robin N. Mitchell-Boyask has written on Freud's detailed knowledge of literature, arguing that his library "was an integral part of his work, as was expressed by the location of his analyst couch in his study surrounded by books"

(Mitchell-Boyask, "Freud's Reading of Classical Literature and Classical Philology," in *Reading Freud's Reading*, eds. Sander L. Gilman, Jutta Birmele, Jay
Geller, and Valerie D. Greenberg [New York: New York University Press, 1994],
24). Addressing the criticism that Freud looked for (and found) the Oedipus
conflict everywhere, Mitchell-Boyask writes that "Freud was merely following
the practice of fin de siècle scholars of mythology and folklore . . . who sought
corroborations for their theories in a variety of texts from different eras and
cultures. Freud was not alone in thinking the Oedipus myth said something
universal about the human condition" (37).

2   Sigmund Freud, *The Interpretation of Dreams* (New York: Avon, 1965), 295.

3   Walker Burkert, *Oedipus, Oracles, and Meaning* (Toronto: University College,
1991), 10.

4   Freud, *Interpretation of Dreams*, 295.

5   Sophocles, *Oedipus the King*, trans. David Grene, in *Greek Tragedies*, eds. David
Grene and Richmond Lattimore (Chicago: University of Chicago Press, 1960),
l. 716. Subsequent quotations from *Oedipus the King* in this chapter are cited
parenthetically by line in the text itself.

6   Another question that never arises is why the herdsman misstates the prophecy that lead to all of this in the first place. When asked why the infant was to be
killed, he replies, "They said that he should kill his parents" (l. 1177), and not
merely his father, as the original prophecy foretold.

7   Or, as William Chase Greene puts it, in what seems to be the first modern
mention of the numerical discrepancy (1929), "The question of brigand or
brigands quietly drops out of view, and the catastrophe is sufficiently promoted
by the discovery of the origin of Oedipus. This establishes him as the son of
Laius; but it does not directly carry forward his knowledge of the fact that he did
on a definite occasion kill Laius beyond the strong presentiment which he felt
when the triple ways were first mentioned" (Greene, "The Murderers of Laius,"
Transactions and Proceedings of the American Philological Association 60 [1929],
81).

Other scholars have noticed the inconsistency in the reports of Laius's murder, but most attribute the variance to carelessness, the unconscious, or to
Sophocles' style. See in particular Gilbert Norwood, who writes that when the
aged Theban is summoned, "it is to settle whether Laius was slain by one man
or by a company; by the time he arrives, this is forgotten, and all wait to know
from whom he received the outcast infant" (Norwood, *Greek Tragedy* [New
York: Hill and Wang, 1960], 149). Rush Rehn makes brief mention of the
numbers game (Rehn, *Greek Tragic Theater* [New York: Routledge, 1992], 115),
but he does not conclude anything particular about the incongruity in the
reporting of the facts behind Laius's murder. Charles Segal also makes mention of this inconsistency ("Sophocles' Oedipus Tyrannus," in *Freud and Forbidden Knowledge*, ed. Peter L. Rudnytsky and Ellen Handler Spitz [New York:

New York University Press, 1994], 74); Karl Reinhardt observes the glitch, too (Reinhardt, "Illusion and Truth in *Oedipus Tyrannus*," in *Sophocles' "Oedipus Rex,"* ed. Harold Bloom [New York: Chelsea House, 1988], 65–102). Frederick Ahl argues that the witness to the event could quite likely be lying on several counts (Ahl, *Sophocles' Oedipus* [Ithaca, N.Y.: Cornell University Press, 1991], 197–201).

The most exhaustive account of this facet of *Oedipus Rex* is Sandor Goodhart's excellent article (Goodhart, "Ληϲταζ Εφαϲχε: Oedipus and Laius' Many Murderers," *Diacritics* 8, no. 1 [spring 1978]: 55–71).

8   See also Jean-Joseph Goux, who writes that Freudian psychoanalysis is obsessed "with the myth of Oedipus which it erroneously takes as a regulatory structure" (Goux, "The Phallus: Masculine Identity and the 'Exchange of Women,'" trans. Maria Amuchastegui, Caroline Benforado, Amy Hendrix, and Eleanor Kaufman, *Differences* 4, no. 1 [1992]: 63). I will discuss the ramifications of this error in greater detail in chapter 4.

9   I am trying to emphasize the fact that the father is not a person, a point I will return to in much greater depth in chapter 5. In *The Four Fundamental Concepts of Psychoanalysis*, Jacques Lacan has occasion to refer to the "father *qua* father, that is to say, no conscious being" (Lacan, *The Four Fundamental Concepts of Psychoanalysis*, trans. Alan Sheridan [New York: Norton, 1978], 59). The fact that no living human male could ever *be* the father will become crucial later on in my discussion.

10 Of the desire to sleep with one's mother and of the representation of that desire, Freud writes: "The straightforward dream of sexual relations with one's mother, which Jocasta alludes to in the *Oedipus Rex*, is a rarity in comparison with all the dreams which psycho-analysis must interpret in the same sense" ("Some Additional Notes on Dream-Interpretation as a Whole," *Standard Edition*, 19:132). Nevertheless, there are a good number of instances in which that desire found clear expression in the ancient world. Herodotus recounts of Hippias's dream that he slept with his mother, which the dreamer interpreted to mean that "he would return to Athens, recover his power, and die peacefully at home in old age" (Herodotus, *The Histories*, trans. Aubrey de Sélincourt [New York: Penguin, 1954], 426). He was wrong. The second-century writer Pausanias reports a similar dream: "In Euhesperides Komon dreamed he was sleeping with his mother's corpse, and when they slept together his mother came back to life. Komon was hoping for a return to Naupaktos with Atyhenian naval power, but the dream showed him the salvation of Messene" (Pausanias, *Guide to Greece*, trans. Peter Levi [New York: Penguin, 1971], 2:162). In his *Interpretation of Dreams*, another second-century writer, Artemidorus, devotes a great deal of exposition to the question of what it means to dream of having sex with one's mother. Artemidorus enumerates a wide variety of considerations, including physical position, the dreamer's occupation, and how often

he sees his mother, crucial to understanding such a dream's significance (Artemidorus Daldianus, *The Interpretation of Dreams*, trans. Robert J. White [Park Ridge, N.J.: Noyes Press, 1975]).

11 Hortense J. Spillers, "All the Things You Could Be by Now, If Sigmund Freud's Wife Was Your Mother: Psychoanalysis and Race," in *Female Subjects in Black and White*, eds. Elizabeth Abel, Barbara Christian, and Helene Moglen (Berkeley: University of California Press, 1997), 146.

12 Peter D. Arnott, *An Introduction to the Greek Theater* (London: Macmillan, 1961), 24. Leo Aylen extends the discussion to the cliché of the "tragic hero," arguing that such a term is "utterly irrelevant to any of the extant Greek tragedies. It enters discussion solely as a result of the misunderstandings of scholars and critics of an earlier generation" (Aylen, *The Greek Theater* [Rutherford, N.J.: Farleigh Dickinson University Press, 1985], 23).

13 Joel D. Schwartz, "Human Action and Political Action in *Oedipus Tyrannos*," in *Greek Tragedy and Political Theory*, ed. Peter Euben (Berkeley: University of California Press, 1986), 184. Rehn seconds Schwartz by arguing that an "insidious form of theatrical reductionism arises from the mistaken belief that the characters in the play are simply puppets in the hands of the gods" (Rehn, *Greek Tragic Theater*, 109). See also E. R. Dodds, who states: "*We* think of two clear-cut alternative views—either we believe in free will or else we are determinsts. But fifth-century Greeks did not think in these terms" (Dodds, "On Misunderstanding the *Oedipus Rex*," in *Sophocles' "Oedipus Rex,"* ed. Harold Bloom [New York: Chelsea House, 1988], 40]); and Thomas Gould: "A belief in fate or the ultimate triumph of divine will does not always make judgments of human excellence impossible or nonsensical" (T. Gould, "The Innocence of Oedipus," in *Sophocles' "Oedipus Rex,"* ed. Harold Bloom [New York: Chelsea House, 1988], 55).

14 Charles Segal, *Interpreting Greek Tragedy* (Ithaca, N.Y.: Cornell University Press, 1986), 25.

15 For detailed accounts of the political tensions in Greece, especially in the seventh through fourth centuries B.C.E., see in particular Oswyn Murray, *Early Greece* (Stanford, Calif.: Stanford University Press, 1980); M. I. Finley, *Economy and Society in Ancient Greece* (New York: Penguin, 1981); Matthew Dillon and Lynda Garland, *Ancient Greece* (New York: Routledge, 1994); and Pierre Vidal-Naquet, *The Black Hunter: Forms of Thought and Forms of Society in the Greek World*, trans. Andrew Szegedy-Masjak (Baltimore: Johns Hopkins University Press, 1986).

16 Cf. Herodotus, who in *The Histories* writes that "Cleisthenes . . . took the people into his party. He then changed the number of Athenian tribes from four to ten, and abolished the old names—previously the four tribes had been called after Geleon, Aegicores, Argades, and Hoples, the four sons of Ion; but now he named the new tribes after other heroes, all native Athenian except Ajax,

whom, though a foreigner, he admitted into the list as a neighbour and ally" (364).

17   Ivan Hannaford argues that Athens's political innovations included eight principal features, among them the idea that all human beings "share in the uncertainties of this transitory life," and that the resolution of difference needs to be accomplished through compromise, persuasion, and critical argument (Hannaford, *Race: The History of an Idea in the West* [Baltimore: Johns Hopkins University Press, 1996], 11–12). See also N. G. L. Hammond, *A History of Greece* (Oxford: Clarendon, 1959), especially 138–45.

18   Vidal-Naquet, *Black Hunter,* 257.

19   Of the importance of discourse in the Greek world Vidal-Naquet writes, "Within the city-state, speech, in the form of persuasion becomes the most basic political tool" (Vidal-Naquet, *Black Hunter,* 257).

20   Jean-Pierre Vernant, "Oedipus Without the Complex," in *Myth and Tragedy in Ancient Greece,* eds. Jean-Pierre Vernant and Pierre Vidal-Naquet, trans. Janet Lloyd (New York: Zone Books, 1988), 92.

21   In his *Structural Anthropology,* Claude Lévi-Strauss recounts a tale in which a young man accused of sorcery concocts a defense that exculpates him by corroborating the theory informing the accusers' attack. Admitting a connection to witchcraft, the young man claims no longer to have his powers, which prompts Lévi-Strauss to remark: "The defendant, who serves as a witness, gives the group the satisfaction of truth, which is infinitely greater and richer than the satisfaction of justice that would have been achieved by his execution. And finally, by his ingenious defense which makes his hearers progressively aware of the vitality offered by his corroboration of their system (especially since the choice is not between this system and another, but between the magical system and no system at all—that is, chaos), the youth . . . became the guardian of its spiritual coherence" (Lévi-Strauss, *Structural Anthropology,* trans. Claire Jacobson and Brooke Schoeff [New York: Basic Books, 1963], 174).

22   Vladimir Propp points out that this incident in the Oedipus tale is unique to Sophocles, but that it retains folkloric characteristics, including the fact that we do not know the identity of the drunken man, nor do we know how he gained this knowledge of Oedipus's identity, a secret that had been carefully guarded by his parents (Propp, "Oedipus in the Light of Folklore," in *Oedipus: A Folklore Casebook,* eds. Lowell Edmunds and Alan Dundes [Madison: University of Wisconsin Press, 1983], 105).

23   On the assumption that Oedipus is guilty, see Ahl, *Sophocles' Oedipus.*

24   Sandor Goodhart, "Ληστας Εφασχε," 61.

25   E. R. Dodds, "Misunderstanding," 39.

26   Bernard Knox argues that "Oedipus, in his character and his mode of action, is a symbolic representation of Periclean Athens. But that Athens was not only the magnificent *polis tyrannos* and the source of law, it was also the center of the

intellectual revolution of the fifth century" (Knox, *Oedipus at Thebes* [New Haven: Yale University Press, 1957], 107).

27 Martha C. Nussbaum challenges traditional Freudian readings of *Oedipus Rex* when she writes that "it seems difficult to avoid the conclusion that the play itself is not very much concerned with sexual desire as such, or with deep-hidden sexual urges toward one's parent, combined with aggressive wishes toward one's parental rival. Its subject matter does very much appear to be that of reversal of fortune" (Nussbaum, "The *Oedipus Rex* and the Ancient Unconscious," in *Freud and Forbidden Knowledge*, eds. Peter L. Rudnytsky and Hellen Handler Spitz [New York: New York University Press, 1994], 43).

28 *Oedipus, Philosopher*, 34–39.

29 Lowell Edmunds concurs that "the Oedipus legend originated from the folk-tale of the hero who wins a bride by slaying a monster" (Edmunds, "The Sphinx in the Oedipus Legend," in *Oedipus: A Folklore Casebook*, eds. Lowell Edmunds and Alan Dundes [Madison: University of Wisconsin Press, 1983], 148). He goes on to point out that neither solving a riddle nor slaying a monster occurred in the original Oedipus legend, and that the Sphinx is a secondary addition to the tale.

30 Knox also points out that "Oedipus is like the great teachers of the fifth century in one respect: he has no master from whom he learned, he is self-taught" (Knox, *Oedipus at Thebes*, 136).

31 As Karl Kerényi reminds us, although every version of the Oedipus story, including very early ones, has Oedipus triumphing over the Sphinx, it is only in later forms that he does so by solving a riddle (Kerényi, "Oedipus: Two Essays," in *Oedipus Variations*, trans. Jon Solomon [Woodstock, Conn.: Spring Publications, 1990], 5–86).

32 Goux, *Oedipus, Philosopher*, 41–42.

33 Ibid., 34.

34 The entire case history can be found in Freud, "From the History of an Infantile Neurosis," in *Three Case Histories* (New York: Collier, 1963), 187–316.

35 Ibid., 238.

36 Ibid., 236–37.

37 Freud, *Interpretation of Dreams*, 549.

38 Freud, *Totem and Taboo* (London: Routledge and Kegan Paul, 1950), 126.

39 I will return to the myth of the primal horde that Freud develops in chapter 5.

40 For example, in the eighteenth century, Voltaire railed against the logical "absurdities" in Sophocles' *Oedipus Rex*. "It is already going against verisimilitude to have Oedipus, who has been reigning so long, not to know how his predecessor died" (Voltaire, "Lettres sur Œdipe," in *Œuvres complètes de Voltaire*, ed. Beuchot [Paris: Garnier Frères, 1877], 2:27; my translation.); "Jocasta doesn't reveal in this scene that she was one day supposed to marry her son. . . . For, when Oedipus says to Jocasta: 'it was predicted that I would soil the bed of my

mother, and that my father would be massacred by my hands,' Jocasta should immediately respond: 'The same thing was predicted of my son.'" (2:33). Voltaire notes that these inconsistencies violate the "rules of common sense."

41 The historical dimensions of Oedipus's contradictory role in this tale are underscored by the fact that, according to Propp, "the prophecy of patricide is unknown in preclass societies; it appears with the rise of the patriarchal system" (Propp, "Oedipus in the Light of Folklore," 88). Propp argues that the earlier versions of the Oedipus drama would have included not a prophecy that Oedipus would kill the *father*, but that he would kill the *king*, which "permits us to submit the hypothesis that the tale arose from historical forms of the struggle for power, or more precisely, from the conflict of two forms of inheritance of power" (84).

42 Jonathan Culler maintains that the "demands of narrative coherence" cause us to conclude that Oedipus is guilty, and that in Sophocles' version of the Oedipus myth "meaning is not the effect of a prior event but its cause" (Culler, *The Pursuit of Signs* [Ithaca, N.Y.: Cornell University Press, 1981], 174).

43 Cynthia Chase, "Oedipal Textuality: Reading Freud's Reading of *Oedipus*," *Diacritics* 9, no. 1 (spring 1979): 58.

44 Bernard Knox, "Sophocles's *Oedipus*," in *Sophocles' "Oedipus Rex,"* ed. Harold Bloom (New York: Chelsea House, 1988), 14.

45 Goux, *Oedipus, Philosopher*, 30.

46 Ibid., 30. In a related formulation based on a somewhat different model, the anthropologist Victor Turner writes that "ceremony is a declaration against indeterminacy. Through form and formality it celebrates man-made meaning, the culturally determinate, the regulated, the named, and the explained" (Turner, "Social Dramas and Stories about Them," in *On Narrative*, ed. W. J. T. Mitchell [Chicago: University of Chicago Press, 1980], 159–60).

47 In *The Four Fundamental Concepts of Psychoanalysis*, Lacan discusses the famous *Fort-da* game that Freud described: "Man thinks with his object. It is with his object that the child leaps the frontiers of his domain, transformed into a well, and begins the incantation. If it is true that the signifier is the first mark of the subject, how can we fail to recognize here—from the very fact that this game is accompanied by one of the first oppositions to appear—that it is in the object to which the opposition is applied in act, the reel, that we must designate the subject" (62).

48 Slavoj Žižek, *Tarrying with the Negative* (Durham, N.C.: Duke University Press, 1993), 171.

49 Judith Butler has written a great deal on the question of identity and its performance. See in particular Butler, *Gender Trouble* (New York: Routledge, 1990), especially 16–25, for a description of how subjects perform identities that can in no way be presumed to pre-exist their expression.

50 As we will see in chapter 3, perhaps the most common way of conceptualizing

racial antagonism has been on an economic level. At the turn of the century, Colonel Robert Bingham wrote that "race antagonism" arose "because as a free man [the Negro] has become the competitor of the white laborer in many fields of activity" (Bingham, "An Ex-Slaveholders [sic] View of the Negro Question in the South," in *Anti-Abolition Tracts and Anti-Black Stereotypes*, ed. John David Smith, vol. 4. [New York: Garland, 1993], 7. First published in European edition of *Harper's Monthly Magazine* [July 1900]: 241–56).

51 Žižek, *Tarrying*, 203.

52 I might also note here that what I am describing as antagonsim finds resonances in Jean-François Lyotard's conception of the figural. Concerning this latter, Anne Tomiche writes: "The figural is the name of an unspeakable other necessarily at work *within* and *against* discourse. It is not opposed to discourse but is the point at which the oppositions by which discourse works are opened to a radical heterogeneity. . . . Insofar as the 'figure' is unrepresentable, heterogeneous to the order of discourse, and inarticulate, insofar as it 'inhabits' discourse while being outside of it at the same time, the figure has the same relation to discourse as the inarticulate phrase has to articulation" (Tomiche, "Rephrasing the Freudian Unconscious: Lyotard's Affect-Phrase," *Diacritics* 24, no. 1 [spring 1994]: 48). Later on, she points out that Lyotard's "differend" is a "dispute, without possibility of linkage, between two parties" (49).

53 Laclau and Mouffe, *Hegemony*, 125. In his *New Reflections on the Revolution of Our Time* Ernesto Laclau elaborates his own theory of antagonism, maintaining that antagonism is the limit of all objectivity, since it has no objective meaning of its own, but instead blocks the complete elaboration of the identity to which it is opposed. He argues that because antagonism is purely oppositional it is also contingent; consequently it is part of the conditions of existence of the identity that it would block (19–22).

54 As John Brenkman puts it, in his description of contemporary psychoanalysis and its theories of masculinity: "With this fantasmal form of the antagonism of father and son there emerge the two primal symbolizations of the struggle's outcome. Either the son will kill the father or the father will castrate the son" (Brenkman, *Straight Male Modern*, 32).

55 Freud, *Ego and the Id*, 24.

56 Sigmund Freud, *The Standard Edition of the Complete Psychological Works of Sigmund Freud* (London: Hogarth Press, 1962–74), 19:32.

57 Freud, *Standard Edition*, 19:176.

58 Freud, *Standard Edition*, 1:265. Letter 71, to Fliess, dated 15 October 1897, is generally accepted as containing Freud's first explicit mention of the Oedipus complex.

59 Freud, *Standard Edition*, 19:174.

60 In "On the Universal Tendency to Debasement in the Sphere of Love," Freud writes that "the excremental is all too intimately and inseparably bound up

with the sexual; the position of the genitals—*inter urinas et faeces*—remains the decisive and unchangeable factor. One might say here, varying a well-known saying of the great Napoleon: 'Anatomy is destiny' " (*Standard Edition*, 11:189); in the "Dissolution of the Oedipus Complex," he writes that "here the feminist demand for equal rights for the sexes does not take us far, for the morphological distinction is bound to find expression in differences of psychical development. 'Anatomy is Destiny,' to vary a saying of Napoleon's" (*Standard Edition*, 19:178).

61 Oedipus emphasizes that he is "a stranger to the story" of what happened at Thebes before his arrival (l. 219), and Teiresias reminds everybody that "in name he is a stranger among citizens" (l. 451).

62 Sigmund Freud, "Some Psychological Consequences of the Anatomical Distinction Between the Sexes," in *Sexuality and the Psychology of Love* (New York: Macmillan, 1925), 187.

63 Among the notable critiques of Freud's work along these lines are: Teresa Brennan, *The Interpretation of the Flesh* (New York: Routledge, 1992) and Brennan, ed., *Between Feminism and Psychoanalysis* (New York: Routledge, 1989); Sander Gilman, G. S. Rousseau, Helen King, Roy Porter, and Elaine Showalter, eds., *Hysteria Beyond Freud* (Berkeley: University of California Press, 1993); Sarah Kofman, *The Enigma of Woman*, trans. Catherine Porter (Ithaca, N.Y.: Cornell University Press, 1985); Rachel Bowlby, *Still Crazy After All These Years* (New York: Routledge, 1992); Elizabeth Abel, Barbara Christian, and Helene Moglen, eds., *Female Subjects in Black and White* (Berkeley: University of California Press, 1997); Barbara Creed, *The Monstrous-Feminine* (New York: Routledge, 1993); Juliana Schiesari, *The Gendering of Melancholia* (Ithaca, N.Y.: Cornell University Press, 1992); Naomi R. Goldenberg, *Returning Words to Flesh* (Boston: Beacon, 1990); Jane Flax, *Thinking Fragments* (Berkeley: University of California Press, 1990), and *Disputed Subjects* (New York: Routledge, 1993); Marianne Hirsch, *The Mother/Daughter Plot* (Bloomington: Indiana University Press, 1989); Jessica Benjamin, *The Bonds of Love* (New York: Pantheon, 1988); Samuel Slipp, *The Freudian Mystique* (New York: New York University Press, 1993); Madelon Sprengnether, *The Spectral Mother* (Ithaca, N.Y.: Cornell University Press, 1990); Charles Bernheimer and Claire Kahane, eds., *In Dora's Case* (New York: Columbia University Press, 1985); Juliet Mitchell, *Psychoanalysis and Feminism* (New York: Vintage, 1974); Jacqueline Rose, *Why War?* (Cambridge, Mass.: Blackwell, 1993); Janice L. Doane, *From Klein to Kristeva* (Ann Arbor: University of Michigan Press, 1992); Patricia Elliot, *From Mastery to Analysis* (Ithaca, N.Y.: Cornell University Press, 1991); Silverman, *Male Subjectivity*; Mary Ann Doane, *Femmes Fatales* (New York: Routledge, 1991); Nancy Chodorow, *Feminism and Psychoanalytic Theory* (New Haven: Yale University Press, 1989); Janet Walker, *Couching Resistance* (Minneapolis: University of Minnesota Press, 1993); Shoshana Felman, *What Does a Woman Want?* (Bal-

timore: Johns Hopkins University Press, 1993); Richard Feldstein and Judith Roof, eds., *Feminism and Psychoanalysis* (Ithaca, N.Y.: Cornell University Press, 1989); Constance Penley, *The Future of an Illusion* (Minneapolis: University of Minnesota Press, 1989); Jane Gallop, *The Daughter's Seduction* (Ithaca, N.Y.: Cornell University Press, 1982); and Renata Salecl, *The Spoils of Freedom* (New York: Routledge, 1994).

64 Freud, "Infantile Neurosis," 291.

65 In her *Acoustic Mirror* Kaja Silverman makes a similar point: "I would like to suggest that this refusal to identify castration with any of the divisions which occur prior to the registration of sexual difference reveals Freud's desire to place a maximum distance between the male subject and the notion of lack. To admit that the loss of the object is also a castration would be to acknowledge that the male subject is already structured by absence prior to the moment at which he registers women's anatomical difference—to concede that he, like the female subject, has already been deprived of being, and already been marked by the language and desires of the Other" (Silverman, *The Acoustic Mirror* [Bloomington: Indiana University Press, 1988], 15).

66 Freud, "The Infantile Genital Organization of the Libido," in *Sexuality and the Psychology of Love* (New York: Collier, 1963), 172.

67 A relatively large number of scholars have pointed out that the people whom westerners have traditionally "racialized"—that is, those to whom an indelible mark of inferiority is attributed, based on morphological features that seem to correlate cultural, intellectual, and moral characteristics—are also generally feminized. Sander Gilman, for example, writes: "Not only did Freud construct a specific image of the feminine onto which the qualities of the male Jew were projected (which reified the image of the female found in the popular and medical literature of his age), but this construction was the result of Freud's assumption of the persona of the male scientist. . . . It was through the assumption of the neutrality of the definition of the (male) scientist that Freud was able in his scientific writing to efface his own anxiety (which he expressed in private) about the limitations ascribed to the mind and character of the Jewish male. Thus the fabrication of the image of the female was a reflex of the central construction of masculinity in Freud's writing" (Gilman, *Freud, Race*, 37). Similarly, Robin Wiegman evokes the numerous comparisons in eighteenth-century taxonomy between the black male and the white female, and moving the discussion to North America, she writes: "By figuring blackness as a feminine racial formation, the possibility of the African(-American) male assuming an equal position with the crusader for advanced civilization, the white male, was thwarted and racial hierarchies became further entrenched according to the corporeal inequalities inscribed by sexual difference" (Wiegman, *American Anatomies: Theorizing Race and Gender* [Durham, N.C.: Duke University Press, 1995], 55).

68 John Brenkman makes a similar point when he writes that "the simple positive Oedipus complex enjoys a privilege by virtue of the fact that it lies on the path to male-dominated heterosexuality: its every manifestation and nuance is socially validated and rewarded. The *normative outcome* it promises is nothing more than the *coercive* appeal it holds in an overwhelmingly homophobic and male-dominated lifeworld" (Brenkman, *Straight Male Modern*, 120).

69 Or, as Judith Butler has phrased a similar formulation, "As a shifting and contextual phenomenon, gender does not denote a substantive being, but a relative point of convergence among culturally and historically specific sets of relations" (Butler, *Gender Trouble*, 10). Similarly, Kathy E. Ferguson writes, "The deconstruction of gender entails stepping back from the opposition of male and female in order to loosen the hold of gender on life and meaning. This theoretical project renders gender more fragile, more tenuous, and less salient both as an explanatory and as an evaluative category. Women's point of view is created in order to reject the male ordering of the world; gender is deconstructed in order to reject the dualism of male and female" (Ferguson, *The Man Question: Visions of Subjectivity in Feminist Theory* [Berkeley: University of California Press, 1993], 4).

70 Jacques Lacan, *Les formations de l'inconscient: Le séminaire*, livre 5 (Paris: Seuil, 1998), 262.

2. MISSING LINKS

1 On whiteness as neutrality or absence, see Richard Dyer, *White* (New York: Routledge, 1997), especially chapters 1 and 2; similarly, Ruth Frankenberg refers to "whiteness as an 'empty' but simultaneously normative space" (Frankenberg, "Local Whitenesses, Localizing Whiteness," 64); and Toni Morrison has written that "whiteness alone, is mute, meaningless, unfathomable, pointless, frozen, veiled, curtained, dreaded, senseless, implacable. Or so our writers seem to say" (Morrison, *Playing in the Dark*, 59). Ross Chambers writes that "there are plenty of unmarked categories (maleness, heterosexuality, and middle classness being obvious ones), but whiteness is perhaps the primary unmarked and so unexamined—let's say "blank"—category" (Chambers, "The Unexamined," in Whiteness: A Critical Reader, ed. Mike Hill [New York: New York University Press, 1997],189).

2 Aristotle's use of the term *tuché* is variously translated as fate, fortune, or necessity. It sometimes refers to the act of a god, or of a human being, but it can also refer to that which is outside of human control. The odd ambiguity is significant here, because it underscores the manner in which determinate material circumstances sometimes owe their determination to human understanding, and not to the natural world. In the *Physics* Aristotle writes that "the things which might act as causes of chance events are bound . . . to be indeter-

minate. That is why chance too is taken to be indeterminate and opaque to people, and why it does make a kind of sense to think that nothing comes about by chance. . . . But in an unqualified sense chance causes nothing." He goes on to claim that "both chance and spontaneity are . . . coincidental causes. . . . Their sphere of operation is events which do not have to happen, either in any case or usually, and they apply to just those cases which might have occurred for some purpose" (Aristotle, *The Physics*, trans. Robin Waterfield (New York: Oxford University Press, 1996), bk. 2, chaps. 4–6, pp. 42–46). The notion of causality as simultaneously part of the material world and distinct from it will become important in the discussion to follow.

3   Lacan, *Four Fundamental Concepts*, 53–54.

4   Ibid., 55.

5   There has been a growing body of work surrounding the question of trauma, but I would like to mention briefly here Kai Erikson's work, in which he argues that " 'trauma' has to be understood as resulting from a *constellation of life experiences* as well as from a discrete happening, from a *persisting condition* as well as from an acute event." For Erikson, "The traumatized mind holds on to that moment, preventing it from slipping back into its proper chronological place in the past, and relives it over and over again in the compulsive musings of the day and the seething dreams of night" (Erikson, "Notes on Trauma and Community," in *Trauma: Explorations in Memory*, ed. Cathy Caruth [Baltimore: Johns Hopkins University Press, 1995], 185). Cathy Caruth applies the notion to epistemological domains. She argues that "through the notion of trauma . . . we can understand that a rethinking of reference is aimed not at eliminating history but at resituating it in our understanding, that is, at precisely permitting *history* to arise where *immediate understanding* may not" (Caruth, *Unclaimed Experience* [Baltimore: Johns Hopkins University Press, 1996], 11).

6   Lacan, *Four Fundamental Concepts*, 54.

7   Congress passed a law in 1790 restricting naturalization to "white persons." For more detailed discussion of this issue, see Ian F. Haney López, *White by Law* (New York: New York University Press, 1996), and Omi and Winant, *Racial Formation*, especially 75ff.

8   *United States v Thind*, 261 US 204 (1922), 209.

9   López points out that "though the courts did not see their decision in this light, the early congruence of and subsequent contradiction between common knowledge and scientific evidence set the terms of a debate about whether race is a social construction or a natural occurrence" (López, *White by Law*, 6).

10 Thucydides, *The Peloponnesian War*, trans. Rex Warner (New York: Penguin, 1984), 242. Thucydides continues: "What used to be described as a thoughtless act of aggression was now regarded as the courage one would expect to find in a party member; to think of the future and wait was merely another way of saying

one was a coward; any idea of moderation was just an attempt to disguise one's unmanly character" (242).

11 For more on how this matter pertained to parentage and heredity, see Davis Bitton, *The French Nobility in Crisis* [Stanford, Calif.: Stanford University Press, 1969], especially 100–3. Virginia has tenaciously held on to racial laws. In 1924 Virginia law held that the "term 'white person' shall apply only to the person who has no trace whatsoever of any blood other than Caucasian, but persons who have one-sixteenth or less of the blood of the American Indian, and no other non-Caucasian blood shall be deemed white persons" (Barbara Bair, "Remapping the Black/White Body," in *Sex, Love, Race,* ed. Martha Hodes [New York: New York University Press, 1999], 399). In 1965, Circuit Judge Leon Bazile defended a state anti-miscegenation law, writing that "Almighty God created the races white, black, yellow, malay and red, and he placed them on separate continents. . . . The fact that he separated the races shows that he did not intend for the races to mix" (Dorothy E. Roberts, "The Genetic Tie," in *Critical White Studies,* ed. Richard Delgado and Jean Stefancic [Philadelphia: Temple University Press, 1997], 186).

12 See in particular F. James Davis, *Who Is Black?: One Nation's Definition* (University Park: Pennsylvania State University Press, 1991), especially 32–35, and Neil Gotanda, "A Critique of 'Our Constitution Is Color-Blind,' " *Stanford Law Review* 44, no. 1 (November 1991): 1–68, especially 6–26.

13 Martha Hodes points out one of the absurdities deriving from the one-drop of blood rule: "The children of white women and black men presented antebellum white Southerners with complexities and confusions of racial categorization. Because Southern statutes stipulated that a child's legal status as slave or free followed the mother, the children of white women and black men were of partial African ancestry but also free, thereby violating the equation of blackness and slavery" (Hodes, *White Women, Black Men* [New Haven: Yale University Press, 1997], 96).

14 *United States v Ozawa,* 260 US 178 (1922). In this vein, Ian F. Haney López argues that the "social construction of Whiteness (and race generally) is manifest in the Court's repudiation of science and its installation of popular knowledge as the appropriate racial meter" (López, "The Social Construction of Race," in *Critical Race Theory,* ed. Richard Delgado [Philadelphia: Temple University Press, 1995], 546).

15 Sally Robinson cautions that the "logics of victimization" combined with what has often been called a "crisis" in masculinity produces a phenomenon of which we should be wary: "the cultural work of *re*centering white masculinity by *de*centering it. In other words, in order for white masculinity to negotiate its position within the field of identity politics, white men must claim a symbolic disenfranchisement" (Robinson, *Marked Men* [New York: Columbia University Press, 2000], 12).

16 Phillip Sloan points out that in the early modern period the word "anthropology" was generally employed "within the context of medical, and specifically anatomical, discussion. The focus of this science was upon those definable and generalizable features of the human *corpus*, delimited by an inquiry into form and function" (Sloan, "The Gaze of Natural History," in *Inventing Human Science*, eds. Christopher Fox, Roy Porter, and Robert Wokler [Berkeley: University of California Press, 1995], 114). Here I will be using the term more broadly to refer to the systematic study of humankind's physical, social, and cultural development and behavior.

17 Lest we think that the time is past when people would refer to an empirically verifiable way of determining race, I might evoke here U.S. Supreme Court Justice Antonin Scalia's reference to the "blood, not background and environment" of the minorities and women petitioning for broadcast licenses in a 1990 hearing: *Metro Broadcasting v FCC*, 110 S. Ct. 2997 (1990), cited by Ruth Marcus, "FCC Defends Minority License Policies: Case Before High Court Could Shape Future of Affirmative Action," *Washington Post*, 29 March 1990, A8.

18 Colette Guillaumin has formulated a similar argument, not for whiteness in particular, but for race in general: "In creating and hypostasizing race, racist ideology set up a metaphysics of relations of social heterogeneity which was adopted as it stood by everyone" (Colette Guillaumin, *Racism, Sexism, Power and Ideology* [New York: Routledge, 1995], 32).

19 Jordan, *White Over Black*, 80. See Jordan: "Why was it that the Puritans rather mindlessly (which was not their way) accepted slavery for Negroes and Indians but not for white men?" (66); Barbara J. Fields, "Slavery, Race and Ideology in the United States of America," *New Left Review* 181 (May/June 1990): 95–118; and Elizabeth Fox-Genovese and Eugene D. Genovese: "When an overseer, in bad humor after a quarrel with his wife, confronted an insolent or merely slow-moving slave, he was not likely to be thinking of double-entry bookkeeping as he laid on the whip" (Fox-Genovese and Genovese, *Fruits of Merchant Capital: Slavery and Bourgeois Property in the Rise and Expansion of Capitalism* [Oxford: Oxford University Press, 1983], 129).

20 Robyn Wiegman offers a similar, compelling argument for going beyond economically determined arguments: "Making the African 'black' reduces the racial meanings attached to flesh to a binary structure of vision, and it is this structure that precedes the disciplinary emergence of the humanities and its methodological pursuits of knowledge and truth. This does not mean that imperialism was not well served by the negative equation between 'blackness' and an ontological difference, but that the framework for such an equation must be approached in terms broader and more historically and culturally comprehensive than the slave trade and its necessity for ideological and economic justification" (Wiegman, *American Anatomies*, 4).

21 Louis Althusser, *Politics and History: Montesquieu, Rousseau, Hegel, and Marx*, trans. Ben Brewster (London: NLB, 1972), 31. Lucien Goldmann refers to this same eighteenth-century phenomenon as "the idea that nature is a book written in mathematical language, that the entire universe is governed by general laws that know no exception" (Goldmann, *The Philosophy of the Enlightenment*, trans. Henry Maas [Cambridge, Mass.: MIT Press, 1973], 24).

22 Louis Althusser writes: "It would be aberrant to look in Hobbes or Spinosa for a real history of the fall of Rome or of the emergence of feudal law. They were not concerned with the *facts*. Rousseau was to say openly that it is essential to start by 'laying facts aside.' They were only concerned with *right*, i.e. with what *ought to be*" (Althusser, *Politics and History*, 28). Bernard Valette agrees with Althusser, but explicitly connects the idea of nature to humans' subjective vision: "Does the idea of nature flow from an observation of reality (what we might call 'the nature of things') or, on the contrary, from a subjective vision, too often systematic, which results from our desires and our fears?" (Valette, "L'Idée de nature." In *Analyses et réflexions sur Montesquieu, "De l'esprit des lois: La nature et la loi"* [Paris: Edition Marketing, 1987], 43; my translation).

23 On early modern verisimilitude and its plausibility and political affiliations, see in particular Gérard Genette, "Vraisemblance et motivation," in *Figures II* (Paris: Seuil, 1969), 2:71–99; and Michael McKeon, *The Origins of the Novel* (Baltimore: Johns Hopkins University Press, 1987). See also my *Dangerous Truths and Criminal Passions* (Stanford, Calif.: Stanford University Press, 1992), especially chapter 2.

24 Peter Gay, *The Enlightenment: An Interpretation* (New York: Knopf, 1969), 458. In the opening lines of his *Social Contract* Rousseau makes a similar point concerning the law's relationship to reality and to ideality when he writes "I want to discover whether in civil order there can be some rule for legitimate and sure administration by taking men as they are, and laws as they might be" (J. Rousseau, *Du contrat social* [Paris: Garnier-Flammarion, 1966], 39; my translation).

25 Ernst Cassirer argues that "the philosophy of the Enlightenment at first holds facts to [the] apriority of the law, to this demand for absolutely universally valid and unalterable legal norms. Even the pure empiricists and the philosophical empiricists are no exception in this respect" (Cassirer, *The Philosophy of the Enlightenment*, trans. Fritz C. A. Koelln and James P. Pettegrove [Princeton: Princeton University Press, 1951], 243).

26 Charles-Louis de Secondat Montesquieu, *Esprit des lois*, XXIII, vol. ii of *Œuvres complètes*, ed. Roger Caillois (Paris: Bibliothèque de la Pléiade, 1958), 683; my translation.

27 Montesquieu, *Les lettres persanes* (Paris: Garnier-Flammarion, 1964), 145; my translation.

28 A number of eighteenth-century studies on law address the juridical capacity to create identity or at least to sketch out zones for it. Frédéric Henri-Strube de Piermont addressed the question of natural law and divine intent in his *Recherche nouvelle de l'origine et des fondemens du droit de la nature* (S. Petersbourg: Académie des sciences, 1740); Jean-Jacques Burlamaqui's *Principes du droit naturel* (Geneva: Barillot, 1747) looks at natural law, international law, and humankind's relationship to law and nature; Gaetano Filangieri's *La Scienza della legislazione* is a treatise on legislation, economics, and ideology in which law is a *practice*, and not so much of a descriptive *taxonomy* (Milan: Galeazzi, 1784).

29 Plato, *The Republic*, trans. G. M. A. Grube (Indianapolis: Hacket, 1974), 461d, p. 123.

30 François Rabelais, *Œuvres complètes*, ed. P. Jourda (Paris: Editions Garnier, 1962), I:19; my translation.

31 Ibid. M. A. Screech informs us that during the Renaissance there raged a heated debate between doctors and lawyers over how long a pregnancy could last, particularly in the case of women whose husbands had died more than nine months before the birth of a child. The debate lasted well into the seventeenth century (Screech, *Rabelais* [Ithaca, N.Y.: Cornell University Press, 1979], 132–34).

32 For an extended discussion of the manner in which human law impinged on matters of identity as well as questions of physiology in the eighteenth century, see François Duchesneau, *La physiologie des lumières* (The Hague: M. Nijhoff, 1982), especially 412–20.

33 I do not mean to suggest, however, that only Europeans and North Africans have exhibited some form of race consciousness or racism. Thomas F. Gossett has written, for example, that Chinese historians from the third century B.C.E. wrote of a "yellow-haired and green-eyed barbarian people" who "resemble monkeys from whom they are descended" (Gossett, *Race: The History of an Idea in America* [New York: Oxford University Press, 1997], 4). Likewise, he continues, the prophet Ezra forbade Jews from marrying Ammonites and Moabites (5), even if it is not entirely clear that such a prohibition resembles racism in the sense we understand it today.

34 See in particular Frank M. Snowden Jr., *Before Color Prejudice*, who argues that "the Africans' color was regarded as their most characteristic and most unusual feature. . . . The Arab historian Ibn Khaldun made a pertinent comment on this practice when he observed that whites did not designate inhabitants of the north, like those of the south, by their color because 'whiteness was something usual and common (to them), and they did not see anything sufficiently remarkable in it to cause them to use it as a specific term' " (Snowden, *Before Color Prejudice: The Ancient View of Blacks* [Cambridge, Mass.: Harvard University Press, 1983], 7).

35 In the *Iliad* the Ethiopians are "blameless," and Zeus and the rest of the gods feast with them (bk. 1, ll. 423–24). In the *Odyssey*, the Ethiopians are the "most distant of men, who live divided, / some at the Setting of Hyperion, some at his rising." (bk. 1, ll. 20–21).

36 Herodotus, *The Histories*, 211, 212.

37 Ibid., 468.

38 Ibid., 332.

39 Snowden states the case in perhaps the baldest possible terms: "In spite of the association of blackness with ill omens, demons, the devil, and sin, there is in the extant records no stereotyped image of Ethiopians as the personification of demons or the devil, no fixed concept of blacks as evil or unworthy of conversion" (Snowden, *Before Color Prejudice*, 107).

40 In her book *The Idea of Race in Science*, Nancy Stepan corroborates this claim: "While Greeks assumed that they were superior to all 'barbarians,' no attempt was made to rank the non-Greek peoples in a hierarchy of inferior and superior types, as judged by some Greek standard of physical and cultural worth" (Stepan, *The Idea of Race*, xi).

41 Aristotle, *The Politics*, trans. T. A. Sinclair (New York: Penguin, 1961), 68–69.

42 Ibid., 72.

43 See Finley, *Economy and Society*, 102; and D. Brendan Nagle, *The Ancient World* (Englewood Cliffs, N.J.: Prentice-Hall, 1979), 161.

44 Rojer Sanjek also makes the point that slavery was not necessarily an identity as it came to be in the U.S., since that condition and the features associated with it did not necessarily pass from one generation to the next: "In earlier and non-Western slavery systems, the populations of slave descendants gradually disappeared. They blended into the dominant cultural group, frequently at low social status, but occasionally in elite circumstances. Since systemic racial ordering did not distinguish slaves and masters (if cultural differences often did), slave descendants could readily acculturate; indeed, they usually had no other choice" (Sanjek, "The Enduring Inequalities of Race,"in *Race*, eds. Steven Gregory and Rojer Sanjek [New Brunswick, N.J.: Rutgers University Press, 1994], 14).

45 Plato, *The Republic*, 129.

46 Cited by Nagle, who goes on to point out that the writer exaggerates, "for as soon as an individual opened his mouth to speak it must have been possible to tell from his accent where he came from" (Nagle, *The Ancient World*, 161).

47 Aristotle, *Nichomachean Ethics*, trans. David Ross (New York: Oxford University Press, 1980), 212.

48 David Brion Davis, *The Problem of Slavery in the Age of Revolution, 1770–1823* (Ithaca, N.Y.: Cornell University Press, 1975), 42.

49 Ptolemy, *Tetrabiblos*, ed. and trans. F. E. Robbins (Cambridge, Mass.: Harvard University Press, 1940), 123.

50 In his seventeenth-century *New History of Ethiopia*, Hiob Ludolf points out that "some authors write, that the *Ethiopians* paint the Devil *white* in disdain of our Complexions" (Ludolf, *A New History of Ethiopia* [London: Samuel Smith, 1682], 72).

51 Snowden, *Before Color Prejudice*, 101.

52 Nancy Stepan, *The Idea of Race*, xii.

53 In Chrétien de Troyes' twelfth-century *Yvain*, for example, the Giant Herdsman is described as being "as black as a blacksmith" ([Paris: Gallimard, 1994], l. 711); In the anonymous *Chanson de Roland* (*La Chanson de Roland*, ed. T. Atkinson Jenkins [n.p.: American Life Foundation, 1977], ll. 1467–76; my translation.) we read the following:

> King Marsile sees the slaughter of his men.
> Then horns and trumpets ring out at his command,
> And he rides on with his assembled host.
> One Saracen rides out in front: Abisme,
> The fiercest man in all that company.
> Evil at heart, and guilty of great crimes,
> He has no faith in Mary's holy Son.
> This pagan's skin is black as melted pitch.
> He'd rather murder or do vile treachery
> Than have the gift of all Galicia's gold.

54 Benoît de Sainte-More, *Chroniques des ducs de Normandie*, ed. Carin Fahlin (Geneva: Droz, 1951), 1:ll.131–43; my translation.

55 John Block Friedman, *The Monstrous Races in Medieval Art and Thought* (Cambridge, Mass.: Harvard University Press, 1981), 172.

56 Stephen Greenblatt reminds us, in reference to such "accidents," that "marks on the body, like marks on paper, may be distinguished from the particular explanations, justifications, and chains of historical causality that led them to be made" (Greenblatt, "Mutilation and Meaning," in *The Body in Parts*, eds. David Hillman and Carla Mazzio [New York: Routledge, 1997], 222).

57 Of course, attempts to distill the natural from its cultural descendants punctuated the seventeenth and eighteenth centuries, at various moments becoming both moral and philosophical obsessions. Not only did early modern and Enlightenment thinkers interrogate institutions and phenomena such as religion, sexuality, the family, and government in order to locate the least common denominators of humanity, they also investigated the state of the body in an attempt to discern its natural condition. Thus, social treatises, in fictive as well as philosophical form, worried through the question of how to disarticulate the natural from the cultural. Leibniz and Locke interrogated the extent to which human practices of nominalization created social categories accepted as natu-

ral; Diderot, Hobbes, and Rousseau investigated fictions of anterior or un-
developed cultures and their relationship to their own contemporary cultures;
Condillac, La Mettrie, and the marquis de Sade wondered how bodily sensation
correlated thought, a preoccupation that in the early modern period extends
back to Bacon, and in history appears almost timeless.

58 The belief that people from other cultures deliberately modified their appearance did not last long, however. In 1875, A. Hoyle Lester would write, "If it were
possible for man to change his own features, the unguent pores of his body, the
color of his skin, flatten his nose, compress his skull, and otherwise disfigure
and degrade his perfect type of nobility, tell me why there were no negroes
found on the American continent when first discovered" (Lester, *The Pre-
Adamite, or Who Tempted Eve?* [Philadelphia: Lippincott, 1875], 81).

59 John Rawlins, "*The Wonderful Recovery of the Exchange of Bristow, from the
Turkish Pirats of Argier, published by John Rawlins, heere abbreviated,*" in *Purchase
His Pilgrimes* (1621; reprint, Glasgow: MacLehose, 1955), 6:153–55.

60 It would appear that circumcision seemed so abhorrent both because it represented a mutilation of the body for European Christians and because of its
association with Islam. In 1602, for example, in his description of the inhabitants of Capo Verde, Pieter de Marees wrote: "Their belief and education are in
the manner of Mahomet, and in many ways not dissimilar in the matter of
circumcision and other foolish practices of that kind" (de Marees, *Description
and Historical Account of the Gold Kingdom of Guinea,* [1602; reprint, Oxford:
Oxford University Press, 1987], 11). Ian Richard Netton argues that for all of the
historical and literary erudition associated with the Arabic language and with
Islam, Islam remained, even for scholars of the field, a profoundly alien entity
(Netton, "The Mysteries of Islam," in *Exoticism in the Enlightenment,* eds. G. S.
Rousseau and Roy Porter [Manchester: Manchester University Press, 1990],
26–31). Following Leo Steinberg, Richard Dyer argues that during the Renaissance artists began to depict the circumcision of Jesus Christ because of the
theological significance of the ritual; they did not, however, represent the results of the operation, mainly out of a "desire not to show Christ as in any way
imperfect, that is, unwhole" (Dyer, *White,* 68).

61 Alden T. Vaughan notes this phenomenon as follows: "Almost without exception, sixteenth-and seventeenth-century writers referred to people of the Old
World as Englishmen, Spaniards, Frenchmen, and so forth, often as Christians, seldom as whites except to distinguish them from blacks. The few excep-
tions suggest that the contrast between Indians' *acquired* color and the Europeans' *natural* hue provided some observers with a handy label for Europeans
of whatever nationality, but such usage remained rare in Indian-European
contexts until the eighteenth century" (Vaughan, *Roots of American Racism*
[New York: Oxford University Press, 1995], 15).

62 John Leo, *Observations of Africa taken out of John Leo his nine Bookes translated by Master Pory, and the most remarkable things hither transcribed,*" in *Purchase His Pilgrimes* (1526; reprint, Glasgow: MacLehose, 1955), 5:488.

63 Jean Barbot, *Barbot on Guinea,* eds. P. E. H. Hair, Adam Jones, and Robin Law (1688; reprint, London: Hakluyt Society, 1992), 1:17–18. Barbot wrote his memoirs in epistolary form, which accounts for the direct address to the reader. There seems to be no evidence that he had any specific correspondent in mind.

64 Ibid., 1:84.

65 *The Jamestown Voyages under the First Charter,* ed. Philip L. Barbour, vol. 1 (Cambridge: Cambridge University Press, 1969), 102–3.

66 I do not mean to imply that no sort of morphological causality or belief in deliberate modification of the body existed prior to the sixteenth or seventeenth centuries. In the *Metamorphoses,* for example, Ovid had accounted for the Ethiopian's darker skin color in the story of Phaëton, who drove his chariot too close to the sun; and Ptolemy had observed that people from warmer climates tended to have darker complexions. The dimension of myth, which although infrequently did occasionally refer to the state of the human body, obviously represents significant exception to the rules I am outlining, but I am interested here in charting this phenomenon in the early modern and modern eras.

67 Anthony Appiah argues that "where race works . . . it works as an attempt at a metonym for culture; and it does so only at the price of biologizing what *is* culture, or ideology. To call it "biologizing" is not to consign our concept of race to biology. What is present there is not our concept but our word only" (Appiah, "The Uncompleted Argument," 36).

68 Bryan Edwards, *History, Civil and Commercial, of the British West Indies,* 5th ed. (1819; reprint, London: G. and W. B. Whittaker, 1966), 2:89.

69 J. G. Grevenbroek, *An Elegant and Accurate Account of the African Race Living Round the Cape of Good Hope,* trans. B. Farrington. (n.p., 1695), 175.

70 Georges-Louis Leclerc Buffon, *De l'homme* (Paris: François Maspero, 1971), 242. A particularly interesting report of people with tails occurs in Linnaeus's *Systema Naturae,* and many eighteenth-century writers commented on the passage (see in particular James Burnett, *Of the Origin and Progress of Language* [1773; reprint, Menston: Scholar Press, 1967], 238–39). Immanuel Kant also passed on stories of people with tails. In his *Physical Geography (Physische Geographie),* he writes: "The people on Formosa, in the interior of Borneo, etc., who possess the beginnings of an ape's tail . . . seem to be not completely fictitious" (Emmanuel Chukwudi Eze, ed., *Race and the Enlightenment* [Cambridge, Mass.: Blackwell, 1997], 63).

71 João dos Sanctos, *Collections out of the Voyage and Historie of Friar João dos Sanctos his Æthiopia Orentalis, and Varia Historia, and out of other Portugals, for the better Knowledge of Africa and the Christianite therein,* in *Purchase His Pil-*

grimes (1559; reprint, Glasgow: MacLehose, 1955), 9:216. Such reports were far from uncommon. Maupertuis, for example, devoted an entire chapter of his *Vénus physique* to the so-called *"nègre blanc."* There he defined this person as "a child about four or five years old who has all the traits of a Negro, traits whose ugliness is only exaggerated by his extremely white and pale skin. His head is covered with a white, almost reddish wool; his pale blue eyes seem wounded by the daylight; his large, poorly formed hands resemble the paws of an animal more than the hands of a man. People assure us that he was born of very black African parents" (Maupertuis, P. L. Moreau de, *Œuvres* [Hildescheim: Georg Olms, 1965], 2:115–16).

72 What we do not generally see before the eighteenth century, or at least what we do not see with any degree of consistency, is a cohesive theory of how individual traits, whether character traits or physical ones, are passed from one generation to the next.

73 Although this is not the place to develop a detailed history of seventeenth-century continental philosophy, it seems important to underscore here that the observations I am describing are perfectly consonant with the philosophy of the period. Mechanistic modes of understanding the world stressed an internal coherence, perhaps best exemplified in Descartes's *Discours de la méthode*, which emphasized the need to proceed analytically from one known quantity to the next, inferring the implicit order that makes things visible to human beings. Isaac Newton's *Principia* envisioned a similar mathematical precision inhering in the universe. Other, perhaps lesser-known thinkers whose philosophies correlated Descartes's and Newton's systems include Naudé, La Motte le Vayer, Pascal, and perhaps Fontenelle.

74 Lacan, *Four Fundamental Concepts*, 22.

75 Ibid.

76 Ibid.

77 Ibid.

78 Žižek, *Metastases*, 30.

79 Žižek provides a familiar example: "Suffice it to recall slips of the tongue when the *automation* of the signifying chain is, for a brief moment, disrupted by the intervention of some traumatic memory" (*Metastases*, 30).

80 David Hume, *A Treatise of Human Nature* (Oxford: Clarendon, 1958), 87.

81 Ibid., 92.

82 Ibid., 93.

83 Immanuel Kant, *Prolegomena to Any Future Metaphysics*, ed. and trans. Gary Hatfield (Cambridge: Cambridge University Press, 1987), 99.

84 Lacan, *Four Fundamental Concepts*, 22.

85 See Leo Groarke and Graham Solomon, "Some Sources for Hume's Account of Cause," *Journal of the History of Ideas* 52, no. 4 (1991): 645–63 for an interesting account of Hume's sources; Peter Jones "Cause, Reason, and Objectivity in

Hume's Aesthetics," in *Hume: A Re-Evaluation*, eds. Donald W. Livingston and James T. King (New York: Fordham University Press, 1976), 323–42 on causality and aesthetics in Hume's work; and Anthony Pike Cavendish, *David Hume* (New York: Dover, 1968) on the influence of skepticism in Hume's work. For Kant, see in particular Paul Guyer, *Kant and the Claims of Knowledge* (Cambridge: Cambridge University Press, 1987).

86 On temporality in the formation of a causal chain, see David Hume, *Human Nature*, especially 69–94; and Kant, *Prolegomena*, especially 95–101.

87 On the notion of body parts and their relationship to corporeal integrity, David Hillman and Carla Mazzio write: "The rhetorical trope in which these relations are configured (and disfigured) is synedoche, a term that signifies the way in which a part is 'taken for' a whole. Insofar as parts were imagined as dominant vehicles for the articulation of culture, the early modern period could be conceptualized as an age of synecdoche" (Hillman and Mazzio, introduction to *The Body in Parts*, xiii–xiv).

88 Butler, *Bodies That Matter*, 11.

89 Ibid.

90 Laqueur, *Making Sex*, 109.

91 Interestingly enough, research on children's perceptions of their own racial markers produced similar conjectures. In her *Race Awareness in Young Children* (1952), Mary Ellen Goodman writes: " 'Why is she that color? Is she sunburned? Can she change?' These questions and more have come from our children [in her study]. They are conspicuously uniform in one respect: These white children do not ask about themselves—*why* their own color or the lack of it. They take it completely for granted, in the fashion of 'primitive' tribesmen, that they are 'the people.' The others, those under the shadow of color, 'they're different' " (Seshadri-Crooks, "Comedy of Domination," 358).

92 Samuel Stanhope Smith, *An Essay on the Causes of the Variety of Complexion and Figure in the Human Species*, ed. Winthrop D. Jordan (1788; reprint, Cambridge, Mass.: Harvard University Press, 1965), 29.

93 Bhabha writes—in this case more broadly of the colonial subject—that "the construction of the colonial subject in discourse, and the exercise of colonial power through discourse, demands an articulation of forms of difference—racial and sexual" (*The Location of Culture* [New York: Routledge, 1994], 67). He also theorizes that "it is in the emergence of the interstices—the overlap and displacement of domains of difference—that the intersubjective and collective experiences of *nationness*, community interest, or cultural value are negotiated. How are subjects formed 'in between,' or in excess of, the sum of the 'parts' of difference (usually intoned as race/class/gender, etc.)?" (2). Lacan argues that "Naming constitutes a pact, by which two subjects simultaneously come to an agreement to recognise the same object. If the human subject didn't name—as Genesis says it was done in earthly Paradise—the major species first, if the

subjects do not come to an agreement over this recognition, no world, not even a perception, could be sustained for more than one instant" (Lacan, *The Ego in Freud's Theory and in the Technique of Psychoanalysis: The Seminaire*, book 2, trans. Sylvana Tomaselli [New York: Norton, 1991], 169–70).

94 By way of interrogating the extent to which power and its denominational practices inflect one another, Butler asks, "To what extent does discourse gain the authority to bring about what it names through citing the conventions of authority?" (Butler, *Bodies That Matter*, 13).

95 Jordan, *White Over Black*, 257. Jordan, however, does not always seem to fully explore the complexity of the issue obtaining here. After describing how medieval bestiaries contained rosters of monsters resembling human beings, he writes that "given this tradition [of associating the ape's likeness to human beings and to sexuality] it was virtually inevitable that Englishmen should discern similarity between the man-like beasts and the beast-like men of Africa" (Jordan, *White Over Black*, 30). The point here would be that there is nothing "inevitable" about making the tremendous cultural leap of associating a particular human group with a species of animal. Furthermore, Jordan's use of the word "discern" implies that such a similarity is somehow natural and pre-exists the connection people made.

96 Alden T. Vaughan, *American Racism*, 6. Further examples abound, but we might note the following recent manifestation of this issue: "The association of black with evil was of course deeply rooted in Western and Christian mythology; it was natural to think of Satan as the Prince of Darkness and of witchcraft as black magic. . . . Carl Gustav Jung has even argued that the Negro became for the European whites a symbol of the unconscious itself—of what he calls 'the shadow'—the whole suppressed or rejected side of the human psyche" (George Frederickson, *The Arrogance of Race: Historical Perspectives on Slavery, Racism, and Social Inequality* [Middletown, Conn.: Wesleyan University Press, 1988], 191).

97 Or, as Barbara J. Fields puts it: "The idea one people has of another, even when the difference between them is embodied in the most striking physical characteristics, is always mediated by the social context within which the two come into contact" (Fields, "Ideology and Race in American History," in *Region, Race, and Reconstruction*, eds. J. Morgan Kousser and James M. McPherson [New York: Oxford University Press, 1982], 148–49).

98 In chapter 5 I will examine more closely the manner in which competing ideological representation stake out segments of a field of vision such that each segment actively blocks the other from view. This phenomenon, which Lacan has analyzed under the heuristic device of the anamorphic lens, can help illustrate not only how believing is seeing, but how one particular account of the way the world works can antagonistically blot out competing versions.

99 See Algirdas Greimas, especially *Structural Semantics*, trans. Daniele McDow-

ell, Ronald Schleifer, and Alan Velie (Lincoln: University of Nebraska Press, 1983) and *On Meaning*, trans. Paul Perron and Frank H. Collins (Minneapolis: University of Minnesota Press, 1987); Thomas Pavel, especially his notion of inference systems and the use readers' make of fiction, as compared to their attempt to make it realistic (Pavel, *Fictional Worlds* [Cambridge, Mass.: Harvard University Press, 1986], 17, 43–48, 60); Marthe Robert, especially her argument that novels simultaneously ask readers to recognize and to ignore the craftwork that went into their production (Robert, *Origins of the Novel*, trans. Sacha Rabinovitch [Bloomington: Indiana University Press, 1980], 35ff); and Didier Coste, *Narrative as Communication*, (Minneapolis: University of Minnesota Press, 1989).

100 As Ernst Cassirer puts it, "Thought no longer wants to accept the world as empirically given; it sets itself the task of analyzing the structure of the universe, in fact, of producing this structure with its own resources" (Cassirer, *Philosophy of the Enlightenment*, 51).

101 By invoking the perhaps oxymoronic phrase "relative equality," I mean to place the attitudes that seventeenth-century Europeans held toward the people they observed in some sort of historical perspective. Given the attitudes that would prevail only a generation or so later, it seems important to underscore that if Europeans did not consider the people of Africa to be their absolute equals, neither did they treat them as a different species barely worthy of the status of human, a not at all uncommon position in the eighteenth century, both in Europe and North America.

102 Grevenbroek, *An Elegant and Accurate Account*, 175.

103 Notable contributions to the idea of natural law were developed by Samuel Pufendorf, in his *De jure naturae et gentium libri* (1672; reprint, Buffalo, N.Y.: William Hein, 1995) and *De officio hominis et civis juxta legem naturalem* (1673; reprint, Buffalo, N.Y.: William Hein, 1995); Richard Cumberland, *De legibus naturae disquisitio philosophica* (London: Typis E. Flesher, 1672); and Locke's *Two Treatises of Government*, ed. Peter Laslett (London: Cambridge University Press, 1970).

104 Hobbes writes: "Nature hath made men so equall, in the faculties of body, and mind; as that though there bee found one man sometimes manifestly stronger in body, or of quicker mind then another; yet when all is reckoned together, the difference between man, and man, is not so considerable, as that one man can thereupon claim to himselfe any benefit, to which another may not pretend, as well as he. For as to the strength of body, the weakest has strength enough to kill the strongest, either by secret machination, or by confederacy with others, that are in the same danger with himselfe" (Hobbes, *Leviathan* [New York: Penguin, 1968], 183).

105 Hobbes, *Leviathan*, 189–90.

106 Ibid., 189.

107 On the concept of natural law in the Enlightenment, see in particular, in addition to the sources already mentioned and to be discussed below, Jean Ehrard, *L'idée de nature en France*, 2 vols (Paris: SEVPEN, 1963), especially 2:333–49 and 2:419–44; Ira O. Wade, *The Intellectual Origins of the French Enlightenment* (Princeton: Princeton University Press, 1971), especially chapter 11; Roger Mercier, *La réhabilitation de la nature humaine* (Villemomble: La Balance, 1960), especially 227–71.

108 Montesquieu, *Esprit des lois I*, i, 2:232.

109 Ibid., iii, 2:237.

110 Paul Hazard, *La crise de la conscience européenne* (Paris: Fayard, 1961), 294; my translation.

111 *Encyclopédie, ou Dictionnaire raisonné des sciences, des arts et des métiers* (Geneva: Briasson, 1754–92), 12:509; my translation.

112 Paul Hazard, *La pensée européenne au XVIIIe siècle* (Paris: Fayard, 1963), 280; my translation. Thomas Hankins has described the transition from seventeenth-century to eighteenth-century epistemologies as follows: "Descartes had concluded in 1638 that with the exception of the human rational soul all natural objects were caused by inert particles of matter in motion. . . . The mechanical philosophy was seductive, but it could explain vital phenomena such as growth, nutrition, and reproduction only by resorting to the most outlandish hypotheses, none of which was confirmable by experiment" (Hankins, *Science and the Enlightenment* [Cambridge: Cambridge University Press, 1985], 114–15).

113 Buffon, *De l'homme*, 223; my translation.

114 Ibid., 227.

115 Ibid., 270.

116 Ibid., 310.

117 Arthur O. Lovejoy, *The Great Chain of Being* (Cambridge, Mass.: Harvard University Press, 1936), 59. Jordan traces the Chain back to medieval bestiaries, which he notes contained reports of unusual creatures resembling humans. The *simia, agnocephali*, and *satyri* are among those he describes (Jordan, *White Over Black*, 28–31).

118 Lovejoy, *Great Chain of Being*, 145. Diderot would later lambaste Leibniz in his *Rêve de d'Alembert*. He writes that "all the delirium surrounding this faculty [imagination] boils down to the talent these charlatans have of taking several chopped up animals and forming a strange new one that no one has ever seen in nature" (Diderot, *Le rêve de d'Alembert*, in *Œuvres philosophiques*, ed. P. Vernière [Paris: Classiques Garnier, 1964], 369; my translation.) Nevertheless, in his "De l'interprétation de la nature," he places stock in "la grande

chaîne qui lie toutes choses (the great chain that unites all things)" (Diderot, "De l'interprétation de la nature," in *Œuvres philosophiques,* ed. P. Vernière [Paris: Classiques Garnier, 1964], 182).

119   It is interesting to note that during the third quarter of the seventeenth century many philosophers and others were interested in constructing human languages based on ideas similar to Leibniz's. John Wilkins's *Essay towards a Real Character and a Philosophical Language* strives toward constructing a language whose character fits in with dominant philosophical concepts. Wilkins asks: "What kind of *Character* or Language may be fixed upon, as most convenient for the expression of all those Particulars above mentioned, belonging to the Philosophy of *Speech*" (Wilkins, *Essay towards a Real Character and a Philosophical Language* [London: Gellibrand, 1668], 385). Furthermore, Wilkins imagines a language in which "the *Names* of things might consist of such *Sounds,* as should bear in them some Analogy to their *Natures;* and the Figure or Character of these Names should bear some proper resemblance to those *Sounds,* that men might easily guess at the sense or meaning of any name or word, upon the first *hearing* or *sight* of it" (386).

120   Sir William Petty, *The Petty Papers* (New York: Houghton Mifflin Co., 1927), 21.

121   Richard Blackmore, *The Lay-Monastery* (London: Pemberton, 1714), 29.

122   James Burnett, *Origin and Progress of Language,* 201–2.

123   Ibid., 202. Burnett did not always find himself writing for the majority of his contemporaries. In another context, he writes, "And I am persuaded, that all nations have at some time or another been cannibals" (Burnett, *Origin and Progress of Language,* 208–9).

124   Even well into the nineteenth century scholars made explicit connections linking humans and beasts. As Sander Gilman writes, in 1817 Georges Cuvier wrote up the autopsy of the famous Hottentot Venus: "Cuvier's description reflected [Henri de] Blainville's two intentions: the comparison of a female of the 'lowest' human species with the highest ape (the orangutan) and the description of the anomalies of the Hottentot's 'organ of generation'" (Gilman, "Black Bodies, White Bodies: Toward an Iconography of Female Sexuality in Late Nineteenth-Century Art, Medicine, and Literature," in *Race, Writing, and Difference,* ed. Henry Louis Gates Jr. [Chicago: University of Chicago Press, 1985], 232).

125   Alexander Pope, *Essay on Man,* epistle 2, ll. 3–8, in *Alexander Pope,* ed. Pat Rogers (Oxford: Oxford University Press, 1993), 281. If Leibniz never explicitly acknowledged the human craftwork involved in the construction of nature, other philosophers and naturalists recognized the extent to which thought created the objects they observed. John Locke wondered whether the human variation that travelers had observed originated from nature or from the observers themselves. Referring to the now-famous reports of people with

tails, he writes: "If it be asked whether these be all *men* or no, all of human species? it is plain, the question refers only to the nominal essence: for those of them to whom the definition of the word man, or the complex idea signified by that name, agrees, are men, and the other not" (John Locke, *An Essay Concerning Human Understanding*, bk. 3, ch. 6, sec. 22, ed. John W. Yolton [New York: Dutton, 1978], 73). Whatever fits the definition of man *is* man, for the obvious reason that that is how nominalization works.

126 Ibid,, sec. 12.

127 S. Smith, *An Essay on the Causes*, 48.

128 Ibid., 5.

129 Ibid., 29.

130 Buffon, *De l'homme*, 304.

131 Ibid., 318.

132 Ibid., 262.

133 Ibid., 304.

134 Barbara J. Fields notes that "there is no reason to doubt that such a striking contrast in color would arrest the attention of Englishmen encountering it for the first time. But surely other circumstances account more powerfully than the psychological impact of color as such for the fact that the English did not tarry over gradations in color" (Fields, "Ideology," 145). Similarly, Ross Chambers has written that "the difference between white and nonwhite depends in crucial ways on there also being differences among the multiple categories that constitute the paradigm of the nonwhite, since it is only by differentiation from a pluralized paradigm that the singularity of whiteness as nonparadigmatic, its undivided touchstone character, can be produced" (Chambers, "The Unexamined," 190).

135 Even at the beginning of the nineteenth century writers still held onto the idea that white was white, and afforded very little variation. In his *Goldsmith's Natural History*, Oliver Goldsmith offers up a taxonomy of the great divisions of the earth. He writes: "The sixth and last division of the Human Race is comprised under the term of EUROPEANS, a set of people who possess those superior advantages which religion and refinement naturally produce.... The inhabitants of countries so remote from each other, of course must vary in their manners and designs; but in their form and persons there is a striking similitude, and little variation in the colour of their skin" (Goldsmith, *Goldsmith's Natural History*, [Philadelphia: Johnson and Warner, 1810], 21–22).

136 S. Smith, *An Essay on the Causes*, 104.

137 Manoel de Almeida, *Some Records of Ethiopia, 1593–1646, Being Extracts from the History of High Ethiopia or Abassia, by Manoel de Almeida*, eds. and trans. C. F. Beckingharm and G. W. B. Huntingford (London: Hakluyt Society, 1954), 57. In the eighteenth century, Kant would write that "when a Negro burns

himself the spot turns white. Long illnesses also turn the Negroes quite white; but a body that has become white through illness turns blacker in death than it ever was before" (Eze, *Race and the Enlightenment*, 60).

138 Andrew Battell, *The Strange Adventures of Andrew Battell of Leigh, in Angola and the Adjoining Regions*, series 2, no. 6. ed. E. G. Ravenstein (London: Hakluyt Society, 1901), 81.

139 Buffon found similar disturbing white people where he did not expect them. Describing white skin where he expected to find black, he writes that "what can persuade us that these white men are only in effect individuals who have degenerated from their species is the fact that they are all much weaker and vigorous than the others, and that their eyes are extremely weak" (Buffon, *De l'homme*, 304).

140 Buffon, *De l'homme*, 286.

141 In the nineteenth century various American racial writing addressed the reality of what they called the "black white man," which was a snide way of arguing that those who claimed Africans and Europeans were the same but for their color were sadly mistaken. As late as 1868, Dr. John H. Van Evrie wrote, in his *White Supremacy and Negro Subordination* that "the Albino, the deformed or monstrous Negro, the seemingly wide departure from the normal standard, still obeys the higher law. All the peculiarities that distinguish him from his race are *sui generis*, without any approximation or resemblance to the white man" (Van Evrie, *White Supremacy and Negro Subordination*, in vol. 3 of *Anti-Black Thought, 1863–1925*, ed. John David Smith [New York: Garland, 1993], 139). I will address these matters in chapter 3.

142 At least from a European perspective. In his *Travels in the Interior Districts of Africa* Mungo Park describes how the women of the seraglio he visited tried to account for his unusual, European appearance: "They rallied me with a good deal of gaiety on different subjects; particularly upon the whiteness of my skin, and the prominency of my nose. They insisted that both were artificial. The first, they said, was produced when I was an infant, by dipping me in milk; and they insisted that my nose had been pinched every day, till it had acquired its present unsightly and unnatural conformation" (Park, *Travels in the Interior Districts of Africa* [London: Bulmer and Co., 1799], 56). In the nineteenth century, Dr. John H. Van Evrie was startled to learn that people had, in fact, sought the cause of whiteness, and he addresses this fact in his *White Supremacy and Negro Subordination:* "Anatomists and physiologists have labored very earnestly to account for or to show the 'cause' of color, not of the Negro alone, but in the case of our own race." Apparently a follower of Kant and the idea of natural necessity, however, he goes on to state that "to speak of [the reason given for the cause of color] is an abuse of terms, for it is simply a fact, and no more a cause than it is an effect" (Van Evrie, *White Supremacy*, 92]).

143 S. Smith, *An Essay on the Causes*, 9.

144 Blackmore, *The Lay-Monastery*, 30.

145 Ibid., 29. In this context Londa Schiebinger writes that the great apes "seemed to confirm the notion of hierarchy and continuity in nature. Humans—part brute, part angel—were thought to link the mortal world to the divine. Might apes be human or the link between humans and brutes, just as asbestos linked minerals and plants; the *Hydra* (water polyp) joined plants and animals; and the flying squirrel linked birds and quadrupeds?" (Schiebinger, *Nature's Body*, 80).

146 Sloan, "The Gaze of Natural History," 123.

147 Buffon, *De l'homme*, 47. Not everyone agreed that animals possessed no reason. Hume writes that "no truth appears to me more evident, than that beasts are endow'd with thought and reason as well as men" (Hume, *Human Nature*, 176).

148 Locke, *Human Understanding*, bk. 2, ch. 11, sec. 10, 207–8.

149 Although most Enlightenment thinkers held that reason is an indivisible attribute of the human being, Locke happened to be one of the few who maintained that, while reason does separate human from beast, it is also available in quantifiable units. Writing of "brutes," he posits: "For if they have any ideas at all, and are not bare machines, (as some would have them,) we cannot deny them to have some reason. It seems as evident to me, that they do [some of them in certain instances] reason, as that they have sense; but it is only in particular ideas, just as they received them from their senses" (bk. 2, ch. 11, sec. 11, 208; bracketed passages are additions to the fourth edition).

150 Some Enlightenment philosophers acknowledged the historically contingent nature of reason. Locke, for example, recognized that regardless of the material composition underlying any given species, divisions and categories reflect human, and not natural, designations. Of the human tendency to produce taxonomies and descriptions he writes: "It is plain that *our distinct species* are *nothing but distinct complex ideas, with distinct names annexed to them*. It is true every substance that exists has its peculiar constitution, whereon depend those sensible qualities and powers we observe in it; but the ranking of things into species (which is nothing but sorting them under several titles) is done by us according to the ideas that *we* have of them" (bk. 3, ch. 6, sec. 13, p. 69). Diderot also argued that reason and philosophy, like any other historically produced discourses, are products of their times. See his *Rêve de d'Alembert;* likewise, Hume's treatises make passing references to the circumstantial nature of human thought.

151 Petty, *Petty Papers*, 21.

152 Ibid., 31.

153 Correlatively, in the nineteenth century in particular the idea that only white

people had a history became something of a commonplace. The author of the anonymous *Six Species of Men* (1866), for example, wrote that "the Caucasian is the only historical race, and is the only one capable of those mental manifestations which have a permanent impression behind. It is the only race that can be said to have a history" (Smith, *Anti-Black Thought, 1863–1925*, ed. John David Smith [New York: Garland, 1993], 1:132). James Hunt, in his *The Negro's Place in Nature* (1868), correlated this view when he wrote that "We now know it to be a patent fact that there are races existing which have no history, and that the Negro is one of these races" (Hunt, *The Negro's Place in Nature*, in vol. 1 of *Anti-Black Thought, 1863–1925*, ed. John David Smith [New York: Garland, 1993], 109).

154 Tracing the development of value as substitution in linguistic, economic, and psychic economies, Jean-Joseph Goux, following Marx, notes that commodities express their values simply, in terms of one commodity, then in uniform fashion, since all commodities express their values in terms of a single commodity; the general form of value is common to all commodities. Of Marx's formulation, Goux writes: "This is an elegant solution; it is *reason* itself" (Goux, *Symbolic Economies*, trans. Jennifer Curtiss Gage [Ithaca, N.Y.: Cornell University Press, 1990], 16). Goux's analysis underscores the historical contingency of reason, as well as the fact that forms of reason are tied to other kinds of substitutions.

155 Although she does not consider, as I do here, the form that European reason took in the development of racial category, Fields also notes a connection. She writes: "Bourgeois 'rationality' tore loose from 'natural' categories the task—which all societies carry out in some form—of identifying and classifying differences among people. The latter had to be recreated from scientific first principles, with the enterprise of classification and identification now subordinated to the practical business of disciplining—and, if need be, institutionalizing—deviance and nonconformity" (Fields, "Ideology," 152).

156 S. Smith, *An Essay on the Causes*, 118.

157 Maxine Sheets-Johnstone has argued more broadly, and indeed, she has made it the thesis of her *Roots of Thinking*, that "there is an indissoluble bond between hominid thinking and hominid evolution, a bond cemented by the living body" (Sheets-Johnstone, *The Roots of Thinking* [Philadelphia: Temple University Press, 1990], 4).

158 Jordan points out that the endurance of stories of beast-like humans "was in itself an indication of the diverse functions it served. The notion has scientific value: it forged a crucial link in the Chain of Being and helped explain the Negro's and the ape's prognathism. On a less rational level the notion gave expression to men's half-conscious realization that they were linked to beasts and bestiality. And just as the concept of the Chain ordered every being on a

vertical scale, the association of the Negro with the ape ordered men's deep, unconscious drives into a tightly controlled hierarchy" (Jordan, *White Over Black*, 238).

159 Richard Feldstein provides a concise way of conceiving these fundamental signifiers: "When a *point de capiton* recasts numerous free-floating signifiers into a unified field of meaning that reads each term in relation to this deterministic signifier, the disarray is recast into coherence" (Feldstein, "Subject of the Gaze for Another Gaze," in *Lacan, Politics, Aesthetics*, eds. Willy Apollon and Richard Feldstein [Albany: State University of New York Press, 1996], 51–52).

160 Thomas Laqueur makes a similar point about gender: "The nature of sexual difference is not susceptible to empirical testing. It is logically independent of biological facts because already embedded in the language of science, at least when applied to any culturally resonant construal of sexual difference, is the language of gender. In other words, all but the most circumscribed statements about sex are, from their inception, burdened with the cultural work done by these propositions" (Laqueur, *Making Sex*, 153).

161 Horkheimer and Adorno's critiques are, of course, extensive, but I might briefly cite here a few key passages: "For the Enlightenment, whatever does not conform to the rule of computation and utility is suspect. So long as it can develop undisturbed by any outward repression, there is no holding it. In the process, it treats its own ideas of human rights exactly as it does the older universals" (Max Horkheimer and Theodor Adorno, *Dialectic of Enlightenment* [New York: Continuum, 1987], 6); "Enlightenment recognizes as being and occurrence only what can be apprehended in unity: its ideal is the system from which all and everything follows" (7); "Enlightenment dissolves the injustice of the old inequality—unmediated lordship and mastery—but at the same time perpetuates it in universal mediation, in the relation of any one existent to any other" (12).

162 Horkheimer and Adorno, *Dialectic of Enlightenment*, 27.

163 Ibid., 68.

3. THE FAIR SEX

1 Buffon, *De l'homme*, 316. Subsequent quotations from *De l'homme* in this chapter are cited by page number in the text.

2 Jordan, *White Over Black*, 158.

3 Later writers would contest the assertion that African children are born white. In his treatise *The Negro's Place in Nature* (1868), Dr. James Hunt wrote: "M. Flourens asserted that the Negro children were born white; but recent observation has shown that this not the case [*sic*]. Benet, ex-physician of Run-

jeet Singh, and Dumontier, affirmed that the children are born chestnut color. M. Pruner Bey confirms this fact from personal observation" (Hunt, *The Negro's Place in Nature*, 107).

4 Oddly enough, Buffon's claim that penises are fundamentally white is directly contradicted by Kant, who in the *Physische Geographie* [Physical Geography] writes: "The Negroes are born white apart from their genitals and a ring around the navel, which are black" (Eze, *Race and Enlightenment*, 60).

5 Schiebinger, *Nature's Body*, 146. Schiebinger goes on to remark that "females were rarely compared across racial lines in the eighteenth century; or, if they were, it was commonly in relation to their sexual parts," and that there was an "assumption that the racial subject was male and that sexual differentiation was primarily about Europeans" (147).

6 Stephen Jay Gould points out that Abraham Lincoln, traditionally championed as the staunchest supporter of racial equality, never abandoned a belief in biological *inequality*. Citing Lincoln's claim that "there is a physical difference between the white and black races which I believe will forever forbid the two races living together on terms of social and political equality" (S. Gould, *The Mismeasure of Man* [New York: Norton, 1996], 66), he writes: "I quote the men who have justly earned our highest respect in order to show that white leaders of Western nations did not question the propriety of racial ranking during the eighteenth and nineteenth centuries. In this context, the pervasive assent given by scientists to conventional rankings arose from shared social belief, not from objective data gathered to test an open question" (66).

7 Kenan Malik, *The Meaning of Race* (New York: New York University Press, 1996), 10.

8 McDowell, "Pecs and Reps," 366.

9 Ian Haney López discusses this operation in the context of court decisions concerning who is white: "The courts constructed the bounds of Whiteness by deciding on a case by case basis who was *not* White. Though the prerequisite courts were charged with defining the term 'white person,' they did so not through an appeal to a freestanding notion of Whiteness, but instead negatively, by identifying who was non-White. Thus, . . . the courts did not establish the parameters of Whiteness so much as the non-Whiteness of Chinese, South Asians, and so on" (López, *White by Law*, 547).

10 In making this claim I am of course not arguing that such knowledge did not exist prior to the eighteenth century or in locales outside of western Europe. Rather, I am trying to determine the particularities of forms of knowledge predicated on the human body and in particular I am striving to demonstrate the historical specificity of what we now somewhat blithely refer to as the white male, as though such an identity did not require archaeological investigation.

11 It is important to point out that the kinds of body-based racial knowledge I am investigating in the early modern period continues. Kimberlé Williams

Crenshaw analyzes race-neutrality in law, and points out that white race-consciousness, which reinforces whites' belief in an American society based on merit, combats the sorts of gains that legal reform is ostensibly meant to bring about. See Crenshaw, "Race, Reform, and Retrenchment," in *Theories of Race and Racism,* eds. Les Back and John Solomos (New York: Routledge, 2000), 549–60.

12 Lacan most fully develops his theory of the four positions of discourse in *L'envers de la psychanalyse: Le Séminaire,* livre 17 (Paris: Seuil, 1991). See also *Encore: Le séminaire,* livre 20 (Paris: Seuil, 1975), especially 19–26.

13 The object a is what is excluded from speech, and it functions simultaneously as the object and the cause of desire. To some extent, it is the difference or remainder belonging to the subject when one removes the realm of meaning *(lettre)* from the realm of being *(l'être).* On this rather difficult Lacanian concept, see in particular Slavoj Žižek, *The Sublime Object of Ideology* (New York: Verso, 1989), especially 52–53.

14 On the Lacanian algebra for the four discourses, see Mark Bracher, "Lacan's Theory in the Four Discourses" *Prose Studies* 11, no. 3 (December 1988): 32–49; and Bruce Fink, *The Lacanian Subject* (Princeton: Princeton University Press, 1995), especiall ch. 9.

15 Fink, *The Lacanian Subject,* 129–30.

16 Writing in a different context, David Theo Goldberg stresses the manner in which the supposedly neutral detachment of taxonomy that claims for itself transparent systemization serves the interests of the master: "*Classification* is basically the scientific extension of the epistemological drive to place phenomena under categories. The impulse to classify data goes back at least to Aristotle. However, it is only with the 'esprits simplistes' of the seventeenth century and the Enlightenment that classification is established as a fundament of scientific methodology. With its catalogues, indices, and inventories, classification establishes an ordering of data; it thereby systemizes observation. But it also claims to reflect the natural order of things" (*Racist Culture* [Cambridge, Mass.: Blackwell, 1993], 49).

17 Lacan, *L'envers,* 70–71; my translation.

18 Ibid., 101.

19 Bracher, "Four Discourses," 35.

20 See in particular Lévi-Strauss, *Structural Anthropology,* especially 31–51.

21 Lacan points out that hidden truth *(une vérité cachée)* implies not that a specific form of discourse hides itself, but that, as one should expect from the etymology of the French word for "hidden"—*cacher* derives from the classical Latin *coactare,* "to compress"—"there is something compressed, which is like a double-exposure, something that must be unfolded in order to be legible" (Lacan, *L'envers,* 90).

22 Lacan, *L'envers,* 102.

23　Nancy Leys Stepan and Sander L. Gilman, "Appropriating the Idioms of Science: The Rejection of Scientific Racism," in *The Bounds of Race*, ed. Dominick LaCapra (Ithaca, N.Y.: Cornell University Press, 1991), 100.

24　Ragland-Sullivan, "Discourse," 134.

25　Lacan, *L'envers*, 34.

26　Ibid., 141.

27　Ibid., 150.

28　In a perhaps typically difficult formulation, Lacan describes this phenomenon as follows: "The subject itself, hysterical, alienates itself from the master signifier as the one that this signifier divides . . . the one that refuses to make it its body" (Lacan, *L'envers*, 107). Mark Bracher interprets Lacan by writing that "the hysterical structure is in force whenever a discourse is dominated by the speaker's symptom—i.e., his or her unique mode of experiencing *jouissance*, a uniqueness which is manifested (in experiences such as shame, meaninglessness, anxiety, and desire) as a failure of the subject, $, to coincide with or be satisfied by the master signifiers offered by society and embraced as the subject's ideals" (Bracher, "Four Discourses," 45). Jan Goldstein puts the matter in somewhat simpler terms: "Hysteria represents in each sex an aspiration to androgyny—that is to say, a protest against conventional gender definitions and an (ultimately failed) attempt to transcend them" (Goldstein, *Uses of Male Hysteria*, 145).

29　Lacan, *Les psychoses: Le séminaire*, livre 3 (Paris: Seuil, 1981), 201; my translation.

30　As Paul Verhaeghe phrases it, "In the end, the only successful master is a dead one, one who has entered eternal silence" (Verhaeghe, *Does the Woman Exist?*, trans. Marc du Ry [New York: Other Press, 1999], 109).

31　In addition to Fink and Bracher on the discourse of the hysteric, see also Colette Soler, "Hysteria and Obsession," in *Reading Seminars I and II*, eds. Richard Feldstein, Bruce Fink, and Maire Jaanus (Albany: State University of New York Press, 1996), 248–82; and Vicente Palomera, "The Ethics of Hysteria and of Psychoanalysis," in *Reading Seminars I and II*, eds. Richard Feldstein, Bruce Fink, and Maire Jaanus (Albany: State University of New York Press, 1996), 387–96.

32　For feminist interpretations of the politics of hysteria, see in particular Bernheimer and Kahane, *In Dora's Case;* Juliet Mitchell and Jacqueline Rose, introductions to *Feminine Sexuality* (New York: W. W. Norton, 1983); Mitchell, *Psychoanalysis and Feminism;* Luce Irigaray, especially "The Blind Spot of an Old Dream of Symmetry," in *Speculum;* Gallop, especially *The Daughter's Seduction;* Copjec, *Read My Desire* (Cambridge, Mass.: MIT University Press, 1994), especially "Cutting Up"; Jann Matlock, *Scenes of Seduction* (New York: Columbia University Press, 1994); David-Ménard, *Hysteria;* Sharon Willis, "A Symptomatic Narrative," *Diacritics* 13, no. 1 (spring 1983): 46–60. For hysteria as a potential agent of social change, see Verhaeghe, *Does the Woman Exist;* Bracher, "Four Discourses"; Fink, *The Lacanian Subject;* and Salecl, *Spoils of Freedom.*

33 In *L'envers de la psychanalyse* he argued that Revolution with its capital R has become another master signifier, and to protesting students at Vincennes in 1969 he maintained that students are products of the university—or perhaps more accurately surplus value—and they leave that place stamped with credits, the defining feature of the institution (Lacan, *L'envers,* 232).

34 Lacan, *L'envers,* 35.

35 Ann Pellegrini, *Performance Anxieties* (New York: Routledge, 1997), 2.

36 Seshadri-Crooks, "Comedy of Domination," 356–57.

37 Butler, *Bodies That Matter,* 18.

38 Ibid., 190.

39 Ibid., 206.

40 Yet I would not argue that this has necessarily always been the case, nor would I argue that this is simply necessarily the case. The point here is that as our master signifiers of race and gender exist and have existed since the eighteenth century; they rely on one another for stability and for dominance. This point will become clearer at the end of this chapter and in chapter 5.

41 Thomas Hankins makes the simplest and perhaps most elegant pronouncement on this score: "Mechanism . . . had failed in physiology because it could not account for the properties of life" (Hankins, *Science and the Enlightenment,* 127). Many others, of course, have addressed this problem. See, for example, Paul Illie, *The Age of Minerva* (Philadelphia: University of Pennsylvania Press, 1995), especially volume 2, chapter 6, on "Theories of Vital Force, Matter, and Fiber"; G. S. Rousseau, *Enlightenment Crossings* (Manchester: Manchester University Press, 1991), especially chapter 5, "Nerves, Spirits, and Fibres"; Andrew Cunningham and Roger French, eds., *The Medical Enlightenment of the Eighteenth Century* (Cambridge: Cambridge University Press, 1990), which contains essays on the interaction between mind and body, the influence of medicine on the Enlightenment, and the relationships between a scientific approach to the body and such concepts as honor and property; Ernst Cassirer, *Philosophy of the Enlightenment;* Leonard Barkan, *Nature's Work of Art* (New Haven: Yale University Press, 1975); Jacques Roger, *Les sciences de la vie dans la pensée française au XVIII siècle* (Paris: Colin, 1963); Leonora Cohen Rosenfield, *From Beast-Machine to Man-Machine* (New York: Octagon, 1968); L. J. Rather, *Mind and Body in Eighteenth-Century Medicine* (Berkeley: University of California Press, 1965); Roy Porter, "Barely Touching: A Social Perspective on Mind and Body," in *The Languages of Psyche,* ed. G. S. Rousseau (Berkeley: University of California Press, 1990), 45–80; and Simon Schaffer, "States of Mind," in *The Languages of Psyche,* ed. G. S. Rousseau (Berkeley: University of California Press, 1990), 233–90.

42 Stepan, *The Idea of Race,* 4.

43 Lacan himself says of the position of master that "we only know it nowadays in a considerably modified form" (*L'envers*, 203).

44 I am including the subjects who identify as white male in the category of racialized subjects, and we will see below how this category pertains to this group, and why it is important to insist on labeling them this way. On this particular issue, Hazel Carby in "The Multicultural Wars" writes: "We need to recognize that we live in a society in which systems of dominance and subordination are structured through processes of racialization that continuously interact with all other forces of socialization. Theoretically, we should be arguing that everyone in this social order has been constructed in our political imagination as a racialized subject. In this sense, it is important to think about the invention of the category of whiteness as well as that of blackness and, consequently, to make visible what is rendered invisible when viewed as the normative state of existence: the (white) point in space from which we tend to identify difference" (193).

45 In specifying that it is *white males* who here perform the discourse of the master, I do not mean to imply that *only* white males are involved in the production of white masculinity. Eve Kosofsky Sedgwick, for example, reminds us that "sometimes masculinity has got nothing to do with . . . men. And when something is about masculinity, it is not always 'about men' " (Sedgwick, " 'Gosh, Boy George, You Must Be Awfully Secure in your Masculinity,' " in *Constructing Masculinity*, eds. Marice Berger, Brian Wallis, and Simon Watson [New York: Routledge, 1995], 12). Nor do I mean to suggest a one-to-one correspondence between white masculinity and the discourse of the master I have been invoking, since it seems fairly clear that such a correspondence would obviate the need to theorize the *function* of that identity in the first place.

46 Sidney Kaplan has written of the intense dramatic potential American playwrights have derived from the question of mixed race, beginning in the nineteenth century in particular, with such plays as Boucicault's *Octoroon*, through the twentieth century. He ascribes the fragmentation implicit in American notions of mixed race to a democratic "fatal flaw" comparable to that found in Aristotelian notions of tragedy. See Kaplan, "*The Octoroon:* Early History of the Drama of Miscegenation," in *American Studies in Black and White*, ed. Allan D. Austin (Amherst: University of Massachusetts Press, 1991), 198–210.

47 Contemporary urban myths as well as tabloid journalism have continued to launch stories concerning people who bizarrely and inexplicable change gender or who perform actions normally attributed to the other gender. "Pregnant Man Gives Birth—Baby Lives!" screamed the banner headline on the April 30, 1991 *Sun* (Ken O'Hara). Joe Berger's report in the *Weekly World News* carried a story in which "easygoing Jean Webb always knew she was a little different," but after she gave birth to a baby she "watched in horror as she slowly became a man!" (Berger, "This Man Gave Birth to a 7-lb. Baby Girl!" *Weekly World News*,

26 September 1989, 3). We will see further examples in chapter 5 of people spontaneously changing race.

48 John Locke, *Human Understanding*, bk. 3, ch. 6, sec. 22, p. 73.

49 Grevenbroek, *An Elegant and Accurate Account*, 207.

50 Battell, *Strange Adventures*, 17–18.

51 In the nineteenth century, observations concerning a purported reversal of appropriate gender roles continued. In *The Negro's Place in Nature*, James Hunt writes: "If the women of Africa are brutal, the men of Africa are feminine." He continues by elaborating the characteristics that contribute to the overall sense of a generalized gender reversal. The faces of the men "are smooth, their breasts are frequently as full as those of European women; their voices are never gruff or deep. Their fingers are long; and they can be very proud of their rosy nails. While the women are nearly always ill-shaped after their girlhood, the men have gracefully moulded limbs, and always are after a feminine type— the arms rounded, the legs elegantly formed, without too much muscular development, and the feet delicate and small" (Hunt, *The Negro's Place in Nature*, 116).

52 Thomas Jefferson, *"Notes on the State of Virginia"* (1787; reprinted in *The Portable Thomas Jefferson*, ed. Merrill D. Peterson (New York: Penguin, 1975), 93.

53 Blumenbach, *De generis humani varietate nativa*, 98.

54 *Relation des costes d'Afrique* (Paris: Denys Thierry, 1669), 214.

55 J. Smith, *Anti-Black Thought*, 1:138. At the end of the eighteenth century, Mungo Park noted in his travels throughout Africa a similar obsession with men's beards and a particular pride of masculine origin. He writes: "Such of the Moors as have long beards, display them with a mixture of pride and satisfaction, as denoting an Arab ancestry. . . . And here I may be permitted to observe, that if any one circumstance excited among them favourable thoughts towards my own person, it was my beard; which was now grown to an enormous length, and was always beheld with approbation or envy. I believe in my conscience, they thought it too good a beard for a Christian" (Park, *Travels in the Interior*, 154).

56 Schiebinger, *Nature's Body*, 89–91. Schiebinger here relies on Charles White, *An Account of the Regular Gradation in Man and in Different Animals and Vegetables* (London: Dilly, 1799).

57 Schiebinger, *De generis*, 91.

58 Writing of the differences generally attributed to sex, Thomas Laqueur makes a point similar to the notion of "believing is seeing" that I have been developing. He argues: "The history of the representation of the anatomical differences between man and woman is thus extraordinarily independent of the actual structures of these organs or of what was known about them. Ideology, not accuracy of observation, determined how they were seen and which differences would matter" (Laqueur, *Making Sex*, 88).

59 Blumenbach, *De generis*, 90. And in a formulation that makes particularly interesting use of the ostensibly neutral third-person masculine pronoun, Johann Friederich Blumenbach goes on to remark that if the clitoris is found in beasts as well as in humans, "The hymen, the guardian of chastity, is adapted to man who is alone endowed with reason" (Blumenbach, "*De Generis Humani Varietate Nativa*," in *The Anthropological Treatises of Blumenbach*, ed. and trans. Thomas Bendyshe [London: Longman, Green, 1865. First published as *De Generis Humani Varietate Nativa* (Goettingase: Typis frid. andr. Rosenbuschii, 1775], 90). Interest in the clitoris seemed briefly, at least, to supersede fascination with African women's enlarged labia, about which more below.

60 Perhaps the most notable display of female genitals would be the dissection of Saartjie Baartman, the famous "Hottentot Venus" the tremendous interest in whom Sander Gilman has analyzed at length. Baartman died in France in 1815, and an autopsy was performed and widely published. Gilman cites Georges Cuvier, who wrote up the autopsy; Cuvier reports that he presented to "the Academy the genital organs of this woman prepared in a way so as to allow one to see the nature of the labia" (Gilman, "Black Bodies," 232–35).

61 Blumenbach, *De generis*, 249.

62 C. White, *Regular Gradation in Man*, 59.

63 And it is impossible to resist pointing out here that in 1996 the alternative rock group King Missile had a moderately successful hit with their song "Detachable Penis."

64 Nor is it necessarily the case that castration involves exclusively the detachability of the male genitals. On the one hand Freud distinguishes the male anxiety about the potential of castration from the female "discovery that she *is* castrated" (Freud, "Femininity," in *New Introductory Lectures on Psychoanalysis*, ed. and trans. James Strachey [New York: Norton, 1965], 111; emphasis mine). On the other hand, however, in Lacanian psychoanalysis castration names the subject's radical split from being. Parveen Adams states that "castration bears down upon both sexes within the registers of the symbolic, the Imaginary, and the Real" (Adams, "Waiving the Phallus," *Differences* 4, no.1 [1992]: 77).

65 John Brenkman argues that to view castration simply as an anatomical phenomenon completely misses the point of the forms of social privilege that appear to inhere in anatomical features: "Because Freud always construes castration in terms of anatomy, he misses the fact, as feminists as varied as Simone de Beauvoir, Juliet Mitchell and Luce Irigaray have demonstrated, that having-a-penis acquires its special value because it 'stands for' something valuable: prestige, privilege, power, property and so on. By the same token, the reason these goods get symbolized by *having-a-penis* is because they are monopolized by men. In having recourse to the anatomical distinction of the sexes, Freud hides and naturalizes this nexus of social relations between men and women" (Brenkman, *Straight Male Modern*, 124–25).

66 Jordan, *White Over Black*, 155–56.

67 Robyn Wiegman, "The Anatomy of Lynching," in *American Sexual Politics*, ed. John C. Fout and Maura Shaw Tantillo (Chicago: University of Chicago Press, 1993), 224. Wiegman further analyzes castration as a white remedy for black men's claims to equality: "Such a remedy becomes necessary in the social transformation from enslavement to freedom, where the measure of the African American's claim to citizenship is precisely his status as man—a status evinced by the penis, but ultimately rewarded in the symbolic exchange between penis and phallus" (227). I will analyze the relationship between penis and phallus below.

68 William Ten Rhyne, *A Short Account of the Cape of Good Hope and of the Hottentots who Inhabit that Region* (Schaffhausen: John Martin Oswald, 1686), 143.

69 Ibid., 115.

70 Olfert Dapper, "*Kaffraria or Land of the Kafirs, Also Named Hottentots*," in *The Early Cape Hottentots*, ed. I. Schapera, trans. I. Schapera and B. Farrington (Cape Town: Van Riebeeck Society, 1993. First published in Amsterdam: Jacob van Meur, 1668), 45. Olfert Dapper writes: "The married women . . . have exceedingly big bosoms, so big that their breasts, which hang loose and uncovered, can be passed back over the shoulders to suckle the children whom as a rule they carry there. . . . The lining of the body appears to be loose, so that in certain places part of it dangles out" (45). Rhyne writes that "the women may be distinguished from the men by their ugliness. And they have this peculiarity to distinguish them from other races, that most of them have dactyliform appendages, always two in number, hanging down from their pudenda" (Rhyne, *Cape of Good Hope*, 115). Peter Kolb refers to a "broad callous Part, growing just above the *Pudenda*, and flapping over and hiding them. It seems intended by Nature for the Concealment of those Parts" (Kolb, *The Present State of the Cape of Good Hope: or, a Particular Account of Several Nations of the Hottentots*, trans. Mr. Medley [1719; reprint, London: St. Paul's, 1731], 118).

71 Isaac Schapera, *The Early Cape Hottentots* (Cape Town: Van Riebeeck Society, 1933), 142 n.45.

72 Grevenbroek, *An Elegant and Accurate Account*, 209. On the practice of circumcision in some parts of Africa, see A. N. N. Ngxamngxa, "The Function of Circumcision among the Xhosa-speaking Tribes in Historical Perspective," in *Man: Anthropological Essays Presented to O. F. Raum*, ed. E. J. DeJager [Cape Town: C. Struik, 1971], 182–204).

73 On the matter of male circumcision and its capacity to mark cultural affinities, Stephen Greenblatt refers to a "detachability," in which the "mark or mutilation" remains separate from the interpretation ascribed to it. He writes: "In the case of male circumcision, which appears to have been a widespread practice throughout the ancient Middle East, Judaism provided a myth of origin that is in effect the expression of this detachability. Without narrative rationalization

or doctrinal justification, God simply commands it of Abraham and his descendants" (Greenblatt, "Mutilation and Meaning," 222).

74 The *Encyclopédie* catalogs the different varieties of circumcision practiced in the world, and it should have been clear, even in the generation preceding publication of that work, that the practice was not limited to Jews. For example, in the article "Circoncision," we read: "The Turks have a manner of circumcising different from that of the Jews; for, after having cut the skin of the prepuce, they touch it no more, whereas the Jews tear the edges of the skin remaining after the *circumcision* in several places: that is why circumcised Jews heal more easily than Turks" (*Encyclopédie*, 3:461). The author of the *Encyclopédie* article "Homme" attributes a purely reasonable rationale for the practice of circumcision: "The prepuce of most of these people would be too long and would inhibit reproduction without circumcision" (8:258).

75 Grevenbroek, *An Elegant and Accurate Account*, 209. In what admittedly appears to be an ironic remark, Kolb attempts to demonstrate how fond of tobacco Hottentot men and women are, and suggests that body parts are less dear to them than tobacco: "A *Hottentot* would rather lose a Tooth than a Corn of Tobacco" (Kolb, *Cape of Good Hope*, 209).

76 Grevenbroek, *An Elegant and Accurate Account*, 209.

77 Kolb, *Cape of Good Hope*, 113–14. Kolb also speculates that the origin of this practice might derive from Jewish circumcision rituals, and wonders whether the removal of a testicle might have somehow been mistaken for the cutting of the foreskin (118). The original edition of Kolb's work was published in 1719.

78 J. G. Grevenbroek finds instances of Hottentots urinating on one another and indicates that this has a healing mechanism: "A very frequent remedy is to turn the patient on his back and on his front and make water on him. They do not allow even his face to escape a bath of urine. Some even take, in a sea-shell or tortoise-shell or some other vessel, the amount of water discharged by one man, mix it with a powder from a certain plant, and administer it to the sick man" (Grevenbroek, *An Elegant and Accurate Account*, 243).

79 I am borrowing the term *defamiliarize* from the Russian formalists. Concerning the unfamiliar in art, Victor Shklovsky writes that "the technique of art is to make objects 'unfamiliar,' to make forms difficult, to increase the difficulty and length of perception because the process of perception is an aesthetic end in itself and must be prolonged" ("Art as Technique," in *Russian Formalist Criticism*, eds. Lee T. Lemon and Marin J. Reis [Lincoln: University of Nebraska Press, 1965], 12).

80 Grevenbroek, *An Elegant and Accurate Account*, 209. I am citing an English translation of 1731.

81 There is of course a considerable body of literature surrounding the development and significance of travel narratives. See in particular Percy Adams, *Travel Literature and the Evolution of the Novel* (Lexington: University Press of

Kentucky, 1983); Syed Manzoorul Islam, *The Ethics of Travel: From Marco Polo to Kafka* (Manchester, N.Y.: Manchester University Press, 1996); Diana Knight, *Barthes and Utopia: Space, Travel, Writing* (New York: Oxford University Press, 1997); Marie-Madeleine Martinet, *Le voyage d'Italie dans les littératures européennes* (Paris: Presses Universitaires de France, 1996); Joseph McMinn, *Jonathan's Travels: Swift and Ireland* (New York: St. Martin's Press, 1994); Sara Mills, *Discourses of Difference: An Analysis of Women's Travel Writing and Colonialism* (New York: Routledge, 1991); and Christopher Mulvey, *Transatlantic Manners: Social Patterns in Nineteenth-Century Anglo-American Travel Literature* (New York: Cambridge University Press, 1990).

82 *Encyclopédie*, 8:320.

83 Buffon's report of the ceremony reads as follows: "After having rubbed the young man with the fat of the entrails of a sheep killed for the occasion, they lay him down on his back on the ground; his hands and feet are tied, and three or four of his friends hold him. Then, the minister (for this is a religious ceremony), armed with a very sharp knife, makes an incision, removes the left testicle, and puts in its place a ball of fat of the same size, which has been prepared with medicinal herbs. Next he sews up the wound with the bone of a small bird serving as needle, and a thread of sheep's nerve. The operation now complete, the patient is untied, but before leaving him, the preacher, rubs him with the hot fat of the killed sheep, or, rather, he drenches his whole body with it with such abundance that, when it cools, it forms a kind of crust. All the while he rubs him so vigorously that the young man, who is already suffering considerably, sweats copiously and smokes like a roasted capon. Next the operator makes furrows in this crust of fat, from one end of the body to the other, and he pisses on top of him as copiously as he can, after which he begins to rub him again, and he covers up with the fat the furrows filled with urine. Immediately after, everyone leaves the patient; he is left alone, more dead than alive, and he must drag himself as best he can to a little hut that has been built for the occasion near the place where the operation took place. There he either dies or recovers his health with no help from anyone, and with no other refreshment or food than the fat which covers his whole body, which he can lick if he wants" (Buffon, *De l'homme*, 286–87).

84 Dana D. Nelson's *National Manhood* looks at a gendered form of national identity not only as an ideological and economic structure, but as one that provides "an affective space, for men individually and in groups" (Nelson, *National Manhood* [Durham: Duke University Press, 1998], 16). Nelson is also interested in the tension separating ideals of gender identity and the reality of lived experience, and she investigates "repeating thematics" of white manhood, including "anxiety and disappointment, longing for and fear of equality and human connection" (23). Nelson strenuously argues against the idea that white manhood is a unified identity position.

85   Encyclopédie, 8:320.

86   Strikingly, Buffon's description of the Hottentots as a people who are "not true Negroes, but men who, in the race of blacks, are beginning to approach white" prefigures Frantz Fanon's attempt to describe the frustration and disorientation experienced by one who is divorced from his own past: "Not yet white, no longer wholly black, I was damned" (Fanon, *Black Skin, White Masks*, trans. Charles Lam Markman [New York: Grove Press, 1967], 138).

87   Buffon, *De l'homme*, 319. In a perhaps related remark of this sort, which might well betray some aspects of Buffon's own cultural prejudices, he notes, apparently without any sort of irony, that the Ethiopians "drink no wine, even though they have vines" (272).

88   Here Buffon was treading on more or less familiar territory. In 1688 Jean Barbot penned the story of his voyages to Guinea. He found the inhabitants of Senegal to be "sensual, knavish, fond of lying, gluttons, abusive, more luxurious than can be imagined" (Barbot, *Barbot on Guinea*, 1:84). Of the women and of the sexual practices of these people in general, he writes: "The wives of the Africans are well-shaped, tall and loose-limbed. They are lively and wanton, and eager to be amused. All of them have a warm temperament and enjoy sexual pleasures, European men being more pleasing to them than their own men. Few of them will refuse the final favour if offered the most trifling gift. This is what makes the black men so jealous" (1:84–85).

89   Michèle Duchet makes explicit the point that Buffon identifies color as a fundamental feature, arguing that on the one hand Enlightenment values required a certain historical organicism, and on the other hand that color allowed Buffon to posit a single form of humanity altered by a form of degeneration, caused by such things as the weather, responsible for the varieties he and others observed (Duchet, *Anthropologie et histoire au siècle des lumières* [Paris: Flammarion, 1977], 201–2).

90   Winthrop Jordan looks at this phenomenon through the specific lens of interracial sex, particularly among free white men and enslaved African Americans: "The perceptual prerequisite for this conflict [desire and aversion for interracial sexual union] is so obvious as to be too easily overlooked: desire and aversion rested on the bedrock fact that white men perceived Negroes as being *both alike and different* from themselves. Without perception of similarity, no desire and no widespread gratification was possible. Without perception of difference, on the other hand, no aversion to miscegenation nor tension concerning it could have arisen" (Jordan, *White Over Black*, 137). He makes this point most forcefully when he writes that "American colonials no more thought Negroes were beasts than did European scientists and missionaries; if they had *really* thought so they would have sternly punished miscenegation for what it would have been—buggery" (232).

91   Gilman, *Freud, Race*, 37.

92 For two pertinent discussions of Gilman's work, see Jean Walton, "Re-placing Race," in *Female Subjects in Black and White*, eds. Elizabeth Abel, Barbara Christian, and Helene Moglen [Berkeley: University of California Press, 1997], 223–51); and Daniel Boyarin, "What Does a Jew Want?; or, The Political Meaning of the Phallus," in *The Psychoanalysis of Race*, ed. Christopher Lane (New York: Columbia University Press, 1998).

93 Concerning the relationship to scientific inquiry about race and sex, Laqueur writes: "Scientific race, for example—the notion that either by demonstrating the separate creation of various races (polygenesis) or by simply documenting difference, biology could account for differential status in the face of 'natural equality'—developed at the same time and in response to the same sorts of pressures as scientific sex" (Laquer, *Making Sex*, 155).

94 Laqueur, *Making Sex*, 149–50. We see evidence of Laqueur's claim in this passage from Buffon: "The testicles of females give birth to sorts of natural protruberances that I have called *glandulous bodies*: these bodies, which grow little by little, and which serve to filter, to perfect, and to contain the seminal liquor, are in a state of continual change" (Buffon, *De l'homme*, 95).

95 Randolph Trumbach, "Sex, Gender, and Sexual Identity in Modern Culture," in *Forbidden History*, ed. John C. Fout (Chicago: University of Chicago Press, 1990), 93.

96 But see Irene Fizer, "Women 'Off' the Market," in *Illicit Sex*, eds. Thomas DiPiero and Pat Gill (Athens: University of Georgia Press, 1997), 89–108, an analysis of feminine economies, particularly in convents, as they are depicted in eighteenth-century literature.

97 George Haggerty, "Beckford's Pederasty," In *Illicit Sex*, ed. Thomas DiPiero and Pat Gill (Athens: University of Georgia Press, 1997), 123–42.

98 William Edmiston, "Shifting Ground," in *Illicit Sex*, ed. Thomas DiPiero and Pat Gill (Athens: University of Georgia Press, 1997), 143–60.

99 Colette Guillaumin pursues this phenomenon in her book *Racism, Sexism, Power, and Ideology*. She writes that "there is a subtle trap laid for us by words whose forms do not alter over time, for we tend to ascribe to them with no hesitation the identity of a fixed meaning" (37). Barbara J. Fields concurs. She writes that "there would be no great problem if, when the things changed, the vocabulary died away as well. But by far the more common situation in the history of ideologies is that instead of dying, the same vocabulary attaches itself, unnoticed, to new things" (Fields, "Ideology," 153).

100 Schiebinger, *Nature's Body*, 146.

101 J. C. Nott and Geo. R. Gliddon, *Types of Mankind: or, Ethnological Researches*, 2d ed. (Philadelphia: Lippincott, Grambo, and Co., 1854), 89.

102 See also Henri Hollard, *De l'homme et des races humaines* (Paris: Labi, 1853); Charles Caldwell, *Thoughts on the Original Unity of the Human Race* (Cincinnati: J. A. and U. P. James, 1852); Thomas Smyth, *Unity of the Human Races*

Proved to be the Doctrine of Scripture, Reason, and Science (Edinburgh: Johnstone and Hunter, 1851); Eusèbe François de Salle, *Histoire générale des races humaines* (Paris: B. Duprat, 1849); and John Bachman, *The Doctrine of the Unity of the Human Race* (Charleston, S.C.: C. Canning, 1850).

103   Stephen Jay Gould, "American Polygeny and Craniometry Before Darwin," in *The Racial Economy of Science*, ed. Sandra Harding (Bloomington: Indiana University Press, 1993), 93. Jean Louis Armand de Quatrefages had as little patience with the polygenists as does Stephen Jay Gould. Writing in 1861, he argued that if American supporters of polygenesis "have designated race by the expression 'hereditary variety,' this difference in wording in no way effects the ideas behind it. The distinction existing in the facts is still translated in language. Thus it is this distinction that the American school seems to forget entirely. For them, there is no longer in nature *race* or *variety;* there are only *species*" (Quatrefages, *Unité de l'espèce humaine* [Paris: Hachette, 1861], 311; my translation).

104   James Cowles Prichard, *Researches into the Physical History of Mankind*, 5 volumes (London: Sherwood, Gilbert, and Piper, 1841 [1837–47]), vol. 1, 109.

105   Lacan, *L'envers*, 102.

106   In a work written just before the American Civil War, the anonymous author of *Abolition Is National Death* perhaps unwittingly provided a useful illustration of how the discourse of the master functions: "The party that elected Mr. Lincoln assume that negroes are *black*-white men, with the same natural right to liberty as their masters, that the relation between them is forced and artificial, and dependent on the *lex loci*, and therefore being wrong, and an evil, that it should be abolished, and 'impartial freedom' secured to all alike. . . . *They suppose the negro to be a black-white man, and they propose to use the government to realize their idea, or transform their theory into fact*" (J. Smith, *Anti-Black Thought*, 1:11]; author's emphasis). What is particularly interesting in this citation is the author's proposition that a political power has the capacity to create facts.

107   Kimberlé Crenshaw and Gary Peller, "Reel Time/Real Justice," in *Reading Rodney King, Reading Urban Uprising*, ed. Robert Gooding-Williams (New York: Routledge, 1993), 56–57. The context in which Crenshaw and Peller are writing is the verdict in what has come to be known as the "Rodney King" trial. They write: "The techniques utilized to convince the Simi Valley jury of the 'reasonableness' of the use of force on Rodney King are linked to the struggle, in a quite different legal arena, over whether to permit race-conscious, affirmative-action programs, and both of those arenas are in turn related to the conflict over whether to see the events in South Central L.A. as an 'insurrection,' as Representative Maxine Waters characterized it, or as a 'riot' of the 'mob,' the official version presented in dominant media and by the

president of the United States" (Ibid.). The conflict, then, according to this argument, is one of meaning.

108 John Forrester, "What Do Men Want?" in *Between Men and Feminism*, ed. David Porter (New York: Routledge, 1992), 108.

109 I realize that my use of the neuter pronoun "its" in these formulations is somewhat unsettling, but I have chosen "its" over "her" or "his" to avoid confusion. In one pointed passage dedicated to the topic, Lacan uses a feminine adjective to refer to the hysteric. He writes: "By saying *industrieuse*, we make the hysteric a woman, but that is not her privilege. Many men enter into analysis who, by this simple fact, are also forced to travel that route through hysterical discourse, since that's the law, the rule of the game" (Lacan, *L'envers*, 36). Since referring to the hysteric in this context as "she" seemed likely to cause confusion, I have chosen "its" to highlight the ambiguity of the male gender position here.

110 Žižek, *Sublime Object*, 113.

111 Žižek writes that "the final moment of the psychoanalytic process is, for the analysand, precisely when he gets rid of this question—that is, when he accepts his being as *non-justified by the big Other*. This is why psychoanalysis began with the interpretation of hysterical symptoms. . . . [I]n the last resort, what is hysteria if not precisely the effect and testimony of a failed interpellation?" (Žižek, *Sublime Object*, 113).

112 Ellie Ragland writes, in fact, that "the discourse of mastery [has] but one goal: to be certain" (Ragland, "The Discourse of the Master," in *Lacan, Politics, Aesthetics*, ed. Willie Apollon and Richard Feldstein [Albany: State University of New York Press, 1996], 141). She also writes that "the master signifier denotes identification with Ideals, with the ideals of society. Such signifiers dictate what one must do to be accepted, to be 'in the know,' at a given moment. Thus, the master discourse is spoken in superego tones, even to the contradictory point that Lacan names: *Jouis* (you *must* enjoy!)" (133–34).

113 Ibid., 134.

4. IN DEFENSE OF THE PHALLUS

1 Jane Gallop, *Thinking Through the Body* (New York: Columbia University Press, 1988), 126.

2 Butler, *Bodies That Matter*, 60.

3 The list of critiques of the Lacanian phallus is extensive. Among the earlier, and perhaps most trenchant critiques are Luce Irigaray, *Speculum of the Other Woman* (originally published in 1974) and *This Sex Which Is Not One*, trans. Catherine Porter (Ithaca, N.Y.: Cornell University Press, 1985; originally published in 1977). See also the following: David Macey, *Lacan in Contexts* (New

York: Verso, 1998), especially chapter 6; Mikkel Borch-Jacobsen, *Lacan: The Absolute Master* (Stanford, Calif.: Stanford University Press, 1991), especially 210–27; Teresa Brennan, *The Interpretation of the Flesh*, especially 72–80; Toril Moi, *Sexual/Textual Politics* (New York: Routledge, 1985), especially 66–70; Jane Flax, *Thinking Fragments*, especially 102–7; Charles Bernheimer writes that "Lacan's refusal to contextualize the phallus is part of his strategy to detach the unconscious from history" (Bernheimer, "Penile Reference in Phallic Theory," *Differences* 4, no.1 [1992]: 124); Catherine Clément, *The Lives and Legends of Jacques Lacan*, trans. Arthur Goldhammer (New York: Columbia University Press, 1983); Jane Gallop, *The Daughter's Seduction;* François Roustang, *Dire Mastery*, Trans. Ned Lukacher (Baltimore: Johns Hopkins University Press, 1982); Madelon Sprengnether says of the phallus that it is "a term which can never successfully be divorced from its association with the biological penis" (Sprengnether, "Mourning Freud," in *Psychoanalysis in Contexts*, eds. Anthony Elliott and Stephen Frosh [New York: Routledge, 1995], 144–45); Kaja Silverman, "The Lacanian Phallus," *Differences* 4, no.1 (1992), 92. Elizabeth Grosz puts the matter in simple, bald terms: "The processes by which the phallus, a signifier, becomes associated with the penis, an organ, involve the procedures by which women are systematically excluded from positive self-definition and a potential autonomy" (Grosz, *Jacques Lacan* [New York: Routledge, 1990], 116). Teresa Brennan strives for a balanced representation of the debate when she writes: "By the fact that it appears more visible, and because it can represent lack, the penis stands in for the would-be neutral phallus. . . . Feminists influenced by Lacan have stressed that both sexes can take up the masculine and feminine places; these shift and slide—no one has the phallus. Yet the tie between phallus and penis exists, and persists" (Brennan, *Between Feminism and Psychoanalysis*, 4). Jacqueline Rose, *Sexuality in the Field of Vision* (London: Verso, 1986) is perhaps one of the more sympathetic feminist criticisms of Lacanian psychoanalysis to issue forth in the 1980s.

4   Reading Jacques Lacan and Jacques Derrida on Edgar Allan Poe's "Purloined Letter," Barbara Johnson wonders, "What kind of logic is it that . . . seems to turn one-upmanship into inevitable one-downmanship?" (Johnson, "The Frame of Reference: Poe, Lacan, Derrida," in *The Purloined Poe*, eds. John P. Muller and William J. Richardson [Baltimore: Johns Hopkins University Press, 1988], 218). She continues: "The rivalry over something neither man will credit the other with possessing, the retrospective revision of the origins of both their resemblances and their differences, thus spirals backward and forward in an indeterminable pattern of cancellation and duplication" (220). It is difficult not to read in Johnson's remarks the object that is the subject of this chapter.

5   In a similar vein, Stephen Frosh writes: "The phallus cannot be known directly, it speaks its name only through its effects. And the primary function of these effects is to produce human subjects who are sexed in their essence—who are

generated along a sexual divide" (Frosh, "Masculine Mastery and Fantasy," in *Psychoanalysis in Contexts,* eds. Anthony Elliott and Stephen Frosh [New York: Routledge, 1995], 176).

6   Jane Flax is not persuaded that Lacan's attempts to separate penis and phallus are in good faith: "Lacan's claims that the phallus exists purely upon a symbolic plane, that it does not signify penis, and that any relationship between signifier and signified is arbitrary are disingenuous. Would we be persuaded by Lacan if he claimed that the mother lacks, say, 'a mouse' or that her desire for the child is to be the 'waxpaper'? (Flax, *Thinking Fragments,* 104).

7   Stephen Frosh is more confident than some that the phallus is a purely structural phenomenon: "Prior to Lacan, no one has understood that the phallus cannot be taken literally, as something to be grabbed and pulled upon. It only works if it is not seen, its message being that there is no centre to power, just the emanation of some remarkable effects. The phallus is a function, something that happens and makes things happen; it is often related to as a fantasy, like the fantasy of mastery, but no one can have it because it is not a thing to be had" (Frosh, "Masculine Mastery and Fantasy," 175).

8   Garber, "Spare Parts," 137.

9   Ibid., 138.

10 Making a parallel point, Lynne Segal writes: "Bolstered by the multifaceted reality of men's power, the phallus, as a symbol, is not, however, available for individual men to possess. It is that which they attempt to possess, or perhaps to reject; or maybe that which they approach with uncertainty and disquiet" (Lynne Segal, *Slow Motion: Changing Men* [London: Virago, 1990], 210).

11 Lacan, *Les psychoses,* 359.

12 Madelon Sprengnether expresses the situation as follows: "Before [the acquisition of language] the infant exists in a diffuse, boundaryless state, in which it does not clearly distinguish between itself and its mother. Her gaze (or the reflecting surface of a mirror) offers the image of a unified self, yet one which the infant does not recognize as a distortion of its actual condition of inner fragmentation. As long as the child remains fixed in this dyadic state it remains outside of the realm of symbolization and hence culture" (Sprengnether, "Mourning Freud," 144).

13 Lacan, *La relation d'objet: Le séminaire,* livre 4 (Paris: Seuil, 1994), 58; my translation.

14 Although examples to demonstrate that claim abound, I am thinking here of the work of Claude Lévi-Strauss, in particular his analysis of dual organizations. In *Structural Anthropology* Lévi-Strauss looks at kinship relations and their connection to, among other things, the way inhabitants of a particular locale understand the physical geography they inhabit. See chapter 8, "Do Dual Organizations Exist?"

15 Maria Torok, "The Meaning of 'Penis Envy' in Women," trans. Nicholas Rand,

Differences 4, no. 1 (1992): 34. Subsequent references to this title are cited in the text of this chapter.

16 Lacan argues that so-called penis envy is symbolic: "It is in so far as the woman is in a symbolic order with an androcentric perspective that the penis takes on this value. Besides, it isn't the penis, but the phallus, that is to say something whose symbolic usage is possible because it can be seen, because it is erected. There can be no possible symbolic use for what is not seen, for what is hidden" (Lacan, *The Ego*, 272).

17 Goux, "The Phallus," 52. Freud observed the same phenomenon in the *Interpretation of Dreams:* "Things that are symbolically connected today were probably united in the prehistoric times by conceptual and linguistic identity. The symbolic relation seems to be a relic and a mark of former identity" (Freud, *Interpretation of Dreams*, 387).

18 Lacan, *The Ego*, 5. In a similar formulation, Lacan writes: "From the moment that a part of the symbolic world comes into existence it does indeed create its own past. But not in the same way as the form at the intuitive level. It is precisely in the confusion of the two planes that the error lies, the error of believing that what science constitutes by the intervention of the symbolic function has always been there, that it is given. This error exists in all knowledge, in as much as it is only a crystallization of the symbolic activity, and once constituted, it forgets it. In all knowledge once constituted there is a dimension of error, which is the forgetting of the creative function of truth in its nascent form" (Lacan, *The Ego*, 18–19).

19 Ferdinand de Saussure had this to say of that peculiar domain: "The characteristic role of a language in relation to thought is not to supply the mental phonetic by which ideas may be expressed. It is to act as intermediary between thought and sound, in such a way that the combination of both necessarily produces a mutually complementary delimitation of units" (de Saussure, *Course in General Linguistics* [Chicago: Open Court, 1986], 110). He goes on to remark that "linguistics . . . operates along this margin, where sound and thought meet. *The contact between them gives rise to a form, not a substance*" (111, Saussure's emphases).

20 Lacan, *Les formations*, 273; my translation.

21 Ibid.

22 Ibid., 180.

23 Lacan, *La relation*, 204–5. On the importance of the father, not only for instituting a symbolic order, but also for organizing and guaranteeing the interchangeability of a nexus of different symbolic systems, see Thomas DiPiero, "Angels in the (Out)Field of Vision," *Camera Obscura* 40–41 (1999): 201–25.

24 Lacan, *Le transfert: Le séminaire*, livre 8 (Paris: Seuil, 1991), 67; my translation.

25 Concerning the embodied, biological father and the purely symbolic variety, Lacan writes in the *Ethics of Psychoanalysis* that "Freud does not neglect the

Name-of-the-Father. To the contrary, he speaks quite eloquently about it, in *Moses and Monotheism*—granted in a contradictory sense in the eyes of those who would not accept *Totem and Taboo* for what it is, that is, a myth" (Jacques Lacan, *L'éthique de la psychanalyse, le séminaire*, livre 7 [Paris: Seuil, 1986], 213).

26 Lacan, *La relation*, 205.

27 Elizabeth Grosz formulates the manner in which cultural determinisms inscribe consistency in the manner in which we perceive and live bodies when she writes: "The body is lived in accordance with an individual's and a culture's *concepts* of biology. This imaginary anatomy has been called a number of other names elsewhere—in Schiller's work, it is the 'postural schema of the body,' in Merleau-Ponty's, it is the 'body-subject' or 'body-image,' in Wallon, the 'corporeal schema' " (Grosz, *Jacques Lacan*, 44).

28 In a somewhat different context, Judith Butler makes a similar point as follows: "The materiality of the signifier will signify only to the extent that it is impure, contaminated by the ideality of differentiating relations, the tacit structurings of a linguistic context that is illimitable in principle. Conversely, the signifier will work to the extent that it is also contaminated constitutively by the very materiality that the ideality of sense purports to overcome. . . . This radical difference between *referent* and *signified* is the site where the materiality of language and that of the world which it seeks to signify are perpetually negotiated" (Butler, *Bodies That Matter*, 69).

29 Two different takes on the paternal metaphor and its relationship to the social order and to individual accession of the symbolic are Judith Roof's and Elizabeth Grosz's. Concerning the former, Roof writes that "the paternal metaphor—the Name-of-the-Father standing in relation to the Law—represents the principle by which the individual relates to the social order: the name of the father that determines the child's lineage and place in society. . . . The paternal metaphor is also metaphorically connected to the social ordering principles of patriarchy, effecting not just a law of division but also a law of connection to the larger sweep of the social rules of kinship exchange" (Roof, "Verdict on Paternal Function," in *Lacan, Politics, Aesthetics*, eds. Willy Apollon and Richard Feldstein [State University of New York Press, 1996], 106–7). Related to the latter (to individual accession to the symbolic), Grosz writes that "the paternal metaphor is the threshold permitting access to the symbolic. It does not presume a Real castration but an acknowledgment by the boy of his willingness to give up his most powerful desires to accept the Law. His 'reward' is the preservation of the penis as a narcissistic organ, and its (provisional) elevation to the position of object of desire for the other" (Grosz, *Jacques Lacan*, 119).

30 Jacques-Alain Miller, "An Introduction to Lacan's Clinical Perspectives," in *Reading Seminars I and II*, eds. Richard Feldstein, Bruce Fink, and Maire Jaanus (Albany: State University of New York Press, 1996), 246.

31 Lacan, *Les formations*, 180.

32 Ibid., 181.

33 François Regnault, "The Name-of-the-Father," in *Reading Seminars I and II*, eds. Richard Feldstein, Bruce Fink, and Maire Jaanus (Albany: State University of New York Press, 1995), 70.

34 Anika Lemaire defines the paternal metaphor as "the representation . . . of a father who is the authority separating the child from its mother" (Lemaire, *Jacques Lacan* [London: Routledge and Kegan Paul, 1970], 235). Lemaire and others concentrate on paternal *authority*, as opposed to the institution of a symbolic link that I have been emphasizing here. The point in common, however, is that paternal authority relies not necessarily or exclusively on force, but on the capacity to structure symbolic views of the world.

35 And it should go without saying here that I recognize our inability to think in symbolic terms about what preceded subjective identity.

36 See for example, the following passages from the fourth seminar: "It is necessary not to confuse phallus and penis. When around the time of the 1920's a great debate that occupied the entire analytic community centered around the notion of phallicism and on the question of the phallic phase, what was in question was to distinguish the penis as a real organ with functions definable by certain real coordinates, and the phallus in its imaginary function" (*La relation* 30–31); later on in the same seminar, Lacan observed: "Freud tells us that in the world of objects, there is one whose function is paradoxically decisive, and that is the phallus. That object is defined as imaginary, and it is in no way possible to confuse it with the penis in its reality; it is strictly speaking its form, the erected image" (*La relation* 70).

37 Lacan, *Les formations*, 346.

38 Lacan, *Écrits: A Selection*, trans. Alan Sheridan (New York: Norton, 1977), 285.

39 Butler, *Bodies That Matter*, 69.

40 Lacan, *The Ego*, 119; Butler, *Bodies That Matter*, 76.

41 Lacan, *The Ego*, 119; Butler, *Bodies That Matter*, 76–77.

42 Butler, *Bodies That Matter*, 77.

43 Lacan, *The Ego*, 119.

44 Ibid., 198; Butler, *Bodies That Matter*, 77.

45 Butler, *Bodies That Matter*, 77.

46 For example, Butler argues that the phallus "is both occasioned by Lacan and exceeds the purview of that form of heterosexist structuralism. It is not enough to claim that the signifier is not the same as the signified (phallus/penis), if both terms are nevertheless bound to each other by an essential relation in which that difference is contained" (Butler, *Bodies That Matter*, 90). She then points out the political implications for the lesbian phallus: "The lesbian phallus offers the occasion (a set of occasions) for the phallus to signify differently, and in so signifying, to resignify, unwittingly, its own masculinist and heterosexist privilege" (Butler, *Bodies That Matter*, 90).

47   Butler finesses the argument concerning the phallus's representation of the penis *and* the clitoris with a long note in which she maintains that the penis and the clitoris symbolize differently, and that while the clitoris is symbolized as penis envy, the penis is symbolized as the castration complex. "The phallus symbolizes the clitoris as not having the penis, whereas the phallus symbolizes the penis through the threat of castration, understood as a kind of dispossession. To have a penis is to have that which the phallus *is* not, but which, precisely by virtue of this not-being, constitutes the occasion for the phallus to signify (in this sense, the phallus requires and reproduces the diminution of the penis in order to signify—almost a kind of master–slave dialectic between them)." She concludes this rather lengthy note by arguing that "the clitoris can never be said, within this view, to be an example of 'having' the phallus" (Butler, *Bodies That Matter*, 263, note 30). Mikkel Borch-Jacobsen takes on the same argument in his *Lacan: The Absolute Master*, 210–18. Parveen Adams addresses that same question, but reaches different conclusions: "The experience of 'having' or 'not having,' just like the experience of 'being' or 'not being' in respect to an organ, exists at the level of identification, of the Imaginary. To experience 'having' it, whatever the organ might be—penis, breast, or womb—is to experience phallic satisfaction. The irony then is that the countercelebration of other candidate organs as the model of female completeness is itself an act of phallic identification" (Adams, "Waiving the Phallus," 77). Here I will simply call attention to the fact that that is not what Lacan claimed; his argument was that the phallus bore a symbolic relationship to both the penis and the clitoris.

48   Butler, *Bodies That Matter*, 83. Kaja Silverman makes a similar argument: "The basis for the comparison between the phallus and "being" [in "Desire and the Interpretation of Desire in *Hamlet*"] seems again to be analogy, and once again that analogy is keyed to the penis. The scale and detachability of that organ permit it to represent the "pound of flesh" which is the price of meaning (Silverman, "The Lacanian Phallus," 92). I will address below the question of the penis's "detachability."

49   Butler, *Bodies That Matter*, 83. Jane Gallop makes a similar point: "By negative, diacritical definition, Lacan is at least explicit as to what the phallus is not. Not a fantasy, not an object, but least of all an organ, least of all the penis. We can gather from this progression that it is in fact closer to being a fantasy or an object than to being the penis as organ" (*Reading Lacan* [Ithaca, N.Y.: Cornell University Press, 1985], 136).

50   Regarding the phallus's status as a signifying wild card, Kaja Silverman adds the notion that "if the phallus has no fixed meaning, that is not because it is a primordial linguistic signifier, and as such radically nonsensical, but rather because of its implicitly visual identity (Silverman, "The Lacanian Phallus," 90).

51 Butler, *Bodies That Matter*, 84.

52 In most accounts of the genealogy, Chaos gave birth to Gaia, who produced Ouranos on her own. The primeval union of Gaia and Ouranos produced the twelve Titan gods, as well as the Cyclops.

53 Diana Fuss has commented on the manner in which Aristotelian metaphysics underwrites an essentialism based on gender, and she argues that the figure of "woman" articulates a contradiction inherent to Aristotelian metaphysics: "On the one hand," she writes, "woman is asserted to have an essence which defines her as woman and yet, on the other hand, woman is relegated to the status of matter and can have no access to essence (the most she can do is to facilitate man's actualizing of his inner potential)" (Fuss, "Essentially Speaking," in *Revaluing French Feminism*, eds. Nancy Fraser and Sandra Lee Bartky [Bloomington: Indiana University Press, 1992], 109).

54 Goux, "The Phallus," 52.

55 Plutarch, *Moralia*, trans. Frank Cole Babbitt (Cambridge, Mass.: Harvard University Press, 1936), 5:135. Subsequent references to Plutarch's *Moralia* are cited parenthetically in the text. Concerning the right triangle, Plutarch continues, "This triangle has its upright of three units, its base of four, and its hypotenuse of five, whose power is equal to that of the other two sides" (Ibid). Horus, incidentally, is the son of Isis, sister and wife of Osiris.

56 In another passage, Plutarch writes that "in the soul Intelligence and Reason, the Ruler and Lord of all that is good, is Osiris, and in earth and wind and water and the heavens and stars that which is ordered, established, and healthy, as evidenced by seasons, temperatures, and cycles of revolution, is the efflux of Osiris and his reflected image" (Plutarch, *Moralia*, 5:121).

57 Specifically, Typhon "is that part of the soul which is impressionable, impulsive, irrational and truculent, and of the bodily part the destructible, diseased and disorderly as evidenced by abnormal seasons and temperatures, and by obscurations of the sun and disappearances of the moon, outbursts, as it were" (5:121). Elsewhere Plutarch writes that "the wiser of the priests call not only the Nile Osiris and the sea Typhon, but they simply give the name of Osiris to the whole source and faculty creative of moisture, believing this to be the cause of generation and the substance of life-producing seed; and the name of Typhon they give to all that is dry, fiery, and arid, in general, and antagonistic to moisture" (5:81).

58 Herodotus describes the same scene as follows: "The Egyptian method of celebrating the festival of Dionysus is much the same as the Greek, except that the Egyptians have no choric dance. Instead of the phallus they have puppets, about eighteen inches high; the genitals of these figures are made almost as big as the rest of their bodies, and they are pulled up and down by strings as the women carry them round the villages. . . . There is a religious legend to account

for the size of the genitals and the fact that they are the only part of the puppet's body which is made to move" (Herodotus, *The Histories,* 149).

59 Goux, "The Phallus," 43. Goux points out that in both psychoanalytic discourse and in the discourses of religious initiation in antiquity the unveiling of the phallus has always marked the end of a process. "Psychoanalysis, therefore, does not determine a new object in naming the phallus. It operates an unveiling on its own account and by its own means, an unveiling that already ordained the mystical ritual. Lacan suggests that at the same time psychoanalysis brings an explanation to this unveiling. It is a double revelation, first of the phallus and secondly of the reasons for its ancient revelation" (Goux, "The Phallus," 43).

60 Lacan, *La relation,* 346.

61 It seems important to point out here that John Wayne Bobbitt, whose wife Lorena sliced off his penis and tossed it out the car window by the side of the road, is the star of an "adult" movie called *John Wayne Bobbitt Uncut.*

62 Goux, "The Phallus," 43.

63 Peter Lehman, *Running Scared* (Philadelphia: Temple University Press, 1993), III.

64 Ibid., 5.

65 Ibid., 10. Peter Lehman cites Barbara de Genevieve's pithy phrase concerning the double standard that celebrates the unveiled female form and all but prohibits the exhibition of the male body: "To unveil the penis is to unveil the phallus is to unveil the social construction of masculinity. And *that* is a real taboo" (5).

66 Ibid., 164.

67 Eva C. Keuls, *The Reign of the Phallus* (Berkeley: University of California Press, 1985), 68. Keuls uses myriad examples drawn from black and red vase painting. One depicts Heracles defeating the attendants of King Busiris, whom the artists depicts with a thick and circumcised penis.

68 Keuls reminds us that "the largest phallus was the one which was carried around the city in the grand and gay parade which preceded the Greater Dionysia, a yearly dramatic festival" (Keuls, *Reign of the Phallus,* 78).

69 Lacan, *Le transfert,* 306. Specifying the difference between phallus and penis, Lacan writes that "the phallus, under the organic function of the penis, is not in the animal world a universal organ. Insects have other means of hooking up" (306).

70 Goux, "The Phallus," 60.

71 Lacan, *La relation,* 351. Goux writes of the tradition of male ancestors as well, emphasizing in the formulation masculine mediation in a symbolic economy: "The phallus has thus the role of a detachable value (it is detachment itself) which arises from the bloody cutting of a vital bond ('symbolic castration') and

which rewards (by a second birth) the metaphoric joining of the paternal ancestors, even if they are only evoked by a name which continues the lineage and
allows admission to the society of males. The effect of a 'deadly' loss for which a
secret gift of paternal origin compensates, the phallic effigy, in which the
subject finally recuperates his integrity, his vital unity, is thus the mediation
which authorizes the transaction which takes the form of the exogamic barter"
(Goux, "The Phallus," 61–62).

72 Goux, "The Phallus," 56.

73 Lacan, *La relation*, 37.

74 Which is why I would continue to stress that a strict separation between penis
and phallus be made. Teresa Brennan writes that "for the embodied subject,
difference can be represented only on the *visual* basis that the father and
mother are different; it depends on the recognition of the visual anatomical
difference between the sexes. Because of this, the neutral phallus is tied to
the male penis" (Brennan, *The Interpretation of the Flesh*, 72). I would argue
that since embodiment belongs to the imaginary realm and hence enjoys a
dimension extending beyond the purely morphological, to suggest that a *visual*
difference—if by visual we mean ocular—is necessary for difference to take
hold is to fail to grasp social difference obtaining in the formation of the
subject.

75 Lacan, *La relation*, 209; my translation.

76 Slavoj Žižek echoes Lacan on this matter: "The 'real' penis turns into the form
of appearance of (the virtual) phallus, and so on. That is the paradox of castration: whatever I do in reality, with my 'real' penis, is just redoubling, following
as a shadow, another virtual penis whose existence is purely symbolic—that is,
phallus as a signifier" (Žižek, *The Plague of Fantasies* [New York: Verso, 1997],
150).

77 Plutarch reminds his readers that cultural objects often cannot name a particular object, but only evoke them through the indirect means of narrative or other
forms of representation. In his introductory material to the story of Isis and
Osiris, he writes: "Whenever you hear the traditional tales which the Egyptians
tell about the gods, their wanderings, dismemberments, and many experiences
of this sort, you must remember what has been already said, and you must not
think that any of these tales actually happened in the manner in which they are
related. The facts are that they do not call the dog by the name of Hermes as his
proper name, but they bring into association with the most astute of their gods
that animal's watchfulness and wakefulness and wisdom" (Plutarch, *Moralia*,
5:29).

78 See in particular Jean-Joseph Goux, *Symbolic Economies*, especially the chapters
on "Numismatics" and "History and the Unconscious."

79 Mark Bracher provides a succinct formulation of the discourse of the master
and its reliance on master signifiers as follows: "When one reads or hears such

a discourse, one is forced, in order to understand the message, to accord full explanatory power and/or moral authority to the proffered master signifiers and to refer all other signifiers (objects, concepts, or issues) back to them. In doing this, the receiver of the message (occupying the position of 'other' in Lacan's schema) enacts the function of knowledge" (Bracher, "Four Discourses," 43).

80   Jean Walton has elegantly called for a psychoanalysis that would account for how race works into the formation of the unconscious. She writes, in part: "Little has been asked throughout the history of psychoanalysis about what kind of knowledge might be produced if articulations of gendered subjectivity were considered in terms of their being dependent upon or imbricated in implicit assumptions about 'whiteness' and 'blackness,' given that perceptions and fantasies of racial difference might form a significant axis of identity formation" (Jean Walton, *Fair Sex, Savage Dreams* [Durham, N.C.: Duke University Press, 2001], 225).

81   Regarding the potential of unveiling the phallus, Kaja Silverman writes that she "will attempt to lift the veil from the phallus, and thereby to call into question its authority as the signifier par excellence of wholeness and privilege, and to expose the sexually differentiating uses to which it is put in certain passages from the *Séminaires* and *Ecrits*" (Silverman, "The Lacanian Phallus," 89).

5. WHITE MEN AREN'T

1   Wiegman, *American Anatomies*, 4.

2   Michael Omi and Howard Winant very cogently make a similar point: "In the United States, the racial category of 'black' evolved with the consolidation of racial slavery. By the end of the seventeenth century, Africans whose specific identity was Ibo, Yoruba, Fulani, etc., were rendered 'black' by an ideology of exploitation based on racial logic—the establishment and maintenance of a 'color line' (Omi and Winant, *Racial Formation*, 64).

3   Wiegman, *American Anatomies*, 9. Wiegman points out along with many of those we observed in chapters 2 and 3 that the competing taxonomies of race and gender led to curious results, one of which was the "feminization" of nonwhite races: "Masculine domination was evidence of advanced civilization. In this way, the binary structure of race—that rigorously defended emphasis on the incommensurabilities between black and white—took on, through anatomic analysis, a double ideological function: the European male's large brain evinced not simply a racial superiority, but a quintessentially masculine one as well. Blackness, in short, was here feminized and the African(-American) male was disaffiliated from the masculine itself" (Wiegman, *American Anatomies*, 54).

4 S. Smith, *An Essay on the Causes*, 58. Stanhope Smith associates Henry Moss's whiteness with disease no doubt because unexpectedly white individuals, generally Africans, were presumed to be white owing to some unexplained illness. Unexpectedly white individuals were often thought to be ill (Manoel de Almeida says that there are some native-born inhabitants of Ethiopia who are "whitish," but then adds that "it is a bloodless white" [Almeida, *Some Records of Ethiopia*, 57]). Sometimes they were deemed to be supernatural, as we noted in chapter 2 in the writings of João dos Sanctos.

5 S. Smith, *An Essay on the Causes*, 58–59. Smith reports another, similar phenomenon, this time involving an Indian youth: "A young indian, about the age of fifteen, who had been brought from his nation five or six years before, was studying the latin and greek languages in the institution. And from carefully observing him during the greater portion of that time I received the most perfect conviction that, if the Anglo-American, and the indian were placed from infancy in the same state of society, in this climate which is common to them both, the principal differences which now subsist between the two races, would, in a great measure, be removed when they should arrive at the period of puberty. . . . A perceptible difference still existed, at the time of his return to his tribe, between him and his fellow students, in the largeness of the mouth and thickness of the lips, in the elevation of the cheek bone, in the darkness of the complexion, and the contour of the face. These differences had sensibly diminished from the period of his coming to the college" (S. Smith, *An Essay on the Causes*, 108).

6 Van Evrie, *White Supremacy*, 108.

7 Hunt, *Negro's Place in Nature*, 116.

8 Lacan, *The Ego*, 166. Lacan himself specifies this interpretation of the famous "mirror stage" text: "What did I try to get across with the mirror stage? That whatever in man is loosened up, fragmented, anarchic, establishes its relation to his perceptions on a plane with a completely original tension. The image of his body . . ." (166).

9 Ibid.

10 The arbitrariness of the sign was extensively theorized by Saussure. In the *Course in General Linguistics* he maintains that "any linguistic entity exists only in virtue of the association between signal and signification," and that linguistic entities arise "only by association with sound patterns" (Saussure, *General Linguistics*, 101). However, "the link between signal and signification is arbitrary. Since we are treating a sign as the combination in which a signal is associated with a signification, we can express this more simply as: *the linguistic sign is arbitrary*" (67). Lacan employs Saussure's notion of the arbitrariness of the sign to examine intrasubjective phenomena.

11 In his second seminar, Lacan writes: "If the object perceived from without has its own identity, the latter places the man who sees it in a state of tension,

because he perceives himself as desire, and as unsatisfied desire. Inversely, when he grasps his unity, on the contrary it is the world which for him becomes decomposed, loses its meaning, and takes on an alienated and discordant aspect" (Lacan, *The Ego*, 166).

12 Certainly whites outside the Ku Klux Klan were also guilty of the violence collectively known as lynching. In 1900 the Atlantan Alex King put himself through rhetorical contortions to defend the practice: "Where a certain course of treatment of a crime has become, if not customary, at least not unusual—and when there is, if not an expressed, at least an implied assertion on the part of a respectable party, that the law should not suppress this course of dealing with these offences, but that the public welfare requires it to be winked at—then in considering the practical remedies suggested for the suppression of this crime, the remedy of instant punishment by the community without judicial pro-cedure demands consideration" (*Race Problems of the South: Report of the Pro-ceedings of the First Annual Conference Held Under the Auspices of the Southern Society for the Promotion of the Study of Race Conditions and Problems in the South*, in vol. 2 of *Anti-Black Thought, 1863–1925*, ed. John David Smith [New York: Garland, 1993], 276–77).

13 Concerning the use of violence, a Mrs. S. E. F. Rose, author of *The Ku Klux Klan, or Invisible Empire*, wrote in 1914 that "The Ku Klux were opposed to the shedding of human blood, and violence was never used except as a last resort. Repeated warnings were given to offenders, and it was only when they were not heeded, that the Ku Klux resorted to extreme measures" (S. Rose, *The Ku Klux Klan, or Invisible Empire* [New Orleans: L. Graham, 1914], 27).

14 Ku Klux Klan, *Papers Read at the Meeting of Grand Dragons at Their First Annual Meeting held at Asheville, North Carolina, July 1923* [n.p., n.d.], 45–46. The article from which this citation is drawn is entitled "The Definition of Klankraft and How to Disseminate it," written by the "Grand Dragon of the Realm of Oklahoma." In 1923, just as the second wave of Ku Klux Klan activity was taking hold, H. L. Mencken and George Jean Nathan set forth an ironic accep-tance of Klan activity in their condemnation of American hypocrisy concerning notions of individual identity: "What could be more fatuous than the current denunciations of the so-called Ku Klux Klan as an anti-American organization? It is, in point of fact, probably the most thoroughly American *verein* ever set going in the Republic. It supports the doctrine that obscure and anonymous men have the right to regulate the most private acts and the most private opinions of their betters; it maintains as a fundamental principle of law that an unpopular man has no rights in the courts; it resists any and every differentia-tion of American from American and insists that all shall be identical. . . . All these notions are the heart's blood of Americanism" (Richard K. Tucker, *The Dragon and the Cross: The Rise and Fall of the Ku Klux Klan in Middle America* [Hamden, Conn.: Archon Books, 199], 14).

15 Michael Eric Dyson lists a series of misconstruals inherent in the construction of whiteness through history, and one of the myths he identifies is that of "whiteness as the false victim of black power." Dyson argues that "this mode of whiteness is the ultimate strategy of preserving power by protesting its usurpation by the real victim" (Dyson, "The Labor of Whiteness, the Whiteness of Labor," In *Race, Identity, and Citizenship,* eds. Rodolfo D. Torres, Louis F. Mirón, Jonathan Xavier Inda [Malden, Mass.: Blackwell, 1999], 221).

16 Ku Klux Klan, *Papers Read,* 42. From the article "The Story of the Ku Klux Klan," by "The Grand Dragon of Georgia." The image of the black heel on the white neck was a popular one at the time (cf. Mrs. S. E. F. Rose: "Union Leagues, whose members were mainly negroes, and the lowest element of whites, were hotbeds for engendering race strife, and negro equality and plans to place the 'black heels on the white necks' " [S. Rose, *The Ku Klux Klan,* 16–17]).

17 Jessie Daniels has shown than the belief that white masculinity is a threatened species continues today: "White men are not uniformly depicted in white supremacist discourse as the embodiment of strength which the warrior imagery indicates. The very notion of 'warrior' is one that exists within a dualistic construction and depends on its juxtaposition to the view of white men as 'victims' " (J. Daniels, *White Lies* [New York: Routledge, 1997], 37).

18 Hunt, *The Negro's Place in Nature,* 105.

19 Ku Klux Klan, "The Practice of Klanishness" (Atlanta: n.p., 1918). The citation is from the eighth and final page of an unpaginated pamphlet.

20 Trelease, *White Terror,* 16. Allen W. Trelease identifies a sort of "black panic" that swept the South during Reconstruction: "White men were confident of winning ultimately in a war of the races, but visions passed across the mind of bands of maddened black men running amuck in the interim, sacking and burning towns, ravishing women, and indiscriminately shooting down persons of every age and description. This was the ultimate horror, and therefore the reaction to any signs of organization or arming among the blacks was immediate and emphatic" (40).

21 See *Race Problems of the South* for their concerns. King argues that "No crime strikes at the integrity of race or so insults its purity as the crime against women" (*Race Problems,* 280).

22 Trudier Harris, *Exorcising Blackness: Historical and Literary Lynching and Burning Rituals* (Bloomington: Indiana University Press, 1984), 20.

23 Wiegman, *American Anatomies,* 96.

24 Charles Carroll, *The Tempter of Eve, or The Criminality of Man's Social, Political, and Religious Equality with the Negro, and the Amalgamation to Which These Crimes Inevitably Lead,* in vol. 6 of *Anti-Black Thought, 1863–1925,* ed. John David Smith (New York: Garland, 1993), 550.

25 Van Evrie, *White Supremacy,* 96.

26 *Race Problems of the South,* 280.

27 Kathleen M. Blee, *Women of the Klan: Racism and Gender in the 1920s* (Berkeley: University of California Press, 1991), 14.

28 Blee, *Women of the Klan,* 12. Much of the rhetoric surrounding the organization of the second Klan in the 1920s focused on comparisons between the U.S. Constitution and the Klan's internal structures. Thus, in the "Harmony Between the Constitution of the United States and the Constitution of the Knights of the Ku Klux Klan" we read: "We must let the world know that the Invisible Empire is constituted and exists with as much verity as the United States of America are constituted and exist" (Ku Klux Klan, *Papers Read,* 30). And, slightly later, we find: "The Constitution of the United States was not formed merely to guard the States against danger arising from foreign nations but mainly to secure union and harmony at home, and safety against injustice from one another. It was designed for the common and equal benefit of all the United States. So was the Constitution of the Invisible Empire designed for the common and equal benefit of all the citizens of the Invisible Empire, and to secure union and harmony within the Empire. Both the Constitution of the United States and of the Invisible Empire were adopted as free and voluntary acts for the protection of its citizens" (32).

29 Blee, *Women of the Klan,* 15–16.

30 Ibid., 15.

31 C. Harris, "Whiteness as Property," Harvard Law Review 106, no. 8 (June 1993): 1725.

32 *Plessy v Ferguson,* 163 U.S. 551.

33 Ibid., 537, 549 (1896), 549. Neil Gotanda argues in an article that also considers the Plessy case that although legal discourse has traditionally used race as a social classifier, there is considerable disagreement about what that means: "In both constitutional discourse and in larger society, race is considered a legitimate and proper means of classifying Americans. Its frequent use suggests that there is a consensus about what the "races" are. For example, racial nonrecognition implies a common understanding of what, exactly, is not considered" (Gotanda, "Our Constitution," 23).

34 C. Harris, "Whiteness as Property," 1734.

35 Ibid., 1737.

36 Ibid., 1724.

37 Ibid., 1731–32.

38 Wiegman, *American Anatomies,* 55.

39 T. Harris, *Exorcising Blackness,* 29. See also William H. Grier and Price M. Cobbs: "The black man . . . is regarded as socially, economically, and politically castrated, and he is gravely handicapped in performing every other masculine role" (Grier and Cobbs, *Black Rage* [New York: Basic Books, 1968], 87).

40 Trudier Harris: "Black males historically, because they could be physically

castrated, had a physical part of themselves identified with their powerlessness" (T. Harris, *Exorcising Blackness*, 188). Wiegman: "In severing the black male's penis from his body, either as a narrative account or a material act, the mob aggressively denies the patriarchal sign and symbol of the masculine, interrupting the privilege of the phallus and thereby reclaiming, through the perversity of dismemberment, the black male's (masculine) potentiality for citizenship" (Wiegman, *American Anatomies*, 83).

41 Jacques-Alain Miller provides a helpful and cogent way of understanding the sexes' relationship to the phallic function: "It has scandalized feminists that Freud said there is only one symbol for both sexes, one symbol of reference, and that is the phallic symbol. He was not choosing between men and women to give the advantage to men. The problem is that this symbol is exterior to both sexes. . . . Nobody would think that men are equal to this symbol. It's rather the measure of their impotence" (Craig Saper, "A Nervous Theory: The Troubling Gaze of Psychoanalysis in Media Studies," *Diacritics* 21, no. 4 [winter 1991]: 45).

42 Lester and Wilson, *Ku Klux Klan*, 56. Similarly, in the 1923 publication of *The Ku Klux Spirit*, J. A. Rogers maintains that "the alliteration and the mysterious affect [of the group's name] made an instant impression" (Rogers, *The Ku Klux Spirit* [reprint, Baltimore: Black Classic Press, 1980], 15).

43 Most authorities cite 1866 as the date of the first Klan's origins, but some argue that it was formed as early as 1865.

44 Rogers, *The Ku Klux Spirit*, 15.

45 Trelease, *White Terror*, 52.

46 The front page of the prescript of the original KKK formed in Tennessee bears the following verses from *Hamlet*, Act 1, scene 4:

> What may this mean,
> That thou, dead corse, again, in complete steel,
> Revisit'st thus the glimpses of the moon,
> Making night hideous; and we fools of nature,
> So horridly to shake our disposition,
> With thoughts beyond the reaches of our souls?

(J. C. Lester and D. L. Wilson, *Ku Klux Klan: Its Origin, Growth, and Disbandment* [(1884), 1905; reprint, New York: AMS Press, 1971], 135).

47 S. Rose, *The Ku Klux Klan*, 43.

48 Lester and Wilson, *Ku Klux Klan*, 74.

49 Ibid.

50 Rogers, *The Ku Klux Spirit*, 17. Mrs. Rose reports the same trick, focusing as well on the silence: "Slowly and silently they marched and countermarched through the streets of the town, thus leaving the impression of great numbers

while in reality there were only a very few. This parade, which lasted for hours, made a great sensation. Not a word was spoken . . ." (S. Rose, *The Ku Klux Klan*, 47).

51 "There were twelve of them. They had on something like an old-fashioned hunting shirt, as they have them in this southern part" (Albion Winegar Tourgée, *The Invisible Empire*, ed. Otto H. Olsen [Baton Rouge: Lousiana State University Press, 1989], 51). It is significant that this witness was also whipped by the group.

52 See, for example, Rogers: "Each individual was left free to choose his own color and cut and each endeavored to make his robe as fantastic as possible" (Rogers, *The Ku Klux Spirit*, 15); Mrs. Rose: "The robes always covered the entire body" (S. Rose, *The Ku Klux Klan*, 43).

53 Tourgée, *The Invisible Empire*, 49.

54 Ibid., 51.

55 Lester and Wilson, *Ku Klux Klan*, 98.

56 Rogers, *The Ku Klux Spirit*, 18.

57 *Testimony Taken by the Joint Select Committee to Inquire Into the Condition of Affairs in the Late Insurrectionary States.* 42nd Cong., 2d sess. Washington: Government Printing Office, 1871–72, no. 41, part 6, pp. 14–15.

58 Ibid., 17.

59 Ibid., 13. Similarly, this same witness indicates no fear of the Klansmen's disguises themselves, but of the violence associated with those disguises: "QUESTION: Does the riding round of these men in disguise terrify the colored people, whether they commit any acts of violence or not? ANSWER: Sometimes they ride round there and never pester anybody at all" (13). Likewise, a seventy-five-year-old formerly enslaved man reports only fearing repeated acts of violence such as those he had already suffered: "I have been stung once, and a burnt child fears the fire" (*Testimony*, no. 41, part 3, 430).

60 Kathleen M. Blee finds that the gender dynamics at work in Klansmen's relationship to race focuses nearly exclusively on lynching practices that included castration of black men: "Sexual torture and emasculation of black men by mobs of Klansmen validated the claim that masculinity ('real manhood') was the exclusive prerogative of white men. The rape of black women by white Klansmen represented the Klan's symbolic emasculation of black men through violating 'their' women while affirming the use of male sexuality as a weapon of power against women" (Blee, *Women of the Klan*, 16).

61 Charles L. Flynn Jr., "The Ancient Pedigree of Violent Repression: Georgia's Klan as a Folk Movement," in *The Southern Enigma: Essays on Race, Class, and Folk Culture*, eds.Walter J. Fraser Jr. and Winfred B. Moore Jr. (Westport, Conn.: Greenwood Press, 1983), 192.

62 Henri Rey-Flaud has exhaustively researched the phenomenon of the *charivari*,

the ancient noisy and disorderly popular demonstrations often associated with licentiousness or with the breaking of some cultural law, most often associated with sexuality. The *charivari* is often associated with different forms of masquerade, often in the form of animals, or cross-dressing. See Henri Rey-Flaud, *Le Charivari* (Paris: Payot, 1985).

63 Natalie Zemon Davis, *Society and Culture* (Stanford, Calif.: Stanford University Press, 1975), 149–50.

64 Flynn, "Ancient Pedigree," 192–93. Davis also points out examples of male transvestitism in England during the reign of Henry VIII. "The most important English examples of the male as grotesque female . . . were the Bessy and Maid Marian. In the northern countries, a Fool-Plough was dragged about the countryside, often on the first Monday after Epiphany, by men dressed in white shirts" (*Society and Culture*, 137–38).

65 Gail Bederman has persuasively shown that Ida B. Wells's anti-lynching campaign inverted the ties linking manhood and white supremacy. She writes that Wells's argument aimed to demonstrate that "black men were far more manly than whites who tolerated lynching" (Bederman, *Manliness and Civilization* [Chicago: University of Chicago Press, 1995], 75). Wells inverted traditional notions of civilization that had been linked to white supremacy and manliness, and in the process produced "an antiracist discourse of manliness" (75).

66 In an extraordinarily penetrating rapprochement of psychoanalysis and racial analysis, Kalpana Seshadri-Crooks argues that Lacan's theory of sexual difference marks the point where language breaks down, and thus marks the human subject as extending beyond the symbolic domain. On the one hand, race is like sex in psychoanalysis, to the extent that it exceeds language; and unlike sex in that it is largely of historical and cultural origin. Seshadri-Crooks writes: "[Race's] symbolical origin . . . does not render it simply historical, for it relies for its effectivity on a phobic object that exceeds biological and historical explanations of identity. What this means is that one encounters the limits of one's subjectivity as an effect of language, and the question of being as not so much that which escapes articulation, but as one that is extinguished or foreclosed. Thus what the study of race offers to psychoanalysis is a view of historicity that is not only about the ungraspable, non-signifiable limit, but about the horrific confrontation of the subject with its own signifying totality, the anxiety of suffering the recognition that there is no enigma to racial difference or to the raced subject" (Seshadri-Crooks, *Desiring Whiteness* [New York: Routledge, 2000], 46).

67 Although I have used specific instances of violence and particular pranks perpetrated by the KKK, I should emphasize that the instability of white racial identity in the years following the American Civil War are not limited to those sorts of examples. Matthew Frye Jacobson has argued that other forms of racial

instability punctuated that same period, and he bolsters his argument by noting that the mere prevalence of various names for what many people took to be the same "race" should tell us something: "The discrepancy in racial usages such as 'white,' 'Celt,' and 'Caucasian' . . . do not denote a mere sloppiness or imprecision in the language of race; such contradictions do not in every case represent insignificant choices among interchangeable synonyms. Rather, they reflect the contending racial schemes in the air at a given moment and the multiplicity of available categories that the culture has generated and is capable of sustaining" (M. Jacobson, *Whiteness of a Different Color* [Cambridge, Mass.: Harvard University Press, 1998], 170).

68   James Baldwin, *Just Above My Head* (New York: Laurel, 1979), 515.

69   Baldwin's Hall Montana is certainly not alone in twentieth-century literature to observe that white people can afford to misrecognize the nature of their identities. Ralph Ellison, for example, writes that "the Negro looks at the white man and finds it difficult to believe that the 'grays'—a Negro term for white people—can be so absurdly self-deluded over the true interrelatedness of blackness and whiteness" (Ellison, "Change the Joke and Slip the Yoke," in *Shadow and Act* [New York: Vintage, 1972], 55).

70   Hazel Carby has noticed this phenomenon. Arguing that the implicit normalcy of whiteness excludes whites from "racialization," she writes that "processes of racialization, when they are mentioned at all in multicultural debate, are discussed as if they were the sole concern of those particular groups perceived to be racialized subjects. Because the politics of difference work with concepts of individual identity, rather than structures of inequality and exploitation, processes of racialization are marginalized and given symbolic and political meaning only when the subjects are black" ("Multicultural Wars," 193).

71   Manthia Diawara notes that mainstream cinema controls the way black characters are represented by causing them to abide by rules slanted against them: "One may note how black male characters in contemporary Hollywood films are made less threatening to whites either by white domestication of black customs and culture—a process of deracination and isolation—or by stories in which blacks are depicted playing by the rules of white society and losing" (Diawara, "Black Spectatorship: Problems of Identification and Resistance," *Screen*, 29, no. 4 [autumn 1988]: 71).

72   Perhaps the best study of unconventional or otherwise marginalized masculinity is Kaja Silverman's *Male Subjectivity at the Margins*, which treats masochism and other nonstandard forms of masculine subjectivity within the framework of what she calls "dominant fictions," a term loosely derived from Althusser's notion of hailing. Another notable examination of nonhegemonic masculinity is David Savran's *Taking It Like a Man*, which traces the effects white masculinity's others have had in shaping the identity of the white American male.

73 Dyer observes that whiteness is not simply difficult to characterize, but that this is, in fact, part of its social and political power. He writes that "white power secures its dominance by seeming not to be anything in particular" and that "this property of whiteness, to be everything and nothing, is the source of its representational power" ("White," *Screen* 29, no. 4 [autumn 1988]: 44, 45).

74 Fred Pfeil has made a similar observation in his analysis of films that seek to redeem white male protagonists from insensitive boorishness and convert them into sensitive men. White men's others are responsible in these films, he maintains, for educating them. Reading *City Slickers*, *Regarding Henry*, and *The Fisher King*, among others, he argues that "the education of our reborn heroes can only be carried out by agents who are secondary Others to the main event of (white middle-class) men versus (white middle-class) women, who . . . might well enjoy both the pleasures of this education *and* the satisfaction of carping at it" (Pfeil, *White Guys* [New York: Verso, 1995], 62).

75 Freud, *Totem and Taboo*, 141, 141–42.

76 Ibid., 142.

77 Freud, *The Ego*, 27.

78 Freud, *Totem and Taboo*, 144.

79 Ibid., 146.

80 Ibid., 143.

81 Ibid., 141.

82 In a critique of Gayle Rubin's "The Traffic of Women: The 'Political Economy' of Sex," Judith Butler makes a similar argument: "This narrative of gender acquisition requires a certain temporal ordering of events which assumes that the narrator is in some position to 'know' both what is before and after the law. And yet the narration takes place within a language which, strictly speaking, is after the law, the consequence of the law, and so proceeds from a belated and retrospective point of view. If this language is structured by the law, and the law is exemplified, indeed, enacted in the language, then the description, the narration, not only cannot know what is outside itself—that is, prior to the law—but its description of that 'before' will always be in the service of the 'after'" (*Gender Trouble*, 74). See also John Brenkman, *Straight Male Modern*, 126–27.

83 Jane Gallop has also pointed out problems in the association with the father and maleness: "If the phallus is the standard of value, then the Father, possessor of the phallus, must desire the daughter in order to give her value. But the Father is a man (a little boy in the anal, the phallic phase) and cannot afford to desire otherness, an other sex, because that opens up his castration anxiety" (Gallop, *The Daughter's Seduction*, 70).

84 Or, as Lacan puts it, to identify with the symbolic domain of a culture is to associate oneself with the *function* of the father: "The only function of the father . . . is to be a myth, always and uniquely the Name-of-the-Father, that is, nothing but the dead father, as Freud explains in *Totem and Taboo*" (Lacan,

L'ethique, 356–57). See also *Les Psychoses*. There Lacan writes that "in order for there to be reality, sufficient access to reality, in order for the feeling of reality to be a just guide, in order for reality not to be what it is in psychosis, the Oedipal complex must have been lived" (224).

85 Juliet Flower MacCannell reads Freud's *Totem and Taboo* in a similar manner. Arguing that "a dramatic act of forgetting" produces a traumatic moment for the brothers, she writes that "the dialectic of the 'Law' thus results in the emergence of an unconscious, misrecognized superego, one which risks again becoming the tyranical, despotic pre-Oedipal Father" (MacCannell, *The Regime of the Brother* [New York: Routledge, 1991], 65).

86 Jane Gaines, "White Privilege and Looking Relations: Race and Gender in Feminist Film Theory," *Screen* 29, no. 4 (autumn 1988): 13.

87 Hortense J. Spillers, "Mama's Baby, Papa's Maybe: An American Grammar Book," *Diacritics* 17, no. 2 (summer 1987): 74.

88 Ibid., 80.

89 Sharon Willis has pointed out that Kasdan's *Grand Canyon* was something of a forerunner in the recent phenomenon of films depicting the "accidental" relationships involving whites and blacks who seem to have no particular affiliation with one another save the random occurrence bringing them together (Willis, *High Contrast*, 187).

90 Hazel Carby has made a similar observation concerning the soundtrack in *Grand Canyon*. She writes that "the words of 'Lawyers, Guns, and Money' evoke with a wry liberal irony memories of the Cold War, of danger to Americans trespassing in exotic locales, and of covert U.S. intervention in other countries. Presumably, the intentions behind the careful selection of this song are the establishment of the liberal credentials of the protagonist, the creation of a mood of empathy for the way in which he has accidentally strayed into alien territory, and an understanding of the gravity of the situation in which he finds himself" ("Encoding White Resentment: *Grand Canyon*—A Narrative for Our Times," in *Race, Identity, and Representation in Education*, eds. Cameron McCarthy and Warren Crichlow [New York: Routledge, 1993], 241).

91 Mack's racial and gender hysterias would seem to come together when he first meets Jane, Dee's friend whom he will later fix up with Simon. When he asks Jane if she would like to meet Simon, she asks what he looks like.

> MACK: Are looks important to you?
> JANE: Somewhat.
> MACK: I was just curious. Actually, he's a very handsome black guy.
> DEE: How are you going to describe Jane?
> MACK: Same way.
> DEE: A very handsome black guy?
> MACK: Yeah.

92 Butler, *Bodies That Matter*, 24.

93 James Baldwin, *The Fire Next Time* (New York: Laurel, 1962), 96.

AFTERWORD

1 Freud, "The Unconscious," in *The Standard Edition of the Complete Psychological Works of Sigmund Freud* (London: Hogarth Press, 1962–74), 14:191.

2 Ibid.

WORKS CITED

Abel, Elizabeth, Barbara Christian, and Helene Moglen. *Female Subjects in Black and White*. Berkeley: University of California Press, 1997.

Adams, Parveen. "Waiving the Phallus," *Differences* 4, no.1 (1992): 76–83.

Adams, Percy G. *Travel Literature and the Evolution of the Novel*. Lexington: University Press of Kentucky, 1983.

Adorno, T. W., E. Frenkel-Brunswick, D. J. Levinson, and R. N. Sanford. *The Authoritarian Personality*. New York: Wiley, 1950.

Ahl, Frederick. *Sophocles' Oedipus*. Ithaca, N.Y.: Cornell University Press, 1991.

Alba, Richard. *Ethnic Identity: The Transformation of White America*. New Haven: Yale University Press, 1990.

Almeida, Manoel de. *Some Records of Ethiopia, 1593–1646, Being Extracts from the History of High Ethiopia or Abassia, by Manoel de Almeida*. Edited and translated by C. F. Beckingharm and G. W. B. Huntingford. London: Hakluyt Society, 1954.

Althusser, Louis. *Politics and History: Montesquieu, Rousseau, Hegel, and Marx*. Translated by Ben Brewster. London: NLB, 1972.

Anderson, Benedict. *Imagined Communities*. New York: Verso, 1991.

Appiah, Anthony. "The Uncompleted Argument: Du Bois and the Illusion of Race." In *Race, Writing, and Difference*, edited by Henry Louis Gates Jr., 21–37. Chicago: University of Chicago Press, 1989.

Ariel [Buckner H. Payne]. *The Negro: What Is His Ethnological Status?* 2d ed. Cincinnati: N.p., 1867.

Aristotle. *The Metaphysics*. Translated by Richard Hope. New York: Columbia University Press, 1952.

——. *The Nicomachean Ethics*. Translated by David Ross. New York: Oxford University Press, 1980.

——. *The Physics*. Translated by Robin Waterfield. New York: Oxford University Press, 1996.

——. *The Poetics*. Translated by T. A. Sinclair. New York: Penguin, 1982.

——. *The Politics*. Translated by T. A. Sinclair. New York: Penguin, 1961.

Arnott, Peter D. *An Introduction to the Greek Theater.* London: Macmillan, 1961.

Artemidorus Daldianus. *The Interpretation of Dreams.* Translated by Robert J. White. Park Ridge, N.J.: Noyes Press, 1975.

Aylen, Leo. *The Greek Theater.* Rutherford, N.J.: Farleigh Dickinson University Press, 1985.

Babb, Valerie. *Whiteness Visible.* New York: New York University Press, 1998.

Bachman, John. *The Doctrine of the Unity of the Human Race.* Charleston, S.C.: C. Canning, 1850.

Bair, Barbara. "Remapping the Black/White Body." In *Sex, Love, Race,* edited by Martha Hodes, 399–419. New York: New York University Press, 1999.

Baldwin, James. *The Fire Next Time.* New York: Laurel, 1962.

——. *Just Above My Head.* New York: Laurel, 1979.

Barbot, Jean. *Barbot on Guinea.* 2 vols. Edited by P. E. H. Hair, Adam Jones, and Robin Law. 1688. Reprint, London: Hakluyt Society, 1992.

Barkan, Leonard. *Nature's Work of Art.* New Haven: Yale University Press, 1975.

Barrett, James R., and David Roediger. "How White People Became White." In *Critical White Studies,* edited by Richard Delgado and Jean Stefancic, 402–6. Philadelphia: Temple University Press, 1992.

Battell, Andrew. *The Strange Adventures of Andrew Battell of Leigh, in Angola and the Adjoining Regions.* Edited by E. G. Ravenstein. London: Hakluyt Society, 1901.

Bederman, Gail. *Manliness and Civilization.* Chicago: University of Chicago Press, 1995.

Beizer, Janet. *Ventriloquized Bodies.* Ithaca, N.Y.: Cornell University Press, 1994.

Benjamin, Jessica. *The Bonds of Love.* New York: Pantheon, 1988.

Berger, Joe. "This Man Gave Birth to a 7-lb. Baby Girl!" *Weekly World News,* 26 September 1989, 3.

Bergner, Gwen. "Myths of Masculinity: The Oedipus Complex and Douglass's 1845 *Narrative.*" In *The Psychoanalysis of Race,* edited by Christopher Lane, 241–60. New York: Columbia University Press, 1998.

Bernheimer, Charles. *Figures of Ill Repute.* Durham, N.C.: Duke University Press, 1997.

——. "Introduction: Part One." In *In Dora's Case,* edited by Charles Bernheimer and Claire Kahane, 1–18. New York: Columbia University Press, 1985.

——. "Penile Reference in Phallic Theory," *Differences* 4, no.1 (1992): 116–32.

Bernheimer, Charles, and Claire Kahane, eds. *In Dora's Case.* New York: Columbia University Press, 1985.

Bhabha, Homi K. "Are You a Man or a Mouse?" In *Constructing Masculinity,* edited by Maurice Berger, Brian Wallis, and Simon Watson, 57–65. New York: Routledge, 1995.

——. *The Location of Culture.* New York: Routledge, 1994.

Bingham, Robert. "An Ex-Slaveholders [sic] View of the Negro Question in the

South." In vol. 4 of *Anti-Black Thought, 1863–1925*, edited by John David Smith. New York: Garland, 1993. First published in European edition of *Harper's Monthly Magazine* (July 1900): 241–56.

Bitton, Davis. *The French Nobility in Crisis*. Stanford, Calif.: Stanford University Press, 1969.

Blackmore, Richard. *The Lay-Monastery*. London: Pemberton, 1714.

Blee, Kathleen M. *Women of the Klan: Racism and Gender in the 1920s*. Berkeley: University of California Press, 1991.

Blumenbach, Johann Friederich. *"De Generis Humani Varietate Nativa."* In *The Anthropological Treatises of Blumenbach*, edited and translated by Thomas Bendyshe. London: Longman, Green, 1865. First published as *De Generis Humani Varietate Nativa* (Goettingase: Typis frid. andr. Rosenbuschii, 1775).

Bonnett, Alastair. "Constructions of Whiteness." In *Race, Identity, and Citizenship*, edited by Rodolfo D. Torres, Louis F. Mirón, Jonathan Xavier Inda, 200–18. Malden, Mass.: Blackwell, 1999.

Borch-Jacobsen, Mikkel. *Lacan: The Absolute Master*. Stanford, Calif.: Stanford University Press, 1991.

Bowlby, Rachel. *Still Crazy After All These Years*. New York: Routledge, 1992.

Boyarin, Daniel. "What Does a Jew Want?; or, The Political Meaning of the Phallus." In *The Psychoanalysis of Race*, edited by Christopher Lane, 211-40. New York: Columbia University Press, 1998.

Bracher, Mark. "Lacan's Theory in the Four Discourses." *Prose Studies* 11, no. 3 (December 1988): 32–49.

Breitenberg, Mark. *Anxious Masculinity in Early Modern England*. Cambridge: Cambridge University Press, 1996.

Brenkman, John. *Straight Male Modern: A Cultural Critique of Psychoanalysis*. New York: Routledge, 1993.

Brennan, Teresa. *The Interpretation of the Flesh*. New York: Routledge, 1992.

———. "Introduction." In *Between Feminism and Psychoanalysis*, edited by Teresa Brennan, 1–24. New York: Routledge, 1989.

———, ed. *Between Feminism and Psychoanalysis*. New York: Routledge, 1989.

Breuer, Joseph, and Sigmund Freud. *Studies on Hysteria*. New York: Penguin, 1988.

Brod, Harry, ed. *Making of Masculinities*. Boston: Allen and Unwin, 1987.

Brousse, Marie-Hélène. "The Imaginary." In *Reading Seminars I and II*, edited by Richard Feldstein, Bruce Fink, and Maire Jaanus, 118–22. Albany, N.Y.: State University of New York Press, 1996.

Brown, Matthew P. "Basketball, Rodney King, Simi Valley." In *Whiteness*, edited by Mike Hill, 102–16. New York: New York University Press, 1997.

Buffon, Georges-Louis Leclerc, Comte de. *De l'homme*. Paris: François Maspero, 1971.

Burkert, Walter. *Oedipus, Oracles, and Meaning*. Toronto: University College, 1991.

Burlamaqui, Jean-Jacques. *Principes du droit naturel*. Geneva: Barillot, 1747.

Burnett, James. *Of the Origin and Progress of Language*. 1773. Reprint, Menston: Scholar Press, 1967 .

Butler, Judith. *Bodies That Matter*. New York: Routledge, 1993.

———. *Gender Trouble*. New York: Routledge, 1990.

Caldwell, Charles. *Thoughts on the Original Unity of the Human Race*. Cincinnati: J. A. and U. P. James, 1852.

Carby, Hazel V. "Encoding White Resentment: *Grand Canyon*—A Narrative for Our Times." In *Race, Identity, and Representation in Education*, edited by Cameron McCarthy and Warren Crichlow, 236–47. New York: Routledge, 1993.

———. "The Multicultural Wars." In *Black Popular Culture*, edited by Gina Dent, 187–99. Seattle, Wash.: Bay Press, 1992.

Carroll, Charles. *The Tempter of Eve, or The Criminality of Man's Social, Political, and Religious Equality with the Negro, and the Amalgamation to Which These Crimes Inevitably Lead*. In vol. 6 of *Anti-Black Thought, 1863–1925*, edited by John David Smith. New York: Garland, 1993. First published in St. Louis: Adamic, 1902.

Caruth, Cathy. *Unclaimed Experience*. Baltimore: Johns Hopkins University Press, 1996.

Cassirer, Ernst. *The Philosophy of the Enlightenment*. Translated by Fritz C. A. Koelln and James P. Pettegrove. Princeton: Princeton University Press, 1951.

Cavendish, Anthony Pike. *David Hume*. New York: Dover, 1968.

Chambers, Ross. "The Unexamined." In *Whiteness: A Critical Reader*, edited by Mike Hill, 187–203. New York: New York University Press, 1997.

Chase, Cynthia. "Oedipal Textuality: Reading Freud's Reading of *Oedipus*." *Diacritics* 9, no. 1 (spring 1979): 54–68.

Chodorow, Nancy. *Feminism and Psychoanalytic Theory*. New Haven: Yale University Press, 1989.

Chrétien de Troyes. *Yvain*. Paris: Gallimard, 1994.

Clément, Catherine. *The Lives and Legends of Jacques Lacan*. Translated by Arthur Goldhammer. New York: Columbia University Press, 1983.

———. *The Weary Sons of Freud*. Translated by Nicole Ball. New York: Verso, 1987.

Clément, Catherine, and Hélène Cixous. *La jeune née*. Paris: Union générale d'éditions, 1975.

Condillac, Etienne Bonnot de. *Essai sur l'origine des connaissances humaines*. Paris: Editions Alive, 1998.

Connell, R. W. *Gender and Power*. Cambridge: Blackwell, 1987.

Copjec, Joan. *Read My Desire*. Cambridge, Mass.: MIT University Press, 1994.

Cornell, Drucilla. *The Imaginary Domain*. New York: Routledge, 1995.

Coste, Didier. *Narrative as Communication*. Minneapolis: University of Minnesota Press, 1989.

Creed, Barbara. *The Monstrous-Feminine*. New York: Routledge, 1993.

Crenshaw, Kimberlé Williams. "Race, Reform, and Retrenchment." In *Theories of*

Race and Racism, edited by Les Back and John Solomos, 549–60. New York: Routledge, 2000.

Crenshaw, Kimberlé, and Gary Peller. "Reel Time/Real Justice." In *Reading Rodney King, Reading Urban Uprising*, edited by Robert Gooding-Williams, 56–70. New York: Routledge, 1993.

Culler, Jonathan. *The Pursuit of Signs*. Ithaca, N.Y.: Cornell University Press, 1981.

Cumberland, Richard. *De legibus naturae disquisitio philosphica*. London: Typis E. Flesher, 1672.

Cunningham, Andrew, and Roger French, eds. *The Medical Enlightenment of the Eighteenth Century*. Cambridge: Cambridge University Press, 1990.

Daniels, Doug. "The White Race Is Shrinking: Perceptions of Race in Canada and Some Speculations on the Political Economy of Race Classification." In *Critical White Studies*, edited by Richard Delgado and Jean Stefancic, 51–54. Philadelphia: Temple University Press, 1997.

Daniels, Jessie. *White Lies*. New York: Routledge, 1997.

Dapper, Olfert. "*Kaffraria or Land of the Kafirs, Also Named Hottentots*." In *The Early Cape Hottentots*, edited by I. Schapera, translated by I. Schapera and B. Farrington. Cape Town: Van Riebeeck Society, 1993. First published in Amsterdam: Jacob van Meur, 1668.

David-Ménard, Monique. *Hysteria from Freud to Lacan*. Ithaca, N.Y.: Cornell University Press, 1989.

Davis, David Brion. *The Problem of Slavery in the Age of Revolution, 1770–1823*. Ithaca, N.Y.: Cornell University Press, 1975.

Davis, F. James. *Who Is Black?: One Nation's Definition*. University Park: Pennsylvania State University Press, 1991.

Davis, Natalie Zemon. *Society and Culture*. Stanford, Calif.: Stanford University Press, 1975.

Derrick, Scott. *Monumental Anxieties*. New Brunswick, N.J.: Rutgers University Press, 1997.

Descartes, René. *Discourse on Method*. Translated by Doland A. Cress. Indianapolis: Hackett, 1998.

Diawara, Manthia. "Black Spectatorship: Problems of Identification and Resistance." *Screen*, 29, no. 4 (autumn 1988): 66–76.

Dickerson, Gary E. *The Cinema of Baseball*. Westport, Conn.: Meckler, 1991.

Diderot, Denis. "De l'interprétation de la nature." In *Œuvres philosophiques*, edited by P. Vernière, 177–244. Paris: Classiques Garnier, 1964.

——. "*Le rêve de d'Alembert*." In *Œuvres philosophiques*, edited by P. Vernière, 285–371. Paris: Classiques Garnier, 1964.

——. *Supplément au voyage de Bougainville*. Paris: Flammarion, 1972.

Dillon, Matthew, and Lynda Garland. *Ancient Greece*. New York: Routledge, 1994.

DiPiero, Thomas. "Angels in the (Out)Field of Vision," *Camera Obscura* 40–41 (1999): 201–25.

———. *Dangerous Truths and Criminal Passions*. Stanford, Calif.: Stanford University Press, 1992.

Doane, Janice L. *From Klein to Kristeva*. Ann Arbor: University of Michigan Press, 1992.

Doane, Mary Ann. *Femmes Fatales*. New York: Routledge, 1991.

Dodds, E. R. "On Misunderstanding the *Oedipus Rex*." In *Sophocles' "Oedipus Rex,"* edited by Harold Bloom, 35–47. New York: Chelsea House, 1988.

dos Sanctos, João. *Collections out of the Voyage and Historie of Friar João dos Sanctos his Æthiopia Orentalis, and Varia Historia, and out of other Portugals, for the better Knowledge of Africa and the Christianite therein*. Vol. 9 of *Purchase His Pilgrimes*. 1559. Reprint, Glasgow: MacLehose, 1955.

Duchesneau, François. *La physiologie des lumières*. The Hague: M. Nijhoff, 1982.

Duchet, Michèle. *Anthropologie et histoire au siècle des lumières*. Paris: Flammarion, 1977.

Dyer, Richard. "White." *Screen* 29, no. 4 (autumn 1988): 44–65.

———. *White*. New York: Routledge, 1997.

Dyson, Michael Eric. "The Labor of Whiteness, the Whiteness of Labor." In *Race, Identity, and Citizenship*, edited by Rodolfo D. Torres, Louis F. Mirón, and Jonathan Xavier Inda, 219–24. Malden, Mass.: Blackwell, 1999.

Edmiston, William. "Shifting Ground." In *Illicit Sex*, edited by Thomas DiPiero and Pat Gill, 143–60. Athens: University of Georgia Press, 1997.

Edmunds, Lowell. "The Sphinx in the Oedipus Legend." In *Oedipus: A Folklore Casebook*, edited by Lowell Edmunds and Alan Dundes, 147–73. Madison: University of Wisconsin Press, 1983.

Edwards, Bryan. *History, Civil and Commercial, of the British West Indies*. 5th ed. 1819. Reprint, London: G. and W. B. Whittaker, 1966.

Ehrard, Jean. *L'idée de nature en France*. 2 vols. Paris: SEVPEN, 1963.

Elliot, Patricia. *From Mastery to Analysis*. Ithaca, N.Y.: Cornell University Press, 1991.

Ellison, Ralph. "Change the Joke and Slip the Yoke." In *Shadow and Act*, 45–59. New York: Vintage, 1972.

Encyclopédie, ou dictionnaire raisonné des sciences, des arts et des métiers. 28 vols. Geneva: Briasson, 1754–92.

Erikson, Kai. "Notes on Trauma and Community." In *Trauma: Explorations in Memory*, edited by Cathy Caruth, 183–99. Baltimore: Johns Hopkins University Press, 1995.

Eze, Emmanuel Chukwudi, ed. *Race and the Enlightenment*. Cambridge, Mass.: Blackwell, 1997.

Fanon, Frantz. *Black Skin, White Masks*. Translated by Charles Lam Markman. New York: Grove Press, 1967.

Fausto-Sterling, Anne. "How to Build a Man." In *Constructing Masculinity*, edited by Maurice Berger, Brian Wallis, and Simon Watson, 127–34. New York: Routledge, 1995.

Feldstein, Richard. "Subject of the Gaze for Another Gaze." In *Lacan, Politics, Aesthetics*, edited by Willy Apollon and Richard Feldstein, 45–61. Albany: State University of New York Press, 1996.

Feldstein, Richard, and Judith Roof. *Feminism and Psychoanalysis*. Ithaca, N.Y.: Cornell University Press, 1989.

Felman, Shoshana. *What Does a Woman Want?* Baltimore: Johns Hopkins University Press, 1993.

Ferguson, Kathy E. *The Man Question: Visions of Subjectivity in Feminist Theory.* Berkeley: University of California Press, 1993.

Fields, Barbara J. "Ideology and Race in American History." In *Region, Race, and Reconstruction*, edited by J. Morgan Kousser and James M. McPherson, 143–77. New York: Oxford University Press, 1982.

———. "Slavery, Race, and Ideology in the United States of America." *New Left Review* 181 (May/June 1990): 95–118.

Filangieri, Gaetano. *La scienza della legislazione*. Milan: Galeazzi, 1784.

Fink, Bruce. *The Lacanian Subject*. Princeton: Princeton University Press, 1995.

Finley, M. I. *Economy and Society in Ancient Greece*. New York: Penguin, 1981.

Fizer, Irene. "Women 'Off' the Market." In *Illicit Sex*, edited by Thomas DiPiero and Pat Gill, 89–108. Athens: University of Georgia Press, 1997.

Flax, Jane. *Disputed Subjects*. New York: Routledge, 1993.

———. *Thinking Fragments*. Berkeley: University of California Press, 1990.

Flynn Jr., Charles L. "The Ancient Pedigree of Violent Repression: Georgia's Klan as a Folk Movement." In *The Southern Enigma: Essays on Race, Class, and Folk Culture*, edited by Walter J. Fraser Jr. and Winfred B. Moore Jr., 189–98. Westport, Conn.: Greenwood Press, 1983.

Fontana, Benedetto. *Hegemony and Power*. Minneapolis: University of Minnesota Press, 1993.

Forrester, John. "What Do Men Want?" In *Between Men and Feminism*, edited by David Porter, 105–17. New York: Routledge, 1992.

Foucault, Michel. *The Archaeology of Knowledge*. Translated by A. M. Sheridan Smith. New York: Pantheon, 1972.

Fox-Genovese, Elizabeth, and Eugene D. Genovese. *Fruits of Merchant Capital: Slavery and Bourgeois Property in the Rise and Expansion of Capitalism*. Oxford: Oxford University Press, 1983.

Franke, Katherine M. "What Does a White Woman Look Like? Racing and Erasing in Law." In *Critical White Studies*, edited by Richard Delgado and Jean Stefancic, 467–70. Philadelphia: Temple University Press, 1997.

Frankenberg, Ruth. "Local Whitenesses, Localizing Whiteness." In *Displacing Whiteness*, edited by Ruth Frankenberg, 1–33. Durham, N.C.: Duke University Press, 1997.

———. "Whiteness and Americanness: Examining Constructions of Race, Culture, and Nation in White Women's Life Narratives." In *Race*, edited by Steven Gregory and Roger Sanjek, 62–77. New Brunswick, N.J.: Rutgers University Press, 1994.

Frederickson, George. *The Arrogance of Race: Historical Perspectives on Slavery, Racism, and Social Inequality.* Middletown, Conn.: Wesleyan University Press, 1988.

Freud, Sigmund. "Analysis of Phobia in a Five-Year-Old Boy." In *The Sexual Enlightenment of Children,* 47–183. New York: Macmillan, 1963.

——. "Contributions to the Psychology of Love." In *Sexuality and the Psychology of Love,* 49–86. New York: Macmillan, 1963.

——. *The Ego and the Id.* Translated by Joan Riviere. New York: Norton, 1960.

——. "Femininity." In *New Introductory Lectures on Psychoanalysis,* edited and translated by James Strachey, 99–119. New York: Norton, 1965.

——. "Fetishism." In *Sexuality and the Psychology of Love,* edited by Philip Rieff, 214–19. New York: Macmillan, 1963.

——. "From the History of an Infantile Neurosis." In *Three Case Histories,* 187–316. New York: Macmillan, 1963.

——. "The Infantile Genital Organization of the Libido." In *Sexuality and the Psychology of Love,* edited by Philip Rieff, 171–75. New York: Macmillan, 1963.

——. *The Interpretation of Dreams.* New York: Avon, 1965.

——. "Some Psychological Consequences of the Anatomical Distinction between the Sexes." In *Sexuality and the Psychology of Love,* edited by Philip Rieff, 183–93. New York: Macmillan, 1963

——. *The Standard Edition of the Complete Psychological Works of Sigmund Freud.* 24 vols. London: Hogarth Press, 1962–74.

——. *Totem and Taboo.* London: Routledge and Kegan Paul, 1950.

Friedman, John Block. *The Monstrous Races in Medieval Art and Thought.* Cambridge, Mass.: Harvard University Press, 1981.

Frosh, Stephen. "Masculine Mastery and Fantasy." In *Psychoanalysis in Contexts,* edited by Anthony Elliott and Stephen Frosh, 166–90. New York: Routledge, 1995.

——. *Sexual Difference: Masculinity and Psychoanalysis.* New York: Routledge, 1994.

Fuss, Diana. "Essentially Speaking." In *Revaluing French Feminism,* edited by Nancy Fraser and Sandra Lee Bartky, 94–112. Bloomington: Indiana University Press, 1992.

Gaillard, Françoise. "Terror of Consensus." In *Terror and Consensus,* edited by Jean-Joseph Goux and Philip R. Wood, 65–74. Stanford, Calif.: Stanford University Press, 1998.

Gaines, Jane. "White Privilege and Looking Relations: Race and Gender in Feminist Film Theory." *Screen* 29, no. 4 (autumn 1988): 12–27.

Gallop, Jane. *The Daughter's Seduction.* Ithaca, N.Y.: Cornell University Press, 1982.

——. "Keys to Dora." In *In Dora's Case,* edited by Charles Bernheimer and Claire Kahane, 200–20. New York: Columbia University Press, 1985.

——. *Thinking Through the Body.* New York: Columbia University Press, 1988.

——. Reading Lacan. Ithaca, N.Y.: Cornell University Press, 1988.

Garber, Marjorie. "Out of Joint." In *The Body in Parts,* edited by David Hillman and Carla Mazzio, 23–52. New York: Routledge, 1997.

——. "Spare Parts: The Surgical Construction of Gender." *Differences* 1, no. 3 (fall 1989): 137–59.

Gay, Peter. *The Enlightenment: An Interpretation.* New York: Knopf, 1969.

Genette, Gérard. "Vraisemblance et motivation." In *Figures II.* Vol. 2: 71–99. Paris: Seuil, 1969.

Gilman, Sander. "Black Bodies, White Bodies: Toward an Iconography of Female Sexuality in Late Nineteenth-Century Art, Medicine, and Literature." In *Race, Writing, and Difference,* edited by Henry Louis Gates Jr., 223–61. Chicago: University of Chicago Press, 1985.

——. *Freud, Race, and Gender.* Princeton: Princeton University Press, 1993.

Gilman, Sander L., G. S. Rousseau, Helen King, Roy Porter, and Elaine Showalter, eds. *Hysteria Beyond Freud.* Berkeley: University of California Press, 1993.

Gobineau, Arthur de. *The Moral and Intellectual Diversity of Races.* Translated by H. Hotz. Philadelphia: J. B. Lippincott and Co., 1856.

Goldberg, David Theo. *Racist Culture.* Cambridge, Mass.: Blackwell, 1993.

Goldenberg, Naomi R. *Returning Words to Flesh.* Boston: Beacon, 1990.

Goldmann, Lucien. *The Philosophy of the Enlightenment.* Translated by Henry Maas. Cambridge, Mass.: MIT Press, 1973.

Goldsmith, Oliver. *Goldsmith's Natural History.* Philadelphia: Johnson and Warner, 1810.

Goldstein, Jan. "The Uses of Male Hysteria: Medical and Literary Discourse in Nineteenth-Century France," *Representations* 34 (spring 1991): 134–65.

Gollobin, Ira. *Dialectical Materialism.* New York: Petras, 1986.

Goodhart, Sandor. "Λησταζ Εφασχε: Oedipus and Laius' Many Murderers." *Diacritics* 8, no. 1 (spring 1978): 55–71.

Gossett, Thomas F. *Race: The History of an Idea in America.* New York: Oxford University Press, 1997.

Gotanda, Neil. "A Critique of 'Our Constitution Is Color-Blind.' " *Stanford Law Review* 44, no. 1 (November 1991): 1–68.

Gould, Stephen Jay. "American Polygeny and Craniometry Before Darwin." In *The Racial Economy of Science,* edited by Sandra Harding, 84–115. Bloomington: Indiana University Press, 1993.

——. *The Mismeasure of Man.* New York: Norton, 1996.

Gould, Thomas. "The Innocence of Oedipus." In *Sophocles' "Oedipus Rex,"* edited by Harold Bloom, 46–63. New York: Chelsea House, 1988.

Goux, Jean-Joseph. *Oedipus, Philosopher.* Translated by Catherine Porter. Stanford, Calif.: Stanford University Press, 1993.

——. "The Phallus: Masculine Identity and the 'Exchange of Women.' " Translated by Maria Amuchastegui, Caroline Benforado, Amy Hendrix, and Eleanor Kaufman. *Differences* 4, no. 1 (1992): 40–75.

——. *Symbolic Economies*. Translated by Jennifer Curtiss Gage. Ithaca, N.Y.: Cornell University Press, 1990.

Greenblatt, Stephen. "Mutilation and Meaning." In *The Body in Parts*, edited by David Hillman and Carla Mazzio, 221–42. New York: Routledge, 1997.

Greene, William Chase. "The Murderers of Laius." *Transactions and Proceedings of the American Philological Association* 60 (1929): 75–86.

Greimas, Algirdas. *Structural Semantics*. Translated by Daniele McDowell, Ronald Schleifer, and Alan Velie. Lincoln: University of Nebraska Press, 1983.

——. *On Meaning*. Trans. Paul Perron and Frank H. Collins. Minneapolis: University of Minnesota Press, 1987.

Grevenbroek, J. G. *An Elegant and Accurate Account of the African Race Living Round the Cape of Good Hope*. Translated by B. Farrington. N.p., 1695.

Grier, William H., and Price M. Cobbs. *Black Rage*. New York: Basic Books, 1968.

Groarke, Leo, and Graham Solomon. "Some Sources for Hume's Account of Cause." *Journal of the History of Ideas* 52, no. 4 (1991): 645–63.

Grosz, Elizabeth. *Jacques Lacan*. New York: Routledge, 1990.

Grotius, Hugo. *Of the Rights of War and Peace*. London: D. Brown, 1715.

Guillaumin, Colette. *Racism, Sexism, Power and Ideology*. New York: Routledge, 1995.

Guyer, Paul. *Kant and the Claims of Knowledge*. Cambridge: Cambridge University Press, 1987.

Haggerty, George. "Beckford's Pæderasty." In *Illicit Sex*, edited by Thomas DiPiero and Pat Gill, 123–42. Athens: University of Georgia Press, 1997.

Halberstam, Judith. *Female Masculinity*. Durham, N.C.: Duke University Press, 1998.

Hammond, N. G. L. *A History of Greece*. Oxford: Clarendon, 1959.

Hankins, Thomas L. *Science and the Enlightenment*. Cambridge: Cambridge University Press, 1985.

Hannaford, Ivan. *Race: The History of an Idea in the West*. Baltimore: Johns Hopkins University Press, 1996.

Harding, Sandra, ed. *The Racial Economy of Science*. Bloomington: Indiana University Press, 1993.

Harris, Cheryl I. "Whiteness as Property." *Harvard Law Review* 106, no. 8 (June 1993): 1707–91.

Harris, Trudier. *Exorcising Blackness: Historical and Literary Lynching and Burning Rituals*. Bloomington: Indiana University Press, 1984.

Hazard, Paul. *La crise de la conscience européenne*. Paris: Fayard, 1961.

——. *La pensée européenne au XVIIIe siècle*. Paris: Fayard, 1963.

Henderson, Robert W. *Ball, Bat, and Bishop: The Origin of Ball Games*. New York: Rockport Press, 1947.

Herodotus. *The Histories*. Translated by Aubrey de Sélincourt. New York: Penguin, 1954.

Hill, Mike. "Introduction: Vipers in Shangri-la: Whiteness, Writing, and Other Ordinary Terrors." In *Whiteness*, edited by Mike Hill, 1–18. New York: New York University Press, 1997.

Hillman, David, and Carla Mazzio. Introduction to *The Body in Parts*, edited by David Hillman and Carla Mazzio, xi–xxix. New York: Routledge, 1997.

Hirsch, Marianne. *The Mother/Daughter Plot*. Bloomington: Indiana University Press, 1989.

Hobbes, Thomas. *Leviathan*. New York: Penguin, 1968.

Hodes, Martha. *White Women, Black Men*. New Haven: Yale University Press, 1997.

Hollard, Henri. *De l'homme et des races humaines*. Paris: Labi, 1853.

Homans, Margaret. " 'Racial Composition': Metaphor and the Body in the Writing of Race." In *Female Subjects in Black and White*, edited by Elizabeth Abel, Barbara Christian, and Helene Moglen, 77–101. Berkeley: University of California Press, 1997.

Homer. *The Iliad*. Translated by Richmond Lattimore. Chicago: University of Chicago Press, 1951.

———. *The Odyssey*. Translated by Richmond Lattimore. New York: Harper, 1965.

hooks, bell. "Representing Whiteness in the Black Imagination." In *Cultural Studies*, edited by Lawrence Grossberg, Cary Nelson, Paula Treichler, 338–46. New York: Routledge, 1991.

Horkheimer, Max, and Theodor Adorno. *Dialectic of Enlightenment*. New York: Continuum, 1987.

Hughes, Langston. "White Man." In *Black on White*, edited by David R. Roediger, 124–25. New York: Schocken, 1998.

Hume, David. *A Treatise of Human Nature*. Oxford: Clarendon, 1958.

Hunt, James. *The Negro's Place in Nature*. In vol. 1 of *Anti-Black Thought, 1863–1925*, edited by John David Smith. New York: Garland, 1993. First published in New York: Van Evrie, 1868.

Hunter, Dianne. "Hysteria, Psychoanalysis, and Feminism." In *Writing on the Body*, edited by Katie Conboy, Nadia Medina, and Sarah Stanbury, 257–76. New York: Columbia University Press, 1997.

Hutchings, Peter. "Masculinity and the Horror Film." In *You Tarzan: Masculinity, Movies, and Men*, edited by Pat Kirkham and Janet Thumin, 84–94. New York: St. Martin's Press, 1993.

Illie, Paul. *The Age of Minerva*. 2 vols. Philadelphia: University of Pennsylvania Press, 1995.

Irigaray, Luce. "Any Theory of the 'Subject' Has Always Been Appropriated by the 'Masculine.'" In *Speculum of the Other Woman*, translated by Gillian C. Gill, 133–46. Ithaca, N.Y.: Cornell University Press, 1985.

———. *Speculum of the Other Woman*. Translated by Gillian C. Gill. Ithaca, N.Y.: Cornell University Press, 1985.

——. *This Sex Which Is Not One*. Translated by Catherine Porter. Ithaca, N.Y.: Cornell University Press, 1985.

Islam, Syed Manzoorul. *The Ethics of Travel*. Manchester, N.Y.: Manchester University Press, 1996.

Jacobson, Matthew Frye. *Whiteness of a Different Color*. Cambridge, Mass.: Harvard University Press, 1998.

Jamestown Voyages Under the First Charter, 1606–1609. 2 vols. Cambridge: Cambridge University Press, 1969.

Jefferson, Thomas. "*Notes on the State of Virginia*." 1787. Reprinted in *The Portable Thomas Jefferson*, edited by Merrill D. Peterson. New York: Penguin, 1975.

Jeffords, Susan. *Hard Bodies: Hollywood Masculinity in the Reagan Era*. New Brunswick, N.J.: Rutgers University Press, 1994.

——. *The Remasculinization of America*. Bloomington: University of Indiana Press, 1989.

Johnson, Barbara. "The Frame of Reference: Poe, Lacan, Derrida." In *The Purloined Poe*, edited by John P. Muller and William J. Richardson, 213–51. Baltimore: Johns Hopkins University Press, 1988.

Jones, Peter. "Cause, Reason, and Objectivity in Hume's Aesthetics." In *Hume: A Re-Evaluation*, edited by Donald W. Livingston and James T. King, 323–42. New York: Fordham University Press, 1976.

Jordan, Winthrop. *White Over Black: American Attitudes Toward the Negro, 1550–1812*. Chapel Hill: University of North Carolina Press, 1968.

Kahane, Claire. "*The Bostonians* and the Figure of the Speaking Woman." In *Psychoanalysis and . . .* , edited by Richard Feldstein and Henry Sussman, 163–74. New York: Routledge, 1990.

——. "Introduction: Part Two." In *In Dora's Case*, edited by Charles Bernheimer and Claire Kahane, 19–31. New York: Columbia University Press, 1985.

——. *Passions of the Voice*. Baltimore: Johns Hopkins University Press, 1995.

Kant, Immanuel. *Prolegomena to Any Future Metaphysics*. Edited and translated by Gary Hatfield. Cambridge: Cambridge University Press, 1987.

Kaplan, Sidney. "*The Octoroon:* Early History of the Drama of Miscegenation." In *American Studies in Black and White*, edited by Allan D. Austin, 198–210. Amherst: University of Massachusetts Press, 1991.

Kerényi, Karl. "Oedipus: Two Essays." In *Oedipus Variations*, translated by Jon Solomon, 5–86. Woodstock, Conn.: Spring Publications, 1990.

Keuls, Eva C. *The Reign of the Phallus*. Berkeley: University of California Press, 1985.

Kimmel, Michael. *Manhood in America*. New York: Free Press, 1997.

Kinsella, W. P. *Shoeless Joe*. New York: Ballantine, 1982.

Kirby, Lynn. "Male Hysteria and Early Cinema." *Camera Obscura* 17 (May 1988): 67–85.

Knight, Diana. *Barthes and Utopia: Space, Travel, Writing*. New York: Oxford University Press, 1997.

Knox, Bernard. *Oedipus at Thebes*. New Haven: Yale University Press, 1957.

——. "Sophocles' *Oedipus*." In *Sophocles' "Oedipus Rex,"* edited by Harold Bloom, 5–22. New York: Chelsea House, 1988.

Kofman, Sarah. *The Enigma of Woman*. Translated by Catherine Porter. Ithaca, N.Y.: Cornell University Press, 1985.

Kolb, Peter. *The Present State of the Cape of Good Hope: or, a Particular Account of Several Nations of the Hottentots*. Translated by Mr. Medley. 1719. Reprint, London: St. Paul's, 1731.

Kovel, Joel. "On Racism and Psychoanalysis." In *Psychoanalysis in Contexts*, edited by Anthony Elliott and Stephen Frosh, 201–22. New York: Routledge, 1995.

Ku Klux Klan. *Papers Read at the Meeting of Grand Dragons at Their First Annual Meeting held at Asheville, North Carolina, July 1923*. N.p., n.d.

Ku Klux Klan. "The Practice of Klanishness." Atlanta: N.p., 1918.

Lacan, Jacques. *Ecrits: A Selection*. Translated by Alan Sheridan. New York: Norton, 1977.

——. *The Ego in Freud's Theory and in the Technique of Psychoanalysis: The seminaire, book 2*. Translated by Sylvana Tomaselli. New York: Norton, 1991.

——. *Encore: Le séminaire*, livre 20. Paris: Seuil, 1975.

——. *L'envers de la psychanalyse: Le séminaire*, livre 17. Paris: Seuil, 1991.

——. *L'éthique de la psychanalyse: Le séminaire*, livre 7. Paris: Seuil, 1986.

——. *Les formations de l'inconscient: Le séminaire*, livre 5. Paris: Seuil, 1998.

——. *The Four Fundamental Concepts of Psychoanalysis*. Translated by Alan Sheridan. New York: Norton, 1978.

——. *Les psychoses: Le séminaire*, livre 3. Paris: Seuil, 1981.

——. *La relation d'objet: Le séminaire*, livre 4. Paris: Seuil, 1994.

——. *Le transfert: Le séminaire*, livre 8. Paris: Seuil, 1991.

La chanson de Roland. Edited by T. Atkinson Jenkins. N.p.: American Life Foundation, 1977.

Laclau, Ernesto. *New Reflections on the Revolution of Our Time*. New York: Verso, 1990.

Laclau, Ernesto, and Chantal Mouffe. *Hegemony and Socialist Strategy*. New York: Verso, 1985.

La Mettrie, Julien Offray de. *L'homme machine*. Edited by Aram Vartanian. Princeton: Princeton University Press, 1960.

Lane, Christopher. *Burdens of Intimacy*. Chicago: University of Chicago Press, 1999.

Laqueur, Thomas. *Making Sex*. Cambridge, Mass.: Harvard University Press, 1990.

Lasch, Christopher. "Origins of the Asylum." In *The World of Nations*, 3–17. New York: Knopf, 1973.

Lee, Harper. *To Kill a Mockingbird*. New York: Warner, 1982.

Lehman, Peter. *Running Scared*. Philadelphia: Temple University Press, 1993.

Leibniz, Gottfried Wilhelm, Freiherr von. *New Essays on Human Understanding*. Edited and translated by Peter Remnant and Jonathan Bennett. New York: Cambridge University Press, 1981.

Lemaire, Anika. *Jacques Lacan*. London: Routledge and Kegan Paul, 1970.

Leo, John. *"Observations of Africa, taken out of John Leo his nine Bookes translated by Master Pory, and the most remarkable things hither transcribed."* Vol. 5 of *Purchase His Pilgrimes*. 1526. Reprint, Glasgow: MacLehose, 1955.

Lester, A. Hoyle. *The Pre-Adamite, or Who Tempted Eve?* Philadelphia: Lippincott, 1875.

Lester, J. C., and D. L. Wilson, *Ku Klux Klan: Its Origin, Growth, and Disbandment*. [1884] 1905; reprint, New York: AMS Press, 1971.

LeVay, Simon. *The Sexual Brain*. Cambridge, Mass.: MIT Press, 1993.

Lévi-Strauss, Claude. *Structural Anthropology*. Translated by Claire Jacobson and Brooke Schoeff. New York: Basic Books, 1963.

Locke, John. *An Essay Concerning Human Understanding*. Edited by John W. Yolton. New York: Dutton, 1978.

——. Two Treatises of Government. Edited by Peter Laslett. London: Cambridge University Press, 1970.

López, Ian F. Haney. "The Social Construction of Race." In *Critical Race Theory*, edited by Richard Delgado, 542–50. Philadelphia: Temple University Press, 1995.

——. *White By Law*. New York: New York University Press, 1996.

Lovejoy, Arthur O. *The Great Chain of Being*. Cambridge, Mass.: Harvard University Press, 1936.

Ludolf, Hiob. *A New History of Ethiopia*. London: Samuel Smith, 1682.

Lukács, Georg. *The Theory of the Novel*. Translated by Anna Bostock. Cambridge, Mass.: MIT Press, 1968.

MacCannell, Juliet Flower. *The Regime of the Brother*. New York: Routledge, 1991.

Macey, David. *Lacan in Contexts*. New York: Verso, 1998.

Malik, Kenan. *The Meaning of Race*. New York: New York University Press, 1996.

Marcus, Ruth. "FCC Defends Minority License Policies: Case Before High Court Could Shape Future of Affirmative Action." *Washington Post*, 29 March 1990: A8.

Marees, Pieter de. *Description and Historical Account of the Gold Kingdom of Guinea*. 1602. Reprint, Oxford: Oxford University Press, 1987.

Martinet, Marie-Madeleine. *Le voyage d'Italie dans les littératures européennes*. Paris: Presses Universitaires de France, 1996.

Matlock, Jann. *Scenes of Seduction*. New York: Columbia University Press, 1994.

Maupertuis, P. L. Moreau de. *Œuvres*. 4 vols. Hildescheim: Georg Olms, 1965.

McDowell, Deborah E. "Pecs and Reps." In *Race and the Subject of Masculinities*, edited by Harry Stecopoulos and Michael Uebel, 361–85. Durham, N.C.: Duke University Press, 1997.

McKeon, Michael. *The Origins of the Novel*. Baltimore: Johns Hopkins University Press, 1987.

McMinn, Joseph. *Jonathan's Travels: Swift and Ireland*. New York: St. Martin's Press, 1994.

Mercier, Roger. *La réhabilitation de la nature humaine.* Villemomble: La Balance, 1960.

Metcalf, Andy, and Martin Humphries. *The Sexuality of Men.* London: Pluto, 1985.

Miller, Jacques-Alain. "An Introduction to Lacan's Clinical Perspectives." In *Reading Seminars I and II,* edited by Richard Feldstein, Bruce Fink, and Maire Jaanus, 241–47. Albany: State University of New York Press, 1996.

Miller, W. "Lower-Class Culture as a Generating Milieu for Gang Delinquency." *Journal of Social Issues* 14 (1958): 5–19.

Mills, Sara. *Discourses of Difference: An Analysis of Women's Travel Writing and Colonialism.* New York: Routledge, 1991.

Mitchell, Juliet. *Mad Men and Medusas.* New York: Basic Books, 2000.

———. *Psychoanalysis and Feminism.* New York: Vintage, 1974.

Mitchell, Juliet, and Jacqueline Rose, eds. *Feminine Sexuality.* New York: W. W. Norton, 1983.

Mitchell-Boyask, Robin N. "Freud's Reading of Classical Literature and Classical Philology." In *Reading Freud's Reading,* edited by Sander L. Gilman, Jutta Birmele, Jay Geller, and Valerie D. Greenberg, 23–46. New York: New York University Press, 1994.

Moi, Toril. "Representation of Patriarchy: Sexuality and Epistemology in Freud's *Dora.*" In *In Dora's Case,* edited by Charles Bernheimer and Claire Kahane, 181–99. New York: Columbia University Press, 1985.

———. *Sexual/Textual Politics.* New York: Routledge, 1985.

Montesquieu, Charles-Louis de Secondat, *Œuvres complètes.* 2 vols. Edited by Roger Caillois. Paris: Bibliothèque de la Pléiade, 1958.

———. *Les lettres persanes.* Paris: Garnier-Flammarion, 1964.

Moravcsik, Julius. *Plato and Platonism.* Cambridge, Mass.: Blackwell, 1992.

Morgan, David H. J. *Discovering Men.* New York: Routledge, 1992.

Morrison, Toni. *Playing in the Dark: Whiteness and the Literary Imagination.* Cambridge, Mass.: Harvard University Press, 1992.

Muller-Hill, Benno. *Murderous Science.* New York: Oxford University Press, 1988.

Mulvey, Christopher. *Transatlantic Manners: Social Patterns in Nineteenth-Century Anglo-American Travel Literature.* New York: Cambridge University Press, 1990.

Murray, Oswyn. *Early Greece.* Stanford, Calif.: Stanford University Press, 1980.

Nagle, D. Brendan. *The Ancient World.* Englewood Cliffs, N.J.: Prentice-Hall, 1979.

Nelson, Dana D. *National Manhood.* Durham, N.C.: Duke University Press, 1998.

Netton, Ian Richard. "The Mysteries of Islam." In *Exoticism in the Enlightenment,* edited by G. S. Rousseau and Roy Porter, 23–45. Manchester: Manchester University Press, 1990.

Newton, Isaac. *Mathematical Principles of Natural Philosophy.* New York: Philosophical Library, 1964.

Ngxamngxa, A. N. N. "The Function of Circumcision among the Xhosa-speaking

Tribes in Historical Perspective." In *Man: Anthropological Essays Presented to O. F. Raum*, edited by E. J. DeJager, 182–204. Cape Town: C. Struik, 1971.

Norwood, Gilbert. *Greek Tragedy.* New York: Hill and Wang, 1960.

Nott, J. C., and Geo. R. Gliddon. *Types of Mankind: or, Ethnological Researches.* 2d ed. Philadelphia: Lippincott, Grambo, and Co., 1854.

Nussbaum, Martha C. "The *Oedipus Rex* and the Ancient Unconscious." In *Freud and Forbidden Knowledge*, edited by Peter L. Rudnytsky and Hellen Handler Spitz, 42–71. New York: New York University Press, 1994.

O'Hara, Ken. "Man Gives Birth and Baby Lives!" *Sun* 9, no. 18 (30 April 1991): 25.

Omi, Michael, and Howard Winant. *Racial Formation in the United States.* New York: Routledge and Kegan Paul, 1986.

Paine, Thomas. *Rights of Man.* New York: Knopf, 1994.

Palomera, Vicente. "The Ethics of Hysteria and of Psychoanalysis." In *Reading Seminars I and II*, edited by Richard Feldstein, Bruce Fink, and Maire Jaanus, 387–96. Albany: State University of New York Press, 1996.

Park, Mungo. *Travels in the Interior Districts of Africa.* London: Bulmer and Co., 1799.

Pausanias. *Guide to Greece.* 2 vols. Translated by Peter Levi. New York: Penguin, 1971.

Pavel, Thomas. *Fictional Worlds.* Cambridge, Mass.: Harvard University Press, 1986.

Pellegrini, Ann. *Performance Anxieties.* New York: Routledge, 1997.

Penley, Constance. *The Future of an Illusion.* Minneapolis: University of Minnesota Press, 1989.

Petty, William. *The Petty Papers.* New York: Houghton Mifflin Co., 1927.

Pfeil, Fred. *White Guys.* New York: Verso, 1995.

Plato. *The Republic.* Translated by G. M. A. Grube. Indianapolis: Hacket, 1974.

Plotinus. *The Enneads.* Edited by John Dillon. Translated by Stephen MacKenna. New York: Penguin, 1991.

Plutarch. *Moralia.* 15 vols. Translated by Frank Cole Babbitt. Cambridge, Mass.: Harvard University Press, 1936.

Pope, Alexander. *Essay on Man.* In *Alexander Pope*, edited by Pat Rogers. Oxford: Oxford University Press, 1993.

Porter, Roy. "Barely Touching: A Social Perspective on Mind and Body." In *The Languages of Psyche*, edited by G. S. Rousseau, 45–80. Berkeley: University of California Press, 1990.

Prichard, James Cowles. *Researches into the Physical History of Mankind.* Vol. 1. London: Sherwood, Gilbert, and Piper, 1841 [1837–47].

Propp, Vladimir. "Oedipus in the Light of Folklore." In *Oedipus: A Folklore Casebook*, edited by Lowell Edmunds and Alan Dundes, 76–121. Madison: University of Wisconsin Press, 1983.

Ptolemy (Claudius Ptolemaeus). *Tetrabiblos.* Edited and translated by F. E. Robbins. Cambridge, Mass.: Harvard University Press, 1940.

Pufendorf, Samuel. *De jure naturae et gentium*. 1672. Reprint, Buffalo, N.Y.: William
Hein, 1995.

——. *De officio hominis et civis juxta legem naturalem libri*. 1673. Reprint, Buffalo,
N.Y.: William Hein, 1995.

Quatrefages de Bréau, Jean Louis Armand de. *Unité de l'espèce humaine*. Paris:
Hachette, 1861.

Rabelais, François. *Œuvres complètes*. 2 vols. Edited by P. Jourda. Paris: Editions Garnier, 1962.

*Race Problems of the South: Report of the Proceedings of the First Annual Conference
Held Under the Auspices of the Southern Society for the Promotion of the Study of
Race Conditions and Problems in the South*. In vol. 2 of *Anti-Black Thought, 1863–
1925*, edited by John David Smith. New York: Garland, 1993. First published in
Richmond: Johnson Publishing Co., 1900.

Ragland, Ellie. "The Discourse of the Master." In *Lacan, Politics, Aesthetics*, edited by
Willie Apollon and Richard Feldstein, 127–47. Albany: State University of New
York Press, 1996.

Ragland-Sullivan, Ellie. "The Sexual Masquerade." In *Lacan and the Subject of Language*, edited by Ellie Ragland-Sullivan and Mark Bracher, 49–80. New York:
Routledge, 1991.

Rather, L. J. *Mind and Body in Eighteenth-Century Medicine*. Berkeley: University of
California Press, 1965.

Rawlins, John. "*The Wonderful Recovery of the Exchange of Bristow, from the Turkish
Pirats of Argier, published by John Rawlins, heere abbreviated*." Vol. 6 of *Purchase
His Pilgrimes*. 1621. Reprint, Glasgow: MacLehose, 1955.

Regnault, François. "The Name-of-the-Father." In *Reading Seminars I and II*, edited
by Richard Feldstein, Bruce Fink, and Maire Jaanus, 65–76. Albany: State University of New York Press, 1996.

Rehn, Rush. *Greek Tragic Theater*. New York: Routledge, 1992.

Reinhardt, Karl. "Illusion and Truth in *Oedipus Tyrannus*." In *Sophocles' "Oedipus
Rex*," edited by Harold Bloom, 65–102. New York: Chelsea House, 1988.

Relation des costes d'Afrique appellées Guinée. Paris: Denys Thierry, 1669.

Rey-Flaud, Henri. *Le Charivari*. Paris: Payot, 1985.

Rhyne, William Ten. *A Short Account of the Cape of Good Hope and of the Hottentots
who Inhabit that Region*. Schaffhausen: John Martin Oswald, 1686.

Ricius and Trigautius. "*A Discourse of the Kingdome of China*." Vol. 12 of *Purchase His
Pilgrimes*. 1579. Reprint, Glasgow: MacLehose, 1955.

Robert, Marthe. *Origins of the Novel*. Translated by Sacha Rabinovitch. Bloomington:
Indiana University Press, 1980.

Roberts, Dorothy E. "The Genetic Tie." In *Critical White Studies*, edited by Richard
Delgado and Jean Stefancic, 186–89. Philadelphia: Temple University Press,
1997.

Robinson, Sally. *Marked Men*. New York: Columbia University Press, 2000.

Roediger, David R. *The Wages of Whiteness*. New York: Verso, 1991.

Roger, Jacques. *Les sciences de la vie dans la pensée française au XVIII siècle*. Paris: Colin, 1963.

Rogers, J. A. *The Ku Klux Spirit*. 1923. Reprint, Baltimore: Black Classic Press, 1980.

Roof, Judith. "Verdict on Paternal Function." In *Lacan, Politics, Aesthetics*, edited by Willy Apollon and Richard Feldstein, 102–23. State University of New York Press, 1996.

Rose, Jacqueline. "Dora: Fragment of an Analysis." In *In Dora's Case*, edited by Charles Bernheimer and Claire Kahane, 128–48. New York: Columbia University Press, 1985.

——. *Sexuality in the Field of Vision*. London: Verso, 1986.

——. *Why War?* Cambridge, Mass.: Blackwell, 1993.

Rose, S. E. F. (Mrs.). *The Ku Klux Klan, or Invisible Empire*. New Orleans: L. Graham, 1914.

Rosenfeld, Leonora Cohen. *From Beast-Machine to Man-Machine*. New York: Octagon, 1968.

Rousseau, G. S. *Enlightenment Crossings*. Manchester: Manchester University Press, 1991.

Rousseau, Jean-Jacques. *Discourse on Inequality*. Translated by Maurice Cranston. New York: Penguin, 1984.

——. *Du contrat social*. Paris: Garnier-Flammarion, 1966.

Roustang, François. *Dire Mastery*. Translated by Ned Lukacher. Baltimore: Johns Hopkins University Press, 1982.

Ruthven, K. K. *Feminist Literary Studies*. New York: Cambridge University Press, 1984.

Sade, Donatien-Alphonse-François, marquis de. *Three Complete Novels*. Translated by Richard Seaver and Austryn Wainhouse. New York: Grove Press, 1965.

Sadoff, Dianne F. *Sciences of the Flesh*. Stanford, Calif.: Stanford University Press, 1998.

Sainte-More, Benoît de. *Chroniques des ducs de Normandie*. 3 vols. Edited by Carin Fahlin. Geneva: Droz, 1951.

Salecl, Renata. *The Spoils of Freedom*. New York: Routledge, 1994.

Salles, Eusèbe François, comte de. *Histoire générale des races humaines*. Paris: B. Duprat, 1849.

Sandys, George. *"Relations of Africa."* Vol. 6 of *Purchase His Pilgrimes*. 1610. Reprint, Glasgow: MacLehose, 1955.

Sanjek, Roger. "The Enduring Inequalities of Race." In *Race*, edited by Steven Gregory and Roger Sanjek, 1–17. New Brunswick, N.J.: Rutgers University Press, 1994.

Saper, Craig. "A Nervous Theory: The Troubling Gaze of Psychoanalysis in Media Studies." *Diacritics* 21, no. 4 (winter 1991): 33–52.

Saussure, Ferdinand de. *Course in General Linguistics*. Chicago: Open Court, 1986.

Savran, David. *Taking It Like a Man*. Princeton: Princeton University Press, 1998.

Saxton, Alexander. *The Rise and Fall of the White Republic*. New York: Verso, 1990.

Schaffer, Simon. "States of Mind." In *The Languages of Psyche*, edited by G. S. Rousseau, 233–90. Berkeley: University of California Press, 1990.

Schapera, Isaac. *The Early Cape Hottentots*. Cape Town: Van Riebeeck Society, 1933.

Schiebinger, Londa. *Nature's Body*. Boston: Beacon Press, 1993.

Schiesari, Juliana. *The Gendering of Melancholia*. Ithaca, N.Y.: Cornell University Press, 1992.

Schneiderman, Stuart. *An Angel Passes*. New York: New York University Press, 1988.

Schwartz, Joel D. "Human Action and Political Action in *Oedipus Tyrannos*." In *Greek Tragedy and Political Theory*, edited by Peter Euben, 183–209. Berkeley: University of California Press, 1986.

Screech, M. A. *Rabelais*. Ithaca, N.Y.: Cornell University Press, 1979.

Sedgwick, Eve Kosofsky. "'Gosh, Boy George, You Must Be Awfully Secure in your Masculinity.'" In *Constructing Masculinity*, edited by Marice Berger, Brian Wallis, and Simon Watson, 11–20. New York: Routledge, 1995.

Segal, Charles. *Interpreting Greek Tragedy*. Ithaca, N.Y.: Cornell University Press, 1986.

——. "Sophocles' *Oedipus Tyrannus*." In *Freud and Forbidden Knowledge*, edited by Peter L. Rudnytsky and Ellen Handler Spitz, 72–95. New York: New York University Press, 1994.

Segal, Lynn. *Slow Motion: Changing Men*. London: Virago, 1990.

Seidler, Victor J. *Recreating Sexual Politics*. London: Routledge, 1991.

——. *Rediscovering Masculinity: Reason, Language, and Sexuality*. London: Routledge, 1989.

Seshadri-Crooks, Kalpana. "The Comedy of Domination: Psychoanalysis and the Conceit of Whiteness." In *The Psychoanalysis of Race*, edited by Christopher Lane, 353–79. New York: Columbia University Press, 1998.

——. *Desiring Whiteness*. New York: Routledge, 2000.

Sheets-Johnstone, Maxine. *The Roots of Thinking*. Philadelphia: Temple University Press, 1990.

Shklovsky, Victor. "Art as Technique." In *Russian Formalist Criticism*, edited by Lee T. Lemon and Marin J. Reis, 1–21. Lincoln: University of Nebraska Press, 1965.

Silverman, Kaja. *The Acoustic Mirror*. Bloomington: Indiana University Press, 1988.

——. "The Lacanian Phallus," *Differences* 4, no.1 (1992): 84–115.

——. *Male Subjectivity at the Margins*. New York: Routledge, 1992.

Slipp, Samuel. *The Freudian Mystique*. New York: New York University Press, 1993.

Sloan, Philip. "The Gaze of Natural History." In *Inventing Human Science*, edited by Christopher Fox, Roy Porter, and Robert Wokler, 112–51. Berkeley: University of California Press, 1995.

Smith, John David, ed. *Anti-Black Thought, 1863–1925.* 11 vols. New York: Garland, 1993.

Smith, Samuel Stanhope. *An Essay on the Causes of the Variety of Complexion and Figure in the Human Species.* Edited by Winthrop D. Jordan. 1788. Reprint, Cambridge, Mass.: Harvard University Press, 1965.

Smyth, Thomas. *The Unity of the Human Races Proved to be the Doctrine of Scripture, Reason, and Science.* Edinburgh: Johnstone and Hunter, 1851.

Snowden, Frank M., Jr. *Before Color Prejudice: The Ancient View of Blacks.* Cambridge, Mass.: Harvard University Press, 1983.

Soler, Colette. "Hysteria and Obsession." In *Reading Seminars I and II,* edited by Richard Feldstein, Bruce Fink, and Maire Jaanus, 248–82. Albany: State University of New York Press, 1996.

Sophocles. *Oedipus the King.* Translated by David Grene. In *Greek Tragedies,* edited by David Grene and Richmond Lattimore. Chicago: University of Chicago Press, 1960.

Spillers, Hortense J. "All the Things You Could Be by Now, If Sigmund Freud's Wife Was Your Mother: Psychoanalysis and Race." In *Female Subjects in Black and White,* edited by Elizabeth Abel, Barbara Christian, and Helene Moglen, 135–58. Berkeley: University of California Press, 1997.

———. "Mama's Baby, Papa's Maybe: An American Grammar Book." *Diacritics* 17, no. 2 (summer 1987): 65–81.

Sprengnether, Madelon. "Mourning Freud." In *Psychoanalysis in Contexts,* edited by Anthony Elliott and Stephen Frosh, 142–65. New York: Routledge, 1995.

———. *The Spectral Mother.* Ithaca, N.Y.: Cornell University Press, 1990.

Springer, Claudia. "Sex, Memories, Angry Women." In *Flame Wars,* edited by Mark Dery, 157–77. Durham, N.C.: Duke University Press, 1994.

Stepan, Nancy. *The Idea of Race in Science: Great Britain 1800–1960.* Hamden, Conn.: Archon, 1982.

Stepan, Nancy Leys. "Race and Gender: The Role of Analogy in Science." In *Anatomy of Racism,* edited by David Theo Goldberg. Minneapolis: University of Minnesota Press, 1990.

Stepan, Nancy Leys, and Sander L. Gilman. "Appropriating the Idioms of Science: The Rejection of Scientific Racism." In *The Bounds of Race,* edited by Dominick LaCapra, 72–103. Ithaca, N.Y.: Cornell University Press, 1991.

Stokes, Mason. *The Color of Sex.* Durham, N.C.: Duke University Press, 2001.

Strube de Piermont, Frédéric-Henri. *Recherche nouvelle de l'origine et des fondemens du droit de la nature.* S. Petersbourg: Académie des sciences, 1740.

Suleiman, Susan. *Authoritarian Fictions.* New York: Columbia University Press, 1983.

Testimony Taken by the Joint Select Committee to Inquire Into the Condition of Affairs in the Late Insurrectionary States. 42nd Cong., 2d sess. Washington: Government Printing Office, 1871–72.

Theweleit, Klaus. *Male Fantasies.* Vol. 1. Translated by Stephen Conway. Minneapolis: University of Minnesota Press, 1987.

Thomson, Ann. "From *L'Histoire naturelle de l'homme* to the Natural History of Mankind." *British Journal for Eighteenth-Century Studies* 9, no. 1 (spring 1986): 73–80.

Thucydides. *The Peloponnesian War.* Translated by Rex Warner. New York: Penguin, 1984.

Tomiche, Anne. "Rephrasing the Freudian Unconscious: Lyotard's Affect-Phrase." *Diacritics* 24, no. 1 (spring 1994): 43–62.

Tomplins, Jane. *West of Everything: The Inner Life of Westerns.* New York: Oxford, 1992.

Torok, Maria. "The Meaning of 'Penis Envy' in Women." Translated by Nicholas Rand. *Differences* 4, no. 1 (1992): 3–39.

Tourgée, Albion Winegar. *The Invisible Empire.* Edited by Otto H. Olsen. Baton Rouge: Lousiana State University Press, 1989.

Trelease, Alan W. *White Terror: The Ku Klux Klan Conspiracy and Southern Reconstruction.* New York: Harper and Row, 1971.

Trumbach, Randolph. "Sex, Gender, and Sexual Identity in Modern Culture." In *Forbidden History,* edited by John C. Fout, 89–107. Chicago: University of Chicago Press, 1990.

Tucker, Richard K. *The Dragon and the Cross: The Rise and Fall of the Ku Klux Klan in Middle America.* Hamden, Conn.: Archon Books, 1991.

Turner, Victor. "Social Dramas and Stories about Them." In *On Narrative,* edited by W. J. T. Mitchell, 137–64. Chicago: University of Chicago Press, 1980.

Valette, Bernard. "L'idée de nature." In *Analyses et réflexions sur Montesquieu, "De l'esprit des lois: La nature et la loi."* Paris: Edition Marketing, 1987.

Van Evrie, John H. *White Supremacy and Negro Subordination.* In vol. 3 of *Anti-Black Thought, 1863–1925,* edited by John David Smith. New York: Garland, 1993. First published in New York: Van Evrie, 1868.

Vaughan, Alden T. *Roots of American Racism.* New York: Oxford University Press, 1995.

Verhaeghe, Paul. *Does the Woman Exist?* Translated by Marc du Ry. New York: Other Press, 1999.

Vernant, Jean-Pierre. "Oedipus Without the Complex." In *Myth and Tragedy in Ancient Greece,* edited by Vernant and Pierre Vidal-Naquet, translated by Janet Lloyd. New York: Zone Books, 1988.

Veyne, Paul. *Writing History.* New York: Harper and Row, 1984.

Vidal-Naquet, Pierre. *The Black Hunter: Forms of Thought and Forms of Society in the Greek World.* Translated by Andrew Szegedy-Masjak. Baltimore: Johns Hopkins University Press, 1986.

Voltaire [François-Marie Arouet]. "Lettres sur Oedipe." In *Œuvres complètes de Voltaire.* Vol. 2. Paris: Badouin Frères, 1828.

Wade, Ira O. *The Intellectual Origins of the French Enlightenment*. Princeton: Princeton University Press, 1971.

Walker, Janet. *Couching Resistance*. Minneapolis: University of Minnesota Press, 1993.

Walton, Jean. *Fair Sex, Savage Dreams*. Durham, N.C.: Duke University Press, 2001.

———. "Re-placing Race." In *Female Subjects in Black and White,* edited by Elizabeth Abel, Barbara Christian, and Helene Moglen, 223–51. Berkeley: University of California Press, 1997.

Westbrook, Deeanne. *Ground Rules: Baseball and Myth*. Urbana: University of Illinois Press, 1996.

White, Charles. *An Account of the Regular Gradation in Man*. London: Dilly, 1799.

Wiegman, Robyn. *American Anatomies: Theorizing Race and Gender*. Durham, N.C.: Duke University Press, 1995.

———. "The Anatomy of Lynching." In *American Sexual Politics,* edited by John C. Fout and Maura Shaw Tantillo, 223–45. Chicago: University of Chicago Press, 1993.

———. "Whiteness Studies and the Paradox of Particularity." *Boundary 2* (26), no. 3 (fall 1999): 115–50.

Wilkins, John. *An Essay towards a Real Character and a Philosophical Language*. London: Gellibrand, 1668.

Williams, Raymond. *Marxism and Literature*. Oxford: Oxford University Press, 1977.

Willis, Sharon. *High Contrast: Race and Gender in Contemporary Hollywood Film*. Durham, N.C.: Duke University Press, 1997.

———. "A Symptomatic Narrative." *Diacritics* 13, no. 1 (spring 1983): 46–60.

Žižek, Slavoj. *The Metastases of Enjoyment*. London: Verso, 1994.

———. *The Plague of Fantasies*. New York: Verso, 1997.

———. *The Sublime Object of Ideology*. New York: Verso, 1989.

———. *Tarrying with the Negative*. Durham, N.C.: Duke University Press, 1993.

Zomchick, John P. *Family and the Law in Eighteenth-Century Fiction*. Cambridge: Cambridge University Press, 1993.

Zupančič, Alenka. "Sophocles' 'Oedipus Tyrannus.'" In *Freud and Forbidden Knowledge,* edited by Peter L. Rudnytsky and Ellen Handler Spitz, 72–95. New York: New York University Press, 1994.

———. "The Subject of the Law." In *Cogito and the Unconscious,* edited by Slavoj Žižek, 41–73. Durham, N.C.: Duke University Press, 1998.

INDEX

Causality (*cont.*)

   philosophical, 76–77, 85, 96,
270 n.142; scientific 61, 81–83, 98;
symbolic, 75, 77, 96, 98

Chalmers, David, 194

Chambers, Ross, 253 n.1, 269 n.134

Chanson de Roland, 260 n.53

Charivari, 204–5, 303–4, n.62

Chase, Cynthia, 39

Chrétien de Troyes, 260 n.53

Circumcision, 69–70, 127–28,
242 n.47, 261 n.60, 281–82 n.73,
282 n.74. *See also* Genital alteration

Cixous, Hélène, 18

Classification. *See* Taxonomy

Clément, Catherine, 18

Cobbs, Price M., 301 n.39

Complexion, 63–64, 66, 70, 83, 86, 91,
102–3, 269 n.134

Connell, R. W., 5

Crenshaw, Kimberlé Williams, 148,
274–75 n.11, 286–87 n.107

Cross-dressing, 204–5, 304 n.64

Culler, Jonathan, 249 n.42

Daniels, Doug, 238 n.23

Daniels, Jessie, 300 n.17

Dapper, Olfert, 126

Davis, David Brion, 65–66

Davis, Natalie Zemon, 204–5, 304 n.64

Diawara, Manthia, 305 n.71

Diderot, Denis, 267–68 n.118, 271 n.150

Dodds, E. R., 31

dos Sanctos, Joao, 73, 91–92

Duchet, Michèle, 284 n.89

Dyer, Richard, 261 n.60, 306 n.73

Dyson, Michael Eric, 300 n.15

Edmiston, William, 141

Edmunds, Lowell, 248 n.29

Edwards, Bryan, 71

Ellison, Ralph, 305 n.69

Encyclopédie, 85, 132, 134, 282 n.74

Enlightenment: as reason, 59, 82–85,
100, 146–47, 273 n.161; subjectivity
in, 59–63

Erikson, Kai, 254 n.5

Ethiopians, 63–64, 66, 92, 136,
257 nn.35 and 39, 260 n.50,
262 n.66

Fanon, Frantz, 284 n.86

Father: as masculine standard, 3–4, 31,
61; name of, 14; symbolic, 62, 154–
55, 160–63, 170, 215, 224, 245 n.9,
291 n.29, 292 n.34. *See also*
Masculinity

Fausto-Sterling, Ann, 10

Feldstein, Richard, 273 n.159

Femininity: endangered, 189–90, 193–
94; and hysteria, 18–20, 111; stabilizing, 192–94, 205

Ferguson, Kathy E., 253 n.69

Fields, Barbara J., 265 n.97, 269 n.134,
272 n.155

Fink, Bruce, 107

Flax, Jane, 289 n.6

Flynn, Charles, 204–5

Fontana, Benedetto, 15

Fontenelle, Bernard le Bovier de, 85

Forrester, John, 148

Fox-Genovese, Elizabeth, 256 n.19

Frankenberg, Ruth, 253 n.1

Frederickson, George, 265 n.96

Freud, Sigmund: *Ego and the Id*, 212; on
fathers, 3–4, 35, 43, 160–61, 212,
214–16, 290–91 n.25; masculine
hegemony in, 49, 280 n.64; Oedipus
complex, 21–23, 25, 44–45, 214–15,
245 n.10, 280 n.65; and race, 139; and
Sophocles, 23–24, 40, 42–43, 50,
243–44 n.1; *Totem and Taboo*, 36–37,
185, 212–15; unconscious, 290 n.17;
Wolfman, 35–36, 47, 54

Friedman, John Block, 67
Frosh, Stephen, 238 n.20, 288–89 n.5, 289 n.7

Gaillard, Françoise, 241 n.41
Gaines, Jane, 217
Gallop, Jane, 19, 151, 293 n.49, 306 n.83
Garber, Marjorie, 13, 153, 239 n.31, 240 n.34
Gay, Peter, 60–61
Gender. *See* Sexual difference
Genital alteration, 126–35, 138–39, 146, 272 n.77
Genovese, Eugene D., 256 n.19
Gill, Joseph, 202
Gilman, Sander, 109, 139, 241 n.47, 252 n.67, 268 n.124, 280 n.60
Glidden, George R., 143–44
Gobineau, Arthur de, 8
Goldberg, David Theo, 275 n.16
Goldmann, Lucien, 257 n.21
Goldsmith, Oliver, 269 n.135
Goldstein, Jan, 276 n.28
Gollobin, Ira, 238 n.24
Goodhart, Sandor, 31, 245 n.7
Goodman, Mary Ellen, 264 n.91
Gossett, Thomas F., 258 n.33
Gotanda, Neil, 301 n.33
Gould, Stephen Jay, 144, 274 n.6
Goux, Jean-Joseph, 32–34; 41, 156, 168–69, 171, 174–75, 245 n.8, 272 n.154, 295 n.59, 295–96 n.71
Grand Canyon, 218–26
Great Chain of Being, 87–91, 93–97, 103–5, 272–73 n.158
Greenblatt, Stephen, 260 n.56, 281–82 n.73
Greene, William Chase, 244 n.7
Grevenbroek, J. G., 72–73, 83, 119, 127–28, 131, 282 n.78
Grier, William H., 301 n.39

Grosz, Elizabeth, 291 nn.27, 29
Guillaumin, Colette, 256 n.18, 285 n.99

Haggerty, George, 141
Hankins, Thomas, 267 n.112, 277 n.41
Hannaford, Ivan, 247 n.17
Harris, Cheryl I., 194
Harris, Trudier, 192, 199, 301–2 n.40
Hazard, Paul, 85–86
Hegemony, 3, 12–15, 22, 42, 49–52, 62, 73, 105, 114, 118, 135, 148
Herodotus, 63–64, 245 n.10, 246–47 n.16, 294–95 n.58
Hillman, David, 264 n.87
Hobbes, Thomas, 84, 266 n.104
Hodes, Martha, 255 n.13
Homans, Margaret, 8
Homer, 1, 63, 259 n.35
Horkheimer, Max, 100–101, 273 n.161
Hottentots, 83, 119, 126–29, 132–35, 280 n.60, 281 n.70, 282 n.78, 284 n.86
Hughes, C. C., 202
Hume, David, 76, 271 n.147
Humphries, Martin, 5
Hunt, James, 191, 272 n.153, 274 n.3, 279 n.51
Hunter, Dianne, 19
Hutchings, Peter, 235 n.4
Hysteria: discourse of, 107, 110, 148, 205, 276 n.28; and femininity, 17–20, 111; masculine, 19–20, 25, 38, 104–5, 118, 135, 143–45, 147, 182, 187, 198, 206, 213, 225, 307 n.91; racial, 135, 143; white, 148, 184, 196–98, 206, 225, 307 n.91. *See also* Mastery

Incest taboo, 36–37
Irigaray, Luce, 12
Isis. *See* Osiris
Islam, 69, 127–28, 261 n.60

Index   333

Jacobson, Matthew Frye, 304–5 n.67
Jefferson, Thomas, 120
Jeffords, Susan, 235 n.1
Johnson, Barbara, 288 n.4
Jordan, Winthrop, 59, 80, 124, 240 n.32, 256 n.19, 265 n.95, 267 n.117, 272–73 n.158, 284 n.90

Kahane, Claire, 18
Kant, Immanuel, 74, 76–77, 82, 262 n.70, 269–70 n.137
Kaplan, Sidney, 278 n.46
Kerényi, Karl, 248 n.31
Keuls, Eva C., 173, 295 nn.67 and 68
Kimmel, Michael, 236 n.7
King, Alex, 192, 193
King Missile, 280 n.63
Knox, Bernard, 40–41, 247 n.26
Kolb, Peter, 129–31, 133, 281 n.70, 282 nn.75, 77
Kovel, Joel, 19
Ku Klux Klan, 189–94, 198–206, 299 nn.12, 14, 301 n.28

Lacan, Jacques: father in, 154–56, 160–63, 176–77, 290–91 n.25, 291 n.29, 306 n.84; the four discourses, 20, 106–12, 145, 277 n.33; hysteria, 20, 287 n.109; mirror stage, 188, 298 n.8; phallus, 6–7, 154, 171, 173, 290 n.16, 295 n.69; and real, 53–55, 307 n.84; subject, 51, 157–58, 249 n.47, 264–65 n.93, 276 n.28, 298–99 n.11, 304 n.66; symbolic, 75, 157, 161, 175–76, 188, 290 n.18, 304 n.66
Laclau, Ernesto, 14, 21, 43, 237 n.14, 239 n.31, 243 n.65, 250 n.53
Laqueur, Thomas, 78, 140, 237 n.13, 273 n.160, 279 n.58, 285 n.93
Law: in Enlightenment, 60–62, 68, 85, 258 n.28; of the father, 216–17,

291 n.29, 292 n.34, 307 n.85; natural, 60, 74, 82–83, 84–85; "one drop" rule, 9, 57, 118, 230, 255 n.11; regulating identity, 55–56, 61–62, 65, 258 n.31; and reproduction, 174–75; and whiteness, 56–57, 195–97, 255 n.11, 274 n.9, 274–75 n.11
Lehman, Peter, 172–73
Leibniz, Gottfried Wilhelm, Freiherr von, 88–89, 268 n.125
Lemaire, Anika, 292 n.34
Leo, John, 70
Lester, J. C., 200–201, 203
LeVay, Simon, 8
Lévi-Strauss, Claude, 108, 247 n.21, 289 n.14
Lincoln, Abraham, 274 n.6
Linnaeus, Carl von, 90, 93–94
Locke, John, 90, 94, 119, 268–69 n.125, 271 nn.149, 150
López, Ian F. Haney, 254 n.9, 255 n.14, 274 n.9
Lovejoy, Arthur O., 88
Lynching, 189–94, 198–99, 299 n.12, 304 n.65
Lyotard, Jean-François, 250 n.52

MacCannell, Juliet Flower, 307 n. 85
Malike, Kenan, 104
Masculinity: conflicted, 3–4, 25, 34–35, 37–38, 45, 170, 236 n.7; foreign, 125, 130–31, 149; fragmentation, 117–18, 123, 125, 133, 205–6; hegemonic, 138, 142, 145, 166, 168–69, 178–79, 181, 226; and insufficiency, 9–10, 117–18, 123, 135, 150, 173, 197; and integrity, 143, 146, 169–72, 184; and male body, 40, 120–21, 125, 145–46, 279 n.55; Oedipus complex, 21, 25, 40; role of father, 25, 34–36, 38, 43, 45, 161–62, 245 n.9, 250 n.54; and social identity, 34, 38, 141; tied to

Phallus (*cont.*)
289 n.7; lesbian, 165–66, 292 n.46;
vs. penis, 151–52, 163–67, 172,
289 n.6, 290 n.16, 292 n.36, 293
nn.47, 48, 295 n.69, 296 n.74; and
reproduction, 174–75, 180; and signification, 151–52, 157–58, 161–62,
167–69, 171–74, 178–79, 295–
96 n.71; as simulacrum, 170–72,
175–76, 294–95 n.58; as standard of
masculinity, 153, 164–65, 172, 175,
238 n.20, 281 n.67, 289 n.10,
306 n.83. *See also* Penis
Plato, 62, 65, 169
Plessy v. Ferguson, 195–96, 301 n.33
Plutarch, 169–71, 294 nn.56 and 57,
296 n.77
Point de capiton. See Master signifier
Polygenesis, 143–46
Pope, Alexander, 90
Prichard, James Cowles, 144–45
Propp, Vladimir, 247 n.22, 249 n.41
Psychoanalysis: masking difference,
49–50, 178, 215, 233; and race, 17–18,
26, 112, 297 n.80, 304 n.66; sexual
difference in, 16, 21–22, 25, 34 , 37,
46–49, 112–13, 178, 211–16
Ptolemy, 66, 262 n.66

Quatrefages, Jean Louis Armand de,
286 n.103

Rabelais, François, 62
Race: and binaries, 183, 297 n.2, and
castration, 123–24, 131–32; and culture, 71, 86, 122, 262 n.66; discursive
structures, 112–14; historical definitions, 144; and morphology, 7–8, 148,
183, 186–88, 264 n.93, 265 n.96,
274 n.6; purity, 134–35, 144, 189–91,
229; and sexual difference, 140, 191,
193, 304 n.66; unstable, 133–34, 186,

198, 298 nn.4 and 5, 304 n.67; variability, 118, 132, 134, 273–74 n.3,
286 n.106
Ragland-Sullivan, Ellie, 109, 287 n.112
Rawlins, John, 69–70
Real: empiricism, 68, 72, 85, 290 n.18;
encounter with, 53–55, 74–75, 77, 87,
98, 225, 253–54 n.2; and sexual differ-
ence, 16, 113–14; and trauma, 53–55
Reason: and the body, 95–97, 272 n.157;
and human classification, 93–95,
97, 105–6, 137, 271 nn.147, 149,
272 n.155, 280 n.59; and real, 88–89
Rehn, Rush, 244 n.7, 246 n.13
Reinhardt, Karl, 245 n.7
Rey-Flaud, Henri, 303–4 n.62
Rhyne, William Ten, 126, 281 n.70
Robinson, Sally, 255 n.15
Roediger, David, 238 n.21
Rogers, J. A., 200, 202–3, 303 n.52
Roof, Judith, 291 n.29
Rose, Jacqueline, 19
Rose, S. E. F., Mrs., 201, 299 n.13,
300 n.16, 302–3 n.50, 303 n.52
Rousseau, Jean-Jacques, 257 n.24

Sadoff, Dianne, 18
Sainte-More, Benoît de, 66–67
Sanjek, Roger, 259 n.44
Saussure, Ferdinand de, 290 n.19,
298 n.10
Savran, David, 235 n.2, 240 n.37,
305 n.72
Scalia, Antonin, 256 n.17
Schiebinger, Londa, 104, 121–22, 142,
271 n.145, 274 n.5
Schwartz, Joel D., 26
Science: discourse of, 107–9; empiri-
cism, 63, 68, 84, 140, 263 n.73;
and racial identity, 57, 116; and real,
55, 73
Screech, M. A., 258 n.31

Thomas DiPiero is Associate Professor of French and of
Visual and Cultural Studies at the University of Rochester.

Library of Congress Cataloging-in-Publication Data
DiPiero, Thomas.
White men aren't / Thomas DiPiero.
p. cm.   Includes bibliographical references and index.
ISBN 0-8223-2933-6 (cloth : alk. paper)
ISBN 0-8223-2961-1 (pbk. : alk. paper)
1. White men—Psychology. 2. Men—Identity. 3. White
men in literature. 4. Masculinity. 5. Masculinity in literature.
I. Title: White men are not. II. Title.
HQ1090 .D567 2002   305.31—dc21   2002002875